lonely planet

Lonely Planet Publications
Melbourne | Oakland | London

Neil Wilson

Prague

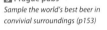

The Top Five

1 Vyšehrad
Watch architectural styles blend in this ancient citadel (p104)

2 Veletržní Palace
Explore four floors of superb Czech and European art (p109)

3 Prague Castle
Stroll the cobbled lanes of the world's biggest castle (p69)

4 Charles Bridge
Cross the Vltava River on this Prague landmark (p80)

5 Prague pubs
Sample the world's best beer in convivial surroundings (p153)

Contents

Published by Lonely Planet Publications Pty Ltd
ABN 36 005 607 983

Australia Head Office, Locked Bag 1, Footscray,
Victoria 3011, ☎ 03 8379 8000, fax 03 8379 8111,
talk2us@lonelyplanet.com.au

USA 150 Linden St, Oakland, CA 94607,
☎ 510 893 8555, toll free 800 275 8555,
fax 510 893 8572, info@lonelyplanet.com

UK 72–82 Rosebery Ave, Clerkenwell, London,
EC1R 4RW, ☎ 020 7841 9000, fax 020 7841 9001,
go@lonelyplanet.co.uk

The Author

Neil Wilson

Neil first succumbed to the pleasures of Prague back in 1995, beguiled, like everyone else, by its ethereal beauty, but also drawn to the darker side of its hidden history. He has returned regularly for a fix of the world's finest beers, and the chance to track down yet another obscure monument. In recent years Neil has been working on Lonely Planet's *Eastern Europe, Czech & Slovak Republics* and *Prague* guides. A full-time freelance writer since 1988, Neil has travelled in five continents and written around 45 travel and walking guides for various publishers. He is based in Edinburgh, Scotland.

NEIL'S TOP PRAGUE DAY

I'd start the day at Ebel Coffee House (p139) in the Týn Courtyard, relaxing with the papers over a giant cappuccino. Then, after browsing the bookshelves at the nearby Anagram (p183) and Big Ben (p184) bookshops, I'd cross the river and spend the rest of the morning wandering through the gardens of Malá Strana (p118), stopping to read for a while on a park bench in either the Wallenstein Garden (p81) or the Palace Gardens beneath Prague Castle (p81).

For lunch I'd grab a riverside table at Rybářský klub (p136) and order the grilled *candát* (pike-perch), and then take the funicular railway up Petřín (p83) for a stroll through the gardens to Strahov Monastery (p76), followed by a visit to the Story of Prague Castle exhibit (p73) in the castle grounds. By this time I'd be more than ready for a beer, so I'd walk east through Letná Park to the Letenský sady beer garden (see the boxed text, p157) and enjoy a Gambrinus or two with a view over the city.

Finally, I'd round off the day with dinner on the terrace at U zlaté studně (p137) – so that I could continue to enjoy the city view as the sun sets – followed by live jazz (and more beer) at U malého Glena (p171).

Introducing Prague

For centuries it has been known as Zlatá Praha or Golden Prague – a glittering jewel of art and architecture nestling snugly at the heart of Europe. Home to emperors and kings, artists and astronomers, this beautiful and fascinating city has worked its subtle magic on generations of visitors, and lent inspiration to musicians and writers from Mozart to Dvořák and Kafka to Klíma.

Kidnapped by communism for 40 years, Prague has returned to the capitalist fold to become one of Europe's most popular tourist destinations. Largely undamaged by the ravages of WWII, its cityscape offers a smorgasbord of stunning architecture, from the soaring verticals of Gothic spires and the buxom exuberance of baroque domes to the sensuous elegance of Art Nouveau maidens and the chiselled cheekbones of Cubist façades.

There are glitzy shopping malls, designer restaurants and cool cocktail bars galore, a feast of film and music festivals, and a packed programme of opera, ballet and drama. Smoky jazz cellars and rock basements compete with DJs and dance clubs into the small hours – no matter how late it is, there's always a party happening some-where – and then, heading home after an all-nighter, there's the mystical silence of the mist-shrouded Charles Bridge at dawn.

As well as its cultural treasures, Prague offers another precious commodity – the liquid gold of Bohemian beer. The Czechs have been brewing since at least the 9th century – they invented Pilsner, the world's first clear, golden lager, in 1842 – and Czech breweries still produce some of the world's finest beers.

Above all, Prague is to be explored at lei-sure, whether venturing along the medieval

lanes and hidden passages of the Old Town, strolling through the many wooded parks or taking a leisurely cruise along the Vltava. Everywhere you go you will uncover some aspect of the city's multilayered history – in its time Prague has been the capital of the Holy Roman Empire, the Habsburg Empire, the first Czechoslovak Republic, the Nazi Protectorate of Bohemia and Moravia, the Communist Republic of Czechoslovakia, and the modern, democratic Czech Republic.

Despite the onslaught of mass tourism, the city's dark and mysterious soul survives, haunted by the shadows of Kafka and communism. For those willing to wander off the beaten track, to risk getting lost in the city's maze of alleyways and courtyards, a deeper, truer experience of Golden Prague awaits.

LOWDOWN

Population 1,184,000

Time zone GMT + 1 hour

Cappuccino 40Kč to 100Kč

3-star double room 4000Kč to 4500Kč

Essential accessory A novel by Kafka or Kundera conspicuously poking from pocket or handbag

Metro/tram ticket 20Kč

No-no Wearing a T-shirt with the slogan 'Czech This Out!'

Portrait by Charles Bridge caricaturist 250Kč

Annual beer consumption 160L per head

Number of bars in Prague Over 11,000

Number of churches in Prague Around 150

City Life

City Life

PRAGUE TODAY

As the 21st century gets into its stride, Prague has almost completely recovered from its communist hangover and is fast becoming like any other big capitalist European city, with all the freedoms and pitfalls that entails. Of all the states that joined the EU in the past few years, the Czech Republic had the highest GDP and highest inward investment, and its capital city has these advantages in spades. Financially speaking, Prague operates on a level significantly above that of the rest of the country.

The rapid transition from communism to capitalism has brought plenty of problems, though. The gap between rich and poor grows wider, and the growth of car culture has led to an increasing gridlock on the city's streets. Since the country joined the EU in 2004, there has also been a significant increase in heavy freight traffic passing through and around the city. Plans to build a ring road floated around for years, but lack of funds – plus objections from the council of every district the road would pass through – held back construction. The project is at last under way, but is not expected to be completed until the end of 2009.

Praguers remain some of the most determined smokers in Europe – around one in three people smoke – but they are having to come to terms with a new law, introduced on 1 January 2006, banning smoking in public places. Weirdly, this includes tram and bus stops in the open air – on average, around 1500 smokers have been fined each month since the ban was introduced, most of them outdoors. Even more weirdly, the new law overturned an older one that banned smoking in restaurants and pubs when food was being served. Now restaurants can allow smoking, although they are supposed to provide a nonsmoking area. The government has also been gradually increasing the tax on cigarettes since 2004; by 2007 the price of a packet of 20 will have increased by 60% to around 80Kč (£2, or US$3.60).

The city continues to suffer from large numbers of British and Irish stag parties attracted by cheap flights, cheap beer and not-so-cheap sex clubs. As a result, Wenceslas Square after dark has become a seedy strip haunted by hookers and strip-club touts, and the city centre is occasionally disrupted by large gangs of noisy lads surfing from pub to pub on a tidal wave of beer and testosterone. Most locals are now heartily pissed off with this phenomenon, and you'll see plenty of signs on pub doors requesting 'Please, no groups of drunken British men allowed'. Hopefully they'll soon move on to pastures new (look out Bratislava and Budapest).

HOT CONVERSATION TOPICS

- Has life improved since we joined the European Union?
- Is it just me, or are the traffic cops demanding higher bribes these days?
- Has Staropramen beer gone downhill since it was taken over by a multinational brewery?
- Have you been to that new shopping mall in [insert random suburb]?
- Have you been fined for smoking at a tram stop yet?

Skating (p179) on the frozen Vltava River

CITY CALENDAR

Prague caters for visitors all year round, and there's no bad time to visit. The city is at its prettiest in spring, when the many parks begin to bloom with flowers, and the budding leaves on the trees are a glowing green.

Periods when the tourist crush is especially oppressive include the holidays at Easter and Christmas to New Year, as well as May (during the Prague Spring festival), June and September. Many Czechs go on holiday in July and August, during which time the supply of budget accommodation actually increases, as student hostels are opened to visitors.

If you can put up with the cold and the periodic smog alerts during weather inversions, hotel space is plentiful in winter (outside Christmas to New Year), and the city looks gorgeous and mysterious under a mantle of snow.

JANUARY
THREE KINGS' DAY (SVÁTEK TŘÍ KRÁLŮ)
Three Kings' Day is Twelfth Night, marking the formal end of the Christmas season on 6 January; it is celebrated with carol singing, bell ringing and gifts to the poor.

ANNIVERSARY OF JAN PALACH'S DEATH
This is a gathering on 19 January in Wenceslas Square in memory of the Charles University student who burned himself to death in 1969 in protest against the Soviet occupation (see the boxed text, p44).

MARCH
ST MATTHEW FAIR (MATĚJSKÁ POUT')
From the Feast of St Matthew (24 February) up to and including Easter weekend, the exhibition grounds at Výstaviště (p107) fill up with rollercoasters, fairground rides, ghost trains, shooting galleries and stalls selling candyfloss and traditional heart-shaped cookies. The fair is open 2pm to 10pm Tuesday to Friday, 10am to 10pm Saturday and Sunday.

PRAGUE WRITERS' FESTIVAL
www.pwf.cz
This is an international meeting of writers from around the world, with public readings, lectures, discussions and bookshop events.

BIRTHDAY OF TOMÁŠ G MASARYK
Commemoration of Czechoslovakia's father figure and first president on 7 March.

EASTER MONDAY (PONDĚLÍ VELIKONOČNÍ)
The city collapses in a mirthful rite of spring – Czech males of all ages chase their favourite girls and swat them on the legs with ribboned willow switches (you'll see them on sale all over the place); the girls respond with gifts of handpainted eggs (likewise on sale), then everyone gets down to some serious partying. This is the culmination of several days of serious spring-cleaning, cooking and visiting.

FEBIOFEST
www.febiofest.cz
This international festival of film, television and video features new works by international film-makers. Shown throughout the Czech Republic and Slovakia.

TOP FIVE BOOKS ABOUT PRAGUE

- *Magic Prague*, Angelo Ripellino (1995) – a literary and cultural odyssey through the history of Prague
- *Prague in Black and Gold*, Peter Demetz (1997) – a personal view of Prague's history and its people
- *Prague Tales*, Jan Neruda (2000) – a collection of Neruda's wry, bittersweet stories of life among the inhabitants of 19th-century Prague
- *The Coasts of Bohemia*, Derek Sayer (2000) – draws on an array of literary, musical, visual and documentary sources to create a sense of Czech society and identity
- *The Spirit of Prague*, Ivan Klíma (1998) – a collection of essays charting five critical decades of the city's history

APRIL

ONE WORLD (JEDEN SVĚT)

www.oneworld.cz

Week-long film festival dedicated to documentaries on the subject of human rights, with screenings held at small cinemas including Kino Aero and Kino Perštýn (p176).

BURNING OF THE WITCHES (PÁLENÍ ČARODĚJNIC)

This is the Czech version of a pre-Christian (pagan) festival for warding off evil, featuring burning brooms at Výstaviště (p107), and all-night, end-of-winter bonfire parties on Kampa island (p82) and in suburban backyards. It's held on 30 April.

MAY

LABOUR DAY (SVÁTEK PRÁCE)

Once sacred to the communists, the 1 May holiday is now just a chance for a picnic or a day in the country. To celebrate the arrival of spring, many couples lay flowers at the statue of the 19th-century romantic poet, Karel Hynek Mácha (Map pp270–1), author of *Máj* (May), a poem about unrequited love. Ex-president Václav Havel has been known to pay homage here.

BOOKWORLD PRAGUE (SVĚT KNIHY)

www.bookworld.cz

This major international book festival is held at the Výstaviště exhibition grounds (p107). Though primarily an industry event, it's open to the general public and has author readings, book launches, exhibits, seminars and lectures, mostly in English.

PRAGUE SPRING (PRAŽSKÉ JARO)

Running from 12 May to 3 June, this international music festival is Prague's most prestigious event, with classical-music concerts in theatres, churches and historic buildings. For details, see the boxed text, p161.

KHAMORO

www.khamoro.cz

This is a festival of Roma culture, with performances of traditional music and dance, exhibitions of art and photography, and a parade through Staré Město, usually held in late May.

JUNE

DANCE PRAGUE (TANEC PRAHA)

www.tanecpha.cz

International festival of modern dance held at theatres around Prague throughout June.

JULY

JAN HUS DAY (DEN JANA HUSA)

Celebrations are held on 6 July to commemorate the 1415 burning at the stake of Bohemian religious reformer Jan Hus. Kicked off with low-key gatherings and bell-ringing at Bethlehem Chapel (p96) the evening before.

AUGUST

FESTIVAL OF ITALIAN OPERA

www.opera.cz

Beginning in August and extending into September, this festival features the works of Verdi and other Italian composers performed at the Prague State Opera (p162); it provides a chance to see quality productions outside the main opera season.

SEPTEMBER

PRAGUE AUTUMN (PRAŽSKÝ PODZIM)

www.prazskypodzim.cz

International classical-music festival and the autumn version of Prague Spring. Most performances held at the Rudolfinum (p161).

OCTOBER

INTERNATIONAL JAZZ FESTIVAL (MEZINÁRODNÍ JAZZOVÝ FESTIVAL)

www.jazzfestivalpraha.cz/jazz

Established in 1964, and based at the Reduta Jazz Club (p162), this two-week festival stretches from late October into early November, with a mix of Czech musicians and star performers from around the world.

DECEMBER

CHRISTMAS–NEW YEAR (VÁNOCE–NOVÝ ROK)

From 24 December to 1 January many Czechs celebrate an extended family holiday. Revelling tourists engulf Prague, and a Christmas market is held in Old Town Square below a huge Christmas tree.

CULTURE

IDENTITY

Despite increasing immigration and a thriving expat community, the Czech capital is still pretty homogeneous – Praguers are almost all Czechs. In addition to Slovak and Roma minorities, there are significant numbers of expatriates – especially Americans and Germans – living and working in Prague. Based on work-permit statistics and educated guesses about the ratio of legal to illegal workers, it's thought there are between 20,000 and 60,000 expatriates living in the city.

The ugly side of the Czech population's homogeneity is an often-vicious racism directed at the Roma minority. The Roma community in Prague is small compared with other parts of the country – many live in the poorer parts of town, including Karlín and western Smíchov. For more on the Czech Republic's Roma community check out www.romove.cz/en.

LIFESTYLE

Prague is an expensive city and much more so for Czechs than for foreigners. The average monthly salary in Prague is around 23,000Kč (that's about €770, £575, or US$1030), and it's common for at least half of that to go on rent. So all those fancy restaurants and stylish bars are out of reach of the majority of Praguers, their custom confined to expats, gangsters, and a small elite of monied entrepreneurs (or corporate thieves, depending on your point of view).

Despite the everyday difficulties of making ends meet, Praguers remain for the most part mild-mannered people with a good sense of humour, and an attachment to old-fashioned values. On the tram even the roughest-looking skinhead will often give up a seat for an elderly passenger, and holding open a door for a lady is still considered the right thing to do. It's customary to say *dobrý den* (good day) to all and sundry when entering a shop, café or quiet bar, and to say *na shledanou* (goodbye) when you leave. If you're invited to someone's home, bring flowers or some other small gift for your host, and remember to remove your shoes when you enter the house.

Financial hardship is never considered an excuse for slackness when it comes to looking your best for a night on the town. When attending a classical concert, opera or play in one of the traditional theatres, men typically wear a suit and tie, and women an evening dress – it's only foreigners who don't. Casual dress is considered OK at performances of modern music, avant-garde plays and so on.

One legacy of the communist era that continues to plague the lives of ordinary Prague citizens is the petty corruption that riddles many areas of public life, ranging from the city council to health care. It's not unusual to bring a small 'gift' when you visit your doctor, just to make sure that any tests or referrals you may need are given the priority they deserve.

Nepotism and cronyism are also rife in business and politics. There's a Czech saying that goes, *Já na bráchu, brácha na mě,* which translates literally as 'I help my brother, my brother helps me', but is used in the wider sense of 'You scratch my back, and I'll scratch yours'. So prevalent is this philosophy in everyday life that the original phrase has evolved into a single word, *jánabráchismus,* which means 'mutual back-scratching, cronyism, corruption'.

The love of beer is just one of several traits that the Czechs share with the British, and it's not unusual to see workers downing a glass at breakfast time on the way to the building site or office. Another shared characteristic is a dark, satirical and often surrealist sense of humour – Monty Python is a big favourite here. Another is a love of dogs; the city's parks are filled with dog-walkers and dog poop, despite a determined effort by the city council to get owners to clean up after their canine companions. The annual dog-licence fee has been increased to help finance a team of Parisian-style 'pooper scoopers' with moped-mounted vacuum cleaners. Whatever; you should still watch your feet when you're strolling in the park.

FASHION

City Life

It must be something in the tap water; spend any time people-watching in Prague and you'll soon notice that there are a lot of gorgeous women here. All those sharp Slavic cheekbones, slim silhouettes and seductive, Mucha-maiden eyes were just made for showing off designer clothes. It's hardly surprising that Czech names – Eva Herzigová, Karolina Kurková, Daniela Peštová, Linda Vojtova and Petra Němcová – litter any list of supermodels.

In recent years Czech names have been popping up on the other side of the catwalk, with Prague fashion designers making names for themselves in Western Europe and opening boutiques across Prague. Names to look out for include Klara Nademlýnská (p185), Helena Fejková (p188), Hana Stocklassa, Martina Nevarilová, Tatiana Kovariková and Lucie Blazková.

Although there is a small Czech contingent that plumps for the nylon-tracksuit and socks-with-sandals look, most Praguers are pretty style-conscious and take pleasure in looking good. Folk here still dress up for dinner, and as for going to the opera in anything but your best, well, you must be a tourist.

Prague Autumn Festival, Old Town Square (p10)

SPORT

Football (Soccer)

Football is a national passion in the Czech Republic. The national team performs well in international competitions, having won the European Championship in 1976 (as Czechoslovakia), and reached the final in 1996 and the semifinal in 2004. Sadly, it crashed out in the first round of the 2006 World Cup in Germany. The latest up-and-coming star is Tomáš Rosický, who began his career with Sparta Praha in 1998 and signed for UK club Arsenal in 2006.

Prague has three teams that play in the Czech First Division – Sparta Praha, Slavia Praha and Viktoria Žižkov (see p177 for details of home stadiums). Sparta is the most successful team, frequently qualifying for the European Champions League. The football seasons run from August to December and February to June.

Ice Hockey

It's a toss-up whether football or ice hockey inspires more passion in the hearts of Prague sports fans, but hockey probably wins. The Czech national team has been rampant in recent years, winning the World Championship three years running (1999 to 2001) and taking the title again in 2005; it reached the final in 2006 but lost to Sweden. It also won Olympic gold in 1998 by defeating the mighty Russians in the final.

Prague's two big hockey teams are HC Sparta Praha and HC Slavia Praha (see p179), both of which compete in the 14-team national league. Promising young players are often lured away by the promise of big money in North America's National Hockey League, and there is a sizeable Czech contingent in the NHL.

Sparta plays at the huge, modern T-Mobile Aréna at Výstaviště in Holešovice; games are fast and furious, and the atmosphere can be electrifying – it's well worth making the effort to see a game. The season runs from September to early April.

Tennis

Tennis is another sport that the Czechs do well in, having produced world-class players such as Jan Kodeš, Ivan Lendl, Petr Korda, Hana Mandlikova, Jana Novotna, Cyril Suk, and up-and-coming star Nicole Vaidisova. Plus, of course, probably the finest woman tennis player ever, Martina Navratilova.

In May the Czech Lawn Tennis Club on Štvanice Island (p180) hosts the Prague Open, a competition that was established in 2001 in the hope of luring international tennis talent back to the Czech capital (Prague no longer hosts the Czech Open, which is now held at Prostějov). In 2005 the Prague Open was joined by a women's WTA tournament, which runs concurrently.

MEDIA

The Czechs are newspaper junkies, and you'll see people with their noses buried in the latest rag in bars, on trams, on park benches, and even walking along the street. Sadly, though, the overall quality of newspaper journalism is low, any lingering tradition of quality investigative reporting having been thoroughly stamped out during the communist era.

There are five national daily newspapers; most are now in the hands of German and Swiss media magnates. The biggest seller is the lurid tabloid *Blesk*, with sales of almost half a million. Second favourite is the centre-right *Mlada Fronta Dnes*, followed by the left-leaning *Právo*, the only national paper still in Czech ownership.

The weekly, English-language *Prague Post* (www.praguepost.cz) is good for local news and features, and has a useful 'Night & Day' arts and entertainment section, with travel tips and concert, film and restaurant reviews.

The *New Presence* (subtitled *Prague Journal of Central European Affairs*; www.new-presence.cz) is a quarterly English translation of the Czech *Nová Přítomnost*, with features and essays on current affairs, politics and business. And look out for the bilingual (Czech and English) monthly magazine *Think Again* (www.thinkagain.cz; free), a youth-oriented mag with an alternative take on music, fashion and art.

LANGUAGE

Naturally enough for the capital of the Czech Republic, the dominant language in Prague is Czech, although you will find that many older Czechs speak some German. Under communism everybody learned Russian at school, but this has now been replaced by English. While you'll have little trouble finding English speakers in central Prague, they're scarce in the suburbs and beyond, as are translated menus.

For more information on Czech and a list of useful words and phrases, see p242.

ECONOMY & COSTS

Prague's economy is largely a service one, and an estimated 60% of the city's cash comes from the pockets of visiting tourists. Although Prague was once an industrial powerhouse, only about 9% of its population is now employed in manufacturing (major industries are textiles, machinery, brewing and food processing); even so, it is still the largest industrial centre in the republic. Although the nationwide unemployment rate is around 9%, in Prague it is only 3%.

The average monthly wage in Prague is about 23,000Kč (€770), enough for a reasonably comfortable life if you live in its outer suburbs; for Prague residents living

HOW MUCH?

1L of petrol 29Kč

Bottled water (1.5L) 12Kč

Guardian newspaper 85Kč

Beer (0.5L) in tourist/nontourist pub 60Kč plus/25Kč

Pork & dumplings 80Kč to 100Kč

Souvenir T-shirt 300Kč

Ticket to Laterna Magika 690Kč

Tour of Municipal House 150Kč

Cinema ticket 90Kč to 170Kč

Vintage car tour 950Kč

in the central tourist zones, however, costs have gone through the roof. And the average wage for the whole country is only 18,900Kč (€670) a month, making the capital expensive for most Czech citizens.

Prague is not a cheap destination for visitors either, unless you're on the backpacker trail. You can expect to pay around 4000Kč to 4500Kč a night for a double room in an attractive central hotel, and budget 500Kč a head for lunch and 1500Kč a head for dinner (without wine) if you plan to sample the best of Prague's restaurants.

GOVERNMENT & POLITICS

As capital of the Czech Republic, Prague is the seat of government, parliament and the president. The city itself is governed separately by the Local Government of the Capital City of Prague, headed by a council and a mayor. The acting body of this government is the municipal office together with the council. Prague is divided into 10 districts and 57 suburbs, governed by district and local governments.

Since 1989 Prague citizens have voted heavily (typically about 60%) for right-of-centre parties, which is more than in the country generally. The June 2006 elections were fought on issues that included the future of the welfare state and the need to stamp out corruption, but resulted in a stalemate. The centre-right Civil Democratic Party (ODS) led the field with 35.4% of the vote (in Prague, the ODS polled 48.2%), followed by the left-of-centre Social Democrats (ČSSD) with 32.3%, the Czech Communist Party (KSČM) with 12.8%, the Christian Democrats (KDU-CSL) with 7.2%, and the Green Party (SZ) with 6.3%.

This gave the ruling coalition exactly 100 seats out of 200 in the Chamber of Deputies. At the time of writing, the ODS and the ČSSD had agreed to form a coalition along with the Greens. But as this was the equivalent of the UK's Labour and Conservative parties forming an unholy alliance, a lot of political horse-trading remained to be done. The Czech government looks to be heading for an unstable and acrimonious few years.

Václav Klaus, the right-wing, eurosceptic former leader of the ODS, succeeded Václav Havel as president of the Czech Republic in 2003. The next presidential election will be held in January 2008.

Despite an overwhelming referendum vote in favour of joining the European Union, the Czechs displayed a degree of apathy in relation to the European Parliament elections in 2004; it is said that more Czechs voted for their favourite candidates in the TV programme *Česko hledá SuperStar* (the Czech equivalent of *Pop Idol* in the UK, or *American Idol* in the USA) than turned out in the European elections.

ENVIRONMENT

In midwinter Prague occasionally suffers from smog, when the air becomes foul with vehicle emissions during temperature inversions. If you're here for just a few days, there's little to worry about, though Prague residents have high rates of respiratory ailments. Radio and TV stations provide bulletins about pollution levels, and if you are an asthma sufferer, the Prague Information Service (p238) should be able to tell you if there's a risk.

THE LAND

Central Prague sits in a sweeping bend of the Vltava, the longest river in the Czech Republic. Low, rocky hills rise immediately above the west bank, while on the east bank is a low-lying basin bounded by the long ridge of Vítkov (or Žižkov Hill) in the north, the riverside crags of Vyšehrad in the south, and the high ground of Vinohrady to the east. North of Vítkov is another low-lying plain, now occupied by the suburbs of Karlín and Libeň, which were badly affected by flooding in 2002 and 2006.

This geography defined the city's layout, with Prague Castle and the fortress of Vyšehrad founded on the hills to the northwest and southeast respectively, and the original settlements of Malá Strana and Staré Město growing up on the riverbanks on either side of the only possible fording place.

The Vltava rises in the Šumava hills near the Czech Republic's southern border with Austria and, along with its tributary the Berounka (which joins the Vltava a short distance upstream from Prague), drains most of southern and western Bohemia. Because of this huge drainage basin, Prague has found itself prone to severe flooding since its earliest days.

A flood washed away the Judith Bridge in 1342 (the Charles Bridge was built as its replacement), and in recent centuries there have been serious floods in 1784, 1827, 1845 and 1890. A carved stone head set into the embankment near the east end of Charles Bridge (on the downstream side, close to the modern flood gauge) marks the height reached by the 1890 flood, as do several metal plaques around Kampa island in Malá Strana (p82).

The construction of the Slapy Dam 20km south of the city in the 1950s was intended to bring the Vltava under human control, but the flood that hit the city in August 2002 proved that the river was still untamed. The flood killed 19 people and caused about €2.4 billion of damage; 18 metro stations were flooded, and the metro remained out of operation for more than six months. The catastrophe was caused by unusually heavy rainfall from thunderstorms in southwestern Bohemia – about 9.7 cubic kilometres of rain fell in the space of just nine days.

Since then, the city has invested in a new flood defence system, consisting of metal barriers than can be erected quickly in times of danger. You can see the metal sockets for these barriers all along the banks of the Vltava; there is even a line of fittings right through the middle of Na Kampě Square in Malá Strana (p82).

GREEN PRAGUE

When it comes to large-scale recycling, sustainable energy and organic farming, the Czech Republic still lags a long way behind Germany, the UK and Scandinavia. All the same, Czech industry has cleaned up its act considerably since the fall of communism, with the annual production of greenhouse gases falling to one-thirtieth of pre-1989 levels.

Czechs have been recycling waste for a long time; you'll find large bins for glass, plastics and paper all over Prague. Most glass bottles are recyclable, and the price of most bottled drinks includes a deposit of between 3Kč and 10Kč, refundable at supermarkets and food shops (some beer bottles only have a 0.40Kč deposit).

Meanwhile, two new commercial developments on opposite sides of the city – the Park, next to Chodov metro station in the south, and River City in Karlín, in the north – are being touted as Prague's first 'green' buildings. Both have been designed to minimise energy consumption, using the sun's warmth to heat the offices in winter and river water to cool them in summer; recycled rainwater feeds the fountains and irrigates gardens.

URBAN PLANNING & DEVELOPMENT

Prague city council's plans for the future are focussed on easing the pressure on the already overcrowded centre by moving development into the inner suburbs, notably Karlín, Smíchov, Pankrác and Holešovice. New developments include the River City office complex in Karlín, the Prague Marina luxury apartment complex at the old river port in Holešovice, and the huge new Palladium shopping centre that is due to open on náměstí Republiky in late 2007.

The River City complex is one of Prague's flagship developments, a whole new district of offices, shops, hotels, restaurants and a riverside park. Situated just east of the Hilton Hotel, it will be linked by pedestrian footbridges to Štvanice Island and the Prague City Market across the river in Holešovice. The complex is due for completion in 2009, but there are longer-term plans to extend redevelopment into the Libeň docks.

Prague's main train station, Praha-hlavní nádraží, has long been an eyesore, a combination of crumbling, soot-stained Art Nouveau and 1970s ugly. After years of complaints about the bad first impression the station creates for travellers arriving in the city, the station is to undergo a major refurbishment and redevelopment in 2007. Another city landmark that is slated for restoration is the Charles Bridge, which will be partly closed to visitors in 2007 and 2008 while work is done to repair its foundations, which were damaged in the 2002 floods.

Plans for a ring road have finally got off the ground afer years of stalling. The city's main traffic routes are descending into gridlock, as anyone who has ever tried to drive across the city (or walk across the freeway at the top of Wenceslas Square) can testify. It has been estimated that car ownership in Prague has increased by more than 75% in the last decade, yet the city still suffers from the communist-era legacy of a poorly planned and hastily executed traffic system that feeds major highways through the congested city centre.

Meanwhile Prague's metro system continues to grow, with line C (which used to end at Nádraží Holešovice) now extending northeast across the river to a new terminus at Ládví, and line A's eastern terminus extended by one more stop to Depo Hoštivar. Line C is being extended to the northeast, with three more stations due to open by 2008. More ambitiously, the city council has agreed to a US$760 million plan to extend metro line A from Dejvická to Ruzyně airport.

Arts

Arts

Ask anyone in the west to name a famous Czech artist, musician and writer, and the odds are that the majority will come up with Alfons Mucha, Antonín Dvořák and Franz Kafka. But to the generation of Czechs which has grown up since 1989, these are names from the distant past. Even Ivan Klíma, who is now in his 70s, is widely dismissed as irrelevant, though he's revered in the west. There are many young Czech writers who don't rate him as a novelist, just as they don't rate Václav Havel – the west's favourite playwright-cum-president.

Enthused by romantic notions of the Czech National Revival, Art Nouveau and the dissident writer struggling against the oppression of the communist regime, Western visitors to Prague have all too often overlooked the vibrant arts scene that has arisen in the city since 1989.

Prague's major art galleries are complemented by dozens of small, independent and commercial galleries where you can begin to appreciate the artistic energy that bubbles away beneath the surface of the city. And the smaller concert venues, jazz clubs and rock bars are a hot-bed of innovation and experimentation.

MUSIC

Prague enjoys a rich and varied musical life, and its concert halls, churches, jazz clubs and rock bars provide an almost unceasing choice of musical entertainment that you can dip into as you choose. Praguers have eclectic musical tastes; they are interested in all kinds of music, ranging from Mozart, who conducted the premiere of *Don Giovanni* here in 1787, to the Rolling Stones, who played to No 1 fan and ex-president Václav Havel in 2003.

One of the Czech Republic's most successful homegrown pop stars of recent years has been Prague singer-songwriter Radůza, who first shot to fame in 1993 when she shared a stage at the Lucerna Music Bar (p172) with Suzanne Vega. But cast aside your preconceptions – Radůza's instrument of choice is...the accordion. Her songs are modern and lyrical, but firmly rooted in Czech folk music and the Bohemian beer-hall tradition. Her latest album *V hoře* (In a Mountain), released in 2005, shot to the top of the Czech charts without the help of an advertising campaign.

At the classical end of the music spectrum, mezzosoprano Magdalena Kožená is a leading light in the younger generation of opera singers. She has carved out a career as a major concert and recital artist – she has performed at the Salzburg, Glyndebourne and Edinburgh festivals, among others – and has recorded best-selling CDs of Mozart arias, French opera and Bach's *St Matthew Passion*.

CLASSICAL

Classical music is hugely popular in Prague, and not only with the crowds of international aficionados who flock to the Prague Spring (see the boxed text, p161) and Prague Autumn (p10) festivals – the Czechs themselves have always been keen fans of classical music. Both locals and visitors can choose from a rich programme of concerts performed by Prague's three main resident orchestras – the Prague Symphony Orchestra (Symfonický orchestr hlavního města Prahy; www.fok.cz), the Czech Philharmonic Orchestra (Česká filharmonie; www.czechphilharmonic.cz) and the world-renowned Czech National Symphony Orchestra (Český národní symfonický orchestr; www.cnso.cz).

Among contemporary composers, the most widely known is probably Milan Slavický (1947–), who teaches at the Prague Academy of Performing Arts. His most famous piece, *Requiem*, premiered in Prague in 2005. Other modern Czech composers worth looking out for include Petr Eben (1927–), best known for his choral and organ music, and Marek Kopelent (1932–), who made his name with his avant-garde compositions of the 1950s and '60s.

Czech classical music first blossomed in the mid-19th century, when the National Revival saw the emergence of several great composers who drew inspiration from traditional Czech folk music in their work.

Bedřich Smetana (1824–84), the first great Czech composer, incorporated folk melodies into his classical compositions. His best-known works are *Prodaná nevěsta* (The Bartered Bride), *Dalibor a Libuše* (Dalibor & Libuše) and the patriotic *Má Vlast* (My Homeland), which opens the Prague Spring festival each year.

Antonín Dvořák (1841–1904) is probably the most famous Czech composer internationally. He spent four years in the USA where he lectured on music and composed the symphony *From the New World*. Among his other well-known works are the two *Slovanské tance* (Slavonic Dances; 1878 and 1881), the operas *Rusalka* and *Čert a Káča* (The Devil & Kate) and his religious masterpiece *Stabat Mater*.

Statue of Antonín Dvořák (left)

Moravian-born Leoš Janáček (1854–1928), who also incorporated folk elements into his heavier music, was a leading 20th-century Czech composer, although he was never as popular as Smetana or Dvořák in his native country. His better-known compositions include the opera *Jenůfa*, the *Glagolská mše* (Glagolitic Mass) and *Taras Bulba*, while one of his finest pieces is *Stories of Liška Bystrouška*.

Other well-known Czech composers include Josef Suk (1874–1935), Dvořák's son-in-law, whose best-known works include *Serenade for Strings* and the *Asrael Symphony*; and Bohuslav Martinů (1890–1959), famed for his opera *Julietta* and his Symphony No 6 (*Fantaisies Symphoniques*).

JAZZ

Jazz was already being played in Prague in the mid-1930s, and has retained a grip on Czech cultural life that is unmatched almost anywhere else in Europe. Czech musicians remained at the forefront of the European jazz scene until the communist takeover in 1948, when controls were imposed on the performance and publication of jazz music, considered to be a corrupting product of the capitalist system. Even so, in the late 1950s Prague Radio still had a permanent jazz orchestra led by Karel Krautgartner.

Restrictions were gradually lifted in the 1960s. One of the top bands in this period was the SH Quartet, which played for three years at Reduta, the city's first professional jazz club. Another leading band was the Junior Trio, with Jan Hamr and the brothers Miroslav and Allan Vitouš, who all left for the USA after 1968. Jan Hamr (keyboards) became prominent in 1970s American jazz-rock as Jan Hammer, while Miroslav Vitouš (bass) rose to fame in several American jazz-rock bands.

One of the most outstanding musicians in today's jazz scene is Jiří Stivín, who in the 1970s produced two excellent albums with the band System Tandem and has since become regarded as one of the most original jazz musicians in Europe. Another is Milan Viklický, who still performs in many of Prague's jazz clubs. Milan Svoboda, as well as being an accomplished pianist, is best known for his conducting abilities.

ROCK & POP

The Prague rock scene has produced some truly original (and unusually long-lived) bands, though it has to be said that not being able to understand the lyrics – which are often bizarre, witty and scatological – tends to diminish their appeal to non-Czechs. A classic example is Už Jsme Doma, formed in 1985 and still touring, whose music has been described as 'intellectual, orchestral punk'; they describe themselves as an 'avant-punk-ska-acid-jazz-Prague-prog-rock' band. Guess you just have to hear them.

Another Prague-based outfit that is worth listening out for is Freak Parade, an indie band with a Blondie-in-1979 sound and mainly live performances, having released only two albums since 1995.

During the communist era, rock (known as *bigbít* in Czech) was often banned by the authorities because of its 'corrupting influence', although certain local bands and innocuous Western groups such as Abba were allowed.

Sputnici, the pioneer of Czech rock, was the best known of several 1960s bands recycling American hits – Malostranská beseda (p172) in Malá Strana was a popular venue – but serious rock remained an underground movement enjoyed by small audiences in obscure pubs and country houses; devotees included many political dissidents such as Václav Havel. Raids and arrests were common – the Czech rock band Plastic People of the Universe (still performing, by the way) achieved international fame after being imprisoned following a 1970s show trial intended to discourage underground music.

Since 1989 rock has really taken off. When Václav Havel – a long-standing rock fan – became president, one of his first acts was to invite Frank Zappa to come and play in Prague. Havel even wanted to appoint Zappa as his special ambassador to the US, but had to settle for the post of unofficial cultural attaché. (Zappa died in 1993, but when the surviving members of his band, the Mothers of Invention, played in Prague in 2004, the gig sold out several times over.)

Popular bands on the home front include pop-oriented Buty; hard-rock bands Lucie and the less-refined Alice; and even a 'country rock' band Žlutý Pes (Yellow Dog). More alternative are several veteran outfits, including the grunge band Support Lesbiens, and Visací Zámek (Padlock). Lucie Bílá, the diva of 1990s Czech pop, started out sounding like a toned-down Nina Hagen, but has turned to rock musicals and Czech versions of American and British hits. Newer talent includes Patti Smith–like Načeva, and avant-garde violinist and vocalist Iva Bittová, who has made first-rate classical and modern recordings.

LITERATURE

Among the emerging generation of Prague writers, one of the most interesting (and commercially successful) is poet and rock lyricist turned novelist Jáchym Topol (1962–). The son of a playwright, Topol signed the dissident manifesto *Charta 77* at the tender age of 15. His 1994 novel *Sestra* (translated into English as *City Sister Silver*) is an exhilarating exploration of post-communist Prague, a stream-of-consciousness odyssey that vividly captures the sense of chaos and social dislocation that swept over the city in the wake of the Velvet Revolution.

To date, very little contemporary Czech literature has been translated into English; apart from Topol, there is *Fingers Pointing Somewhere Else,* a collection of beautifully

TOP FIVE READS

- *City Sister Silver,* Jáchym Topol (1994) – a postmodern stream-of-consciousness novel that takes the reader on an exhilarating exploration of post-communist Prague
- *I Served the King of England,* Bohumil Hrabal (1974) – a humorous and deceptively simple tale of one man's rise to riches and ultimate fall into poverty, mirroring Czech history from 1918 to the communist era
- *Mendelssohn Is on the Roof,* Jiří Weil (1960) – a moving and often wryly humorous memoir of Jewish life in Prague during WWII
- *The Trial,* Franz Kafka (1915) – perhaps Kafka's most famous story: a man is put on trial by an incomprehensible bureaucracy, not even knowing what crime he has been accused of
- *The Widow Killer,* Pavel Kohout (2000) – a gripping thriller set in Nazi-occupied Prague, in which a Czech detective and a Gestapo agent combine forces to track down a serial killer

crafted short stories by Daniela Fischerová; Michal Viewegh's *Bringing Up Girls in Bohemia,* a satirical snapshot of present-day Prague society; and the gutsy, fast-paced novels of Prague-based author Iva Pekárková. Keep your fingers crossed that someday soon you will be able to enjoy the funny, Prague-centred stories of Emil Hakl and the biting social satire of Miloš Urban.

The roots of Czech literature go back to the National Revival. Karel Hynek Mácha, possibly the greatest of all Czech poets, was the leading representative of Romanticism in the early 19th century; his most famous lyrical work is *Máj* (May). Mid-19th-century romanticism produced several outstanding works about life in the country, especially *Grandmother* by Božena Němcová (the first major female Czech writer), and *Flowers* by Karel Erben.

The radical political journalist Karel Havlíček Borovský criticised the Habsburg elite and wrote excellent satirical poems. Two poets of the time who took much inspiration from Czech history were Jan Neruda (who also wrote *Povídky malostranské*, or Prague Tales, a collection of stories about daily life in Malá Strana) and Svatopluk Čech.

At the end of the 19th century Alois Jirásek wrote a compendium of stories from the arrival of the Czechs in Bohemia to the Middle Ages, *Staré pověsti české* (Old Czech Legends), as well as nationalistic historical novels, his best being *Temno* (Darkness).

One of the best-known Czech writers of all is Franz Kafka. Along with a circle of other German-speaking Jewish writers in Prague, he played a major role in the literary scene at the beginning of the 20th century (see the boxed text, p68). His two complex and claustrophobic masterpieces are *The Trial* and *The Castle*. Others in the same circle were critic Max Brod and journalist Egon Erwin Kisch.

Among their Czech-speaking contemporaries was Jaroslav Hašek, now best known for *Dobrý voják Švejk* (The Good Soldier Švejk), which is full of good lowbrow WWI humour about the trials of Czechoslovakia's literary mascot, written in instalments from Prague's pubs.

The post-WWI Czech author Karel Čapek is famous for a science-fiction drama, *RUR* (Rossum's Universal Robots), from which the word 'robot' first entered the English language. Well-known poets of the interwar years are Jaroslav Seifert (awarded the Nobel Prize for Literature in 1984) and Vítěslav Nezval.

The early communist period produced little of literary value, although the 1960s saw a resurgence of writing as controls were relaxed. Writers such as Václav Havel, Josef Škvorecký, Milan Kundera and Ivan Klíma produced their first works in the years preceding the 1968 Soviet-led invasion. Klíma's best-known novel is *A Ship Named Hope*.

After the invasion some, including Havel, stayed and wrote for the *samizdat* (underground press) or had manuscripts smuggled to the West. Others left, producing their best work in exile. Kundera's best novel is probably *The Joke*; two other well-known works are *The Unbearable Lightness of Being* and *The Book of Laughter and Forgetting*. Two good reads by Škvorecký are *Cowards* and *The Bride of Texas*. Other important figures of this time are philosopher Jan Patočka and poet Jiří Kolář.

Until his accidental death – in traditional Czech fashion, he died after falling from a window – the Czech Republic's leading modern novelist was Bohumil Hrabal (1914–97). One of his most notable novels, *The Little Town Where Time Stood Still,* is a humorous portrayal of the interactions of a small, close-knit community. Another popular Hrabal work is *Closely Watched Trains,* which was made into an Oscar-winning film in 1966.

Swing band busking on Charles Bridge (p80)

VISUAL ARTS

Think visual arts in Prague and most visitors will be thinking of Alfons Mucha, but the city has much more to offer than Mucha's sultry maidens. Prague has a rich tradition of public sculpture ranging from the baroque period to the present day – David Černý (p24) is still creating controversy – and there is always something new and fascinating to see in the Veletržní Palace (p109) and the Futura Gallery (p112).

PAINTING

The luminously realistic, 14th-century paintings of Magister Theodoricus (Master Theodoric), whose work hangs in the Chapel of the Holy Cross at Karlštejn Castle (p211) and in the Chapel of St Wenceslas in St Vitus Cathedral (p71), influenced art throughout Central Europe.

Another gem of Czech Gothic art is a late-14th-century altar panel by an artist known only as the Master of the Třeboň Altar; what remains of it is in the Convent of St George (p74) in Prague Castle.

The Czech National Revival in the late 18th and early 19th centuries witnessed the appearance of a Czech style of realism, in particular by Mikuláš Aleš and father and son Antonín and Josef Mánes. Alfons Mucha is well known for his late-19th-century Art Nouveau posters. Czech landscape art developed in the works of Anton Kosárek, followed by a wave of Impressionism and Symbolism at the hands of Antonín Slavíček, Max Švabinský and others. The earliest notable woman painter, Zdenka Braunerová, concentrated on painting and sketching Prague and the Czech countryside.

In the early 20th century Prague developed as a centre of avant-garde art, concentrated in a group of artists called Osma (The Eight). Prague was also a focus for Cubist painters, including Josef Čapek. The functionalist movement flourished between WWI and WWII in

ALFONS MUCHA

Alfons Mucha (1860–1939) is probably the most internationally famous visual artist to come out of the Czech lands, although his reputation within the Czech Republic is less exalted than it is abroad.

Mucha's life and career changed almost overnight after a chance meeting in a print shop led to him designing a poster for the famous actress Sarah Bernhardt, promoting her new play *Giselda*; you can see the original lithograph in the Mucha Museum (p97). The poster, with its tall narrow format, muted colours, rich decoration and sensual beauty, created a sensation.

Mucha quickly became the most talked-about and sought-after artist in Paris. He signed a six-year contract with Bernhardt during which time he created nine superb posters for her in the style that became known as *le style Mucha*. He also designed jewellery, costumes and stage sets, and went on to produce many more famous posters promoting, among other things, Job cigarette papers, Möet & Chandon champagne, and tourism in Monaco and Monte Carlo.

Although firmly associated in the public mind with Art Nouveau, Mucha himself claimed that he did not belong to any artistic movement, and saw his own work as a natural evolution of traditional Czech art. His commitment to the culture and tradition of his native land was expressed in the second half of his career, when he worked without payment on the decoration of the Lord Mayor's Hall in Prague's Municipal House (p93), designed new stamps, banknotes and police uniforms, and created a superb stained-glass window for the nave of St Vitus Cathedral (p71).

He also devoted 18 years of his life (1910–28) to creating his *Slovanské epopej* (Slav Epic), which he then gifted to the Czech nation. The 20 monumental canvasses encompass a total area of around 0.5 sq km and depict events from Slavic history and myth. Although very different in style from his famous Paris posters, they retain the same mythic, romanticised quality, full of wild-eyed priests, medieval pageantry and battlefield carnage, all rendered in symbolic tints – in the artist's own words: 'Black is the colour of bondage, blue is the past, yellow the joyous present, orange the glorious future'. (The *Slav Epic* is on display in the town of Moravský Krumlov, near Brno, 200km southeast of Prague.)

When the Nazis occupied Czechoslovakia at the beginning of WWII, Mucha was one of the first people to be arrested and interrogated by the Gestapo. He was released but died a few days later, shortly before his 79th birthday. He is buried in the Slavín at Vyšehrad Cemetery (p107).

Mucha's granddaughter, Jarmila Plockova, uses elements of his paintings in her work – those interested can check out Art Décoratif; see p184.

a group called Devětsil, led by the adaptable Karel Teige. Surrealists followed, including Zdeněk Rykr and Josef Šíma.

Forty years of communism brought little art of interest, at least through official channels. Underground painters of the time included Mikuláš Medek (whose abstract, Surrealist art was exhibited in out-of-the-way galleries) and Jiří Kolář, an outstanding graphic artist and poet. Some of the works of art that were not exhibited by artists of the postwar years have surfaced since 1989.

Window in the Municipal House (Obecní dům; p93)

SCULPTURE

Public sculpture has always played a prominent role in Prague, from the baroque saints that line the parapets of Charles Bridge to the monumental statue of Stalin that once stood on Letná terrace. And, more often than not, that role has been a political one.

In the baroque era, religious sculptures sprouted in public places; they included 'Marian columns' erected in gratitude to the Virgin for protection against the plague or victory over anti-Catholic enemies – one such Marian column stood in Old Town Square from 1650 until 1918. The placing of the statue of St John of Nepomuk on Charles Bridge in 1683 was a conscious act of propaganda designed to create a new – and Catholic – Czech national hero who would displace the Protestant reformer Jan Hus from popular memory. As such it was successful – John of Nepomuk was canonised in 1729 and the Nepomuk legend, invented by the Jesuits, passed into the collective memory.

The period of the Czech National Revival saw Prague sculpture take a different tack – to raise public awareness of Czech tradition and culture. One of the most prolific sculptors of this period was Josef Václav Myslbek, whose famous statue of St Wenceslas, the Czech patron saint, dominates the upper end of Wenceslas Square (p98). He also created the four huge statues of the mythical Czech characters Libuše, Přemysl, Šárka and Ctirad that now grace the gardens in Vyšehrad fortress (p106).

The Art Nouveau sculptor Ladislav Šaloun was responsible for one of Prague's most iconic sculptures, the monument to Jan Hus that was unveiled in the Old Town Square (p85) in 1915. The figure of Hus – standing firm and unmoving, while the events of history swirl around him – symbolised the Czech nation which, three years later, would be independent for the first time in its history. For three short years he stared across the square at a statue of the Virgin Mary – symbol of the Habsburg victory over the Czechs – until a mob toppled her soon after independence was declared in 1918. Šaloun's works grace the façade of the Municipal House, the Grand Hotel Evropa and City Hall, and he also created the bust of Antonín Dvořák that adorns the composer's tomb in Vyšehrad cemetery.

Probably the most imposing and most visible sculpture in Prague is the huge, mounted figure of Hussite hero Jan Žižka – reputedly the biggest equestrian statue in the world – that dominates the skyline above Žižkov (the district was named after him). Created by sculptor Bohumil Kafka (no relation to the writer) in 1950, it was originally intended to form part of the National Monument (p110) in memory of the Czechoslovak legions who had fought in WWI. But it was hijacked by the communist government and made to serve instead as a political symbol of Czech peasants and workers.

TOP FIVE GALLERIES

- Convent of St Agnes (p89)
- House at the Golden Ring (p88)
- Mánes Gallery (p102)
- Sternberg Palace (p75)
- Veletržní Palace (p109)

The city's long tradition of politically charged sculpture continues today with the controversial and often wryly amusing works of David Černý (see the boxed text, p24).

23

DAVID ČERNÝ – ARTIST-PROVOCATEUR

Czech artist David Černý (1967–) first made international headlines in 1991 when he painted Prague's memorial to WWII Soviet tank crews bright pink (see the boxed text, p105). Since then he has cultivated a reputation as the *enfant terrible* of the Prague arts scene – his works often turn into major media events, occasionally with police involved. He strongly supported the Czech Republic's entry into the EU, and is virulently anticommunist – when the Rolling Stones played Prague in 2003, Keith Richards wore a Černý-designed T-shirt with the slogan 'Fuck the KSČM' (KSČM is the Communist Party of Bohemia and Moravia). He also incurred the wrath of older-generation Czechs by describing them as 'an unmixed, uninteresting, slightly dumplingish, untanned mass'.

Since the 'pink tank' episode Černý has become internationally famous. He lived for a time in the USA and his art has been exhibited in New York, Chicago, Berlin, Dresden, Stockholm and London. Many of his works are on display throughout Prague (see the boxed text, p84).

You can find more details of Černý's work on his website at www.davidcerny.cz.

CINEMA

The pioneer of Czech cinema was the architect Jan Křiženecký, who made three comedies in American-slapstick style that were shown at the 1898 Exhibition of Architecture & Engineering.

The domestic film industry took off in the early years of the 20th century and Czechs were leading innovators. The first film ever to show full-frontal nudity was Gustaf Machatý's *Extase* (Ecstasy; 1932). It was a hit (and a scandal) at the 1934 Venice Film Festival. Revealing all was one Hedvige Kiesler, who went on to Hollywood as Hedy Lamarr. Hugo Haas directed a fine adaptation of Karel Čapek's anti-Nazi science-fiction novel *Bílá nemoc* (White Death) in 1937. Fear of persecution drove him to Hollywood, where he made and starred in many films.

The Nazis limited the movie industry to nationalistic comedies, while under communism the focus was on low-quality propaganda films. A 'new wave' of Czech cinema rose between 1963 and the Soviet-led invasion in 1968. Its young directors escaped censorship because they were among the first graduates of the communist-supervised Academy of Film. It was from this time that Czech films began to win international awards.

Among the earliest outstanding works was *Černý Petr* (Black Peter, known in the USA as *Peter & Paula*; 1963) by Miloš Forman, who fled the country after 1968 and became a successful Hollywood director with films such as *One Flew over the Cuckoo's Nest* (1975) and *Amadeus* (1984). Other prominent directors were Jiří Menzel, Věra Chytilová and Ivan Passer.

Some post-1968 films critical of the regime were banned or production was stopped. Probably the best film of the following two decades was Menzel's internationally screened 1985 comedy *Vesničko má středisková* (My Sweet Little Village), a subtle look at the workings and failings of socialism in a village cooperative.

Directors in the post-communist era struggle to compete with Hollywood films, as well as the good Czech films of the '60s. So far the only one who has succeeded is Jan Svěrák, whose 1994 hit *Akumulátor* was the most expensive Czech film produced to date. In 1996 it was surpassed at the box office by the internationally acclaimed *Kolja*, about a Russian boy raised by a Czech bachelor. A year later *Kolja* won the award for best foreign film at the Cannes Film Festival and the US Academy Awards.

Věra Chytilová continues to produce good films and win prizes at film festivals. In 2000 another brilliant young director, David Ondříček, released *Samotáři*, the story of a group of seven people trying to find love and a partner in the 1990s.

TOP FIVE CZECH FILMS

- Černý Petr (Peter & Paula; 1963) Director: Miloš Forman
- Kolja (1996) Director: Jan Svěrák
- Musíme Si Pomáhat (Divided We Fall; 2000) Director: Jan Hřejbek
- Ostre sledované vlaky (Closely Watched Trains; 1966) Director: Jiří Menzel
- Vesničko má středisková (My Sweet Little Village; 1985) Director: Jiří Menzel

František Palacký Memorial (p101)

Jan Hřejbek's superb black comedy *Musíme Si Pomáhat* (Divided We Fall; 2000), exploring the conflicting loyalties of small-town Czechs during WWII, won an Oscar nomination for best foreign film. In 2001 Jan Svěrák, director of *Kolja*, produced *Dark Blue World*, a story of two Czech fighter pilots who return home after WWII only to be sent to labour camps by the communist authorities.

The Czech film studios at Barrandov in southwestern Prague are known for their world-class animated and puppet films, many of which were made from the 1950s to the 1980s. *A Midsummer Night's Dream* (1959) was the best of the puppet films, and was produced by the talented Jiří Trnka.

THEATRE

Czech-language theatre did not develop fully until the 16th century. Themes were mostly biblical and the intent was to moralise. At Prague's Karolinum, Latin drama was used for teaching. The best plays were written by Jan Ámos Komenský (John Comenius) in the years before the Thirty Years' War, after which plays in Czech were banned. German drama and Italian opera were popular during the 17th and 18th centuries, when many theatres were built.

In 1785 Czech drama reappeared at the Nostitz Theatre, now the Estates Theatre (Stavovské divadlo; p161), and Prague became the centre of Czech-language theatre. Major 19th-century playwrights were Josef Kajetán Tyl and Ján Kolář. Drama, historical plays and fairy tales flourished as part of the Czech National Revival. In 1862 the first independent Czech theatre, the Prozatimní divadlo (Temporary Theatre), opened in Prague.

Drama in the early years of Czechoslovakia was led by the brothers Karel and Josef Čapek, and also František Langer. Actor and playwright EF Burian later became known for his experimental dramas.

Under communism classical theatrical performances were of a high quality, but the modern scene was stifled. Exceptions included the pantomime of the Černé divadlo (Black Theatre) and the ultramodern Laterna Magika (Magic Lantern), founded by Alfréd Radok.

Many fine plays, including those by Václav Havel, were not performed locally as a result of their anti-government tone, but appeared in the West. In the mid-1960s free expression was explored in Prague's Theatre on the Balustrade (divadlo na Zábradlí; p174), with works by Havel, Ladislav Fialka and Milan Uhde, and performances by the comedy duo of Jiří Suchý and Jiří Šlitr.

Marionette performances have been popular in Prague since the 16th century. A major figure of this art form was Matěj Kopecký (1775–1847).

Marionette theatres opened in Prague and Plzeň in the early 20th century. Josef Skupa's legendary Spejbl & Hurvínek (the Czech Punch and Judy) attracted large crowds, and still does.

Even during communism, puppet and marionette theatre was officially approved and popular, and Czech performances were ranked among the best in the world, especially in the films of Jiří Trnka.

Architecture ■

Architecture

Prague is a living textbook of 1000 years of European architecture. The city's historic core is unparalleled in Europe, having escaped damage in WWII and avoided large-scale redevelopment. It records a millennium of continuous urban development, with baroque façades encasing Gothic houses perched on top of Romanesque cellars, all following a street plan that emerged in the 11th century. Malá Strana (Little Quarter), Staré Město (Old Town) and Nové Město (New Town) were given Unesco World Heritage status in 1992; of more than 3500 buildings, over 1500 are designated cultural monuments.

ROMANESQUE

The oldest surviving buildings in Prague date back to the era of the Přemysl dynasty, which began with the founding of Prague Castle by Prince Bořivoj in 870. In the crypt of St Vitus Cathedral (p71) are the sparse remains of the Rotunda of St Vitus, built for Duke Wenceslas (the 'Good King Wenceslas' of Christmas carol fame) in the early 10th century.

What to See

Several stone-built Romanesque rotundas (circular churches dating from the 10th and 11th centuries) survive intact in Prague, though most have since been incorporated into larger churches. Examples include the Rotunda of St Longinus (early 12th century; p102) in Nové Město, the Rotunda of the Holy Cross (mid-12th century; p96) in Staré Město, and the Rotunda of St Martin (late 11th century; p106) at Vyšehrad.

Prague's finest Romanesque structure, however, is the Basilica of St George (p74) at Prague Castle. Although its exterior is hidden behind an elaborate 17th-century baroque façade, the interior exhibits the heavy walls and plain columns, barrel-vaulted ceilings, and small doors and windows with semicircular arches that typify the Romanesque style.

GOTHIC

The Gothic style, which flourished in Prague from the 13th to the 16th centuries, represented not just a new aesthetic but also a revolution in architectural design that allowed architects to build thinner walls and higher vaults. Gothic architecture is characterised by tall, pointed arches, ribbed vaults and columns, external flying buttresses (to support the weight transmitted from the ribbed vaults) and tall, narrow windows with intricate tracery supporting great expanses of stained glass. As time went by Gothic designs became ever taller, pointier and more elaborately decorated.

Spires of St Vitus Cathedral (p71)

AT THE WEIRD & THE WONDERFUL

One of the most distinctive features of Prague's street scene is the colourful and often unusual house signs that adorn the façades of many of the older buildings. Before 1770 (when house signs were banned by Josef II in favour of street numbers) merchants, tradesmen and other notable citizens would have their initials, a symbol of their trade, or some other distinctive device carved on the front of their house which served in place of an address.

Nerudova (see p78) in Malá Strana is particularly rich in surviving examples. Here you will find U bílé labutí (At the White Swan; No 49), U dvou sluncŭ (At the Two Suns; No 47), U zeleného raka (At the Green Lobster; No 43), U zlaté podkovy (At the Golden Horseshoe; No 34), U tří houslíček (At the Three Fiddles; No 12) and U červeného orla (At the Red Eagle; No 6).

Old Town Square (see p85) is graced by U kamenného zvonu (At the Stone Bell; No 13), U kamenného beránka (At the Stone Lamb; No 17), on the corner with U bílého koníčká (At the Little White Horse), U zlatého jednorožce (At the Golden Unicorn; No 20) and U modré hvězdy (At the Blue Star; No 25), while nearby Karlova has U zlatého hada (At the Golden Snake) at No 18.

The tradition is carried on today in the naming of many of Prague's pubs and restaurants, with unusual and inventive names ranging from U modré kachničky (At the Blue Duckling; see p136) to U vystřeleného oka (At the Shot-Out Eye; see p158).

What to See

Czech Gothic architecture flourished during the rule of Charles IV, especially in the hands of German architect Petr Parler (Peter Parléř), best known for the eastern part of St Vitus Cathedral (p71) at Prague Castle. Begun by Matyáš z Arrasu (Matthias of Arras) in 1344, work on the cathedral continued under Parler, the most influential mason in Prague at that time, until his death in 1399. His bold experiments with the design of the cathedral's vaults – note the dazzling star-, fan- and diamond-shaped formations of the ribbed vaults in the choir – laid the foundations for the even more impressive achievements of German architects in the 15th century, while the open-work staircase that Parler installed on the outside of the Great Tower was later copied in the cathedrals of Strasbourg and Ulm.

Parler was also responsible for the Gothic design of the Charles Bridge (Karlův most; p80), the Old Town Bridge Tower (p88), the Church of Our Lady of the Snows (p99) and the Cathedral of St Barbara in Kutnv Hora (p219).

Another master builder of the Gothic period was Benedikt Rejt, who was summoned to Prague Castle to improve the fortifications and the royal living quarters. His finest legacy to the city is the petal-shaped vaulting of the Vladislav Hall (1487–1500; p73) in the Old Royal Palace. Its flowing, intertwined ribs are a beautiful example of late-Gothic craftsmanship, while the huge windows on the south wall are considered to be the earliest example of Renaissance style in Bohemia.

Other fine Gothic buildings in the city include the Convent of St Agnes (1234–1380; p89), and the late-Gothic Powder Gate (1475; p94) by Matěj Rejsek.

RENAISSANCE

When the Habsburgs took over the Bohemian throne in the early 16th century they invited Italian designers and architects to Prague to help create a royal city worthy of their status. The Italians brought a new enthusiasm for classical forms, an obsession with grace and symmetry and a taste for exuberant decoration.

The mixture of local and Italian styles gave rise to a distinctive 'Bohemian Renaissance' style, featuring heavy ornamental stucco decorations and paintings of historical or mythical scenes. The technique of *sgraffito* – from the Italian word meaning 'to scrape' – was much used, creating patterns and pictures by scraping through an outer layer of pale plaster to reveal a darker surface underneath.

The rebuilding of Hradčany and Malá Strana after a devastating fire in 1541 (see p40 for details) was undertaken almost entirely in Renaissance style, with the emphasis firmly on luxurious palaces, pleasure gardens and merchant houses rather than on churches and religious buildings.

What to See

The Summer Palace, or Belvedere (1538–60; p71) in the gardens to the north of Prague Castle was built for Queen Anna, the consort of Ferdinand I, Prague's first Habsburg ruler. It is almost pure Italian Renaissance in style, with features that will strike a chord with anyone familiar with the buildings of Brunelleschi in Florence.

Other fine examples of Renaissance buildings are the Ball-Game House (1569; p71) in Prague Castle, the Schwarzenberg Palace (1546–67; p75) in Hradčany, with its striking, Venetian-style *sgraffito* decoration, the House at the Minute (1564–1610; p88) in Staré Město, and the Star Summer Palace (1556; p116).

BAROQUE

In the aftermath of the Thirty Years' War (1618–48), the triumphant Habsburg empire embarked on a campaign of reconstruction and re-Catholicisation of the Czech lands. The baroque style of architecture, with its marble columns, florid sculpture, *trompe l'oeil* paintings, frescoed ceilings and rich, gilded ornamentation full of curves and ovals, was consciously used by the Catholic Church as an instrument of propaganda – the extravagant and awe-inspiring interiors of baroque churches were designed to impress the faithful with the splendour of the divine, while the elaborate façades were visual symbols of the Church's triumph over the Protestant reformers.

This was the grandest period in Prague's architectural development, responsible for the largely baroque face that you see in Prague today. Not only were churches built in the baroque style, but also palaces, villas, town houses, ornamental gardens and country chateaux. From the early 17th century onwards, noble families such as Schwarzenberg, Nostitz, Liechtenstein, Kolovrat and Czernin decided that they needed a base in the city, and began building their palaces and gardens close to the castle in Hradčany and Malá Strana.

By the early 18th century a distinctively Czech baroque style had emerged. Its best-known practitioners were the Bavarian father and son Kristof and Kilian Ignatz Dientzenhofer (see the boxed text, opposite), the Italian Giovanni Santini and the Bohemian František Kaňka.

What to See

The most impressive example of Prague baroque is the Dientzenhofers' Church of St Nicholas (1704–55; p80) in Malá Strana, one of the finest baroque buildings in central Europe. Its massive green dome dominates Malá Strana in a fitting symbol of the Catholic Church's dominance over 18th-century Prague. You enter through the western door at the foot of an undulating, tripartite façade decorated with the figures of saints, into a fantasy palace of pale pink, green and gold, where a profusion of pilasters, sinuous arches and saintly statues leads your eye ever upward towards the luminous glow of the dome. The magnificent fresco that adorns the ceiling of the nave – at 1500 sq m it is one of the biggest in Europe – depicts the Apotheosis of St Nicholas, and portrays the saint (among other things) rescuing shipwrecked sailors, saving three unjustly condemned men from the death sentence, and saving women from prostitution by throwing them bags of gold.

The final flourish of the late baroque period was the rococo style, a sort of 'super baroque' with even more (and even more elaborate) decoration. The Goltz-Kinský Palace (1755–65; p87), overlooking Old Town Square, has a rococo façade.

Goltz-Kinský Palace (p87)

CZECH NATIONAL REVIVAL

The success of the Czech National Revival (p41) in the second half of the 19th century – when Prague gained a measure of self-government within the Habsburg empire and Czech political parties won control of the city council – saw the commissioning of many public buildings where the designs evoked the elegance and grandeur of the Renaissance era.

The architecture of this period sought to achieve a distinctively Czech style that would reflect the reviving confidence of Czech culture and stand in contrast to the baroque that had come to symbolise, for many Czechs, the domination of the Habsburg empire.

The National Theatre in particular was deeply tied up with the National Revival. A group of Czech patriots, led by historian František Palacký, petitioned the Habsburg emperor to be allowed to build an independent Czech-language theatre, to be funded entirely by public donation, and designed and decorated by the leading Czech artists of the period. So strongly did these plans fire the Czech imagination that when the theatre was seriously damaged by a fire before it had even opened, it took only six weeks to raise enough money to rebuild it. The theatre opened officially in 1883 with a performance of Smetana's patriotic opera *Libuše*.

What to See

Buildings in the so-called neo-Renaissance style include the National Museum (1891; p100) on Wenceslas Square, the Rudolfinum (1876–84; p89) on náměstí Jana Palacha, and, most impressive of all, the National Theatre (1883; p101) on Národní třída, all designed by Josef Zítek and Josef Schulz.

ART NOUVEAU

As the 19th century drew to a close Czech architecture came under the spell of Art Nouveau, with its sinuous, botanical lines and colourful renderings of flowers and (mostly female) human figures. The term came from the French *l'art nouveau* (New Art) and was known as *secese* in Bohemia, *Sezessionstil* in Austria and *Jugendstil* in Germany.

THE DIENTZENHOFER DYNASTY

No two men did more to give Prague its overwhelmingly baroque face than the Bavarian architects Kristof Dientzenhofer (1655–1722) and his son Kilian Ignatz Dientzenhofer (1689–1751). Born into a large family of German builders and architects from Aibling on the borders of Bavaria and Austria, Dientzenhofer senior arrived in Prague at the age of 23 in the hope of making his fortune amid the spate of building activity that accompanied the Counter-Reformation.

He married a German widow and moved into a house at No 2 Nosticova in Malá Strana, where his son Kilian was born in 1689, but he also made several study trips to Austria, Italy and France in his quest to become one of the leading architects of his time. His son attended Malá Strana's Jesuit school and went on to read mathematics and philosophy at Charles University, before spending nine years studying architecture in Vienna under the famous Austrian architect Johann Lukas von Hildebrandts.

Working in collaboration with his father until the latter's death, and later on his own, Kilian Dientzenhofer created more than 250 superb buildings, not only in Prague but also elsewhere in Bohemia, Austria, Italy, France and Hungary. His religious buildings are characterised by undulating façades, an interplay of convex and concave surfaces, and a soaring and harmonious composition that both impresses and inspires, conveying both the spiritual and the material power of the Catholic Church. But despite being a favourite architect of the imperial court, he was often paid poorly or not at all, and when he died his family was left in poverty.

The most prominent Dientzenhofer contributions to Prague's cityscape:

- Church of St John Nepomuk (1720–29; p121)
- Church of St Margaret, Břevnov (1720; p115)
- Church of St Nicholas, Staré Město (1732–35; p87)
- Goltz-Kinský Palace (1755–65; p87)
- Loreta (1711–51; p76)
- St Nicholas Church, Malá Strana (1704–55; p80)
- Vila Amerika (Dvořák Museum; 1717–20; p103)

Museum of Decorative Arts (p90)

The building of the Palace of Industry (p107) for the Jubilee Exhibition of 1891 saw the first arrival of Art Nouveau in Prague, and over the next two decades it became the favoured style of the city's middle classes.

When the Jewish ghetto of Josefov was cleared in the late 19th century and the broad boulevard of Pařížská was driven through the former slums, fashionable new apartment blocks in Art Nouveau style were built along its length. Similar blocks were built in the expanding middle-class suburb of Vinohrady, notably along the desirable streets just to the east of Riegrovy sady.

What to See

The Art Nouveau style was applied to upmarket hotels including the Hotel Central (1899–1901) on Hybernská in Nové Město, where the façade is decorated with stuccoed foliage, ornate lamps and a glass cornice beneath a decorated gable. The more famous Grand Hotel Evropa (1906; see the boxed text, p99), on Wenceslas Square, is even grander and more ornate (on the outside, at least; its accommodation leaves a lot to be desired), while the Hotel Paříž (1904; p200) has retained its interior as well as exterior splendour.

Architect Josef Fanta was responsible for the old, Art Nouveau section of Prague Main Train Station (Praha hlavní nádraží; 1901–09; p98), whose dome and twin towers rise above the busy freeway of Wilsonova, and also for the pretty House of the Hlahol Choir (1906; p101), on the banks of the Vltava.

But the city's finest expression of Art Nouveau architecture is the magnificent Municipal House (Obecní dům; 1906–12; p93). Like the National Theatre before it, it was envisaged as a symbol of a resurgent Czech culture, with every aspect of the building's decoration designed by the leading Czech artists of the time, most famously the Lord Mayor's Hall, which was decorated by Alfons Mucha.

CUBIST

In a period of just 10 years (1910–20), barely half a dozen architects bequeathed to Prague a unique legacy of buildings – mostly private homes and apartment blocks – that were influenced by the Cubist movement in art.

The Cubist style spurned both the regular lines of traditional architecture and the sinuous forms of Art Nouveau in favour of triangular, polygonal and pyramidal forms, emphasising diagonals rather than horizontals and verticals, and achieving a jagged, faceted, almost crystalline effect, where the appearance changes as the angle of the sun moves through the day.

What to See

Some of Prague's finest Cubist façades were designed by Josef Chochol between 1912 and 1914, and can be seen in the neighbourhood below the Vyšehrad fortress; check out the buildings at the corner of Vnislavova and Rašínovo nábřeží, Rašínovo nábřeží 6–10 and Neklanova 30 (see the boxed text, above). Other appealing examples include the House of the Black Madonna (1912; p94) in Staré Město, which

CUBIST HOUSES

If you plan to visit Vyšehrad (p104), don't miss the opportunity to see some of Prague's finest Cubist buildings. Cubist architecture, with its eye-catching use of elementary geometric forms, is more or less unique to the Czech Republic, and particularly to Prague.

Neklanova, northeast of the Vyšehrad citadel, is a dingy street of sooty, pastel-hued neoclassical façades lifted out of the ordinary by the striking planes and angles of the apartment block at **Neklanova 30**, designed by that master of Czech Cubist style, Josef Chochol. Other buildings by Chochol are the **Villa Libušina** at the corner of Vnislavova and Rašínovo nábřeží, and an elegant terrace of three houses at **Rašínovo nábřeží 6–10**, just before it tunnels beneath Vyšehrad rock. All date from around 1912 to 1913. Other Cubist works by lesser lights are scattered around the neighbourhood.

houses the Museum of Czech Cubism, and the twin houses on Tychonova in Dejvice (p121), all by Josef Gočár, and a 1921 apartment building at Elišky Krasnohorské 10–14 in Staré Město, created by Otakar Novotný.

Less well known, but still showing strong Cubist influences, are the early-20th-century apartment blocks along and around Křížkovského (Map pp278–9), on the border between Žižkov and Vinohrady, just east of Riegrovy sady.

After WWI Cubism evolved into another unique Prague architectural style as architects such as Pavel Janák and Josef Gočár added colour and decorative elements to their angular façades in another attempt to define a Czech national style. The more rounded forms that characterise these buildings led to the name 'rondocubism'. This short-lived style is seen in Janák's monumental Adria Palace (1922–25; p100), on Národní třída, and in the tall, narrow apartment building at No 4 Jungmannovo náměstí, but its finest expression is seen in Gočár's Legiobank (Bank of the Czechoslovak Legions; 1921–23) at Na poříčí 24, with its hypnotic alternation of rounded and right-angled features.

The latter is a celebration of the achievements of the Czechoslovak Legions, who fought against the German and Austrian armies in WWI. The façade, which contrasts strongly with the smooth, Functionalist façade (1937–39) to its left, is enlivened by four muscular sculptures topping the street-level pillars and representing, from left to right, the Legions in the Trenches; Defiance and Courage; Waiting and Yearning for Home; and Throwing Grenades and Defence Against Gas Attack. The frieze above, by Otto Gutfreund, illustrates the Legions' victorious homecoming.

House of the Black Madonna (Museum of Czech Cubism; p94)

PANELÁKY

Prague's outer suburbs consist mainly of huge 1970s and '80s housing estates characterised by serried ranks of high-rise apartment blocks, known in Czech as *paneláky* (singular *panelák*) because they were built using prefabricated, reinforced concrete panels. Each block contains hundreds of identical flats, and each estate contains dozens of identical blocks.

Western visitors often assume that these concrete suburbs must be sink estates, filled with the city's poor and riddled with crime and drugs. Nothing could be further from the truth. The *panelák* suburbs are home to a broad spectrum of Czech society, from students to surgeons, from lawyers to street sweepers. Local services and public transport are good, there is plenty of open parkland, and there is a surprisingly strong sense of community. Since the fall of communism, the few who can afford it have moved away from the concrete suburbs to detached houses and villas on the edge of the city. But as Prague property prices have boomed, rent-controlled *panelák* flats continue to offer affordable accommodation within reasonable commuting distance of the city centre. Many tenants have ripped out the flimsy partition walls, laid laminate floors and installed new kitchens and bathrooms to create more attractive, open-plan living spaces. There is even a magazine called *Panel Story* that is devoted to DIY *paneláky* projects.

Although perhaps lacking in aesthetic appeal, Prague's *paneláky* were neither particularly cheap nor quick to build, in contrast to the often shoddy residential blocks of similar vintage that blight many Russian cities. Rather, the prime motive for their construction was ideological. Their very uniformity was the antithesis of bourgeois individuality and spoke of a new order where all were to be equal.

The biggest conglomeration of *paneláky* is in Jižní Město (Map pp262–3) on the southeastern edge of the city, comprising the suburbs of Háje, Opatov and Chodov. Take the metro to Háje at the end of line C for a stroll among the concrete canyons.

During this period Cubist designs were extended both into the field of decorative arts – examples of Cubist furniture, ceramics, and glassware can be seen in the Museum of Decorative Arts (p90) and the Museum of Czech Cubism (p94) – and the more mundane domain of street furniture: Prague must be the only city in the world with a Cubist lamppost (p120). Even Franz Kafka's tombstone (p110), designed by Leopold Ehrmann in 1924, evokes the Cubist style in its crystaline prismatic pillar.

MODERNIST

The creation of an independent Czechoslovakia in 1918 was followed by a wave of excitement and creativity. The architecture of this period was influenced by new technology and materials, and by the streamlined forms of modern transportation such as cars, steam locomotives and ocean liners. Form and purpose were merged dramatically in a new movement that became known as Functionalism. Functionalist buildings were typified by their extreme geometric simplicity, clean lines, and the use of modern materials such as reinforced concrete, plate glass and steel.

One of the more idiosyncratic architects to leave his mark on Prague during this period was the Slovenian Joze Plečnik, a friend of President Tomáš Masaryk, who was commissioned to update and renovate parts of Prague Castle. Plečnik also designed the remarkable Church of the Most Sacred Heart of Our Lord (1928–32; p111), a building that was inspired by the forms of early Christian basilicas and Egyptian temples, and one that still defies classification.

Prague's apartment blocks (boxed text, above)

National Theatre and Nová Scéna (p101)

What to See

A classic example of Functionalism is the Baťa shoe store (1929; see the boxed text p99) on Wenceslas Square, which was the city's first concrete-framed building. Its seven-storey façade consists almost entirely of glass, and there are few structural members to impede the open sales areas on each floor.

The city's first Functionalist building was the vast Veletržní Palace (1926–28; p109), built as an exhibition space and now home to Prague's main gallery of modern art. The huge central space, overlooked by six levels of galleries lined with stainless-steel guardrails, has the feel of a cruise liner's decks.

Other Functionalist masterpieces include the Mánes Gallery (1927–30; p102) in Nové Město and Villa Müller (1930; p115) in Střešovice.

The architectural legacy of the communist era consists mostly of concrete monstrosities, such as the Congress Centre (1981; p128) in Vyšehrad, as well as the serried ranks of mass-produced apartment blocks that comprise the city's outer suburbs (see the boxed text, opposite). More imposing monuments to communism include the Stalinist tower of the Hotel Crowne Plaza (1954; see p113), the extraordinary Hotel Praha (1981; see p208) and Žižkov's space-age TV Tower (1985–92; see p111).

POST-1989

Prague's post-1989 architecture is a mixed bag, some quite out of keeping with its surroundings, some simply ugly and some surprisingly attractive.

One of Prague's most idiosyncratic and appealing examples of new architecture is the Dancing Building (1992–96; p101) on Rašínovo nábřeží in Nové Město, designed by the Prague architect Vlado Milunič and the American Frank O Gehry. Built on a gap site left by a stray WWII American bomb, it drew much criticism from the older generation of Czechs. In contrast to the bland, mass-produced, functional architecture of the communist era, and the spate of historic renovations that characterised post-1989 Prague, this was a bold, innovative and individualistic project.

The building's striking resemblance to a pair of dancers soon saw it acquire the nickname 'Fred and Ginger', after the legendary dancing duo Astaire and Rogers. Some critics, however, have likened the wasp-waisted Ginger to 'a crushed Coke can', while some have compared the building's effect on the Prague cityscape to a second American bomb. But Prague's younger generation are more positive, seeing the Dancing Building as an expression of personal freedom. A poll found that 68% of Praguers liked Fred and Ginger, with only 16% actively disliking it.

The architect Milunič claims that his original idea for the building back in the early 1990s was to create a symbol of the new Czechoslovakia – a dialogue between old and new, static and dynamic, the past dancing with the future. Despite its boldly modern lines, the Dancing Building somehow blends in perfectly with its surroundings.

By contrast, the bland, glass-and-metal façade of the Mýslbek Building (1996), designed by the French firm Caisse des Dépots et Consignations in collaboration with local architects, clashes unpleasantly with its *fin-de-siècle* neighbours on Na příkopě. On the other hand the building's rear façade, on Ovocný trh, blends in masterfully.

The building boom that began in the mid-1990s continues apace, with new shopping centres, office buildings and apartment blocks appearing all over the city. Most are undistinguished but a few stand out, notably the swooping glass façade of the Anděl Center (by French architect Jean Nouvel) and the huge Nový Smíchov shopping mall by local design agency D3A, both in Smíchov.

The latest architectural story to cause controversy is a proposal to build a huge, seven-storey Palace of Art, which will house a permanent collection of around 1500 works by Spanish surrealist Salvador Dalí. The building, which will occupy a site on the banks of the Vltava at the north end of Revoluční, has been designed by Polish-born architect Daniel Libeskind, famous for the Jewish Museum in Berlin and the design for the Freedom Tower that is to be built on the site of the World Trade Center in New York. If approved, the gallery could be open by 2008.

TOP FIVE NOTABLE BUILDINGS

- Dancing Building (p101)
- House of the Black Madonna (p94)
- Municipal House (p93)
- National Theatre (p101)
- St Vitus Cathedral (p71)

History

History

THE RECENT PAST

Despite the city's turbulent history, Prague's progress in recent years has been more stately than revolutionary. The booming tourism sector and a solid industrial base have left its citizens in better economic shape than the rest of the country. Unemployment is minimal, the shops are full, and façades that were crumbling a decade ago have been given face-lifts. Big new shopping malls and multiplex cinemas are popping up all over the place, there's a huge new sporting and events arena, the metro system is being extended and a new flood-protection system has been installed.

There are downsides, of course. Rumours of corruption in City Hall are rife, affordable housing remains in short supply, the health system is under strain, and traffic congestion and crime rates are up. Despite this, the mood of the city remains buoyant.

Václav Havel's 13 years as president came to an end in February 2003, when his place was taken by hard-nosed, right-wing economist Václav Klaus. More change was to come: the decision on whether the Czech Republic should join the European Union was settled by a referendum – with 77% voting in favour – and on 1 May 2004 the Czech Republic became a member of the EU.

However, the parliamentary elections of June 2006 ended in stalemate – it looks like a rocky road ahead for Czech politics in the next few years.

FROM THE BEGINNING

The oldest evidence of human habitation in the Prague valley dates from 600,000 BC, but more numerous clues were left by hunters during the last Ice Age, about 25,000 years ago. Permanent communities were established around 4000 BC in the northwestern parts of Prague, and the area was inhabited continuously by various Germanic and Celtic tribes before the arrival of the Slavs. The name Bohemia came from a Celtic tribe called Boii, and is still used today for the western part of the Czech Republic.

FOUNDATION OF PRAGUE

In the 6th century, two Slav tribes settled on opposite sides of a particularly appealing stretch of the Vltava River. The Czechs built a wooden fortress where the residential area Hradčany stands today, and the Zlíčani built theirs upstream at what is now Vyšehrad. They had barely dug in when nomadic Avars thundered in, to rule until the Frankish trader Samo united the Slav tribes and drove the Avars out. Samo held on for 35 years before the Slavs reverted to squabbling.

In the 9th century Prague was part of the short-lived Great Moravian Empire. Under its second ruler, Rastislav (r 846–70), emissaries were invited to come from Constantinople, and Christianity took root in the region. The Moravians (the ancient lands of Moravia now form the eastern part of the Czech Republic) were ultimately undone by internal conflicts, especially with the Czechs, who finally broke away from the empire.

Prague Castle (Pražský hrad, or just *hrad* to the Czechs; p69) was built in the 870s by Prince Bořivoj as the main seat of the Přemysl dynasty. Vyšehrad (p104) sometimes served as an alternative in the 10th and 11th centuries.

Christianity became the state religion under the rule of the pious Wenceslas (Václav in Czech), duke of Bohemia (r c 925–29), now the chief patron saint of the Czech people.

TIMELINE **6th century**   **870s**

First settlement on Vyšehrad hill	Founding of Prague Castle

Student memorial on Národní třída (p100)

Wenceslas was the 'Good King Wenceslas' of the well-known Christmas carol written in 1853 by English clergyman John Mason Neale. Neale, a scholar of eastern European church history, had read about St Wenceslas' legendary piety, and based his carol on the story of the duke's page finding strength and warmth by following in the footsteps of his master as they carried food, wine and firewood to a poor peasant on a freezing cold Boxing Day. The unfortunate Wenceslas was murdered by his own brother, Boleslav; the Chapel of St Wenceslas in St Vitus Cathedral (see p71) is decorated with scenes from the saint's life.

In 950 the German king Otto I conquered Bohemia and incorporated it into the Holy Roman Empire. By 993 Přemysl princes had forged a genuine Slav alliance, and ruled Bohemia on the Germans' behalf until 1212, when the pope granted Otakar I the right to rule as a king. Otakar bestowed royal privileges on the Staré Město (Old Town), and Malá Strana (Little Quarter) was established in 1257 by Otakar II.

Přemysl lands stretched at one point from modern-day Silesia (a region on the Czech–Polish border) to the Mediterranean Sea. Their Austrian and Slovenian domains, however, were lost when Otakar II died and his army was thrashed at the 1278 Battle of Moravské Pole (fought near modern-day Dürnkrut in Austria) by the Austrian Habsburgs.

GOLDEN AGE

The murder of Wenceslas III in 1306 left no male heir to the Přemysl throne. Two Habsburg monarchs briefly ruled Bohemia until the Holy Roman emperor John of Luxembourg (Jan Lucemburský to the Czechs) also became king of Bohemia by marrying Wenceslas III's daughter Elyška in 1310. Under the rule of John's son Charles (Karel) IV (r 1346–78) as king and Holy Roman emperor, Prague grew into one of the continent's largest and most prosperous cities, acquiring its fine Gothic face, and landmarks including the Karolinum (Charles University), Charles Bridge and St Vitus Cathedral.

HUSSITE REVOLUTION

The late 14th and early 15th centuries witnessed the Church-reform movement led by Jan Hus (see the boxed text, p40). Hus' eventual conviction for heresy and his death at the stake in 1415 sparked a nationalist rebellion in Bohemia led by the Hussite preacher Jan Želivský. In 1419 several Catholic councillors were flung from the windows of Prague's New Town Hall by Želivský's followers, thus introducing the word 'defenestration' (the act of throwing someone or something out of a window) to the political lexicon.

1415	1419
Jan Hus burned at the stake	First Defenestration of Prague; Catholic councillors thrown from New Town Hall (Novoměstská radnice)

JAN HUS

Jan Hus was the Czech lands' foremost, and one of Europe's earliest, Christian reformers, anticipating Martin Luther and the Lutheran Reformation by a century.

Hus was born into a poor family in southern Bohemia in 1372. At the age of 18 he enrolled at the Karolinum (Charles University) and two years after graduating he started work as a teacher there. Five years later he was made dean of the philosophy faculty, at a time when the university was caught up in a struggle against German influence.

Like many of his Czech colleagues, Hus was inspired by the English philosopher and radical reformist theologian John Wycliffe. The latter's ideas on reform of the Roman Catholic clergy meshed nicely with growing Czech resentment at the wealth and corruptness of the higher clergy – who together owned about half of all Bohemia – and its heavy taxation of the peasantry.

In 1391 Prague reformers had founded the Bethlehem Chapel (see p96), where sermons were given in Czech rather than Latin. Hus preached here for about 10 years, while continuing his duties at the university.

Because German masters at the university enjoyed three votes to the Czech masters' one, anti-reform attitudes officially prevailed there. In 1403 the masters declared many of Wycliffe's writings to be heresy. During the Great Schism (1378–1417), when Roman Catholics had two popes, the masters opposed the 1409 Council of Pisa that was called to sort things out. This so infuriated Wenceslas IV that he abrogated the university constitution and gave the Czech masters three votes to the Germans' one, leading to a mass exodus of Germans from Prague.

In the chaos surrounding the Great Schism, one pope was persuaded to prohibit preaching in private chapels such as the Bethlehem Chapel. Hus refused to obey and was excommunicated, though he continued to preach at the chapel and teach at the university. A disagreement with Wenceslas IV over the sale of indulgences cost him the king's support. The Council of Constance, called to put a final end to the Great Schism, convicted Hus of heresy, and Hus was burned at the stake in 1415.

After the death in 1419 of Holy Roman emperor and king of Bohemia Wenceslas IV, Prague was ruled by various Hussite committees. In 1420 combined Hussite forces led by military commander Jan Žižka successfully defended Prague against the first anti-Hussite crusade, launched by Sigismund, the Holy Roman emperor, during the Battle of Vítkov Hill.

In the 1420s a split developed in the Hussite ranks between radical Taborites, who advocated total war on Catholics, and moderate Utraquists, who consisted mainly of nobles who were more concerned with transforming the Church. In 1434 the Utraquists agreed to accept Sigismund's rule in return for religious tolerance; the Taborites kept fighting, only to be defeated in the same year at the Battle of Lipany.

Following Sigismund's death, George of Poděbrady (Jiří z Poděbrad) ruled as Bohemia's one and only Hussite king, from 1452 to 1471, with the backing of Utraquist forces. He was centuries ahead of his time in suggesting a European council to solve international problems by diplomacy rather than war, but he couldn't convince the major European rulers or the pope. After George's death two weak kings from the Polish Jagiellonian dynasty ruled Bohemia, though real power lay with the Utraquist nobles, the so-called Bohemian Estates.

HABSBURG RULE

In 1526 the Austrian Catholic Habsburgs were again asked by the Czech nobility to rule Bohemia. In the second half of the century the city enjoyed great prosperity under Emperor Rudolf II, and was made the seat of the Habsburg empire. Rudolf established great art collections, and renowned artists and scholars were invited to his court.

A huge fire in 1541 laid waste many sections of Malá Strana and Hradčany. The fire started on Hradčany Square, on the site now occupied by the Sternberg Palace (see p75), and swept through the largely wooden houses of merchants and artisans, destroying most of the district. The rebuilding that took place following the fire gave Hradčany and Malá Strana much of the beautiful Renaissance and baroque architecture that still graces their streets.

1618	1620
Second Defenestration of Prague kicks off the Thirty Years' War	Habsburg victory at Battle of Bílá Hora

An ill-fated uprising of the Bohemian Estates in 1618, which began when two Habsburg councillors and their secretary were flung from an upper window in Prague Castle, dealt a blow to Czech fortunes for the next 300 years. This 'Second Defenestration of Prague' sparked off the Thirty Years' War, devastating much of Europe, and Bohemia in particular – a quarter of the Bohemian population perished.

The following year the Bohemian Estates elected Frederick of the Palatinate as their ruler. But because of ineffective leadership, low morale among their heavily mercenary army, and limited international support, the crucial Battle of Bílá Hora (White Mountain) on 8 November 1620 was lost by the Protestants to the Habsburgs almost before the first shots were fired. The 'Winter King' (so-called because he ruled Bohemia for just one winter) fled and, in 1621, the 27 nobles who had instigated the revolt were executed in Old Town Square; for those with a stomach for these things, the sword of the executioner, Jan Mydlář, is displayed in the museum in the Lobkowicz Palace (p74).

The defeat slammed the door on Czech independence for almost three centuries. Czechs lost their privileges, rights and property, and almost their national identity due to forced Catholicisation and Germanisation (part of the wider Counter-Reformation movement). During the Thirty Years' War, Saxons occupied Prague from 1631 to 1632, and Swedes seized Hradčany and Malá Strana in 1648. Staré Město, though unconquered, suffered months of bombardment. Prague's population declined from 60,000 in 1620 to 24,600 in 1648. The Habsburgs moved their throne back to Vienna, reducing Prague to a provincial town, although it did get a major baroque face-lift over the next century, particularly after a great fire in 1689.

In the 18th century the city was again on the move, economically and architecturally. The four towns of Prague – Staré Město, Nové Město, Malá Strana and Hradčany – were joined into a single, strong unit by imperial decree in 1784.

CZECH NATIONAL REVIVAL

In the 19th century Prague became the centre of the so-called Czech National Revival (České národní obrození), which found its initial expression not in politics – political activity was forbidden by the Habsburgs – but in Czech-language journalism, literature and drama. Important figures included linguists Josef Jungmann and Josef Dobrovský, and František Palacký, author of *Dějiny národu českého* (History of the Czech Nation). A distinctive architecture also took form; Prague landmarks of this period include the National Theatre (p101) and the National Museum (p100).

While many of the countries in post-Napoleonic Europe were swept up by similar nationalist sentiments, social and economic factors gave the Czech revival particular strength. Educational reforms by Empress Maria Theresa (r 1740–80) had given even the poorest Czechs access to schooling, and a vocal middle class was emerging with the Industrial Revolution. Austrian economic reforms, plus changes in industrial production, were forcing Czech labourers into the bigger towns, cancelling out the influence of large German minorities there.

Prague also joined in the 1848 democratic revolutions that swept Europe, and the city was the first in the Austrian empire to rise in favour of reform. Yet like most of the others, Prague's uprising was soon crushed. In 1861, however, Czechs defeated Germans in Prague council elections and edged them out of power forever, though the shrinking German minority still wielded substantial influence well into the 1880s.

INDEPENDENCE

Czechs had no interest in fighting for their Austrian masters in WWI, and neighbouring Slovaks felt the same about their Hungarian rulers. Many defected to renegade legions fighting against the Germans and Austrians.

1648	1784
Swedish army occupies Prague Castle; end of Thirty Years' War	Prague's four towns united as a single city

THE JEWS OF PRAGUE

Prague's Jewish community was first moved into a walled ghetto in about the 13th century, in response to directives from Rome that Jews and Christians should live separately. Subsequent centuries of pogroms and official repression culminated in a threat from Ferdinand I (r 1526–64), only grudgingly withdrawn, to throw all Jews out of Bohemia.

The reign of Rudolf II saw honour bestowed on Prague's Jews, a flowering of Jewish intellectual life, and prosperity in the ghetto. Mordechai Maisel (or Maisl), mayor of the ghetto, Rudolf's finance minister and Prague's wealthiest citizen, bankrolled some lavish redevelopment. Another major figure was Judah Löw ben Bezalel (Rabbi Löw), a prominent theologian, chief rabbi, student of the mystical teachings of the cabbala, and nowadays best known as the creator of the mythical golem – a kind of proto-robot made from the mud of the Vltava River.

When they helped to repel the Swedes on Charles Bridge in 1648, Prague's Jews won the favour of Ferdinand III, to the extent that he had the ghetto enlarged. But a century later they were driven out of the city for over three years, to be welcomed back only because Praguers missed their business.

In the 1780s Emperor Joseph II outlawed many forms of discrimination, and in 1848 the ghetto walls were torn down and the Jewish quarter – named Josefov in honour of Joseph II – was made a borough of Prague.

The demise of the quarter (which had slid into squalor as its population fell) came between 1893 and 1910 when it was cleared, ostensibly for public-health reasons, split down the middle by Pařížská třída (Paris Ave) and lined with Art Nouveau apartment buildings.

The community itself was all but eliminated by the Nazis, and the communist regime slowly strangled what remained of Jewish cultural life. Thousands emigrated. Today only about 6000 Jews live in Prague.

Meanwhile Tomáš Garrigue Masaryk, Edvard Beneš and the Slovak Milan Štefánik began to argue the case – especially in the USA with President Wilson – for the Czechs' and Slovaks' long-cherished dream of independence. Wilson's interest was in keeping with his own goal of closer ties with Europe under the aegis of the League of Nations (the unsuccessful precursor to the United Nations). The most workable solution appeared to be a single federal state of two equal republics, and this was spelled out in agreements signed in Cleveland in 1915 and then in Pittsburgh in 1918.

As WWI drew to a close Czechoslovakia declared its independence, with Allied support, on 28 October 1918. Prague became the capital, and the popular Masaryk, a writer and political philosopher, became the republic's first president.

On 1 January 1922 Greater Prague was established by the absorption of several surrounding towns and villages, growing to a city of 677,000. Like the rest of the country, Prague experienced an industrial boom until the Great Depression of the 1930s. By 1938 the population had grown to one million.

GERMAN OCCUPATION

Unfortunately the new country was not left in peace. Most of the three million German speakers of Bohemia and Moravia wished to join Greater Germany, and in October 1938 the Nazis occupied the Sudetenland (the border regions with Germany and Austria), with the acquiescence of Britain and France in the infamous Munich Agreement. On 15 March 1939 Germany occupied all of Bohemia and Moravia, declaring the region a 'protectorate', while Slovakia proclaimed independence as a Nazi puppet state.

Prague suffered little physical damage during the war, although the Germans destroyed the Czech resistance – and hundreds of innocent Czech villagers – in retaliation for the assassination in Prague of SS General and Reichsprotektor Reinhard Heydrich (see the boxed text, opposite).

Prague's pre-WWII community of some 120,000 Jews was all but wiped out by the Nazis. Almost three-quarters of them – and some 90% of all the Jews in Bohemia and Moravia – died of starvation or were exterminated in camps from 1941.

28 October 1918	1939
Republic of Czechoslovakia proclaimed in Prague's Municipal House (Obecní dům)	Nazis invade Czech lands; Prague becomes capital of Protectorate of Bohemia and Moravia

On 5 May 1945 the population of Prague rose against the German forces as the Red Army approached from the east. US troops had reached Plzeň, but held back in deference to their Soviet allies. The only help for Prague's lightly armed citizens came from Russian soldiers of the so-called Vlasov units, former POWs who had defected to the German side and now defected in turn to the Czech cause (they subsequently retreated to western Bohemia and surrendered to the Americans). Many people died before the Germans began pulling out on 8 May, having been granted free passage out of the city by the Czech resistance movement (in return for which the Germans left without destroying any more buildings or bridges).

Most of Prague was thus liberated by its own residents before Soviet forces arrived the following day. Liberation Day is now celebrated on 8 May; under communism it was 9 May.

In 1945 Czechoslovakia was re-established as an independent state. One of the government's first acts was the expulsion of Sudeten Germans from the borderlands. By 1947 nearly 2.5 million Sudetenlanders had been stripped of their Czechoslovak citizenship and their land, and forcibly expelled to Germany (mainly Bavaria) and Austria. Thousands died during forced marches.

Despite a 1997 declaration of mutual apology for wartime misdeeds by the Czech Republic and Germany, the issue still brings emotions to the boil. Most Sudeten survivors feel their Czech citizenship and property were taken illegally. Many Czechs, on the other hand, remain convinced that Sudetenlanders forfeited their rights when they sought help from Nazi Germany, and that a formal apology by President Václav Havel in January 1990 was unwarranted.

COMMUNISM & THE PRAGUE SPRING

In the 1946 elections the Communist Party of Czechoslovakia (KSČ) became the republic's dominant party with 36% of the popular vote, and formed a coalition government with other socialist parties.

Tension grew between democrats and communists, and in February 1948 the communists staged a coup d'état with the backing of the Soviet Union. A new constitution established the KSČ's dominance, and government was organised along Soviet lines. Thousands of noncommunists fled the country.

The 1950s was an era of harsh repression and decline, as communist economic policies nearly bankrupted the country. Many people were imprisoned. Hundreds were executed and thousands died in labour camps, often for little more than a belief in democracy. In a series of Stalin-style purges organised by the KSČ, many people, including top members of the party itself, were executed.

In the late 1960s Czechoslovakia enjoyed a gradual liberalisation under Alexander Dubček, the reformist general secretary of the KSČ. These reforms reflected a popular desire

THE ASSASSINATION OF HEYDRICH

In 1941, in response to strikes and sabotage by the increasingly well-organised Czech underground movement, the German government replaced its Reichsprotektor in Bohemia and Moravia with the SS general and antisubversion specialist Reinhard Heydrich, who cracked down on resistance activities with a vengeance.

In a clandestine operation, Britain trained a number of Czechoslovak paratroopers for an attempt to assassinate Heydrich. Astonishingly, it succeeded. Two paratroopers, Jan Kubiš and Jozef Gabčík, managed, on 27 May 1942, to bomb and shoot Heydrich as he rode in his official car in the city's Libeň district. He later died of his wounds. The assassins and five co-conspirators fled but were betrayed in their hiding place in the Church of SS Cyril & Methodius (kostel sv Cyril a Metoděj); in the ensuing siege all were killed or committed suicide.

The Nazis reacted with a frenzied wave of terror, including the annihilation a month later of two entire Czech villages, Lidice and Ležáky (see p215 for more on the grim fate of Lidice), and the shattering of the underground movement.

9 May 1945	1948
Red Army enters Prague	Communist Party takes control of government in putsch known as 'Victorious February'

for full democracy and an end to censorship – 'socialism with a human face', as the party called it in its April 1968 'Action Programme'.

But Soviet leaders grew alarmed at the prospect of a democratic society within the Soviet bloc, and its certain domino effect on Poland and Hungary. The brief 'Prague Spring' was crushed by a Soviet-led Warsaw Pact invasion on the night of 20–21 August 1968. Prague was the major objective; Soviet special forces with help from the Czechoslovak secret service, the StB (Státní bezpečnost, or State Security), secured Ruzyně airport for Soviet transport planes. At the end of the first day, 58 people had died. Passive resistance followed; street signs and numbers were removed from buildings throughout the country to disorient the invaders.

In 1969 Dubček was replaced by the orthodox Gustav Husák and exiled to the Slovak forestry department. Around 14,000 party functionaries and 280,000 members who refused to renounce their belief in 'socialism with a human face' were expelled from the party and lost their jobs. Many other educated professionals became street cleaners and manual labourers.

In January 1977 a group of 243 writers, artists and other intellectuals signed a public demand for basic human rights, Charta 77, which became a focus for opponents of the regime. Prominent among them was the poet and playwright Václav Havel (see the boxed text, opposite).

VELVET REVOLUTION … & DIVORCE

The communist regime remained in control until the breaching of the Berlin Wall in November 1989. On 17 November Prague's communist youth movement organised an officially sanctioned demonstration in memory of nine students who were executed by the

STUDENT SACRIFICES

Throughout Czech history – from the time of Jan Hus to the Velvet Revolution – Prague's university students have not been afraid to stand up for what they believe; many of them sacrificed their lives for their beliefs. Two student names that have gone down in 20th-century history are Jan Opletal and Jan Palach.

On 28 October 1939 – the 21st anniversary of the declaration of Czechoslovak independence – Jan Opletal, a medical student, was shot and fatally injured by police attempting to break up an anti-Nazi demonstration. After his funeral, on 15 November Prague students again took to the streets, defacing German street signs, chanting anti-German slogans and taunting the police. The Nazi retaliation was swift and savage.

In the early hours of 17 November – a day now known in Czech as *den boje studentů za svobodu a demokracii* (the day of the students' fight for freedom and democracy) – the Nazi authorities raided Prague's university dormitories and arrested around 1200 students before carting them off to various concentration camps. Some were executed and many others died in the camps. Prague's universities were closed down for the duration of WWII.

The street in northwestern Staré Město called 17.listopadu (17 November; Map pp268–9) was named in honour of the students who suffered death and deportation on 17 November 1939. Exactly 50 years later, on 17 November 1989, students marching along Národní třída in memory of that day were attacked and clubbed by police. The national outrage triggered by this event pushed the communist government towards its final collapse a few days later. There's a memorial plaque inside the arcade at Národní třída 16 (see p100).

Thirty years after Opletal's death, on 16 January 1969, university student Jan Palach set himself on fire on the steps of the National Museum (Národní muzeum; p100) in protest at the Warsaw Pact invasion of Prague. He staggered down the steps in flames and collapsed on the pavement at the foot of the stairs. The following day around 200,000 people gathered in the square in his honour.

It was three agonising days before he died, and his body was buried in the Olšany Cemeteries in Žižkov (see p111). But his grave became a focus for demonstrations and in 1974 his remains were moved to his home village. By popular demand he was re-interred in Olšanské hřbitovy in 1990. A cross-shaped monument set into the pavement to the left of the fountain in front of the National Museum marks the spot where he fell.

1968	20-21 August 1968
Alexander Dubček ushers in reforms known as Prague Spring	Soviet-led Warsaw Pact troops and tanks invade Prague

VÁCLAV HAVEL

Václav Havel was born in October 1936, the son of a wealthy Prague restaurateur. His family's property was confiscated after the communist coup of 1948, and as the child of bourgeois parents he was denied easy access to education. He nevertheless finished high school and studied for a time at university before landing a job at the age of 23 as a stagehand at the Theatre on the Balustrade (p174). Nine years later he was its resident playwright.

His enthusiasm over the liberal reforms of the 'Prague Spring', and his signature on the Charta 77 declaration, made him an enemy of the Husák government. His works – typically focusing on the absurdities and dehumanisation of totalitarian bureaucracy – were banned, his passport was seized and altogether he spent some four years in jail for his activities on behalf of human rights in Czechoslovakia.

The massive demonstrations of November 1989 thrust Havel into the limelight as a leading organiser of the noncommunist Civic Forum movement, which pressed for democratic reforms and ultimately negotiated a new government of national reconciliation. Havel himself was elected president of the country the following month, and the first president of the new Czech Republic in 1993.

In 2003, after two terms as president, Havel was replaced by former prime minister Václav Klaus. The lack of a credible successor to Havel was emphasised by the fact that it took three attempts before the Czechs were able to elect a new president, and the uncharismatic Klaus is far from being the popular leader that Havel once was.

Nazis in 1939 (see the boxed text, opposite). But the peaceful crowd of 50,000 was cornered in Národní třída, where hundreds were beaten by police and about 100 were arrested.

Czechs were electrified by this wanton official violence, and the following days saw nonstop demonstrations by students, artists and finally most of the populace, peaking in a rally on Letná plain by some 750,000 people. Leading dissidents, with Havel at the forefront, formed an anticommunist coalition, which negotiated the government's resignation on 3 December. A 'Government of National Understanding' was formed, with the communists as a minority group. Havel was elected president of the republic by the federal assembly on 29 December.

The days following the 17 November demonstration have become known as the 'Velvet Revolution' (Sametová revoluce) because of its almost totally nonviolent character.

Free elections to the federal assembly in 1990 were won by Civic Forum (OH) and its Slovak counterpart, People Against Violence (VPN). But the OH soon split, over economic policy, into the right-of-centre ODS led by Václav Klaus and the left-of-centre OH led by Jiří Dienstbier. Klaus forced through tough economic policies, and their success gave the ODS a slim victory in the 1992 elections.

Meanwhile, separatists headed by Vladimír Mečiar won the 1992 elections in Slovakia, depriving the ODS of a parliamentary majority. The very different economic positions of Mečiar and Klaus made compromise almost impossible, with Mečiar favouring gradual transformation and independence for Slovakia. The two leaders decided that splitting the country was the best solution, and on 1 January 1993, Czechoslovakia ceased to exist for the second time in that century.

Prague became the capital of the new Czech Republic, and Havel was elected as its first president.

Since 1993 Czech politics have been plagued by instability – no election since the Velvet Divorce has produced a government with a majority of more than a single seat. The decade leading up to 2002 was characterised by an unlikely coalition between the nominally right-wing ODS of Václav Klaus (Czech president since 2003), and the supposedly left-wing ČSSD – the equivalent of an alliance between the Conservative and Labour parties in the UK, or between Republicans and Democrats in the USA.

In January 1998 Václav Havel was re-elected as president, by a margin of just one vote. He described the unholy coalition of right and left in the Czech parliament as a deal struck between 'a left-wing party that has for years fought against a government of embezzlers,

1977	3 December 1989
Dissidents sign Charta 77, a demand for basic human rights	Velvet Revolution marks the end of communist rule

and a right-wing party that has called for mobilisation against a left allegedly attempting a return to communism'.

The 2006 elections did nothing to improve the situation, resulting in an even split of 100 seats each for the ruling and opposition coalitions. Protracted political wrangling resulted yet again in an unholy alliance between the ODS and ČSSD, and the future of Czech politics – for the short term, at least – looks to be one dominated by crisis management.

In the international arena the Czech Republic has joined the big league: along with Poland and Hungary it became a member of NATO in 1999. The Lower House of the Czech parliament voted 154 to 38 in favour of NATO membership, though there was little public debate on the subject and no public referendum, as was held in Hungary (where 85% voted in favour). Even more momentously, the Czech Republic became one of 10 nations to join the European Union on 1 May 2004.

Relations with Germany and Austria have in recent years been strained by the Czechs' refusal to decommission the ageing Temelin nuclear power station in southern Bohemia, and their continued upholding of the Beneš Decree, which saw the forced expulsion of Sudeten Germans from postwar Czechoslovakia. Despite the apologies of 1990 and 1997, these were just political gestures – the Czech Parliament voted to uphold the decree in 2002 and it remains law, preventing Sudeten Germans from reclaiming their property.

1993	1 May 2004
Czech and Slovak republics part company in Velvet Divorce	Czech Republic joins the European Union

Food & Drink

Food & Drink

Traditional Czech cuisine is a cardiologist's nightmare, a cholesterol-laden menu of meat, fat, salt and more meat, accompanied by high-calorie dumplings and washed down with copious quantities of beer. When it comes to food, the ultimate Czech put-down is to describe it as *neslaný* or *nemaslý* ('not salty' or 'not fatty').

But if you put aside your notions of healthy eating for a few days (you're on holiday, after all – live a little!), you'll find traditional Czech food to be very tasty. The country can boast some top-notch produce, from game to cheese to smoked meats to wild mushrooms, and Prague's top chefs are beginning to reinvent Czech cuisine with a lighter, more inventive touch.

Czech beer is, of course, world famous and beer-heads come to Prague from all over the world to worship at the motherlode of all lagers. What is less well known is that Czech wines have improved enormously in recent years, and are well worth getting to know.

CULTURE & ETIQUETTE

Although the vast majority of Prague's tourist-oriented restaurants have long since adopted international manners, a dinner in a Czech home or a traditional eatery still demands traditional Czech etiquette.

To the Czech way of thinking, only barbarians would begin a meal without first saying *dobrou chut'* (the Czech equivalent of *bon appetit* – the correct response is to repeat the phrase); even the waiters in tourist restaurants will murmur *dobrou chut'* as they place the plates on your table. And the first drink of the evening is always accompanied by a toast – usually *na zdraví* (nahz-drah-*vee*; literally, 'to health') – as you clink first the tops and then the bottoms of your glasses, and finally touch the glass to the table before drinking.

It's felt to be bad manners to talk while eating, and especially to distract a guest while they are enjoying their food, so conversation is usually kept to a minimum while food is being consumed; the time for talk is between courses and after the meal.

STAPLES & SPECIALITIES

The first course of a meal is usually a hearty *polévka* (soup) – often *bramboračka* (potato soup), *houbová polévka* (mushroom soup) or *hovězí vývar* (beef broth). Ones worth looking out for are *cibulačka* (onion soup), a delicious, creamy concoction of caramelised onions and herbs, and *česnečka* (garlic soup), a powerfully pungent broth that is curiously addictive.

Other common appetisers include *Pražská šunka* (Prague ham), for which the capital is famous. It is cured in brine and smoked; the best stuff is *šunka od kosti* (ham off the bone).

FUNNY, I DON'T REMEMBER ORDERING THAT!

Keep in mind that nothing comes for free in Prague restaurants – if the waiter offers you fries with that, and you accept, you'll be charged for them. Bread, mayonnaise, mustard, vegetables…everything has a price tag. Many restaurants also have a cover charge or *couvert*, which every diner must pay regardless of what they eat and even if they eat nothing. It's not a scam, it's just the way things are done. If the menu has no prices, ask for them. Don't be intimidated by the language barrier; know exactly what you're ordering. If something's not available and the waiter suggests an alternative, ask for the price. Immediately return anything you didn't order and don't want, such as bread, butter or side dishes; don't just leave it to one side or, chances are, they'll appear on your bill. Most importantly, though, don't let paranoia ruin your meal. The majority of overcharging happens at tourist-oriented restaurants in the city centre. If you're not eating in Old Town Square or Wenceslas Square, or if you're at a new place run by young Czechs, you're unlikely to have any problems.

VEGETARIAN MEALS

Bezmasá jídla ('meatless' dishes) are advertised on many traditional Czech menus, but some of these may be cooked in animal fat or even contain pieces of ham or bacon! If you ask, most chefs can whip up something genuinely vegetarian. Fortunately there are several good vegetarian restaurants in Prague – see the boxed text, p138.

Useful phrases include the following:

I'm a vegetarian.	*Jsem vegetarián/ka.* (m/f)	ysem ve-ge-ta-ri-aan/-ka
I don't eat meat.	*Nejím maso.*	ne-yeem ma-so
I don't eat fish/chicken/ham.	*Nejím rybu/kuře/šunku.*	ne-yeem ri-bu/ku-rzhe/shun-ku

Some common meatless dishes:

knedlíky s vejci	kned-lee-ki s-vey-tse	fried dumplings with egg
omeleta se sýrem a bramborem	o-me-le-ta se seer-em a bram-bo-rem	cheese and potato omelette
smažené žampiony	sma-zhe-ne zham-pi-o-nee	fried mushrooms
smažený květák	sma-zhe-nee kvye-taak	fried cauliflower with egg and onion
smažený sýr	sma-zhe-nee seer	fried cheese with potatoes and tartar sauce

What roast beef and Yorkshire pudding is to the English, so *vepřová pečeně s knedlíky a kyselé zelí* – roast pork with dumplings and sauerkraut – is to the Czechs; it's a dish so ubiquitous that it is often abbreviated to *vepřo-knedlo-zelo*. The pork is rubbed with salt and caraway seeds, and roasted long and slow – good roast pork should fall apart, meltingly tender, at the first touch of fork or finger.

The dumplings should be light and fluffy – *houskové knedlíky* (bread dumplings) are made from flour, yeast, egg yolk and milk, and are left to rise like bread before being cooked in boiling water and then sliced. The best *knedlíky* are homemade, but the ones you'll find in most pubs and restaurants will be factory-produced. Alternatively, you may be served *bramborové knedlíky* (potato dumplings); if you thought bread dumplings were filling, just wait till you try these stodge-bombs.

Other staples of Czech restaurant menus include *svíčková na smetaně* (slices of marinated roast beef served with a sour-cream sauce garnished with lemon and cranberries); *guláš* (a casserole of beef or pork in a tomato, onion and paprika gravy); and *vepřový řízek* (Wiener schnitzel, a thin fillet of pork coated in breadcrumbs and fried, served with potato salad or *hranolky* – French fries).

Poultry is another popular main course, either roasted or served as *kuře na paprice* (chicken in spicy paprika-cream sauce). *Kachna* (duck), *husa* (goose) and *krůta* (turkey) usually come roasted, with gravy, dumplings and sauerkraut. A few restaurants specialise in game; the most common are *jelení* (venison), *bažant* (pheasant), *zajíc* (hare) and *kanec* (boar) – fried or roasted and served in a mushroom sauce or as *guláš*.

Seafood is found only in a handful of expensive restaurants, but freshwater fish – usually *kapr* (carp) or *pstruh* (trout) – are plentiful. *Štika* (pike) and *úhoř* (eel) are found on more specialised menus. Note that the price of fish on the menu is sometimes not for the whole fish but per 100g. Ask how much the trout weighs before you order it!

Café patrons

SPANISH BIRDS & MORAVIAN SPARROWS

Many Czech dishes have names that don't offer a clue as to what's in them, but certain words will give you a hint: *šavle* (sabre; something on a skewer); *tajemství* (secret; cheese inside rolled meat or chicken); *překvapení* (surprise; meat, capsicum and tomato paste rolled into a potato pancake); *kapsa* (pocket; a filling inside rolled meat); and *bašta* (bastion; meat in spicy sauce with a potato pancake).

Two strangely named dishes that are familiar to all Czechs are *Španělský ptáčky* (Spanish birds; sausage and gherkin wrapped in a slice of veal, served with rice and sauce) and *Moravský vrabec* (Moravian sparrow; a fist-sized piece of roast pork). But even Czechs may have to ask about *Meč krále Jiřího* (the sword of King George; beef and pork roasted on a skewer), *Tajemství Petra Voka* (Peter Voka's mystery; carp with sauce), *Šíp Malínských lovců* (the Malín hunter's arrow; beef, sausage, fish and vegetables on a skewer) and *Dech kopáče Ondřeje* (the breath of grave-digger Andrew; fillet of pork filled with extremely smelly Olomouc cheese).

The classic Czech dessert is *ovocné knedlíky* (fruit dumplings), but once again the best are to be found at domestic dinner tables rather than in restaurants. Large, round dumplings made with sweetened, flour-based dough are stuffed with berries, plums or apricots, and served drizzled with melted butter and a sprinkle of sugar.

Desserts on offer in traditional restaurants and pubs consist of *kompot* (canned/preserved fruit), either on its own or *pohár* – in a cup with *zmrzlina* (ice cream) and whipped cream. *Palačinky* or *lívance* (pancakes) are also very common. Other desserts include *jablkový závin* (apple strudel), *makový koláč* (poppy-seed cake) and *ovocné koláče* (fruit slices). For cakes and pastries it is better to go to a *kavárna* (café) or *cukrárna* (cake shop).

A typical Czech breakfast (*snídaně*) is a light affair consisting of *chléb* (bread) or *rohlík* (bread roll) with butter, cheese, jam or yogurt, washed down with tea or coffee. A hotel breakfast buffet will normally also include cereals, eggs, ham or sausage. Some Czechs eat breakfast at self-service *bufety*, which are open between 6am and 8am – these serve up soup or hot dogs, which are washed down with coffee or even beer. Some eateries serving Western-style breakfasts are noted in the boxed text on p148.

You can also go to a *pekárna* or *pekařství* (bakery), or to one of the French or Viennese bakeries, for *loupáčky* (like croissants but smaller and heavier). Czech bread, especially rye, is excellent and varied.

Oběd (lunch) is traditionally the main meal of the day and, Sunday excepted, it's often a hurried affair. Because Czechs are early risers they may sit down to lunch as early as 11.30am, though latecomers can still find leftovers in many restaurants at 3pm.

Having stuffed themselves at lunchtime, for many Czechs *večeře* (dinner) is a light meal, perhaps only a platter of cold meats, cheese and pickles with bread.

Coffee & Tea

Káva (coffee) and *čaj* (tea) are very popular. Homemade Czech coffee is the strong *turecká* (Turkish) – hot water poured over ground beans that end up as sludge at the bottom of your cup. *Espreso* means 'black coffee', and is sometimes a fair equivalent of the Italian version; *espreso s mlékem* is coffee with milk. *Vídeňská káva* (Viennese coffee) is topped with whipped cream.

Many hotels – even expensive ones – dish up thermos flasks of dismal instant coffee at breakfast. Fortunately, there are lots of cafés that serve excellent coffee, including *caffe latte* and cappuccino.

Tea tends to be weak and is usually served with a slice of lemon; if you want it with milk, ask for *čaj s mlékem*. *Čajovná* (tea houses) have proliferated in recent years; they serve a wide range of Indian, Sri Lankan, Chinese and herbal teas.

CZECH BEER

The Czech Lands have been famous for centuries for producing some of the finest amber nectar in the world. The first-ever historical mention of beer-making and hop-growing dates back to 1088 and the founding charter of Opatovice monastery in East Bohemia. Apparently the taste of beer was quite different in those days and by today's standards it would be considered undrinkable. It was not until 1842 that a smart group of Plzeň brewers pooled their experience, installed 'modern' technology and founded a single municipal brewery, with spectacular results. Their golden lager beer, labelled Plzeňský Prazdroj (*prazdroj* is old Czech for 'the original source') – Pilsner Urquell in German – is now one of the world's best, and most imitated, beers.

Even in these times of encroaching coffee culture, *pivo* (beer) remains the lifeblood of Prague. Czechs drink more beer per capita than anywhere else in the world (around 157L per head per year, easily beating both Germany and Australia), and the local *hospoda* or *pivnice* (pub or small beer hall) remains the social hub of the neighbourhood. Many people drink at least one glass of beer every day – local nicknames for beer include *tekutý chleb* (liquid bread) and *živá voda* (life-giving water) – and it's still possible to see people stopping off for a small glass of beer on their way to work in the morning.

Most Czech beers are bottom-fermented lagers, naturally brewed using Moravian malt and hand-picked hops from Žatec in northwestern Bohemia. The whole brewing and fermentation process uses only natural ingredients – water, hops, yeast and barley; as in neighbouring Germany, strict regulations prevent the use of chemicals in the beer-making process.

There are two main varieties of beer – *světlé* (light) and *tmavy* or *černé* (dark). The *světlé* is a pale amber or golden, lager-style beer with a crisp, refreshing, hoppy flavour. Dark beers are sweeter and more full-bodied, with a rich, malty or fruity flavour.

Draught beers are often labelled either *dvanáctka* (12°) or *desítka* (10°). This indicator of specific gravity is known as the Balling rating, and was invented by Czech scientist Karl Josef Balling in the 19th century. One degree Balling represents 1% by weight of malt-derived sugar in the brewing liquid before fermentation. However, not all the sugar turns to alcohol, so the Balling rating gives an indication of the 'body' as well as the likely alcohol content of the finished beer – 12° is richer in flavour, as well as being stronger in alcohol, than 10°, with a slight malty sweetness that cuts the bitterness of the hops.

In 1997 Czech law adopted a new system to indicate the alcohol-by-volume (ABV) content of beer, which recognises three categories – *výcepni pivo* (less than 4.5% ABV), *ležák* (4.5% to 5.5% ABV), and *special* (more than 5.5% ABV). However, tradition dies hard and most breweries and pubs still use the *dvanáctka* and *desítka* labels.

Czechs like their beer served at cellar temperature (around 6°C to 10°C) with a tall, creamy head (known as *pěna*, meaning foam). Americans and Australians may find it a bit warm, but this improves the flavour. Most draught beer is sold in *půl-litr* (0.5L) glasses; if

PUB ETIQUETTE

There's an etiquette to be observed if you want to sample the atmosphere in a traditional *hospoda* without drawing disapproving stares and grumbles from the regulars. First off, don't barge in and start rearranging chairs and tables – if you want to share a table or take a spare seat, ask *je tu volno?* (is this free?) first. It's normal practice in crowded Czech pubs to share tables with strangers. Take a beer-mat from the rack and place it in front of you, and wait for the bar staff to come to you; waving for service is guaranteed to get you ignored.

You can order without saying a single thing – it's automatically assumed that you're here for the beer. When the waiter approaches, just raise your thumb for one beer, thumb and index finger for two, etc – providing you want a 0.5L glass of the pub's main draught ale. Even just a nod will do. The waiter will keep track of your order by marking a slip of paper that stays on your table; whatever you do, don't write on it or lose it (you'll have to pay a fine if you do). As soon as the level of beer in your glass falls to within an inch of the bottom, the eagle-eyed waiter will be on their way with another; but never, as people often do in Britain, pour the dregs of the old glass into the new – this is considered to be deeply uncivilised behaviour.

If you don't want any more beer brought to your table, place a beer-mat on top of your glass. When you want to pay up and go, get the waiter's attention and say *zaplatím* (I'll pay). He or she will tot up the marks on your slip of paper, and you pay there, at the table (try to have some smallish change; handing over a 2000Kč note will prompt a huge display of amateur dramatics). It's normal to leave a tip.

you prefer a small beer, ask for a *malé pivo* (0.3L). Some bars confuse the issue by using 0.4L glasses, while others offer a German-style 1L mug known as a *tuplák*.

The world-famous Pilsner Urquell and Budvar (Budweiser) beers are brewed in the provincial towns of Plzeň (West Bohemia) and České Budějovice (South Bohemia) respectively, but Prague has its own native brews. The largest concern is Prague Breweries, which operates the Staropramen (see p112) and Braník breweries in Prague, and the Ostravar brewery in Ostrava (Northern Moravia). Its brands include the traditional Staropramen lager and the newer Kelt stout and Velvet bitter, and account for around 13% of the domestic beer market.

Prague Breweries is now owned by the Belgian company InBev, the largest brewery group in the world, and Pilsner Urquell is a subsidiary of SABMiller. In fact, the Budweiser Budvar Brewery in Ceské Budějovice, which is still partly owned by the state, is the

Popular Czech beers (left)

only major brewery in the country that is still 100% Czech-owned.

The takeover of the Czech Republic's breweries by multinational companies has been accompanied by a resurgence in interest in traditional beer-making, which has seen a wave of microbreweries – beer halls that brew their own beer on the premises – springing up all over the country. There are several microbreweries in Prague – see the boxed text, p155 for details.

WINE

Grapes have been grown in the Czech Lands since the 14th century, when Charles IV imported vines from Burgundy; their descendants are still thriving on the slopes beneath Mělník Chateau (p213).

The standard of Czech wine has soared since the fall of communism, as small producers have concentrated on the quality end of the market. From 12,000 hectares in 1989, the total area of land given over to viticulture increased to 19,000 hectares in 2004. The main wine-growing region in the country is South Moravia, which accounts for more than 90% of Czech vineyards, with several smaller areas scattered across northern Bohemia.

BREWERY TOURS

The Staropramen Brewery in the Prague suburb of Smíchov offers tours to visitors (see p112), but there are several other breweries within reach of the capital, including the following:

Budweiser Budvar Brewery (☎ 387 705 341; www.budvar.cz; cnr Pražská & K Světlé, České Budějovice; tour 100Kč; ☺ 9am-4pm) One-hour tours for a minimum of eight persons; must be booked in advance. České Budějovice is two hours south of Prague.

Pilsner Urquell Brewery (☎ 377 062 888; www.beerworld.cz; U Prazdroje 7, Plzeň; tour 120Kč; ☺ 10am-9pm Mon-Sat, to 8pm Sun) One-hour guided tours (with beer tasting). Tours in English or German begin at 12.30pm and 2pm daily; no advance booking needed. Plzeň is 1½ hours west of Prague.

Velké Popovice Brewery (☎ 323 683 425; www.kozel.cz; Ringhofferova 1, Velké Popovice; tour 60Kč; ☺ 10am-3pm Mon-Fri) Ninety-minute tours can be booked for groups of 10 or more; individuals can tag along with larger groups. Velké Popovice is just 20km southeast of Prague.

PITHY PIVO PROVERBS

According to an old Czech saying, *'kde se pivo vaří, tam se dobře daří* (where beer is brewed, life is good; it's one of the few that rhymes in both Czech and English). And the beer-fuelled good life has spawned a whole range of lager-related epithets.

These include, 'A fine beer may be judged with only one sip, but it's safer to be thoroughly sure'; indeed there are many who might rewrite that opening phrase as 'A fine beer may be judged with only one glass…'

Czechs are certainly not oblivious to the effect that beer-drinking has on their bodies – a beer belly is referred to in Czech as a *pivní mozol* (literally a 'beer callus') – but they rather seem to like the effect; one of their favourite sayings is *'pivo dělá hezká těla'* (beer makes beautiful bodies).

And finally, trust the Czechs to come up with a near-nonsensical proverb extolling the virtues of their national drink – *není pivo jako pivo* (there's no beer like beer!). That one's worthy of Homer Simpson, no less.

Although Czech red wines – such as the South Moravian speciality, Svatovavřinecké (St Lawrence) – are mostly pretty average, Czech whites can be very good indeed. The varieties to look out for are Veltinské zelené (Grüner Veltlin), Rýnský ryzlink (riesling) and Müller-Thurgau. Mělník, northeast of Prague, produces decent whites such as Ludmila bílá, a dry wine with a fruity nose and a hint of pear drops. Czech sparkling wines are good value – try Bohemia Sekt Brut or Demi-Sekt.

Although not as popular as beer, *víno* (wine) is widely available in *vinárny* (wine bars), restaurants and pubs – but not in many beer halls. *Suché víno* is dry wine and *sladké* is sweet; a sign advertising *sudové víno* means that it is served straight from the barrel.

For about three weeks each year from the end of September to mid-October, you will see shops and street stalls selling *burčák*. This is 'young wine', freshly extracted grape juice in the early stages of fermentation. It is sweet and refreshing, more reminiscent of fruit juice than wine, but contains around 3% to 5% alcohol; beware – the stuff sneaks up on you.

Later in the year, as winter sets in and the weather gets colder, you'll notice the *svařák* stalls appearing in the streets. Short for *svařené víno* (mulled wine), *svařák* is what you would expect – red wine heated and flavoured with sugar and spices.

SPIRITS

Probably the most distinctive of Czech *lihoviny* (spirits) is Becherovka. Produced in the West Bohemian spa town of Karlovy Vary, famous for its 12 sulphurous, thermal springs, the bitter, herbal liqueur is famously known as the '13th spring' – a few shots will leave you feeling sprightlier than a week's worth of spa treatment. It is often served as an apéritif, and is increasingly used as an ingredient in cocktails.

The fiery and potent *slivovice* (plum brandy) is said to have originated in Moravia, where the best brands still come from. The best commercially produced *slivovice* is R Jelínek from Vizovice. Other regional spirits include *meruňkovice* (apricot brandy) and juniper-flavoured *borovička*.

The deadliest locally produced spirit is Hills Liquere absinthe from Jindřichův Hradec. While it's banned in many countries, in part because of its high alcohol content, absinthe is legal in the Czech Republic. Unfortunately, connoisseurs of absinthe consider Hills little better than highly alcoholic mouthwash.

Spirits are traditionally drunk neat and usually chilled (an exception is *grog,* a popular year-round hot drink: half rum, half hot water or tea, with a slice of lemon).

NONALCOHOLIC DRINKS

The best-known and most widespread brand of mineral water is Mattoni which, like Becherovka liqueur, comes from the spa town of Karlovy Vary. Other good local brands include Aquila and Dobrá Voda; *perlivá* means sparkling, *neperlivá* means still.

Most Western brands of soft drinks are widely available, but there is one local brand that stands out – Semtex is an 'energy drink', the Czech equivalent of Red Bull, named in honour of the infamous plastic explosive made in the Czech town of Pardubice.

FESTIVALS & CELEBRATIONS

Christmas is the most important celebration on the Czech domestic calendar, and food and drink, as you might expect, play an important part. Christmas Eve (Štědrý den, or 'generous day') is a day of abstinence from meat, with people saving their appetite for the evening meal that is traditionally *smažený kapr* (crisp, fried carp) served with *bramborový salát* (potato salad). The carp are farmed in medieval *rybníky* (fishponds) in the countryside, mostly in South Bohemia, and are brought in December to city markets where they are sold, live, from water-filled barrels. In many homes, the Christmas carp then gets to swim around in the bathtub until it's time for the frying pan.

There is no national tradition as to what is served on Christmas Day (*vánoce*), but meat is definitely back on the menu; *pečená kachna* (roast duck), served with gravy and dumplings, is a widespread favourite. There are also Christmas cookies – *vánoční cukroví* – baked according to traditional family recipes, and *vánočka,* Bohemia's answer to Christmas cake, though it's actually made with bread dough, sweetened with sugar, flavoured with lemon, nutmeg, raisins and almonds, and plaited; it is usually served after the Christmas Eve dinner.

New Year's Eve (Silvestr) is also a big celebration. These days few people still prepare the traditional New Year's Eve dinner of *vepřový ovar* (boiled pig's head) served with grated horseradish and apple, but the day is still a big party day, with plates of *chlebíčky* (small, open sandwiches), *brambůrky* (potato pancakes) and other snacks, and bottles of *šampaňské* or other sparkling wine on hand to toast the bells at midnight.

Sights

Sights

As you can see on the map, the Vltava River winds through the middle of Prague like a giant question mark, with the city centre straddling its lower half. There is little method in Prague's haphazard sprawl – it's a city that has grown organically from its medieval roots, snagging villages and swallowing suburbs as it spread out into the wooded hills of central Bohemia.

The oldest parts of the city cluster tightly just south of the river bend – **Hradčany**, the medieval castle district, and **Malá Strana** (Little Quarter) on the western bank; **Staré Město** (Old Town), **Nové Město** (New Town) and the ancient citadel of **Vyšehrad** on the eastern bank.

Beyond the centre lie the mostly 19th- and 20th-century suburbs, just a 10-minute tram ride away – elegant **Vinohrady** and grungy **Žižkov** and **Karlín** to the east, **Holešovice**, **Bubeneč** and **Dejvice** to the north and northwest, and formerly industrial **Smíchov** to the south. We have also gathered outlying districts such as Troja, Střešovice and Zbraslav together under the heading 'Beyond the Centre'. You can find details of public transport under each district heading and on p226.

ITINERARIES

One Day

Prague in a day? Ambitious. Get up early and take a wander through Prague Castle's court-yards before the main sights open, then spend the morning visiting **St Vitus Cathedral** (p71), the **Old Royal Palace** (p73) and the **Basilica of St George** (p74), timing things to catch the **Changing**

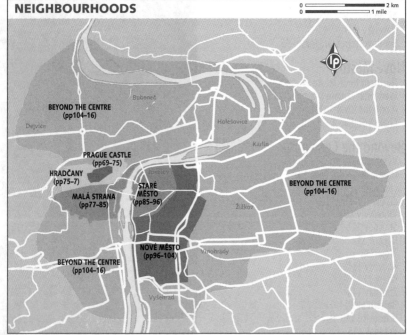

NEIGHBOURHOODS

0 — 2 km
0 — 1 mile

BEYOND THE CENTRE
(pp104–16)

Bubeneč

Dejvice

Holešovice

Karlín

PRAGUE CASTLE
(pp69–75)

HRADČANY
(pp75–7)

Josefov

MALÁ STRANA
(pp77–85)

STARÉ MĚSTO
(pp85–96)

BEYOND THE CENTRE
(pp104–16)

Žižkov

NOVÉ MĚSTO
(pp96–104)

Vinohrady

BEYOND THE CENTRE
(pp104–16)

Vyšehrad

of the Guard (p70) at noon. Descend to Malá Strana through the **Palace Gardens beneath Prague Castle** (p81), and walk through the **Wallenstein Garden** (p81) on your way to lunch on the riverside terrace at **Hergetova Cíhelná** (p135). In the afternoon, visit the Kafka Museum (p81) then stroll across **Charles Bridge** (p80) and continue along Karlova to the **Old Town Square** (p85); after watching the **Astronomical Clock** (p86) do its thing, head to the **Municipal House** (p92) and have a coffee while you admire the Art Nouveau décor. Choose somewhere special for dinner – **U Zlaté Studně** (p137) or **Bellevue** (p138).

TOP FIVE VIEWPOINTS

- Great Tower, St Vitus Cathedral (p71)
- Letná Gardens (p108)
- Petřín Lookout Tower (p84)
- TV Tower (p111)
- Vyšehrad Citadel (p104)

Three Days

Much better – you can devote a day each to Malá Strana, Staré Město, and Nové Město. Spend your first morning at the **castle** (p69), and after lunch with a view at **U Zlaté Studně** (p137) enjoy a leisurely afternoon exploring the sights of **Malá Strana** (p77) before rounding off the day with a romantic dinner at **Kampa Park** (p135) and an evening stroll across **Charles Bridge** (p80).

On day two, kick off with a wander round the **Old Town Square** (p85), then devote an hour or two to the various sights that make up the **Jewish Museum** (p88). Have lunch at a nearby restaurant – **Dinitz** (p139) would be good – then go on the guided tour of the **Municipal House** (p93) that you booked in the morning, followed by a look around the **Mucha Museum** (p97). Have dinner at **V zátiší** (p141) then head for an Old Town **jazz club** (p162).

Your final day is for **shopping** (p182), exploring the passages and arcades around **Wenceslas Square** (p98), and taking a metro ride out to **Vyšehrad** (p104) to explore the ancient citadel. Round off a memorable three days with a **classical concert** (p161) and dinner at **Divinis** (p139).

One Week

Cover the sights mentioned in the three-day itinerary, but spend more time on the places that take your fancy. Add in visits to the **Veletržní Palace** (p109) and the **Prague City Museum** (p98), and set aside a day to do the **walking tour** (p118) from Letná to Troja; get the boat back into town (see p58 for details). You'll have time for a day trip to **Kutná Hora** (p219), and for more of that essential Prague activity of just sitting around in cafés and pubs, soaking up the atmosphere (and the beer).

ORGANISED TOURS

Pragotur and various private companies operating from kiosks along Na příkopě offer three-hour city bus tours for around 600Kč per person. They're OK if your time is short, but the castle and other sights get so crowded that you often can't enjoy the tour; we suggest one of our self-guided walking tours (see p118) instead.

Bicycle

CITY BIKE Map pp268-9

☎ 776 180 284; www.citybike-prague.com; Královdorská 5, Staré Město; ⏰ 9am-7pm Apr-Oct; metro Náměstí Republiky

Two-hour guided tours cost 480Kc, departing at 11am, 2pm and 5pm May to Sep-

tember, 11am and 2pm April and October. Tours take in the Old Town, the Vltava River and Letná park, and include a stop at a riverside pub.

PRAHA BIKE Map pp268-9

☎ 732 388 880; www.prahabike.cz; Dlouhá 24, Staré Město; 2hr tour 420Kč; ⏰ 9am-7pm; metro Náměstí Republiky

A two-hour guided cycling tour through the city, or an easy evening pedal through the parks. Tours depart at 2.30pm mid-March to October, and also at 11.30am and 5.30pm May to mid-September. Trips outside the city can also be arranged. Helmets and locks provided, and bikes are available for private rental (see p225).

Boat
EVROPSKÁ VODNÍ DOPRAVA
Map pp268-9

EVD; ☎ 224 810 030; www.evd.cz; Čechův most, Staré Město; tram 17

EVD operates large cruise boats based at the quay beside Čechův most (Bohemia Bridge), and offers a one-hour return cruise departing hourly from 10am to 6pm (220/110Kč per adult/child); a two-hour return cruise including lunch and live music, departing at noon (690/380Kč per adult/child); a two-hour return cruise to Vyšehrad (350/270Kč), departing at 3pm; and a three-hour evening return cruise with dinner and music (790/500Kč), departing at 7pm. All cruises run year-round.

PRAGUE VENICE Map pp268-9

☎ 603 819 947; www.prague-venice.cz; Platnéřská 4, Staré Město; adult/child 270/135Kč; ⏲ 10.30am–11pm Jul & Aug, to 8pm Mar-Jun, Sep & Oct, to 6pm Nov-Feb; tram 17

Operates entertaining 45-minute cruises in small boats under the hidden arches of Charles Bridge and along the Čertovka millstream in Kampa. Boats depart every 15 minutes from jetties at the western end of Platnéřská, on the Čertovka stream in Malá Strana (Map pp264–5), and at the western end of Mánesův most (Mánes Bridge; Map pp264–5), near Malostranská metro station.

PRAGUE PASSENGER SHIPPING
Map pp272-3

Pražská paroplavební společnost, PPS; ☎ 224 930 017; www.paroplavba.cz; Rašínovo nábřeží 2, Nové Město; metro Karlovo Náměstí

From April to October PPS runs cruises along the Vltava, departing from the central quay on Rašínovo nábřeží (Map pp272–3). Most photogenic is a one-hour jaunt taking in the National Theatre, Střelecký island and Vyšehrad, departing at 11am, 2pm, 4pm, 5pm and 6pm April to September (170Kč).

At 9am on Saturday and Sunday from May to August, a boat goes 37km south (upstream) through a wild, green landscape to the Slapy Dam at Třebenice. This fine, all-day escape costs 300Kč return, arriving back in the city at 6.30pm.

Boats making the 1¼-hour trip to Troja (near the zoo; 100/190Kč one way/return) depart 8.30am on weekdays in May and June only, at 9.30am, 12.30pm and 3.30pm daily May to August, and at weekends and holidays September and October. Returning boats depart Troja 11am, 2pm and 5pm.

Other more expensive trips go up and down the river while you snack, dine and dance to disco or country-and-western music.

Bus & Tram
NOSTALGIC TRAM NO 91

☎ 233 343 349; www.dpp.cz; Muzeum MHD (Public Transport Museum), Patočkova 4, Střešovice; adult/child 25/10Kč; ⏲ departs hourly noon-6pm Sat, Sun & hols Apr–mid-Nov

Vintage tram cars dating from 1908 to 1924 trundle along a special route, starting at the Public Transport Museum (Map pp264–5) and going via stops at Prague Castle, Malostranské náměstí, National Theatre, Wenceslas Square, náměstí Republiky and Štefánikův most to finish at Výstaviště. You can get on and off at any stop, and buy tickets on board; ordinary public transport tickets and passes can't be used on this line.

PRAGUE SIGHTSEEING TOURS

☎ 222 314 661; www.pstours.cz; Klimentská 52, Nové Město; 'Informative Prague' 2hr adult/child 390/300Kč, 'Grand City' 3½hr 660/330Kč

A whole range of tours is offered. The 'Informative Prague' bus tour (departing 11am,

Vintage tram car (right)

(Continued on page 67)

1 The rococo Archbishop's Palace (p75) in Hradčany Square
2 Stained-glass windows by Alfons Mucha in St Vitus Cathedral (p71)
3 Winding streets through the Prague Castle complex (p69)
4 Bell tower at the Loreta (p76)

previous page Charles Bridge (p80), with the Church of St Francis Seraphinus (p92) and the Old Town Bridge Tower (p88)

1 *Battling Titans and castle guards at Prague Castle's main gate (p70)* **2** *St Vitus Cathedral (p71), Prague Castle* **3** *Baroque exterior of the Romanesque Basilica of St George (p74)* **4** *Colourful cottages on Golden Lane (p74), on the castle's northern wall*

1 Christmas market outside Church of Our Lady Before (p86) **2** Old Town Square heart of Prague since the century **3** Astronomical Cl (p86), Old Town Hall

1 *Goltz-Kinský Palace (p87)*
2 *The Art Nouveau Municipal House (Obecní dům; p93)*
3 *Transport through the Old Town Square (p85)* 4 *The medieval Powder Gate (p94)*

1 *Moorish interior of the Spanish Synagogue (p92)* **2** *Window in the Museum of Decorative Arts (p90)* **3** *Josefov's Old Jewish Cemetery (p91)* **4** *Detail of Torah, Old-New Synagogue (p91)*

1 *IP Pavlova metro station (p226)*
2 *Shoppers stroll along Na příkopě, Staré Město (p85)* **3** *The neo-Renaissance National Theatre (p101)* **4** *Inverted version of St Wenceslas and his horse by David Černý, Lucerna Palace (p99)*

1 Rooftops of Malá Strana from leafy Petřín (p83) 2 Snow-covered houses on the island of Kampa (p82) 3 Carved emblem on Nerudova, Malá Strana (p77) 4 Cobbled street on Kampa (p82)

(Continued from page 58)

1.30pm and 4pm from April to October)
takes in all of Prague's important historical
sites, and the 'Grand City' tour (departing
9.30am and 2pm from April to October)
combines a bus tour of the main sites with a
walk through Prague Castle. The tours depart
from the yellow kiosk near the metro entrance on náměstí Republiky (Map pp268–9).

Jewish Interest

PRECIOUS LEGACY TOURS Map pp268-9

☎ 222 321 954; www.legacytours.net; Kaprova
13, Staré Město; per person 630Kč; ⊙ tours begin
10.30am Sun-Fri, also at 2pm by arrangement
Offers guided tours of places of interest
to Jewish visitors, including a three-hour
walking tour of Prague's Josefov district (fee
includes admission to four synagogues, but
not the Staronová Synagogue – this is 200Kč
extra). There's also a daily six-hour excur-
sion to Terezín (1160Kč per person; departs
10am); for more information on Terezín see
p215. Customised, private tours can be arranged for €50 an hour for two people.

WITTMANN TOURS Map pp272-3

☎ 222 252 472; www.wittmann-tours.com;
Mánesova 8, Vinohrady; adult/student 630/500Kč;
⊙ tours 10.30am & 2pm Sun-Fri May-Oct, 10.30am
Apr, Nov & Dec
This outfit's three-hour walking tour of
Josefov starts from the square in front of
the Hotel Inter-Continental on Pařížská.
Wittmann also runs seven-hour day trips to
Terezín (see p215) for 1150/1000Kč per adult/
student. In our opinion, the Wittmann tours
are better than the Precious Legacy ones.

Personal Guides

PRAGOTUR Map pp268-9

☎ 236 002 562; guides@pis.cz; Old Town Hall,
Staroměstské náměstí 1; 3hr tour per person
1000Kč, per 2 persons 1200Kč plus 300Kč per
additional person; ⊙ 9am-6pm Mon-Fri, to 4pm
Sat & Sun
An affiliate of the Prague Information
Service (PIS), Pragotur can arrange personal
guides fluent in all major European lan-
guages. Its desk is in the PIS office in the
Old Town Hall (p88).

Vintage Car

A couple of businesses offer tours around
the city in genuine vintage Czech cars dating from the late 1920s and early 1930s.
There are pick-up points at various city
centre locations; tours depart as available,
or whenever you ask, if it's quiet. Tours last
about 40 minutes.

3 VETERANS

☎ 603 521 700; www.3veterani.cz; 1-2 persons
950Kč, 3-4 persons 1300Kč; ⊙ 9am-6pm
This operation has a small fleet of Praga
Piccolos and early Škodas, all from the
early 1930s. Pick-up points in Staré Město
are on Rytířská, in Malé náměstí, and at
the junction of Pařížská and Staroměstské
náměstí; and on Malostranské náměstí in
Malá Strana.

OLD TIMER HISTORY TRIP

☎ 776 829 897; www.historytrip.cz; 1-2 persons
950Kč, 3-6 persons 1300Kč; ⊙ 9am-6pm Apr-Nov
Rattle along the city's cobblestone streets in
a 1928 Praga Piccolo, or a larger 1929 Praga
Alfa. Pick-up points in Staré Město are in
Malé náměstí, on Karlova and on Malostranská náměstí in Malá Strana. There's also a
two-hour night-time tour (from 1890Kč).

Walking

The corner of Old Town Square outside
the Old Town Hall is usually clogged with
dozens of people touting for business as
walking guides; quality varies, but the best
are listed here. Most operators don't have
an office – you can join a walk by just turn-
ing up at the starting point and paying your
money, though it's best to phone ahead to
be sure of a place. Most walks begin at the
Astronomical Clock (Map pp268–9).

GEORGE'S GUIDED WALKS

☎ 607 820 158; www.praguemaster.com; per 2
persons 1500Kč, per additional person 300Kč
Lots of travellers have recommended
George, whose intimate, personalised
tours include a four-hour History Walk (if
you have been to Prague before, he'll take
you off the beaten track), a two-hour Iron
Curtain Walk, and a five-hour pub crawl,
including dinner in a Czech pub. George
will meet you at your hotel, or anywhere
else that's convenient.

KAFKA'S PRAGUE

Although he wrote in German, Franz Kafka (1883–1924) was very much a son of the Czech capital. He lived in Prague all his life, haunting the city and being haunted by it, both hating it and needing it. His novel *The Trial* can be seen as a metaphysical geography of Staré Město, whose maze of alleys and passageways break down the usual boundaries between outer streets and inner courtyards, between public and private, new and old, real and imaginary.

For most of his life Kafka lived close to Old Town Square, growing up and going to school, working and meeting friends at the addresses listed below; in his own words, 'this narrow circle encompasses my entire life'. Rather than describe some arbitrary walking trail, we have listed them in chronological order, so that you can wander between them by whichever route you feel like, as Kafka would have done himself.

- U Radnice 5 (Map pp268–9; 1883–88) is where Kafka was born on 3 July 1883 in an apartment beside the St Nicholas Church; all that remains of the original building is the stone portal. It now houses a Kafka Exhibition, in reality a thinly disguised souvenir shop.
- Celetná 2 (Map pp268–9; 1888–89), 'The Sixt House', was Kafka's childhood home for a brief period.
- Dům U minuty (Map pp268–9; 1889–96) is where Kafka lived as a schoolboy, in the Renaissance corner building that's now part of the Old Town Hall. In a letter he recalled attending primary school in Masná street, and being dragged reluctantly across the square each day by the family cook, whose duty it was to deposit him in class.
- Goltz-Kinský Palace (Map pp268–9) is where Kafka attended high school, at the Old Town State Gymnasium, on the 2nd floor of the palace, between 1893 and 1901. For a time his father ran a clothing shop on the ground floor there.
- Celetná 3 (Map pp268–9; 1896–1907), House at the Three Kings, is where Kafka first had a room to himself, and where he wrote his first story. His bedroom window looked out onto the Church of Our Lady Before Týn.
- Assicurazioni Generali (Map pp272–3; 1907–8) was the Italian insurance firm, at No 19 Wenceslas Square, where Kafka took his first job as an insurance clerk after earning a law degree from Charles University in 1906. Long hours, poor pay and bureaucratic boredom took its toll, and he quit after only nine months.
- Workers' Accident Insurance Co (Map pp268–9), an office at Na poříčí 7 in Nové Město, is where Kafka toiled on the 5th floor for 14 years, from 1908 until his retirement due to ill health in 1922.
- U Jednoržce (At the Unicorn; Map pp268–9), a house on the southern side of Old Town Square at No 17, was owned by Otto Fanta and his wife Berta, who hosted a regular literary salon to which she invited fashionable European thinkers of the time, including Kafka and fellow writers Max Brod (Kafka's friend and biographer), Franz Werfel and Egon Erwin Kisch.
- Pařížská 36 (Map pp268–9; 1907–13), an apartment overlooking the river beside the Čech Bridge (the building no longer exists), where Kafka wrote *The Judgement* and began work on *Metamorphosis*.
- Pařížská 1 (Map pp268–9; 1913–14), a luxurious top-floor apartment in the Oppelt House, across from the Church of St Nicholas, was the last place Kafka lived with his parents – and the setting for his horrific parable *Metamorphosis*.
- Bilková 22 (Map pp268–9; 1914–15), where, at the age of 31, Kafka moved out of his parental home for the first time, into a flat in this street, where he began work on *The Trial*.
- Dlouhá 16 (Map pp268–9; 1915–17), where Kafka rented a place of his own, at the narrow corner with Masná. He moved around a lot in the next few years, visiting Berlin and Vienna, and staying with his parents at the Oppelt House when he returned to Prague.
- Zlatá ulička 22 (Map p70) was Kafka's sister's rented cottage in the castle grounds. During the winter of 1916–17 Kafka stayed here to escape the noise and distraction of the his Old Town flat, and produced more than a dozen stories.
- Tržiště 15 (Map pp264–5; 1917), the Schönborn Palace in Malá Strana (now the US embassy), where Kafka took a flat for a few months. He was happy here for a while until he suffered a lung haemorrhage, a symptom of the tuberculosis that would eventually kill him. He spent the rest of his life either seeking medical treatments or staying with his parents, and died in Vienna on 3 June 1924. He was buried in the Jewish Cemetery in Žižkov (see p110).

PRAGUE SEGWAY TOURS

☎ 777 070 784; www.prague-segwaytours.com; per person 1500Kč

Not quite a walking tour, but a Segway – a neat, electrically powered, two-wheeled

'personal transportation system' – allows you to cover more ground in less time than on foot. Two-hour guided tours, taking in the Old Town, Mala Strana, Kampa and the National Theatre, depart daily at 10.30am,

2pm and 5pm from April to October, from the Astronomical Clock – look for the orange umbrella.

PRAGUE WALKS

☎ 222 322 309; www.praguewalks.com; per person 300-1000Kč

Interesting walks with themes ranging from Prague architecture to everyday life, Žižkov pubs and the Velvet Revolution. Meet at the Astronomical Clock, or you can arrange to be met at your hotel.

PRAGUE CASTLE

Prague Castle – Pražský hrad, or just *hrad* to Czechs, and almost a small town in itself – is Prague's most popular attraction. According to *Guinness World Records*, it's the largest ancient castle in the world – 570m long, an average of 128m wide and covering a total area bigger than seven football fields.

Its history begins in the 9th century when Prince Bořivoj founded a fortified settlement here. It grew haphazardly as rulers made their own additions, creating an eclectic mixture of architectural styles. The castle has always been the seat of Czech rulers as well as the official residence of the head of state, although the Czech Republic's first president, Václav Havel, chose to live in his own house on the outskirts of the city.

Prague Castle has seen four major reconstructions, from that of Prince Soběslav in the 12th century to a classical face-lift under Empress Maria Theresa (r 1740–80). In the 1920s President Masaryk hired a Slovene architect, Jože Plečník, to renovate the castle; his changes created some of its most memorable features, and made the complex more tourist-friendly.

TRANSPORT - PRAGUE CASTLE

Metro The nearest metro station is Malostranská, but from here it's a stiff climb up the Old Castle Steps to the eastern end of the castle. Hradčanská station is about 10 minutes' walk from the castle, but it's an easy, level walk.

Tram Take tram No 22 or 23 from Národní třída on the southern edge of Staré Město, Malostranská náměstí in Malá Strana, or Malostranská metro station to the Pražský hrad stop. If you want to explore Hradčany first, stay on the tram until Pohořelec, the next stop but one.

Tickets & Opening Hours

Entry is free to the castle courtyards and gardens, and to the nave of St Vitus Cathedral. There are six different tickets (valid for two days), which allow entry to various combinations of sights (see the boxed text, below); you can buy tickets at the **information centre** (☎ 224 373 368, 224 372 434; www .hrad.cz; ☎ 9am-5pm Apr-Oct, to 4pm Nov-Mar) in the Third Courtyard (opposite the main entrance to St Vitus Cathedral), or from ticket offices at the entrance to each of the main sights (St Vitus Cathedral, Old Royal Palace and Basilica of St George).

Concession prices are for those aged seven to 16, students and disabled visitors; children aged six or under get in free. The family ticket is valid for two adults and any children aged 16 or under.

Tickets listed here do not include admission to other art galleries and museums within the castle grounds (those admission costs are listed in the individual reviews).

From April to October the castle grounds are open from 5am to midnight, and the

---

PRAGUE CASTLE TICKETS

Ticket A (adult/concession/family 350/175/520Kč) Includes St Vitus Cathedral, Great Tower, Old Royal Palace, Story of Prague Castle, Basilica of St George, Powder Tower, Golden Lane and Daliborka.

Ticket B (adult/concession/family 220/110/330Kč) Includes St Vitus Cathedral, Great Tower, Old Royal Palace, Golden Lane and Daliborka.

Ticket C (adult/family 50/100Kč) Admission to Golden Lane and Daliborka only.

Ticket D (adult/concession/family 50/25/100Kč) Admission to Basilica of St George only.

Ticket E (adult/concession/family 50/25/100Kč) Admission to Powder Tower only.

Ticket F (adult/concession/family 100/50/150Kc/v) Admission to Convent of St George only.

gardens 10am to 6pm. The cathedral and other historic buildings accessible by ticket are open 9am to 5pm. From November to March the grounds open 6am to 11pm, and the historic buildings open from 9am to 4pm; the gardens are closed.

One-hour guided tours are available in Czech (200Kč for up to five people, plus 40Kč per additional person), and in English, French, German, Italian, Russian and Spanish (450Kč, plus 90Kč per additional person) Tuesday to Sunday. Alternatively you can rent an audio guide (cassette player and headphones) for 145/180Kč for two/three hours. Ask at the information centre.

There's a **post office** (8am-7pm Mon-Fri, 10am-7pm Sat), **currency exchange** (8.10am-6.10pm) and ATM next to the information centre. You can buy tickets for concerts and other special events at the **box office** (224 373 483; 9am-5pm Apr-Oct, to 4pm Nov-Mar) in the Chapel of the Holy Cross in the Second Courtyard.

Orientation

We've organised the castle description starting with the main entrance at the western end, then moving through the various courtyards and sights before exiting at the eastern end. You'll need at least two hours to see the main sights, and all day if you want to visit everything.

The following areas are wheelchair-accessible: the main entrance to St Vitus Cathedral, the Old Royal Palace, Vladislav Hall, Basilica of St George, Ball-Game House, Prague Castle Gallery and the castle gardens. There's a wheelchair-accessible toilet to the right of the cathedral entrance.

FIRST COURTYARD

The castle's main gate on Hradčany Square (Hradčanské náměstí) is flanked by huge, baroque statues of **battling Titans** (1767–70), which dwarf the castle guards who stand beneath them. After the fall of communism in 1989, then-president Václav Havel hired his old pal Theodor Pistek, the Czech costume designer on the film *Amadeus* (1984), to replace their communist-era khaki uniforms with the stylish pale-blue kit they now wear, which harks back to the army of the first Czechoslovak Republic of 1918–38.

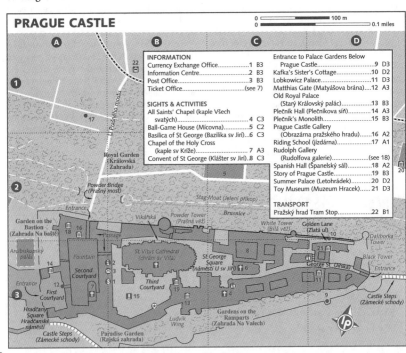

PRAGUE CASTLE

The **changing of the guard** takes place every hour on the hour, but the longest and most impressive display is at noon, when banners are exchanged while a brass band plays a fanfare from the windows of the **Plečník Hall** (Plečníkova síň), which overlooks the First Courtyard.

This impressive hall, which opens off the left side of the baroque **Matthias Gate** (Matyášova brána; 1614), was created by Slovenian architect Jože Plečník as part of the 1920s restoration of the castle; the pointy flagpoles in the First Courtyard are also Plečník's. As you pass through the gate, note the contrast between the gilded baroque staircase to your right and the Doric simplicity of Plečník's stair to the left.

SECOND COURTYARD

You pass through the Matthias Gate into the Second Courtyard, centred on a baroque fountain and a 17th-century well with beautiful Renaissance latticework. On the right, the **Chapel of the Holy Cross** (kaple sv Kříže; 1763) was once the treasury of St Vitus Cathedral; today it houses the castle's box office and souvenir shop.

The magnificent **Spanish Hall** (Španělský sál) and **Rudolph Gallery** (Rudolfova galerie) in the northern wing of the courtyard are reserved for state receptions and special concerts; they are open to the public just two days a year, usually on Liberation Day (8 May) and Republic Day (28 October).

PRAGUE CASTLE GALLERY Map p70
Obrazárna pražského hradu; ☎ 224 373 531; Pražský hrad, II. nádvoří; adult/concession 100/50Kč; ☼ 10am-6pm; metro Malostranská
The same Swedish army that looted the famous bronzes in the Wallenstein Garden (p81) in 1648 also took Rudolf II's art collection. This gallery, housed in the beautiful Renaissance stables at the northern end of the Second Courtyard, is based on the Habsburg collection that was begun in 1650 to replace the lost paintings. The display of 16th- to 18th-century European art includes works by Rubens, Tintoretto and Titian.

ROYAL GARDEN

The gate on the northern side of the Second Courtyard leads to the **Powder Bridge** (Prašný most; 1540), which spans the **Stag Moat** (Je-

lení příkop) and leads to the **Royal Garden** (Královská zahrada), which started life as a Renaissance garden built by Ferdinand I in 1534. The most beautiful of the garden's buildings is the **Ball-Game House** (Míčovna; 1569), a masterpiece of Renaissance *sgraffito* where the Habsburgs once played a primitive version of badminton. To the east is the **Summer Palace** (Letohrádek; 1538–60), or Belvedere, the most authentic Italian Renaissance building outside Italy, and to the west the former **Riding School** (jízdárna; 1695). All three are used as venues for temporary exhibitions of modern art.

A footpath to the west of the Powder Bridge (on the castle side) leads down into the moat, and doubles back through a modern, arty (and rather Freudian), red-brick tunnel beneath the bridge. If you then follow the path east along the moat you'll eventually end up at Malostranská metro station. A gate on the outer wall of the castle, overlooking the moat, leads to a bomb shelter started by the communists in the 1950s but never completed. Its tunnels run under most of the castle.

ST VITUS CATHEDRAL

As you pass through the passage on the eastern side of the Second Courtyard, the huge western façade of **St Vitus Cathedral** soars directly above you. At first glance it may appear impressively Gothic, but in fact the triple doorway dates only from 1953, one of the last parts of the church to be completed.

You enter the cathedral through the western door; everything between here and the crossing was built during the late 19th and early 20th centuries. Inside, the nave is flooded with colour from beautiful **stained-glass windows** created by eminent Czech artists of the early 20th century – note the one by Art Nouveau artist Alfons Mucha (third chapel on the northern side), depicting the lives of SS Cyril and Methodius (1909). Nearby is a wooden sculpture of the **crucifixion** (1899) by František Bílek.

The cathedral's foundation stone was laid in 1344 by Emperor Charles IV, on the site of a 10th-century Romanesque rotunda built by Duke Wenceslas. Charles' original architect Matthias of Arras (Matyáš z Arrasu) began work in 1344 on the choir in the French Gothic style, but died eight years later.

His German successor, Petr Parler – a veteran of Cologne's cathedral – completed

Royal Garden (p71)

most of the eastern part of the cathedral in a freer, late-Gothic style before he died in 1399. Renaissance and baroque details were added over the following centuries, but it was only in 1861 during the Czech National Revival that a concerted effort was made to finish the cathedral; it was finally consecrated in 1929.

Walk up to the crossing, where the nave and transept meet, and look at the huge **south window** (1938) by Max Švabinský, depicting the Last Judgement – note the fires of Hell burning brightly in the lower right-hand corner. In the **north transept** are three carved wooden doors.

Just to the right of the south transept is the entrance to the 96m-tall **Great Tower** (☎ last entry 4.15pm Apr-Oct, closed during bad weather). You can climb the 297 slightly claustrophobic steps to the top for excellent views, and you also get a close look at the clockworks (1597). The tower's Sigismund Bell, made by Tomáš Jaroš in 1549, is Bohemia's largest bell.

You'll need your castle admission ticket (A or B) to enter the eastern end of the cathedral, where the graceful late-Gothic vaulting dates from the 14th century. In the centre lies the ornate **Royal Mausoleum** (1571–89) with its cold marble effigies of Ferdinand I, his wife Anna Jagellonská and son Maximilián II.

On the ambulatory's northern side, just beyond the old sacristy and the confessional booths, a **wooden relief** (1630) by Caspar Bechterle shows Protestant Frederick of the Palatinate (in his horse-drawn coach) legging it out of Prague after the Catholic victory at the battle of Bílá Hora.

As you round the far end of the ambulatory you pass the **tomb of St Vitus** – the brass crosiers set in the floor mark the tombs of bishops – and reach the spectacular, baroque silver **tomb of St John of Nepomuk**, its draped canopy supported by chubby, silver angels (the tomb contains two tonnes of silver in all).

The nearby **Chapel of St Mary Magdalene** contains the grave slabs of Matthias of Arras and Petr Parler. Beyond is the ornate, late-Gothic **Royal Oratory**, a fancy balcony with ribbed vaulting carved to look like tree branches.

Stairs in the corner of the Chapel of the Holy Rood lead down to the crypt, where you can see the remains of earlier churches that stood on the site of the cathedral, including an 11th-century Romanesque basilica. Beyond, you can crowd around the entrance to the **Royal Crypt** to see the marble sarcophagi (dating only from the 1930s), which contain the remains of Czech rulers including Charles IV, Wenceslas IV, George of Poděbrady (Jiří z Poděbrad) and Rudolf II.

The biggest and most beautiful of the cathedral's numerous side chapels is Parler's **Chapel of St Wenceslas**. Its walls are adorned with gilded panels containing polished slabs of semiprecious stones. Wall paintings from the early 16th century depict scenes from the life of the Czechs' patron saint, while even older frescoes show scenes from the life of Christ.

On the southern side of the Chapel of St Wenceslas, a small door – locked with seven locks – hides a staircase leading to the Coronation Chamber above the Zlatá brána, where the Czech **crown jewels** are kept. Rarely exhibited to the public, the jewels include the gold crown of St Wenceslas, which was made for Charles IV in 1346 from the gold of the original Přemysl crown (for details on the Přemysl dynasty see p38).

THIRD COURTYARD

South of the cathedral is the Third Courtyard, which contains a granite **monolith** (1928) dedicated to the victims of WWI, designed by Jože Plečník, and a copy of a 14th-century bronze **statue of St George** slaying the dragon; the original statue is in the Convent of St George.

The southern doorway of the cathedral is known as the **Golden Gate** (Zlatá brána), an elegant, triple-arched Gothic porch designed by Petr Parler. Above it is a **mosaic of the Last Judgment** (1370–71) – on the left, the godly rise from their tombs and are raised into Heaven by angels; on the right, sinners are cast down into Hell by demons. In the centre, Christ reigns in glory, with six Czech saints – Procopius, Sigismund, Vitus, Wenceslas, Ludmila and Adalbert – below. Beneath them, on either side of the central arch, Charles IV and his wife kneel in prayer.

To the left of the gate is the **Great Tower**, which was left unfinished by Parler's sons in the 15th century; its soaring Gothic lines are capped by a Renaissance gallery added in the late 16th century, and a bulging spire that dates from the 1770s.

OLD ROYAL PALACE Map p70

Starý královský palác; admission tickets A or B only; ☉ 9am-5pm Apr-Oct, to 4pm Nov-Mar
The Old Royal Palace, at the courtyard's eastern end, is one of the oldest parts of the castle, dating from 1135. It was originally used only by Czech princesses, but from the 13th to the 16th centuries it was the king's own palace.

At its heart is the **Vladislav Hall** (Vladislavský sál), famous for its beautiful, late-Gothic vaulted roof (1493–1502) designed by Benedikt Rejt. Though around 500 years

old, the flowing, interpenetrating lines of the vaults have an almost Art Nouveau feel, in contrast to the rectilinear form of the Renaissance windows. The vast hall was used for banquets, councils and coronations, and also for indoor jousting tournaments – hence the **Riders' Staircase** (Jezdecké schody) on the northern side, designed to admit a mounted knight. All the presidents of the republic have been sworn in here.

A door in the hall's southwestern corner leads to the former offices of the **Bohemian Chancellery** (České kanceláře). On 23 May 1618, in the second room, Protestant nobles rebelling against the Bohemian estates and the Habsburg emperor threw two of his councillors and their secretary out of the window. They survived, as their fall was broken by the dung-filled moat, but this so-called Second Defenestration of Prague sparked off the Thirty Years' War (see p40).

At the eastern end of the Vladislav Hall you'll come to a balcony that overlooks **All Saints' Chapel** (kaple Všech svatých); a door to the right leads you to a terrace with great views across the city. To the right of the Riders' Staircase you'll spot an unusual Renaissance doorway framed by twisted columns that leads to the **Diet** (Sněmovna), or Assembly Hall, which displays another beautifully vaulted ceiling. To the left, a spiral staircase leads you up to the **New Land Rolls Room** (Říšská dvorská kancelář), the old repository for land titles, where the walls are covered with the clerks' coats of arms.

STORY OF PRAGUE CASTLE Map p70

☎ 224 373 102; www.pribeh-hradu.cz; admission included in ticket A, or adult/child 140/50Kč; ☉ 9am-5pm
Housed in the Gothic vaults beneath the Old Royal Palace, this huge and impressive collection of artefacts is the most interesting exhibit in the entire castle. It traces 1000 years of the castle's history, from the building of the first wooden palisade to the present day, illustrated by large models of the castle at various stages in its development, and includes precious items such as the helmet and chain mail worn by St Wenceslas, illuminated manuscripts, and the Bohemian crown jewels. Anyone with a serious interest in Prague Castle should visit here first, as orientation. If you don't have ticket A, you can buy individual tickets at the entrance to the exhibit (cash only).

ST GEORGE SQUARE

St George Square (Náměstí U sv Jiří), the plaza to the east of the cathedral, lies at the heart of the castle complex.

BASILICA OF ST GEORGE Map p70

Bazilika sv Jiří; adult/concession/family 50/25/100Kč; ☉ 9am-5pm Apr-Oct, to 4pm Nov-Mar

The striking, brick-red, early-baroque façade that dominates the square conceals the Czech Republic's best-preserved Romanesque church, established in the 10th century by Vratislav I (the father of St Wenceslas). What you see today is mostly the result of restorations made between 1887 and 1908.

The austerity of the Romanesque nave is relieved by a baroque double staircase leading to the apse, where fragments of 12th-century frescoes survive. In front of the stairs lie the tombs of Prince Boleslav II (d 997; on the left) and Prince Vratislav I (d 921), the church's founder. The arch beneath the stairs allows a glimpse of the 12th-century crypt; Přemysl kings (see p38) are buried here and in the nave.

The tiny baroque chapel beside the entrance is dedicated to St John of Nepomuk (his tomb lies in St Vitus Cathedral).

CONVENT OF ST GEORGE Map p70

Klášter sv Jiří; ☎ 257 320 536; Jiřské náměstí 33; adult/concession 50/20Kč; ☉ 10am-6pm Tue-Sun

The very ordinary-looking building to the left of the basilica was Bohemia's first convent, established in 973 by Boleslav II. Closed and converted to an army barracks in 1782, it now houses a branch of the National Gallery with an excellent collection of Renaissance and baroque art.

POWDER TOWER Map p70

Prašná věž; adult/concession 50/20Kč; ☉ 9am-5pm Apr-Oct, to 4pm Nov-Mar

A passage to the north of St Vitus Cathedral leads to the Powder Tower (also called Mihulka), which was built at the end of the 15th century as part of the castle's defences. Later it became the workshop of the cannon- and bell-maker Tomáš Jaroš, who cast the bells for St Vitus Cathedral. Alchemists employed by Rudolf II also worked here. Today the 1st floor houses a rather dull exhibition of 17th- and 18th-century weaponry.

GEORGE ST

George St (Jiřská) runs from the Basilica of St George to the castle's eastern gate.

GOLDEN LANE Map p70

Zlatá ulička; Zlatá ul; admission ticket A, B or C; ☉ 9am-5pm

Golden Lane is a picturesque, cobbled alley running along the northern wall of the castle. Its tiny, colourful cottages were built in the 16th century for the sharpshooters of the castle guard, but were later used by goldsmiths. In the 18th and 19th centuries they were occupied by squatters, and then by artists, including the writer Franz Kafka (who stayed at his sister's house at No 22 from 1916 to 1917) and the Nobel-laureate poet Jaroslav Seifert. Today, the lane is an overcrowded tourist trap lined with craft and souvenir shops.

At its eastern end is the **Daliborka**, a round tower named after the knight Dalibor of Kozojedy, imprisoned here in 1498 for supporting a peasant rebellion, and later executed. During his imprisonment, according to an old tale, he played a violin which could be heard throughout the castle. Composer Bedřich Smetana (p18) based his 1868 opera *Dalibor* on the tale.

LOBKOWICZ PALACE Map p70

Lobkovický palác; ☎ 257 535 979; Jiřská 3; adult/concession 20/10Kč; ☉ 9am-5pm Tue-Sun

Built in the 1570s, this aristocratic palace now houses a branch of the National Museum, with a good collection on Czech history from prehistoric times until 1848. Exhibits include the sword of executioner Jan Mydlář (who lopped off the heads of 27 rebellious Protestant nobles in Old Town Square in 1621) and some of the oldest marionettes in the Czech Republic, but to be honest this is a place for history buffs only.

TOY MUSEUM Map p70

Muzeum hraček; ☎ 224 372 294; Jiřská 6; adult/concession 50/30Kč; ☉ 9.30am-5.30pm

In the tower of the Burgrave's Palace (Nejvyšší Purkrabství), across the street from the Lobkowicz Palace, is the second-largest toy museum in the world. It's an amazing collection – with exhibits dating back to ancient Greece – but sure to be frustrating for kids as most displays are hands-off.

GARDEN ON THE RAMPARTS

At the castle's eastern gate, you can either descend the Old Castle Steps to Malostranská metro station, or turn sharp right and wander back to Hradčanské náměstí through the Garden on the Ramparts (Zahrada Na Valech; Apr-Oct only). The terrace garden enjoys superb views across the roof-tops of Malá Strana and permits a peek into the back garden of the British embassy.

Alternatively, you can descend to Malá Strana through the terraced Palace Gardens beneath Prague Castle (Palácové zahrady pod Pražským hradem; p81).

HRADČANY

Eating p133; Drinking p153; Shopping p183; Sleeping p195

Hradčany is the attractive and peaceful residential area stretching west from Prague Castle to Strahov Monastery. It became a town in its own right in 1320, and twice suffered heavy damage – once in the Hussite wars and again in the Great Fire of 1541 – before becoming a borough of Prague in 1598. After this, the Habsburg nobility built many palaces here in the hope of cementing their influence with the rulers in Prague Castle.

TRANSPORT - HRADČANY

Tram Nos 22 and 23 stop at Pohořelec, at the western end of Hradčany.

HRADČANY SQUARE

Hradčany Square (Hradčanské náměstí), facing the castle entrance, has retained its shape since the Middle Ages, with a central plague column by Ferdinand Brokoff (1726) and several former canons' residences (Nos 6 to 12) with richly decorated façades.

ARCHBISHOP'S PALACE Map pp264-5

Arcibiskupský palác; Hradčanské náměstí 16; only on the day before Good Friday; tram 22, 23

Opposite the Schwarzenberg Palace is the rococo Archbishop's Palace, bought by Archbishop Antonín Brus of Mohelnice in 1562, and the seat of archbishops ever since. The exterior was given a rococo makeover between 1763 and 1765.

SCHWARZENBERG PALACE Map pp264-5

Schwarzenberský palác; Hradčanské náměstí 16; tram 22, 23

The Renaissance Schwarzenberg Palace, acquired by the powerful Schwarzenberg family in 1719, sports a striking black-and-white *sgraffito* façade. It is being refitted by the National Gallery, and is due to re-open in November 2007.

STERNBERG PALACE Map pp264-5

Šternberský palác; ☎ 220 514 599; www.ngprague .cz; adult/child 60/30Kč; 10am-6pm Tue-Sun; tram 22, 23

Tucked behind the Archbishop's Palace is the baroque Sternberg Palace, home to the National Gallery's valuable collection of 14th- to 18th-century European art, including works by Goya and Rembrandt. Fans of medieval altarpieces will be in heaven; there are also several Rubens, some Rembrandt and Breughel, and a large collection of Bohemian miniatures. Pride of the collection is the glowing *Feast of the Rosary* by Albrecht Dürer, an artist better known for his engravings. Painted in Venice in 1505 as an altarpiece for the church of San Bartolomeo, it was brought to Prague by Rudolf II; in the background, beneath the tree on the right, is the figure of the artist himself. It's worth a trip to the back of the 1st floor to see van Heemskerck's *The Tearful Bride,* who seems to have stepped right out of a drag-queen show.

LORETA SQUARE

From Hradčany Square it's a short walk west to Loreta Square (Loretánské náměstí), created early in the 18th century when the imposing Černín Palace was built. At the northern end of the square is the Capuchin Monastery (1600–02), which is Bohemia's oldest working monastery.

ČERNIN PALACE Map pp264-5

Černínský palác; Loretánské náměstí; closed to the public

The late-17th-century palace facing the Loreta has the city's largest monumental façade. This imposing building has housed the foreign ministry since the creation of Czechoslovakia in 1918, except during WWII when it served as the SS headquarters. In 1948, Jan Masaryk – son of the Czechoslovak republic's founding father, Tomáš Masaryk, and the only noncommunist in the new Soviet-backed government – fell to his death from one of the top-floor windows. Did he fall, or was he pushed?

LORETA Map pp264-5

☎ 224 510 789; Loretánské náměstí 7; adult/concession 90/70Kč; ⏰ 9.15am-12.15pm & 1-4.30pm; tram 22, 23

The square's main attraction is the Loreta, a baroque place of pilgrimage founded by Benigna Kateřina Lobkowicz in 1626, and designed as a replica of the supposed Santa Casa (Sacred House; the home of the Virgin Mary). Legend says that the original Santa Casa was carried by angels to the Italian town of Loreto as the Turks were advancing on Nazareth. The duplicate **Santa Casa**, with fragments of its original frescoes, is in the centre of the courtyard.

Behind the Santa Casa is the **Church of the Nativity of Our Lord** (kostel Narození Páně), built in 1737 to a design by Kristof Dientzenhofer (for more information on this designer see the boxed text, p31). The claustrophobic interior includes two skeletons – of the Spanish saints Felicissima and Marcia – dressed in nobles' clothing with wax masks over their skulls.

At the corner of the courtyard is the startling **Chapel of Our Lady of Sorrows** (kaple Panny Marie Bolestné), featuring a cruci-fied bearded lady. She was St Starosta, pious daughter of a Portuguese king who promised her to the king of Sicily against her wishes. After a night of tearful prayers she awoke with a beard, the wedding was called off, and her father had her crucified. She was later made patron saint of the needy and the godforsaken.

The most eye-popping attraction is the **treasury** (1st floor). It's been ransacked several times over the centuries, but some amazing items remain. Most over-the-top is the 90cm-tall **Prague Sun** (Pražské slunce), made of solid silver and gold and studded with 6222 diamonds.

Above the Loreta's entrance 27 bells, made in Amsterdam in the 17th century, play *We Greet Thee a Thousand Times* every hour.

Photography is not allowed, and the rule is enforced with a 1000Kč fine.

STRAHOV MONASTERY

In 1140 Vladislav II founded Strahov Monastery (Strahovský klášter; Map pp264–5) for the Premonstratensian order. The present monastery buildings, completed in the 17th and 18th centuries, functioned until the communist government closed them down and imprisoned most of the monks, who returned in 1990.

Inside is the 1612 **Church of St Roch** (kostel sv Rocha), which is now an exhibition hall. The **Church of the Assumption of Our Lady** (kostel Nanebevzetí Panny Marie) was built in 1143, and heavily decorated in the 18th century in the baroque style. Mozart is said to have played the organ here.

MINIATURE MUSEUM Map pp264-5

Muzeum miniatur; ☎ 233 352 371; Strahovské II.nádvoří; adult/child 50/30Kč; ⏰ 10am-5pm; tram 22, 23

The 'write your name on a grain of rice' movement may have undermined the respectability of miniature artists, but Siberian technician Anatoly Konyenko will restore your faith with his microscopic creations. Konyenko used to manufacture tools for eye microsurgery, but these days he'd rather spend seven-and-a-half years crafting a pair of golden horseshoes for a flea. See those, plus the world's smallest book and strangely beautiful silhouettes of cars on the leg of a mosquito. Weird.

Entrance to the Loreta (above)

STRAHOV LIBRARY Map pp264-5

Strahovská knihovna; ☎ 233 107 718; www
.strahovmonastery.cz; Strahovské I.nádvoří;
adult/concession 80/50Kč; ☺ 9am-noon & 1-5pm;
tram 22, 23

The biggest attraction of Strahov Monastery is the Strahov Library, the largest monastic library in the country, with its two magnificent baroque halls. You can peek through the doors but, sadly, you can't go into the halls themselves – it was found that fluctuations in humidity caused by visitors' breath was endangering the frescoes.

The stunning interior of the two-storey-high **Philosophy Hall** (Filozofický sál; 1780–97) was built to fit around the carved and gilded, floor-to-ceiling walnut shelving that was rescued from another monastery in South Bohemia (access to the upper gallery is via spiral staircases concealed in the corners). The feeling of height here is accentuated by a grandiose ceiling fresco, the *Struggle of Mankind to Gain True Wisdom* – the figure of Divine Providence is enthroned in the centre amid a burst of golden light, while around the edges are figures ranging from Adam and Eve to the Greek philosophers.

The lobby outside the hall contains an 18th-century **Cabinet of Curiosities**, displaying the grotesquely shrivelled remains of sharks, skates, turtles and other sea creatures; these flayed and splayed corpses were prepared by sailors, who flogged them to credulous landlubbers as 'sea monsters'. Another case (beside the door to the corridor) contains historical items, including a miniature coffee service made for the Habsburg empress Marie Louise in 1813, which fits into four false books.

The corridor leads to the older but even more beautiful **Theology Hall** (Teologiský sál; 1679). The low, curved ceiling is thickly encrusted in ornate baroque stuccowork, and decorated with painted cartouches depicting the theme of 'True Wisdom', which was acquired, of course, through piety; one of the mottoes that adorns the ceiling is *initio sapientiae timor domini*; 'the beginning of wisdom is the fear of God'.

On a stand outside the hall door is a facsimile of the library's most prized possession, the **Strahov Evangeliary**, a 9th-century codex in a gem-studded 12th-century binding. A nearby bookcase houses the **Xyloteka** (1825), a set of booklike boxes, each one bound in the wood and bark of the tree it describes, with samples of leaves, roots, flowers and fruits inside.

In the connecting corridor, look out for the two long, brown, leathery things beside the model ship and narwhal tusk – if you ask, the prudish attendant will tell you they're preserved elephants' trunks, but they're actually whales' penises.

STRAHOV PICTURE GALLERY
Map pp264-5

Strahovská obrazárna; ☎ 220 517 278; www.strahov
monastery.cz; Strahovské II.nádvoří; adult/child
50/20Kč; ☺ 9am-noon & 12.30-5pm Tue-Sun; tram
22, 23

In Strahov Monastery's second courtyard is the Strahov Picture Gallery, with a valuable collection of Gothic, baroque, rococo and romantic art on the 1st floor, and temporary exhibits on the ground floor. Some of the medieval works are extraordinary – don't miss the very modern-looking 14th-century Jihlava Crucifix.

MALÁ STRANA

Eating p134; Drinking p153; Shopping p183; Sleeping p196

Malá Strana (Little Quarter) is clustered around the foot of Prague Castle. Most tourists climb up to the castle along the Royal Way (p92), on Mostecká and Nerudova, but the narrow side streets of this baroque district also have plenty of interest. Almost too picturesque for its own good, Malá Strana is now much in demand as a film location.

Malá Strana started out initially as a market settlement in the 8th or 9th century. In 1257 Přemysl Otakar II granted the area town status. The district was almost destroyed on two separate occasions: during battles between the Hussites and the Prague Castle garrison in 1419, and then in the Great Fire of 1541. Following this massive devastation Renaissance buildings

Sights

MALÁ STRANA

TRANSPORT

Metro Malostranská metro station is in northern Malá Strana, about five minutes' walk from Malostranské náměstí.
Tram Nos 12, 20, 22 and 23 run along Újezd and through Malostranské náměstí.

and palaces replaced the destroyed houses, followed by the baroque churches and palaces in the 17th and 18th centuries that give Malá Strana much of its charm.

PRAGUE CASTLE TO CHARLES BRIDGE

Following the tourist crowds downhill from the castle via Ke Hradu, you soon arrive at Nerudova, architecturally the most important street in Malá Strana; most of its old Renaissance façades were 'baroquefied' in the 18th century. It's named after the Czech poet Jan Neruda (famous for his short stories, *Tales of Malá Strana*), who lived at the **House of the Two Suns** (dům U dvou slunců; Nerudova 47) from 1845 to 1857.

The **House of the Golden Horseshoe** (dům U zlaté podkovy; Nerudova 34) is named after the relief of St Wenceslas above the doorway – his horse was said to be shod with gold. From 1765 Josef of Bretfeld made his **Bretfeld Palace** (Nerudova 33) a centre for social gatherings, with guests such as Mozart and Casanova. The baroque **Church of Our Lady of Unceasing Succour** (kostel Panny Marie ustavičné pomoci; Nerudova 24) was a theatre from 1834 to 1837, and staged Czech plays during the Czech National Revival.

Most of the houses bear emblems of some kind (see the boxed text, p29). Built in 1566, **St John of Nepomuk** (Nerudova 18) is named after one of the Czech patron saints, whose image was added around 1730. The **House of the Three Fiddles** (dům U tří houslíček; Nerudova 12), a Gothic building rebuilt in Renaissance style during the 17th century, once belonged to a family of violin makers.

Little Quarter Square (Malostranské náměstí; Map pp264–5), Malá Strana's main square, is divided into an upper and lower part by St Nicholas Church, the district's most distinctive landmark. The square has been the hub of Malá Strana since the 10th century, though it lost some of its character when Karmelitská street was widened early in the 20th century. Today, it's a mixture of official buildings and touristy restaurants, with a tram line through the middle of the lower square.

The nightclub and bar at No 21, **Malostranská beseda** (see p172), was once the old town

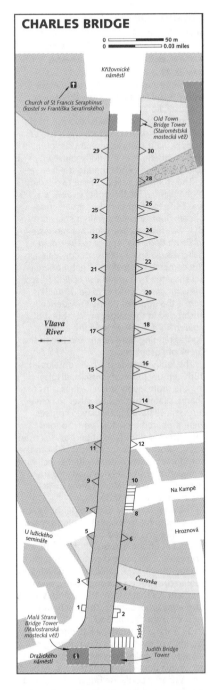

CHARLES BRIDGE

Křižovnické náměstí

Church of St Francis Seraphinus (kostel sv Františka Serafínského)

Old Town Bridge Tower (Staroměstská mostecká věž)

Vltava River

Na Kampě

Hroznová

U lužického semináře

Čertovka

Malá Strana Bridge Tower (Malostranská mostecká věž)

Saská

Judith Bridge Tower

Dražického náměstí

CHARLES BRIDGE STATUES

The bridge's first monument was the crucifix near the eastern end, erected in 1657. The first and most popular statue – the Jesuits' 1683 monument to St John of Nepomuk – inspired other Catholic orders, and over the next 30 years a score more went up, like ecclesiastical billboards. New ones were added in the mid-19th century, and one (plus replacements for some lost to floods) in the 20th century.

As most of the statues were carved from soft sandstone, several weathered originals have been replaced with copies. Some originals are housed in the Casemates (p104) at Vyšehrad; others are in the Lapidárium (p108) in Holešovice.

Starting from the western (Malá Strana) end, the statues that line the bridge are as follows:

1 SS Cosmas & Damian (1709) Charitable 3rd-century physician brothers.

2 St Wenceslas (sv Václav; 1858) Patron saint of Bohemia.

3 St Vitus (sv Víta; 1714) Patron saint of Prague (and of dogs, dancers, actors and comedians).

4 SS John of Matha & Félix de Valois (1714) 12th-century French founders of the Trinitarian order, for the ransom of enslaved Christians (represented by a Tatar standing guard over a group of them), with St Ivo (No 30).

5 St Philip Benizi (sv Benicius; 1714) Miracle worker and healer.

6 St Adalbert (sv Vojtěch; 1709) Prague's first Czech bishop, canonised in the 10th century. Replica.

7 St Cajetan (1709) Italian founder of the Theatine order in the 15th century.

8 The Vision of St Luitgard (1710) Agreed by most to be the finest piece on the bridge, in which Christ appears to the blind saint and allows her to kiss his wounds.

9 St Augustine (1708) Reformed hedonist, famous for his *Confessions*, theological fountainhead of the Reformation. Also, patron saint of brewers. Replica.

10 St Nicholas of Tolentino (1706) Patron of Holy Souls. Replica.

11 St Jude Thaddaeus (1708) Apostle and patron saint of hopeless causes. Further on the right, beyond the railing, is a column with a statue of the eponymous hero of the 11th-century epic poem *Song of Roland* (Bruncvík).

12 St Vincent Ferrer (1712) A 14th-century Spanish priest, and St Procopius, Hussite warrior-priest.

13 St Anthony of Padua (1707) The 13th-century Portuguese disciple of St Francis of Assisi.

14 St Francis Seraphinus (1855) Patron of the poor and abandoned.

15 St John of Nepomuk (1683) Bronze. Patron saint of Czechs: according to the legend illustrated on the base of the statue, Wenceslas IV had him trussed up in a suit of armour and thrown off the bridge in 1393 for refusing to divulge the queen's confessions (he was her priest), though the real reason had to do with the bitter conflict between church and state; the stars in his halo allegedly followed his corpse down the river. Legend has it that if you rub the bronze plaque, you will one day return to Prague.

16 St Wenceslas as a boy (c 1730) With his grand-mother and guardian St Ludmilla, patroness of Bohemia.

17 St Wenceslas (1853) With St Sigismund, son of Charles IV, and St Norbert, 12th-century German founder of the Premonstratensian order.

18 St Francis Borgia (1710) A 16th-century Spanish priest.

19 St John the Baptist (1857) Further along on the right, a bronze cross on the parapet marks the place where St John of Nepomuk was thrown off (see No 15).

20 St Christopher (1857) Patron saint of travellers.

21 SS Cyril & Methodius (1938) The newest statue. These two introduced Christianity and a written script (Cyrillic) to the Slavs in the 9th century.

22 St Francis Xavier (1711) A 16th-century Spanish missionary celebrated for his work in the Orient. Replica.

23 St Anne with Madonna & Child (1707) St Anne is the mother of the Virgin Mary.

24 St Joseph (1854) Husband of the Virgin Mary.

25 Crucifix (1657) Gilded bronze. With an invocation in Hebrew saying 'holy, holy, holy Lord' (funded by the fine of a Jew who had mocked it in 1696); the stone figures date from 1861.

26 Pietá (1859) Mary holding the body of Christ following the crucifixion.

27 Madonna with St Dominic (1709) Spanish founder of the Dominicans in the 12th century, and St Thomas Aquinas. Replica.

28 SS Barbara, Margaret & Elizabeth (1707) St Barbara (2nd-century patron saint of miners); St Margaret (3rd- or 4th-century patron saint of expectant mothers); and St Elizabeth, a 13th-century Slovak princess who renounced the good life to serve the poor.

29 Madonna with St Bernard (1709) Founder of the Cistercian order in the 12th century. Replica.

30 St Ivo (1711) An 11th-century bishop of Chartres. Replica.

hall. Here in 1575 non-Catholic nobles wrote the so-called *České konfese* (Czech Confession), a pioneering demand for religious tolerance addressed to the Habsburg emperor and eventually passed into Czech law by Rudolf II in 1609. On 22 May 1618 Czech nobles gathered at the **Smiřický Palace** (Malostranské náměstí 18) to plot a rebellion against the Habsburg rulers – the next day they flung two Habsburg councillors out of a window in Prague Castle.

CHARLES BRIDGE Map pp264-5 & pp268-9
Karlův most

Strolling across Charles Bridge is everybody's favourite Prague activity. However, by 9am it's a 500m-long fairground, with an army of tourists squeezing through a gauntlet of hawkers and buskers, beneath the impassive gaze of the imposing baroque statues that line the parapets (see the boxed text, p79). If you want to experience the bridge at its most atmospheric it's best appreciated at dawn.

In 1357 Charles IV commissioned Petr Parler (architect of St Vitus Cathedral) to replace the 12th-century Judith Bridge, which had been washed away by floods in 1342. (You can see the only surviving arch of the Judith Bridge by taking a boat trip with Prague Venice; see p58 for details.)

The new bridge was completed around 1400, and only took Charles' name in the 19th century – before that it was known simply as Kamenný most (Stone Bridge). Despite occasional flood damage, it withstood wheeled traffic for 600 years – thanks, legend says, to eggs mixed into the mortar – until it was made pedestrian-only after WWII.

In the crush, don't forget to look at the bridge itself (climb one of the bridge towers for a great view) and the grand vistas up and down the river. Gangs of pickpockets work the bridge day and night, so keep track of your purse or wallet.

HISTORICAL PHARMACY EXHIBITION
Map pp264-5

Expozice Historických lékáren; ☎ 257 531 502; Nerudova 32; adult/child 20/10Kč; ☾ 11am-6pm Tue-Fri, 10am-5pm Sat & Sun Apr-Sep, 10am-5pm Tue-Fri, 10am-5pm Sat & Sun Oct-Mar; tram 12, 20, 22, 23

Hradčany's first pharmacy was opened here in 1749; the building now houses the Historical Pharmacy exhibition, with a small

Statues on Charles Bridge (left)

collection of pharmaceutical paraphernalia and original furnishings dating from the 19th century.

MALÁ STRANA BRIDGE TOWER
Map pp264-5

Malostranská mostecká věž; Charles Bridge; adult/child 40/30Kč; ☾ 10am-6pm Apr-Nov; tram 12, 20, 22, 23

There are actually two towers at the Malá Strana end of Charles Bridge. The lower one was originally part of the long-gone 12th-century Judith Bridge (left), while the taller one was built in the mid-15th century in imitation of the one at the Staré Město end (see p88). The taller tower is open to the public and houses an exhibit on the history of Charles Bridge, though like its Staré Město counterpart the main attraction is the view from the top.

ST NICHOLAS CHURCH Map pp264-5
Kostel sv Mikuláše; Malostranská náměstí 38; adult/child 60/30Kč; ☾ 9am-5pm Mar-Oct, to 4pm Nov-Feb; tram 12, 20, 22, 23

Malá Strana is dominated by the huge green cupola of the St Nicholas Church, one of Central Europe's finest baroque buildings. (Don't confuse it with the other Church of St Nicholas on Old Town Square.) It was begun by Kristof Dientzenhofer; his son Kilian continued the work and Anselmo Lurago finished the job in 1755.

On the ceiling, Johann Kracker's 1770 *Apotheosis of St Nicholas* is Europe's largest fresco (clever *trompe l'oeil* technique has made the painting merge almost seamlessly with the architecture). In the first chapel on the left is a mural by Karel Škréta, which includes the church official who kept track of the artist as he worked; he is looking out through a window in the upper corner.

Mozart himself tickled the ivories on the 2500-pipe organ in 1787, and was honoured with a requiem mass here (14 December 1791). Take the stairs up to the gallery to see Škréta's gloomy 17th-century Passion Cycle paintings and the scratchings of bored 1820s tourists and wannabe Franz Kafkas on the balustrade.

NORTHERN MALÁ STRANA

From the northern side of Malostranské náměstí, Thunovská and the Castle Steps (Zámecké schody) lead up to the castle. At the eastern end of Thunovská, on Sněmovní, is the Czech Parliament House (Sněmovna), seat of the lower house of today's parliament, and formerly of the national assembly that deposed the Habsburgs from the Czech throne on 14 November 1918.

FRANZ KAFKA MUSEUM Map pp264-5
Muzeum Franzy Kafky; ☎ 257 535 507; www.kafkamuseum.cz; Hergetova Cíhelná, Cihelná 2b; adult/child 120/60Kč; ✆ 10am-6pm; tram 12, 20, 22, 23

This much-hyped exhibition on the life and work of Prague's most famous literary son opened here in 2005 after three years in Barcelona and three years in New York. Entitled 'City of K', it explores the intimate relationship between the writer and the city that shaped him through the use of original letters, photographs, quotations, period newspapers and publications, and video and sound installations. Does it vividly portray the claustrophobic bureaucracy and atmosphere of brooding menace that characterised Kafka's world? Or is it a load of pretentious old bollocks? You decide.

PALACE GARDENS BENEATH PRAGUE CASTLE Map pp264-5
Palácové zahrady pod Pražským hradem; ☎ 257 010 401; Valdštejnské náměstí 3; adult/child 79/49Kč; ✆ 10am-9pm Jun & Jul, to 8pm Aug, to 7pm May & Sep, to 6pm Apr & Oct; tram 12, 20, 22, 23

These beautiful terraced gardens on the steep southern slope of the castle hill date from the 17th and 18th centuries, when they were created for the owners of the adjoining palaces. They were restored in the 1990s and contain a Renaissance loggia with frescoes of Pompeii and a baroque portal with sundial that cleverly catches the sunlight reflected from the water in the triton fountain in front of it.

PRAGUE JEWELLERY COLLECTION Map pp264-5
Pražský kabinet šperku; ☎ 221 451 333; Cihelná 2b; adult/child 60/50Kč; ✆ 10am-6pm; tram 12, 20, 22, 23

This museum, next door to the Franz Kafka Museum, provides a showcase for some of the finest items of jewellery in the collection of the Museum of Decorative Arts (p90). There are exquisite Art Nouveau and Art Deco designs, as well as several pieces by Tiffany and Fabergé.

WALLENSTEIN GARDEN Map pp264-5
Valdštejnská zahrada; Letenská 10; admission free; ✆ 10am-6pm Apr-Oct; metro Malostranská

This huge walled garden lurks behind the Wallenstein Palace. Its finest feature is the huge loggia decorated with scenes from the Trojan Wars, flanked to one side by a fake stalactite grotto full of hidden animals and grotesque faces. The bronze statues of Greek gods lining the avenue opposite the loggia are copies – the originals were carted away by marauding Swedes in 1648 and now stand outside the royal palace of Drottningholm near Stockholm.

At the eastern end of the garden is the Wallenstein Riding School (Valdštejnská jízdárna), home to changing exhibitions of modern art and a picturesque pond full of giant carp. There are entrances to the garden on Letenská, beside Malostranská metro station and via the Wallenstein Palace (see the walking tour on p118).

WALLENSTEIN PALACE Map pp264-5
Valdštejnský palác; ☎ 257 071 111; Valdštejnské náměstí 4; admission free; ✆ 10am-4pm Sat & Sun; tram 12, 20, 22, 23

Wallenstein Square (Valdštejnské náměstí), the small square to the northeast of Malostranské náměstí, is dominated by a monumental palace built in 1630 by Albrecht of

Wallenstein, generalissimo of the Habsburg armies. The palace displaced 23 houses, a brickworks and three gardens, and was financed by the confiscation of properties from Protestant nobles defeated at the Battle of Bílá Hora (White Mountain) in 1620. The palace now houses the Senate of the Czech Republic, but you can visit some of the rooms on weekends. The fresco on the ceiling of the Baroque Hall shows Wallenstein glorified as a warrior at the reins of a chariot, while the unusual oval Audience Hall is capped with a fresco of Vulcan at work in his forge.

SOUTHERN MALÁ STRANA

The southern part of Malá Strana centres on pretty Maltese Square (Maltézské náměstí; Map pp264–5), which takes its name from the Knights of Malta who, in 1169, established a monastery beside the austere, early-Gothic towers of the Church of Our Lady Below the Chain (kostel Panny Marie pod řetězem). (The knights were charged with protecting the bridge across the river – the chain refers to the barrier they used.)

To the east of the square is Kampa (Map pp264–5 and pp270–1), an 'island' created by the Čertovka (Devil's Stream), and the most peaceful and picturesque part of Malá Strana. In the 13th century the town's first mill, the Sovovský mlýn (now Kampa Museum), was built on the island, and other mills followed. Kampa was once used as farmland (the name Kampa comes from campus, Latin for 'field'), but the island was settled in the 16th century after being raised above flood level. In 1939 the river was so low that it was again joined to the mainland and many coins and items of jewellery were found in the dry channel.

The area where the Čertovka passes under Charles Bridge is sometimes called Prague's Venice – the channel is often crowded with dinky little tour boats. Cafés beckon from Na Kampě, the little square south of the bridge, though the summer sun is ferocious here. The southern part of Kampa, beyond the square, is a pleasant wooded park with views across to Staré Město.

Near the southern end of Kampa lies one of Malá Strana's oldest Gothic buildings, the Church of St John at the Laundry (kostel sv Jana Na prádle; Map pp270–1), built in 1142 as a local parish church. Inside are the remains of 14th-century frescoes.

Střelecký ostrov (Marksmen's Island; Map pp270–1), just south of Kampa, is crossed by the Legion Bridge (Legií most). The island's name originates in its use in the 16th century as a cannon and rifle target for the Prague garrison. During summer it has an open-air bar and cinema (see the boxed text, p157), and there's a little beach at the northern end.

CHILDREN'S ISLAND Map pp270-1
Dětský ostrov; access from Nábřežní; admission free; 🕒 24hr; metro Anděl
Prague's smallest island offers a leafy respite from the hustle and bustle of the city, with a selection of swings, slides climbing frames and sandpits to keep the kids busy, as well as a rope swing, skateboard ramp, mini football pitch, netball court, and lots of open space for older siblings to run wild. There are plenty of benches to take the strain off weary parental legs, and a decent bar and restaurant at the southern end.

JOHN LENNON WALL Map pp264-5
Velkopřevorské náměstí; tram 12, 20, 22, 23
After his murder on 8 December 1980 John Lennon became a pacifist hero for many young Czechs. An image of Lennon was painted on a wall in a secluded square opposite the French Embassy (there is a niche on the wall that looks like a tombstone), along with political graffiti and Beatles lyrics. Despite repeated coats of whitewash, the secret police never managed to keep it clean for long, and the Lennon Wall became a political focus for Prague youth (most Western pop music was banned by the communists, and some Czech musicians were even jailed for playing it). Post-1989 weathering and lightweight graffiti ate away at the political messages and images, until little remained of Lennon but his eyes. Since 1998 the wall has been whitewashed several times, but it quickly gets repainted with Lennon images, peace messages and inconsequential tourist graffiti of the 'we woz ere' variety.

KAMPA MUSEUM Map pp270-1
Muzeum Kampa ☎ 257 286 147; www.museum kampa.cz; U sovových mlýnů 2; adult/child 120/60Kč; 🕒 10am-6pm; tram 12, 20, 22, 23
Housed in a renovated mill building, this gallery is devoted to 20th-century and

contemporary art from Central Europe. The highlights of the permanent exhibition are extensive collections of bronzes by Cubist sculptor Otto Gutfreund, and paintings by František Kupka, a pioneer of abstract art. The most impressive canvas is Kupka's *Cathedral*, a pleated mass of blue and red diagonals suggesting a curtain with a glimpse of darkness beyond.

MUSEUM OF THE INFANT JESUS OF PRAGUE Map pp264-5

Muzeum Pražského Jezulátka; ☎ 257 533 646; www.pragjesu.info; Karmelitská 9; admission by donation; ☺ 10am-5.30pm Mon-Sat & 1-5pm Sun, closed 25 Dec & Easter Mon; tram 12, 20, 22, 23
The Church of Our Lady Victorious (kostel Panny Marie Vítězné), built in 1613, has on its central altar a 47cm-tall waxwork figure of the baby Jesus brought from Spain in 1628. Known as the Infant Jesus of Prague (Pražské jezulátko), it is said to have protected Prague from the plague and from the destruction of the Thirty Years' War, and is visited by a steady stream of pilgrims, especially from Italy, Spain and Latin America. An 18th-century German prior, ES Stephano, wrote about the miracles, kicking off what eventually became a worldwide cult. It was traditional to dress the figure in beautiful robes, and over the years various benefactors donated richly embroidered dresses. Today the Infant's wardrobe consists of more than 70 costumes donated from all over the world; these are changed regularly in accordance with a religious calendar.

At the back of the church is the museum, displaying a selection of the frocks used to dress the Infant; shops in the street nearby sell copies of the wax figure. Looking at all this, you can't help thinking about the Second Commandment ('Thou shalt not make unto thee any graven image…') and the objectives of the Reformation. Jan Hus must be spinning in his grave.

VRTBOV GARDEN Map pp264-5

Vrtbovská zahrada; ☎ 257 531 480; www.vrtbovska .cz; Karmelitská 25; adult/child 40/25Kč; ☺ 10am-6pm Apr-Oct; tram 12, 20, 22, 23
This 'secret garden', hidden along an alley at the corner of Tržiště and Karmelitská, was built in 1720 for the earl of Vrtba, the senior chancellor of Prague Castle. It's a formal baroque garden, climbing steeply up the hillside to a terrace graced with baroque statues of Greek mythological figures by Matthias Braun – see if you can spot Vulcan, Diana and Mars. Below the terrace (on the right, looking down) is a tiny studio once used by Czech painter Mikuláš Aleš, and above is a little lookout with good views of Prague Castle and Malá Strana.

PETŘÍN

This 318m-high hill is one of Prague's largest single green spaces. It's great for quiet, tree-shaded walks and fine views over the 'city of 100 spires'. There were once vineyards here, and a quarry that provided the stone for most of Prague's Romanesque and Gothic buildings.

Petřín is easily accessible from Hradčany and Strahov, or you can ride the funicular railway (lanová dráha; every 10 to 20 minutes 9.15am to 8.45pm) from Újezd up to the top. The funicular uses ordinary public transport tickets – remember to validate your ticket at the bottom station if it's not already stamped. You can also get off two-thirds of the way up at Restaurant Nebozízek (p135).

Vrtbov Garden (above) and the rooftops of Malá Strana

WEIRD ART

David Černý's sculpture is often controversial, occasionally outrageous, and always amusing. Here are six of his best-known works that are permanently on view in Prague. See also the boxed text, p24.

- Quo Vadis (1991) – found in the garden of the German Embassy in Malá Strana (Map pp264–5). A Trabant (an East German car) on four human legs, a monument to the thousands of East Germans who fled the communist regime in 1989 prior to the fall of the Berlin Wall, and camped out in the embassy garden as they sought political asylum.
- Viselec (Hanging Out; 1997) – above Husova street in Staré Město (Map pp272–3). A bearded, bespectacled chap with a passing resemblance to Sigmund Freud, casually dangling by one hand from a pole way above the street.
- Kun (Horse; 1999) – in the Lucerna Palace shopping arcade, Nové Město (Map pp272–3). Amusing alternative version of the famous St Wenceslas Statue in Wenceslas Square, only this time the horse is dead.
- Miminka (Mummy; 2000) – on the TV Tower, Žižkov (Map pp278–9). Creepy, giant, slot-faced babies crawling all over a TV transmitter tower; something to do with consumerism and the media, methinks.
- Instalace (Installation; 2003) – in the Futura Gallery, Smíchov (Map pp270–1). Stick your head up a statue's backside and watch a video of the Czech president and the director of the National Gallery feeding each other baby food.
- Proudy (Piss; 2004) – in the courtyard of Hergetova Cihelná, Malá Strana (Map pp264–5). Two guys pissing in a puddle (whose irregular outline, you'll notice, is actually the map outline of the Czech Republic) and spelling out famous quotations from Czech literature with their pee (yes, the sculpture moves! It's computer controlled).

In the peaceful **Kinský Garden** (Kinského zahrada), on the southern side of Petřín, is the 18th-century wooden **Church of St Michael** (kostel sv Michala), transferred here, log by log, from the village of Medved'ov in Ukraine. Such structures are rare in Bohemia, though still common in Ukraine and northeastern Slovakia.

MIRROR MAZE Map pp270-1
Bludiště; adult/child 40/30Kč; ⏰ 10am-10pm May, to 8pm Jun-Aug, to 7pm Apr & Sep, to 6pm Oct, to 5pm Sat & Sun Nov-Mar; funicular railway
Below the lookout tower is the Mirror Maze, also built for the 1891 Prague Exposition. As well as the maze, which is good for a laugh, is a diorama of the 1648 battle between Praguers and Swedes on Charles Bridge. Opposite is the **Church of St Lawrence** (kostel sv Vavřince), which contains a ceiling fresco depicting the founding of the church in 991 at a pagan site with a sacred flame.

MUSAION Map pp270-1
☎ 257 325 766; Kinského zahrada 98; adult/child 80/40Kč; ⏰ 10am-6pm Tue-Sun May-Sep, 9am-5pm Tue-Sun Oct-Apr; tram 6, 9, 12, 20
This recently renovated summer palace houses the National Museum's ethnographic collection, with exhibits covering traditional Czech folk culture and art, including music, costume, farming methods and handicrafts. There are regular folk

concerts and workshops demonstration traditional crafts such as blacksmithing and woodcarving.

PETŘÍN LOOKOUT TOWER Map pp270-1
Petřínská rozhledna; adult/child 50/40Kč; ⏰ 10am-10pm May, to 8pm Jun-Aug, to 7pm Apr & Sep, to 6pm Oct, to 5pm Sat & Sun Nov-Mar; funicular railway
To the north of the observatory is Petřínská rozhledna, a 62m-tall Eiffel Tower looka-like built in 1891 for the Prague Exposition. You can climb its 299 steps for some of the best views of Prague; on clear days you can see the forests of Central Bohemia. On the way to the tower you cross the **Hunger Wall** (Hladová zed'), running from Újezd to Strahov. These fortifications were built in 1362 under Charles IV, and are so named because they were built by the poor of the city in return for food – an early job-creation scheme.

ŠTEFÁNIK OBSERVATORY Map pp270-1
Štefánikova hvězdárna; ☎ 257 320 540; www.observatory.cz; adult/child 30/20Kč; ⏰ 6-8pm Tue-Fri, 10am-noon & 2-8pm Sat & Sun Nov-Feb; 7-9pm Tue-Fri, 10am-noon, 2-6pm & 7-9pm Sat & Sun Mar & Oct; 2-7pm & 9-11pm Tue-Fri, 10am-noon, 2-7pm & 9-11pm Sat & Sun Apr-Aug; 2-6pm & 8-10pm Tue-Fri, 10am-noon, 2-6pm & 8-10pm Sat & Sun Sep; funicular railway

Just south of the funicular's top station is this 'people's observatory', opened in 1928 to further public awareness of astronomy and other sciences. There are exhibitions on astronomy, but the main attraction is the double Zeiss astrograph telescope, which also dates from 1928 and allows observation of the sun and sunspots. On clear nights you can also observe the moon, stars and planets.

STARÉ MĚSTO

Eating p137; Drinking p154; Shopping p183; Sleeping p197

By the 10th century a settlement and marketplace existed on the Vltava River's eastern bank. In the 12th century this was linked to the castle district by the Judith Bridge, the forerunner of the Charles Bridge (p80 for details), and in 1231 Wenceslas I honoured it with a town charter and the beginnings of a fortification. This 'Old Town' – Staré Město in Czech – has been Prague's working heart ever since. The town walls are long gone, but their line is still traced by the streets Národní třída, Na příkopě and Revoluční, and the main gate – the Powder Gate – still survives.

Staré Město shared in the boom when Charles IV gave Prague a Gothic face befitting its new status as capital of the Holy Roman Empire. Charles founded Charles University in 1348, and commissioned the Charles Bridge in 1357. When Emperor Joseph II united Prague's towns into a single city in 1784 the Old Town Hall (Staroměstská radnice) became its seat of government.

To ease the devastation of frequent flooding by the Vltava River, the level of the town was gradually raised, beginning in the 13th century, with new construction simply rising on top of older foundations (many of Staré Město's buildings have Gothic interiors and Romanesque cellars). A huge fire in 1689 contributed to an orgy of rebuilding during the Catholic Counter-Reformation of the 17th and 18th centuries, giving the formerly Gothic district a heavily baroque face.

The only intrusions into Staré Město's medieval layout have been the appropriation of a huge block in the west for the Jesuits' massive college, the Klementinum, in the 16th and 17th centuries, and the 'slum clearance' of Josefov, the Jewish quarter, at the end of the 19th century.

At the centre of everything is Old Town Square. If the maze of narrow streets around the square can be said to have a 'main drag' it's the so-called Royal Way (Královská cesta), the ancient coronation route to Prague Castle, running from the Powder Gate along Celetná to Old Town Square and Malé náměstí, then along Karlova and across Charles Bridge.

OLD TOWN SQUARE

One of Europe's biggest and most beautiful urban spaces, the Old Town Square (Staroměstské náměstí, often called Staromák) has been Prague's principal public square since the 10th century, and was its main marketplace until the beginning of the 20th century.

Despite the over-the-top commercialism, crowded pavement cafés and swarms of tourists, it's impossible not to enjoy the spectacle – tour leaders thrusting through the crowd, umbrellas borne aloft like battle standards, with clients straggling behind like a gaggle of ducklings; students dressed as frogs and chickens handing out flyers for a drama production; middle-aged couples

TOP FIVE STARÉ MĚSTO

- Municipal House (p93)
- Museum of Czech Cubism (p94)
- Museum of Decorative Arts (p90)
- Old Town Square (below)
- Prague Jewish Museum (p88)

Sights

STARÉ MĚSTO

TRANSPORT - STARÉ MĚSTO

Metro Staroměstská station is a few minutes' walk northwest of Old Town Square, and Můstek station is five minutes' walk to the south.

Tram No trams run close to Old Town Square. Nos 17 and 18 run along the western edge of Staré Město near the river, while Nos 5, 8 and 14 stop at náměstí Republiky across the street from the Municipal House. Tram Nos 6, 9, 18, 21, 22 and 23 run along Národní třída on the southern edge of Staré Město.

in matching, too-short shorts and sensible shoes, frowning at pink-haired, leather-clad punks with too many piercings; gangs of red-faced lads in football shirts slopping beer and ice cream on the cobblestones; and a bored-looking guy with a placard advertising a museum of torture instruments.

There are also busking jazz bands and alfresco concerts, political meetings, and even fashion shows, all watched over by Ladislav Šaloun's brooding Art Nouveau **sculpture of Jan Hus** (see the boxed text, p40). It was unveiled on 6 July 1915, the 500th anniversary of Hus' death at the stake. The steps at its base – once the only place in the square where you could sit down without having to pay for something – have now been protected by a ring of flower beds, but the police seem to have given up on ordering people to keep off.

The brass strip on the ground nearby is the so-called **Prague Meridian**. Until 1915 the square's main feature was a 17th-century plague column (see the boxed text, p105), whose shadow used to cross the meridian at high noon.

CHURCH OF OUR LADY BEFORE TÝN
Map pp268-9
Kostel Panny Marie před Týnem; Staroměstské náměstí; admission free; ☺ services at 4.30pm Mon-Fri, 1pm Sat, 11.30am & 9pm Sun; metro Staroměstská

The distinctive, spiky-topped Týn Church is early Gothic, though it takes some imagination to visualise the original in its entirety because it's partly hidden behind the four-storey Týn School (not a Habsburg plot to obscure this 15th-century Hussite stronghold, but almost contemporaneous with it). The church's name originates from a courtyard called **Týnský dvůr**, or just **Týn**, behind the church on Štupartská. Originally a sort of medieval caravanserai for visiting foreign merchants, the attractively renovated courtyard now houses shops, restaurants and hotels.

Though Gothic on the outside, the church's interior is smothered in heavy baroque. Two of the most interesting features are the huge rococo **altar** on the northern wall, and the **tomb of Tycho Brahe**, the Danish

THE ASTRONOMICAL CLOCK

The Old Town Hall tower was given a clock in 1410 by the master clockmaker Mikuláš of Kadaně; this was improved in 1490 by one Master Hanuš, producing the mechanical marvel you see today. Legend has it that Hanuš was afterwards blinded so he could not duplicate the work elsewhere, and in revenge crawled up into the clock and disabled it. (Documents from the time suggest that he carried on as clock master for years, unblinded, although the clock apparently didn't work properly until it was repaired in about 1570.)

Four figures beside the clock represent the deepest civic anxieties of 15th-century Praguers: Vanity (with a mirror), Greed (with his money bag; originally a Jewish moneylender, cosmetically altered after WWII), Death, and Pagan Invasion (represented by a Turk). The four figures below these are the Chronicler, Angel, Astronomer and Philosopher.

On the hour, Death rings a bell and inverts his hourglass, and the 12 Apostles parade past the windows above the clock, nodding to the crowd. On the left side are Paul (with a sword and a book), Thomas (lance), Jude (book), Simon (saw), Bartholomew (book) and Barnabas (parchment); on the right side are Peter (with a key), Matthew (axe), John (snake), Andrew (cross), Philip (cross) and James (mallet). At the end, a cock crows and the hour is rung.

On the upper face, the disk in the middle of the fixed part depicts the world known at the time – with Prague at the centre, of course. The gold sun traces a circle through the blue zone of day, the brown zone of dusk (Crepusculum in Latin) in the west (Occasus), the black disc of night, and dawn (Aurora) in the east (Ortus). From this the hours of sunrise and sunset can be read. The curved lines with black Arabic numerals are part of an astrological 'star clock'.

The sun-arm points to the hour (without any daylight-saving time adjustment) on the Roman-numeral ring; the top XII is noon and the bottom XII is midnight. The outer ring, with Gothic numerals, reads traditional 24-hour Bohemian time, counted from sunset; the number 24 is always opposite the sunset hour on the fixed (inner) face.

The moon, with its phases shown, also traces a path through the zones of day and night, riding on the offset moving ring. On the ring you can also read which houses of the zodiac the sun and moon are in. The hand with a little star at the end of it indicates sidereal (stellar) time.

The calendar-wheel beneath all this astronomical wizardry, with 12 seasonal scenes celebrating rural Bohemian life, is a duplicate of one painted in 1866 by the Czech Revivalist Josef Mánes. You can have a close look at the beautiful original in the Prague City Museum (p98). Most of the dates around the calendar-wheel are marked with the names of their associated saints; 6 July honours Jan Hus.

astronomer who was one of Rudolf II's most illustrious 'consultants' (he died in 1601 of a burst bladder following a royal piss-up – he was too polite to leave the table to relieve himself). On the inside of the southern wall of the church are two small windows – they are now blocked off, but once opened into the church from rooms in the neighbouring house at Celetná 3, where the teenage Franz Kafka once lived (from 1896 to 1907).

As for the exterior of the church, the **north portal** overlooking Týnská ulička is topped by a remarkable 14th-century tympanum showing the Crucifixion, carved by the workshop of Charles IV's favourite architect Petr Parler (this is a copy, as the original is in the Lapidárium; see p108).

The entrance to the church is along a passage from the square, through the second (from the left) of the Týn School's four arches. It's only open for services and occasional concerts, not ordinary tourist visits, but you can peer at the interior through the glass doors. The Týn Church is an occasional concert venue and has a very grand-sounding pipe organ.

CHURCH OF ST JAMES Map pp268-9
Kostel sv Jakuba; Malá Štupartská 6; admission free; ⏰ 9.30am-12.30pm & 2.30-4pm Mon-Sat; metro Staroměstská

The great Gothic mass of kostel sv Jakuba, to the east of Týnský dvůr, began in the 14th century as a Minorite monastery church, but was given a beautiful baroque face-lift in the early 18th century. Pride of place inside goes to the over-the-top tomb of Count Jan Vratislav of Mitrovice, an 18th-century lord chancellor of Bohemia, in the northern aisle.

In the midst of the gilt and stucco is a grisly memento: on the inside of the western wall (look up to the right as you enter) hangs a shrivelled human arm. The story goes that around 1400 a thief tried to steal the jewels from the statue of the Virgin. Legend claims the Virgin grabbed his wrist in such an iron grip that his arm had to be lopped off. (The truth may not be far behind: the church was a favourite of the guild of butchers, who may have administered their own justice.)

It's well worth a visit to enjoy St James' splendid pipe organ and famous acoustics. Recitals – free ones at 10.30am or 11am after Sunday Mass – and occasional concerts are

Church of St Nicholas (below)

not always advertised by ticket agencies, so check the noticeboard outside.

CHURCH OF ST NICHOLAS Map pp268-9
Kostel sv Mikuláše; Staroměstské náměstí; admission free; ⏰ noon-4pm Mon, 10am-4pm Tue-Sat, noon-3pm Sun; metro Staroměstská

The baroque wedding cake in the northwestern corner of the square is the Church of St Nicholas, built in the 1730s by Kilian Dientzenhofer (not to be confused with at least two other St Nicholas churches in Prague, including the Dientzenhofers' masterwork in Malá Strana). Considerable grandeur has been worked into a very tight space; originally the church was wedged behind the Old Town Hall's northern wing (destroyed in 1945). Chamber concerts are often held beneath its stucco decorations, a visually splendid (though acoustically mediocre) setting.

GOLTZ-KINSKÝ PALACE Map pp268-9
Palác Kinských; ☎ 224 810758; Staroměstské náměstí 12; adult/child 100/50Kč; ⏰ 10am-5.30pm; metro Staroměstská

Fronting the late-baroque Goltz-Kinský Palace is probably Prague's finest rococo façade, finished in 1765 by the redoubtable Kilian Dientzenhofer (see the boxed text, p31). Alfred Nobel, the Swedish inventor of dynamite, once stayed here; his crush on pacifist Bertha Kinský may have influenced him to establish the Nobel Peace Prize.

87

Many living Praguers have a darker memory of the place, for it was from its balcony in February 1948 that Klement Gottwald proclaimed communist rule in Czechoslovakia. These days it's a branch of the National Gallery, housing temporary art exhibitions.

HOUSE AT THE GOLDEN RING
Map pp268-9

Dům u zlatého prstenu; ☎ 224 827 022; Týnská 6; adult/child 90/50Kč; ☺ 10am-6pm Tue-Sun; metro Staroměstská

The restored Renaissance House at the Golden Ring, on the corner of Týnská just outside the western entrance to Týn courtyard, is another branch of the Prague City Gallery, with a fine collection of 20th-century Czech art. Note the original painted ceiling beams in some rooms.

HOUSE AT THE STONE BELL Map pp268-9

Dům u kamenného zvonu; ☎ 224 827 526; Staroměstské náměstí 13; adult/child 90/50Kč; ☺ 10am-6pm Tue-Sun; metro Staroměstská

Next door to the Goltz-Kinský Palace is this elegant medieval building, its 14th-century Gothic dignity rescued in the 1960s from a second-rate baroque renovation (the stucco façade stripped to reveal the original stonework). Inside, two restored Gothic chapels now serve as branches of the Prague City Gallery, with changing exhibits of modern art, and as chamber-concert venues.

OLD TOWN BRIDGE TOWER Map pp268-9

Staroměstská mostecká věž; Charles Bridge; adult/child 40/30Kč; ☺ 10am-6pm; metro Staroměstská

Perched at the eastern end of Charles Bridge, the elegant late-14th-century tower was, like the bridge itself, designed by Petr Parler. Here, at the end of the Thirty Years' War, an invading Swedish army was finally repulsed by a band of students and Jewish ghetto residents. Today, it houses a fairly humdrum collection of vintage musical instruments, but the main attraction is the amazing view from the top.

Looking out from the eastern face of the tower towards Karlova are the figures of SS Adalbert and Procopius, and below them Charles IV, St Vitus and Wenceslas IV. The tower also features a bit of 'Gothic porn': look below these worthies on the left-hand corner of the tower, just above the bridge parapet, and you'll find a stone carving of a man with his hand up the skirt of what appears to be a nun. Naughty.

OLD TOWN HALL Map pp268-9

Staroměstská radnice; ☎ 12 444; Staroměstské náměstí 1; adult/child 40/30Kč, separate tickets for historic halls, Gothic chapel & tower; ☺ 11am-6pm Mon, 9am-6pm Tue-Sun Apr-Oct, 9am-5pm Tue-Sat, 11am-5pm Sun Nov-Mar; metro Staroměstská

Prague's Old Town Hall, founded in 1338, is a hotchpotch of medieval buildings presided over by a tall Gothic tower, acquired piecemeal over the years by a town council that was short of funds. Most notable is **House at the Minute** (dům U minuty), the arcaded building on the corner covered with Renaissance *sgraffito* – Franz Kafka lived here (1889–96) as a child just before the building was bought for the town hall.

History hangs heavy here. A plaque on the town hall's eastern face lists the 27 Protestant nobles beheaded in 1621 after the Battle of Bílá Hora; white crosses on the ground mark where the deed was done. Another plaque commemorates a critical WWII victory by Red Army and Czechoslovak units at Dukla Pass in Slovakia, and yet another the Czech partisans who died during the Prague Rising on 8 May 1945. If you look at the neogothic eastern gable, you can see that its right-hand edge is broken – the wing that once extended north from here was blown up by the Nazis in 1945, on the day before the Soviet army marched into the city.

This is one of the most crowded corners of Old Town Square, especially during the hourly show put on by the town hall's splendid **Astronomical Clock** (see the boxed text, p86). You can see the interior workings, including parade of Apostles from behind the scenes, by buying a ticket for the Gothic chapel. Apart from the clock, the town hall's best feature is the view from the 60m-tall **tower**, which is certainly worth the climb. There's a lift that allows access for wheelchair users.

JOSEFOV

The slice of Staré Město bounded by Kaprova, Dlouhá and Kozí contains the remains of the once-thriving quarter of Josefov, Prague's former Jewish ghetto, where half-a-dozen old synagogues and the town hall survive along with the powerfully

MENDELSSOHN IS ON THE ROOF

The roof of the Rudolfinum – a complex of concert halls and offices built in the late 19th century – is decorated with statues of famous composers. It housed the German administration during WWII, when the Nazi authorities ordered that the statue of Felix Mendelssohn – who was Jewish – should be removed.

In *Mendelssohn Is on the Roof*, a darkly comic novella about life in wartime Prague, the Jewish writer Jiří Weil weaves a wryly amusing story around this true-life event. The two Czech labourers given the task of removing the statue can't tell which of the two dozen or so figures is Mendelssohn – they all look the same, as far as they can tell. Their Czech boss, remembering his lectures in 'racial science', tells them that Jews have big noses. 'Whichever one has the biggest conk, that's the Jew.'

So the workmen single out the statue with the biggest nose – 'Look! That one over there with the beret. None of the others has a nose like his' – sling a noose around its neck, and start to haul it over. As their boss walks across to check on their progress, he gapes in horror as they start to topple the figure of the only composer on the roof that he does recognise – Richard Wagner.

melancholy Old Jewish Cemetery. In an act of grotesque irony, the Nazis preserved these places as part of a planned 'museum of an extinct race'. Instead they have survived as a memorial to seven centuries of oppression.

Six Jewish monuments clustered together in Josefov are now part of the **Prague Jewish Museum**, holding what is probably the world's biggest collection of sacred Jewish artefacts, many of them saved from demolished Bohemian synagogues: the Maisel Synagogue; the Pinkas Synagogue; the Spanish Synagogue; the Klaus Synagogue; the Ceremonial Hall; and the Old Jewish Cemetery (see the boxed text, p91, for admission details). There is also the Old-New Synagogue, which is still used for religious services, and the Jewish Town Hall.

Despite being built during the slum clearances of old Josefov, Pařížská třída (Paris Ave) and the adjacent streets are themselves a kind of museum. When the ghetto was cleared at the turn of the 20th century, this broad Parisian-style boulevard was driven in a straight line through the heart of the old slums. It was a time of widespread infatuation with the French Art Nouveau style, and the avenue and its side streets were lined with elegant apartment buildings adorned with stained glass and sculptural flourishes. In recent years Pařížská has become a glitzy shopping strand, studded with expensive brand names, such as Dior, Louis Vuitton and Fabergé (see p183).

Jan Palach Square (Náměstí Jana Palacha; Map pp268–9) is named after the young Charles University student who in January 1969 set himself alight in Wenceslas Square in protest against the Soviet invasion (see

the boxed text, p44). On the eastern side of the square, beside the entrance to the philosophy faculty building where Palach was a student, is a bronze memorial plaque with a ghostly death mask.

Presiding over the square is the Rudolfinum, home to the Czech Philharmonic Orchestra. This and the National Theatre (p100), both designed by architects Josef Schulz and Josef Zítek, are considered Prague's finest neo-Renaissance buildings. Completed in 1884, the Rudolfinum served between the wars as the seat of the Czechoslovak parliament, and during WWII as the administrative offices of the occupying Nazis (see the boxed text, above).

CONVENT OF ST AGNES Map pp268-9
Klášter sv Anežky; ☎ 224 810 628; www.ngprague .cz; U milosrdných 17; adult/child 100/50Kč; ⏰ 10am-6pm Tue-Sun; tram 5, 8, 14

In the northeastern corner of Staré Město is the former Convent of St Agnes, Prague's oldest surviving Gothic building, now restored and used by the National Gallery. The1st-floor rooms hold the National Gallery's permanent collection of medieval art (1200–1550) from Bohemia and Central Europe.

In 1234 the Franciscan Order of the Poor Clares was founded by the Přemysl king Wenceslas I, who made his sister Anežka (Agnes) its first abbess. Agnes was beatified in the 19th century, and with timing that could hardly be accidental Pope John Paul II canonised her as St Agnes of Bohemia just weeks before the revolutionary events of November 1989.

In the 16th century the buildings were handed over to the Dominicans, and after

Joseph II dissolved the monasteries, they became a squatter's paradise. They've only been restored in the last few decades.

The complex consists mainly of the cloister, a sanctuary and a church in French Gothic style. The graves of St Agnes and of Wenceslas I's Queen Cunegund are in the Chapel of the Virgin Mary in the Sanctuary of the Holy Saviour. Alongside this is the smaller Church of St Francis, where Wenceslas I is buried. Part of its ruined nave and other rooms have been rebuilt as a chilly concert hall.

The gallery is fully wheelchair accessible, and the ground-floor cloister has a tactile presentation of 12 casts of medieval sculptures with explanatory text in Braille.

KLAUS SYNAGOGUE Map pp268-9
Klauzová synagóga; U Starého hřbitova 1; Prague Jewish Museum ticket; metro Staroměstská

The baroque Klaus Synagogue beside the exit from the Old Jewish Cemetery houses a good exhibit on Jewish ceremonies of birth and death, worship and special holy days. The nearby **Ceremonial Hall** (Obřadní Síň) was built around 1906. Inside is an exhibit on Jewish traditions, similar to that in the synagogue.

MAISEL SYNAGOGUE Map pp268-9
Maiselova synagóga; Maiselova 10; Prague Jewish Museum ticket; metro Staroměstská

The neogothic Maisel Synagogue replaced a Renaissance original built by Maisel and de-

Museum of Decorative Arts (right)

stroyed by fire. It houses another exhibit of ceremonial silver, textiles, prints and books.

MUSEUM OF DECORATIVE ARTS
Map pp268-9

Umělecko-průmyslové muzeum; ☎ 251 093 111; www.upm.cz; 17.listopadu 2; permanent collection adult/child 80/40Kč, temporary exhibitions 80/40Kč, combined 120/60Kč; ☯ 10am-6pm Tue-Sun; metro Staroměstská

This neo-Renaissance museum, opened in 1900, arose as part of a European movement to encourage a return to the aesthetic values sacrificed to the Industrial Revolution. Its four halls are a feast for the eyes, full of 16th- to 19th-century artefacts including furniture, tapestries, porcelain and a fabulous collection of glasswork.

The building itself is a work of art, the façade decorated with reliefs representing the various decorative arts and the Bohemian towns that are famous for them. The staircase leading up from the entrance hall to the main exhibition on the 2nd floor is beautifully decorated with colourful ceramics, stained-glass windows and frescoes representing graphic arts, metalworking, ceramics, glass-making and goldsmithing. It leads to the ornate **Votive Hall**, which houses the **Karlštejn Treasure**, a hoard of 14th-century silver found hidden in the walls of Karlštejn Castle (see p211) in the 19th century.

To the right is a textiles exhibit and a fascinating collection of clocks and watches, but the good stuff is to the left in the **glass and ceramics hall** – exquisite baroque glassware, a fine collection of Meissen porcelain, and a range of Czech glass, ceramics and furniture in Cubist, Art Nouveau and Art Deco styles, the best pieces by Josef Gočár and Pavel Janák. The graphic arts section has some fine Art Nouveau posters, and the gold and jewellery exhibit contains some real curiosities – amid the Bohemian garnet brooches, 14th-century chalices, diamond-studded monstrances and Art Nouveau silverware you will find a Chinese rhino-horn vase in a silver mount, a delicate nautilus shell engraved with battle scenes, and a silver watchcase in the shape of a skull.

Labels are in Czech but detailed English and French texts are available in each room. What you see is only a fraction of the collection; other bits appear now and then in single-theme exhibitions.

PRAGUE JEWISH MUSEUM

All six monuments that make up the **Prague Jewish Museum** (Židovské muzeum Praha; ☎ 222 317
191; www.jewishmuseum.cz; ☺ 9am-6pm Sun-Fri
Apr-Oct, to 4.30pm Sun-Fri Nov-Mar, closed on Jewish hols) can be visited with a single ticket costing
300/200Kč for an adult/child under 15. Admission to
the Old-New Synagogue requires a separate ticket
costing 200/140Kč. You can buy tickets for the Jewish
Museum, including a joint ticket (costing 500/340Kč)
that gives entry to the Old-New Synagogue as well,
at the Spanish Synagogue, the Pinkas Synagogue and
the Ceremonial Hall.

OLD-NEW SYNAGOGUE Map pp268-9

Staronová synagóga; ☎ 224 819 456; Červená 2;
adult/child 200/140Kč; ☺ 9.30am-5pm Sun-Thu,
9am-4pm Fri; metro Staroměstská

Completed around 1270, the Old-New
Synagogue is Europe's oldest working synagogue and one of Prague's earliest Gothic
buildings. You step down into it because it
predates the raising of Staré Město's street
level to guard against floods. Men must
cover their heads (a hat or bandanna will
do; paper yarmulkes are handed out at the
entrance). Around the central chamber are
an entry hall, a winter prayer hall and the
room from which women watch the men-
only services. The interior, with a pulpit
surrounded by a 15th-century wrought-iron
grill, looks much as it would have 500 years
ago. The 17th-century scriptures on the
walls were recovered from under a later
'restoration'. On the eastern wall is the Holy
Ark that holds the Torah scrolls. In a glass
case at the rear, little lightbulbs beside the
names of the prominent deceased are lit on
their death days.

With its steep roof and Gothic gables,
this looks like a place with secrets, and at
least one version of the golem legend ends
here. Left alone on the Sabbath, the creature runs amok; Rabbi Löw rushes out in
the middle of a service, removes its magic
talisman and carries the lifeless body into
the synagogue's attic, where some insist it
still lies.

Across the narrow street is the elegant
16th-century **High Synagogue** (Vysoká synagóga), so-called because its prayer hall
(closed to the public) is upstairs. Around
the corner is the **Jewish Town Hall** (Židovská
radnice; ☺ closed to the public), built by
Maisel in 1586 and given its rococo façade
in the 18th century. It has a clock tower
with one Hebrew face where the hands, like
the Hebrew script, run 'backwards'.

OLD JEWISH CEMETERY Map pp268-9

Starý židovský hřbitov; entrance from Široká;
Prague Jewish Museum ticket; metro Staroměstská

Founded in the early 15th century, the Old
Jewish Cemetery is Europe's oldest surviving Jewish graveyard. It has a palpable
atmosphere of mourning even after two
centuries of disuse (it was closed in 1787).
Some 12,000 crumbling stones (some
brought from other, long-gone cemeteries)
are heaped together, but beneath them
are perhaps 100,000 graves, piled in layers
because of the lack of space. Most bear
the name of the deceased and his or her
father, the date of death (and sometimes of
burial), and poetic texts. Elaborate markers
from the 17th and 18th centuries have bas-
reliefs and sculptures, some of it indicating
the deceased's occupation and lineage.
The oldest standing stone (now replaced
by a replica), dating from 1439, is that of
Avigdor Karo, a chief rabbi and court poet
to Wenceslas IV.

The most prominent graves, marked by
pairs of marble tablets with a 'roof' between them, are near the main gate. They
include those of Mordechai Maisel and
Rabbi Löw. Since the cemetery was closed,
burials have taken place at Olšany Cemetery (p111) in Žižkov. There are remnants
of another old Jewish burial ground at the
foot of the TV tower in Žižkov (see p111).

You enter the cemetery through the
Pinkas Synagogue and exit through a gate
between the Klaus Synagogue and the
Ceremonial Hall. Remember that this is one
of Prague's most popular sights, so if you're
hoping to have a moment of quiet contem-
plation you'll probably be disappointed (try
one of the Žižkov cemeteries for a more
solitary experience).

PINKAS SYNAGOGUE Map pp268-9

Pinkasova synagóga; Široká 3; Prague Jewish
Musem ticket; metro Staroměstská

The handsome Pinkas Synagogue was built
in 1535 and used for worship until 1941.
After WWII it was converted into a moving
memorial, wall after wall inscribed with
the names, birth dates, and dates of disap-
pearance of the 77,297 Czech victims of

Sights

STARÉ MĚSTO

the Nazis. It also has a collection of paintings and drawings by children held in the Terezín concentration camp (see p215) during WWII.

SPANISH SYNAGOGUE Map pp268-9
Španělská synagóga; Vězeňská 1; Prague Jewish Musem ticket; metro Staroměstská
Named after its striking Moorish interior, the Spanish Synagogue, dating from 1868, has an exhibit on Jews in the Czech Republic from emancipation to the present day.

ALONG THE ROYAL WAY
The Royal Way (Královská cesta) was the processional route followed by Czech kings on their way to St Vitus Cathedral for coronation. The route leads from the Powder Gate (Prašná brána; Map pp268–9) along Celetná, through Old Town Square and Malé náměstí, along Karlova and across Charles Bridge to Malostranské náměstí, before climbing up Nerudova to the castle.

Pedestrianised Celetná, leading from the Powder Gate to Old Town Square, is an open-air museum of pastel-painted baroque façades covering Gothic frames resting on Romanesque foundations, deliberately buried to raise Staré Město above the floods of the Vltava River. But the most interesting building – Josef Gočár's delightful House at the Black Madonna (now the Museum of Czech Cubism) – dates only from 1912.

Little Square (Malé náměstí; Map pp268–9), the southwestern extension of Old Town Square, has a Renaissance fountain and 16th-century wrought-iron grill. Here several fine baroque and neo-Renaissance exteriors adorn some of Staré Město's oldest structures. The most colourful is the VJ Rott Building (1890), decorated with wall paintings by Mikuláš Aleš, and now housing four floors of crystal, garnet and jewellery shops.

A dog-leg from the southwestern corner of the square leads to narrow, cobbled Karlova (Charles St; Map pp268–9), which continues as far as Charles Bridge – this section is often choked with tourist crowds. On the corner of Liliová is the house called At the Golden Snake (U zlatého hada), the site of Prague's first coffee house, opened in 1708 by an Armenian named Deomatus Damajan.

Karlova sidles along the massive southern wall of the Klementinum (below) before opening out at the riverside on Křižovnické náměstí. To the right (north) of the Old Town Bridge Tower is the 17th-century Church of St Francis Seraphinus (kostel sv Františka Serafinského), its dome decorated with a fresco of the Last Judgment. It belongs to the Order of Knights of the Cross, the only Bohemian order of Crusaders still in existence.

Just south of the bridge, at the site of the former Old Town mill, is Novotného lávka (Map pp268–9), a riverside terrace full of sunny, overpriced vinárny (wine bars) with great views of the bridge and castle, its far end dominated by a statue of composer Bedřich Smetana.

CZECH MUSEUM OF FINE ARTS
Map pp268-9
České muzeum výtvarních umění; ☎ 222 220 218; www.cmvu.cz; Husova 19-21; adult/child 50/20Kč; ☧ 10am-6pm Tue-Sun; metro Staroměstská
Housed in three beautifully restored Romanesque and Gothic buildings, this often-overlooked little gallery stages temporary exhibitions of 20th-century and contemporary art, though it's worth the admission fee just for a look at the architecture.

KLEMENTINUM Map pp268-9
Entrances to courtyards on Křížovnická, Karlova & Mariánské náměstí; metro Staroměstská
To boost the power of the Roman Catholic Church in Bohemia, the Habsburg emperor Ferdinand I invited the Jesuits to Prague in 1556. They selected one of the city's choicest pieces of real estate and in 1587 set to work on the Church of the Holy Saviour (kostel Nejsvětějšího Spasitele), Prague's flagship of the Counter-Reformation and the Jesuits' original church. The western façade faces Charles Bridge, its sooty stone saints glaring down at the traffic jam of trams and tourists on Kižovnické náměstí.

After gradually buying up most of the adjacent neighbourhood, the Jesuits started building their college, the Klementinum, in 1653. By the time of its completion a century later it was the largest building in the city after Prague Castle. When the Jesuits fell out with the pope in 1773, it became part of Charles University.

The Klementinum is a vast complex of beautiful baroque and rococo halls, now occupied by the Czech National Library. Most of it is closed to the public, but you can visit the baroque **Library Hall & Astronomical Tower** (☎ 221 663 111; adult/child 100/30Kč; ☿ 2-7pm Mon-Fri, 10am-7pm Sat & Sun) on a guided tour. Gates on Křižovnická, Karlova and Seminářská allow free access to the Klementinum's courtyards, which offer a less crowded alternative to Karlova if you're walking to or from Charles Bridge.

The Klementinum's **Chapel of Mirrors** (Zrcadlová kaple) is a popular concert venue (programme and tickets are available at most ticket agencies). Dating from the 1720s, the interior is an ornate confection of gilded stucco, marbled columns, fancy frescoes and ceiling mirrors – think baroque on steroids.

There are two other interesting churches. The **Church of St Clement** (kostel sv Klimenta; ☿ services 8.30am & 10am Sun), lavishly redecorated in the baroque style from 1711 to 1715 to plans by Kilian Dientzenhofer, is now a Greek Catholic chapel. Conservatively dressed visitors are welcome to attend the services. And then there's the elliptical Italian **Chapel of the Assumption of the Virgin Mary** (Vlašská kaple Nanebevzetí Panny Marie), built in 1600 for the Italian artisans who worked on the Klementinum (it's still technically the property of the Italian government).

MARIONETTE MUSEUM Map pp268-9
Muzeum loutek; ☎ 222 220 928; www.puppetart .com; Karlova 12; adult/child 100/50Kč; ☿ noon-8pm; tram 17, 18

Rooms peopled with a multitude of authentic, colourful marionettes illustrate the evolution of this wonderful Czech tradition from the late-17th to early-19th centuries. The star attractions are the Czech children's favourites, Spejbl and Hurvínek – kids and adults alike can enjoy the Czech equivalent of Punch and Judy at the Spejbl & Hurvínek Theatre (p174).

MUNICIPAL HOUSE Map pp268-9
Obecní dům; ☎ 222 002 100; www.obecni-dum.cz; náměstí Republiky 5; guided tours 150Kč; ☿ bldg 7.30am-11pm, information centre 10am-6pm; metro Náměstí Republiky

Prague's most exuberant and sensual building stands on the site of the Royal Court, seat of Bohemia's kings from 1383 to 1483

(when Vladislav II moved to Prague Castle), and demolished at the end of the 19th century. Between 1906 and 1912 the Municipal House was built in its place – a lavish joint effort by around 30 of the leading artists of the day, creating a cultural centre that was to be the architectural climax of the Czech National Revival. Restored in the 1990s after decades of neglect during the communist era, the entire building was a labour of love, every detail of the design and decoration carefully considered, every painting and sculpture loaded with symbolism.

The mosaic above the entrance, *Homage to Prague,* is set between sculptures representing the oppression and rebirth of the Czech people; other sculptures ranged along the top of the façade represent history, literature, painting, music and architecture. You pass beneath a wrought-iron and stained-glass canopy into an interior that is Art Nouveau down to the doorknobs (you can look around the lobby and the downstairs bar for free). The restaurant (see p140) and the *kavárna* (café) flanking the entrance are like walk-in museums of Art Nouveau design.

Upstairs are half a dozen over-the-top halls and assembly rooms that you can visit by guided tour. You can book tours at the building's **information centre**, which is through the main entrance, and around to the left of the stairs.

First stop on the tour is the **Smetana Hall**, Prague's biggest concert hall, with seating for 1200 ranged beneath an Art Nouveau glass dome. The stage is framed by sculptures representing the Vyšehrad legend (to the right) and Slavonic dances (to the left).

Following are several impressive official apartments, but the highlight of the tour is the octagonal **Lord Mayor's Hall** (Primatorský sál), whose windows overlook the main entrance. Every aspect of its decoration was designed by Alfons Mucha, who also painted the superbly moody murals that adorn the walls and ceiling. Above you is an allegory of *Slavic Concord,* with intertwined figures representing the various Slavic peoples watched over by the Czech eagle. Figures from Czech history and mythology, representing the civic virtues, occupy the spaces between the eight arches, including Jan Hus as *Spravedlnost* (justice), Jan Žižka as *Bojovnost* (militancy), and the Chodové (medieval Bohemian border guards) as beady-eyed *Ostražitost* (vigilance).

On 28 October 1918 an independent Czechoslovak Republic was declared in the Smetana Hall, and in November 1989 meetings took place between Civic Forum and the Jakeš regime. The Prague Spring (Pražské jaro) music festival always opens on 12 May, the anniversary of Smetana's death, with a procession from Vyšehrad to the Municipal House followed by a gala performance of his symphonic cycle *Má Vlast* (My Country) in the Smetana Hall.

MUSEUM OF CZECH CUBISM Map pp268-9
Muzeum Českého kubismu; ☎ 224 301 003; Ovocný trh 19; adult/child 100/50Kč; ✆ 10am-6pm Tue-Sun; metro Náměstí Republiky
Though dating from 1912, Josef Gočár's House of the Black Madonna (dům U černé Matky Boží) – Prague's first and finest example of Cubist architecture – still looks modern and dynamic. It now houses three floors of Czech Cubist paintings and sculpture, as well as furniture, ceramics and glassware in Cubist designs.

POWDER GATE Map pp268-9
Prašná brána; Na příkopě; adult/child 40/30Kč; ✆ 10am-6pm May-Oct; metro Náměstí Republiky
The 65m-tall Powder Gate was begun in 1475 on the site of one of Staré Město's original 13 gates. Built during the reign of King Vladislav II Jagiello as a ceremonial entrance to the city, it was left unfinished after the king moved from the neighbouring Royal Court to Prague Castle in 1483. The name comes from its use as a gunpowder magazine in the 18th century. Josef Mocker rebuilt, decorated and steepled it between 1875 and 1886, giving it its neo-gothic icing. There are great views from the top, and an exhibit about Prague's medieval towers.

SMETANA MUSEUM Map pp268-9
Muzeum Bedřicha Smetany; ☎ 222 220 082; adult/child 50/20Kč; ✆ 10am-noon & 12.30-5pm Wed-Mon; metro Staroměstská
This small museum is devoted to Bedřich Smetana, Bohemia's favourite composer. It isn't that interesting unless you're a Smetana fan, and only has limited labelling in English. There's a good exhibit on popular culture's feverish response to Smetana's opera *The Bartered Bride* – it seems Smetana was the Andrew Lloyd Webber of his day.

HAVELSKÉ MĚSTO

In about 1230 a market district named Havelské Město (St Gall's Town; Map pp268-9), named after the 7th-century Irish monk who helped introduce Christianity to Europe, was laid out for the pleasure of the German merchants invited to Prague by Wenceslas I.

Modern-day Rytířská and Havelská were around that time a single plaza, surrounded by arcaded merchants' houses. Specialist markets included those for coal (Uhelný trh) at the western end of the plaza and for fruit (Ovocný trh) at the eastern end. In the 15th century an island of stalls was built down the middle.

All that remains of St Gall's market today is the touristy open-air market on Havelská, and the clothes hawkers in adjacent V kotcích. Though no match for the original, it's still Prague's most central open-air market.

At the eastern end of Havelská is the **Church of St Gall** (kostel sv Havla), as old as St Gall's Town itself, where Jan Hus and his predecessors preached religious reform. The Carmelites took possession of it in 1627, and in 1723 added its present shapely baroque façade. The Czech baroque painter Karel Škréta (1610–74) is buried in the church.

At the western end of Havelská is the former Uhelný trh (coal market), and nearby is the plain 12th-century **Church of St Martin in the Wall**, a parish church enlarged and Gothicised in the 14th century. The name comes from its having had the Old Town wall built right around it. In 1414 the church was the site of the first-ever Hussite communion service *sub utraque specie* (with both bread and wine), from which the name 'Utraquist' derives.

CHARLES UNIVERSITY (KAROLINUM)
Univerzita Karlova; www.cuni.cz
Central Europe's oldest university, founded by Charles IV in 1348, was originally housed in the so-called **Rotlev House** (Železná 9; Map pp268-9). With Protestantism and Czech nationalism on the rise, the reforming preacher Jan Hus became rector in 1402 and soon persuaded Wenceslas IV to slash the voting rights of the university's German students – thousands of them left Bohemia when this was announced.

The facilities of the ever-expanding university were concentrated here in 1611,

Philosophy Hall, Strahov Library (p77)

and by the 18th century the old burgher's house had grown into a sizable complex known as the Karolinum. After the Battle of Bílá Hora it was handed over to the Jesuits, who gave it a baroque makeover. When they were booted out in 1773 the university took it back. Charles University now has faculties all over Prague, and the Karolinum is used only for some medical faculty offices, the University Club and occasional academic ceremonies.

Among pre-university Gothic survivals is the **Chapel of SS Cosmas & Damian** (kaple sv Kosmas a Damian), with its extraordinary oriel window protruding from the southern wall. Built around 1370, it was renovated in 1881 by Josef Mocker.

ESTATES THEATRE Map pp268-9
Stavovské divadlo; ☎ 224 215 001; www.narodni -divadlo.cz; Ovocný trh 1; metro Náměstí Republiky
Beside the Karolinum is Prague's oldest theatre and finest neoclassical building, the Estates Theatre, where the premiere of Mozart's *Don Giovanni* was performed on 29 October 1787, with the maestro himself conducting. Opened in 1783 as the Nostitz Theatre (after its founder, Count Anton von Nostitz-Rieneck), it was patronised by upper-class German citizens and thus came to be called the Estates Theatre – the Estates being the traditional nobility.

After WWII it was renamed the Tylovo divadlo (Tyl Theatre) in honour of the 19th-century Czech playwright Josef Kajetán Tyl. One of his claims to fame is the Czech

national anthem, *Kde domov můj?* (Where Is My Home?), which came from one of his plays. In the early 1990s the theatre's name reverted to Estates Theatre. Around the corner is the 17th-century **Kolowrat Theatre** (Ovocný trh 6), now also a National Theatre venue. See also p161 for more information on classical-music venues.

SOUTHWESTERN STARÉ MĚSTO
The meandering lanes and passageways between Karlova and Národní třída are Prague's best territory for aimless wandering. When the crowds thin out late in the day, this area can cast such a spell that it's quite a surprise to return to the 21st century outside its borders.

The charm goes a bit cold along Bartolomějská, however, and not just because it is lined with police offices. Before November 1989, the block was occupied by the StB (Státní bezpečnost, or State Security), the hated secret police. Older Czechs are still understandably twitchy about police of any shade and it's a common suspicion that a few former StB officers are still around, just wearing new uniforms.

Backing onto Bartolomějská is an old convent and the once-lovely 18th-century **Church of St Bartholomew**, for a time part of the StB complex but now returned to the Franciscans. Although the church is closed to the public, the enterprising Pension Unitas (p201) has rented space from the nuns, and guests can now spend the night in refurbished StB prison cells, including the one where former dissident (and now former president) Václav Havel once spent a night.

BETHLEHEM CHAPEL Map pp272-3

Betlémská kaple; ☎ 224 2448 595; Betlémské náměstí 3; adult/child 40/20Kč; ◷ 9am-6.30pm Tue-Sun Apr-Oct, to 5.30pm Nov-Mar; tram 6, 9, 18, 21, 22, 23

On Bethlehem Square (Betlémské náměstí) is one of Prague's most important churches, the Bethlehem Chapel, true birthplace of the Hussite cause. In 1391, Reformist Praguers won permission to build a church where services could be held in Czech instead of Latin, and proceeded to construct the biggest chapel Bohemia had ever seen, able to hold 3000 worshippers. Architecturally it was a radical departure, with a simple square hall focused on the pulpit rather than the altar. Jan Hus preached here from 1402 to 1412, marking the emergence of the Reform movement from the sanctuary of the Karolinum (where he was rector).

In the 18th century the chapel was torn down. Remnants were discovered around 1920, and from 1948 to 1954 – because Hussitism had official blessing as an ancient form of communism – the whole thing was painstakingly reconstructed in its original form, based on old drawings, descriptions, and traces of the original work. It's now a national cultural monument.

Only the southern wall of the chapel is brand new. You can still see some original parts in the eastern wall: the pulpit door, several windows and the door to the preacher's quarters. These quarters, including the rooms used by Hus and others, are also original; they are now used for exhibits. The wall paintings are modern, and are based on old Hussite tracts. The indoor well predates the chapel.

The chapel has an English text available at the door. Every year on the night of 5 July, the eve of Hus' burning at the stake in 1415, a commemorative celebration is held here, with speeches and bell ringing.

CHURCH OF ST GILES Map pp268-9

Kostel sv Jiljí; cnr Zlatá & Husova; tram 6, 9, 18, 21, 22, 23

With stocky Romanesque columns, tall Gothic windows, and an exuberant baroque interior, St Giles is a good place to ponder the architectural development of Prague's religious buildings. The church was founded in 1371. The proto-Hussite reformer Jan Milíč of Kroměříž preached here before the Bethlehem Chapel was built. The Dominicans gained possession during the Counter-Reformation, built a cloister next door and 'baroquefied' it in the 1730s. Václav Reiner, the Czech painter who created the ceiling frescoes, is buried here.

NÁPRSTEK MUSEUM Map pp272-3

Náprstkovo muzeum; ☎ 224 497 500; www.aconet .cz/npm; Betlémské náměstí 1; adult/child 80/40Kč; ◷ 9am-5.30pm Tue-Sun; tram 6, 9, 18, 21, 22, 23

The small Náprstek Museum houses an ethnographical collection of Asian, African and American cultures founded by Vojta Náprstek, a 19th-century industrialist with a passion for both anthropology and modern technology (his technology exhibits are now part of the National Technical Museum in Holešovice; p107).

ROTUNDA OF THE HOLY CROSS

Map pp272-3

Kaple sv kříže; Konviktská; ◷ services 5pm Sun & Tue, in English 5.30pm on 1st Mon of each month; tram 6, 9, 18, 21, 22, 23

This tiny Romanesque rotunda is one of Prague's oldest buildings, starting out as a parish church in about 1100. Saved from demolition and restored in the 1860s by a collective of Czech artists, it still has the remnants of some 600-year-old wall frescoes, though you may have to attend Mass to see them.

NOVÉ MĚSTO

Eating p142; Drinking p156; Shopping p187; Sleeping p201

Nové Město means 'New Town', although this crescent-shaped district to the east and south of Staré Město was only new when it was founded by Charles IV in 1348. It extends eastwards from Revoluční and Na příkopě to Wilsonova and the main railway line, and south from Národní třída to Vyšehrad.

Most of Nové Město's outer fortifications were demolished in 1875 – a section of wall still survives in the south, facing Vyšehrad – but the original street plan of the area has been essentially preserved,

TOP FIVE NOVÉ MĚSTO

- Lucerna Palace (p99)
- Mucha Museum (right)
- National Theatre (p100)
- Prague City Museum (p98)
- Wenceslas Square (p98)

with three large market squares that once provided the district's commercial focus – Senovážné náměstí (Hay Market), Wenceslas Square (Václavské náměstí; originally called Koňský trh, or Horse Market) and Karlovo náměstí (Charles Square; originally called Dobytčí trh, or Cattle Market).

Though originally medieval, most of the surviving buildings in this area are from the 19th and early 20th centuries, and many of them are among the city's finest. Many blocks are honeycombed with pedestrian-only passages, and are lined with shops, cafés and theatres.

NORTHERN NOVÉ MĚSTO

The northern part of Nové Město stretches from the Vltava River down to Wenceslas Square. The area is mostly rather nondescript, but there are a few gems hidden away among the bland façades.

JINDŘIŠSKÁ TOWER Map pp268-9

Jindřišská věž; ☎ 224 232 429; www.jindrisskavez.cz; Jindřišská 1; adult/child 60/20Kč; 🕙 9am-7pm Mon-Fri, 10am-7pm Sat & Sun; tram 3, 9, 14, 24
This Gothic bell tower, dating from the 15th century but rebuilt in the Gothic style in the 1870s, dominates the end of Jindřišská, a busy street running northeast from Wenceslas Square. Having stood idle for decades, the tower was renovated and reopened in 2002 as a tourist attraction, complete with exhibition space, shop, café and restaurant, and a lookout gallery on the 10th floor.

JUBILEE SYNAGOGUE Map pp268-9

Jubilejní synagóga; Jeruzalémská 7; admission 30Kč; 🕙 1-5pm Sun-Fri, closed on Jewish hols; metro Hlavní nádraží
The colourful Moorish façade of the Jubilee Synagogue, also called the Velká (Great) synagóga, dates from 1906. Note the names of the donors on the stained-glass windows, and the grand organ above the entrance.

MUCHA MUSEUM Map pp272-3

Muchovo muzeum; ☎ 221 451 333; www.mucha.cz; Panská 7; adult/child 120/60Kč; 🕙 10am-6pm; metro Můstek
This fascinating (and busy) museum features the sensuous Art Nouveau posters, paintings and decorative panels of Alfons Mucha (1860–1939), as well as many sketches, photographs and other memorabilia. The exhibits include countless artworks showing Mucha's trademark Slavic maidens with flowing hair and piercing blue eyes, bearing symbolic garlands and linden boughs; photos of the artist's Paris studio, one of which shows a trouserless Gaugin playing the harmonium; a powerful canvas entitled *Old Woman In Winter;* and the original of the 1894 poster of actress Sarah Bernhardt as Giselda, which shot him to international fame. The fascinating 30-minute video documentary about Mucha's life is well worth watching, and helps to put his achievements in perspective. For more information on Mucha see the boxed text, p22.

POSTAL MUSEUM Map pp268-9

Poštovní muzeum; ☎ 222 312 006; Nové mlýny 2; adult/child 25/10Kč; 🕙 9am-5pm Tue-Sun; tram 5, 18, 14
Philatelists will love this tiny museum with its letter boxes, mail coach and drawers of old postage stamps, including a rare Penny Black. Look for the beautiful stamps created in the early 20th century by Czech artists Josef Navrátil and Alfons Mucha.

Across the street is the Petrská vodárenská věž (Petrská Waterworks Tower), built about 1660 on the site of earlier wooden ones. From here, wooden pipes once carried river water to buildings in Nové Město.

TRANSPORT - NORTHERN NOVÉ MĚSTO

Metro The city's three metro lines all intersect in Nové Město, at Muzeum and Můstek stations at the eastern and western ends (respectively) of Wenceslas Square. Florenc station on lines B and C is in northern Nové Město, while Karlovo náměstí station on Line B serves southern Nové Město.
Tram Cutting across the middle of Wenceslas Square, tram Nos 3, 9, 14 and 24 run along Vodičkova and Jindřišská. Nos 17 and 21 run along the river embankment in the west.

PRAGUE CITY MUSEUM Map pp278-9
Muzeum hlavního města Prahy; ☎ 224 816 773;
www.muzeumprahy.cz; Na poříčí 52; adult/child
80/30Kč, 1st Thu of each month 1Kč; ⏱ 9am-6pm
Tue-Sun, to 8pm 1st Thu of each month; metro Florenc

This excellent museum, built between 1896 and 1898, is devoted to the history of Prague from prehistoric times to the 20th century. Among the many intriguing exhibits are the brown silk funeral cap and slippers worn by astronomer Tycho Brahe when he was interred in the Týn Church in 1601 (they were removed from his corpse in 1901), and the Astronomical Clock's original 1866 calendar-wheel with Josef Mánes' beautiful painted panels representing the months – that's January at the top, toasting his toes by the fire, and August near the bottom, sickle in hand, harvesting the corn.

But what everybody comes to see is Antonín Langweil's astonishing 1:480 scale model of Prague as it looked between 1826 and 1834. The display is most rewarding after you get to know Prague a bit, as you can spot the changes – look at St Vitus Cathedral, for example, still only half-finished.

Most labels are in English as well as Czech, but you'll need the English text (available at the ticket desk) for Room I (prehistory to medieval).

PRAGUE MAIN TRAIN STATION

Map pp272-3
Praha hlavní nádraží; Wilsonova; ⏱ closed 12.40-3.15am; metro Hlavní nádraží

What? The train station is actually a tourist attraction? Perhaps not all of it, but it's worth heading up to the top floor for a look at the grimy, soot-blackened splendour of the original Art Nouveau building designed by Josef Fanta and built between 1901 and 1909. The domed interior is adorned with two nubile ladies framing a mosaic with the words *Praga: mater urbium* (Prague, Mother of Cities) and the date '28. října r:1918' (28 October 1918, Czechoslovakia's Independence Day).

WENCESLAS SQUARE & AROUND

Originally a medieval horse market, and more a broad, sloping boulevard than a classical square, Wenceslas Square (Václavské náměstí, also called Václavák) got its present name during the nationalist revival of the mid-19th century. Since then it has witnessed a great deal of Czech history – a giant Mass was held in the square during the revolutionary upheavals of 1848, and in 1918 the creation of the new Czechoslovak Republic was celebrated here.

Following the police attack on a student demonstration on 17 November 1989 (see the boxed text, p44), angry citizens gathered here in their thousands night after night. A week later, in a stunning mirror-image of Klement Gottwald's 1948 proclamation of communist rule in Old Town Square, Alexander Dubček and Václav Havel stepped onto the balcony of the Melantrich Building to a thunderous and tearful ovation, and proclaimed the end of communism in Czechoslovakia.

At the southern end of the square is Josef Myslbek's muscular equestrian **statue of St Wenceslas** (sv Václav; Map pp272–3), the 10th-century pacifist duke of Bohemia and the 'Good King Wenceslas' of Christmas carol fame – he was never a king, but was definitely good. Flanked by other patron saints of Bohemia – Prokop, Adalbert, Agnes, and Ludmila – he has been plastered with posters and bunting at every one of the square's historical moments. Near the statue, a small **memorial to the victims of communism** bears photographs and handwritten epitaphs to Jan Palach and other anticommunist rebels.

Church of Our Lady of the Snows (opposite)

Sights

NOVÉ MĚSTO

TOUR OF WENCESLAS SQUARE

Despite the parade of garish ads and globalised brand names, Wenceslas Square still manages to retain some architectural dignity, having preserved some of the city's finest early-20th-century buildings. Here are the edited highlights, starting at the northern (uphill) end and working down, with even numbers on the western side:

- No 25 Grand Hotel Evropa (1906) is perhaps the most beautiful building on the square, Art Nouveau inside and out; have a peep at the French restaurant at the rear of the ground floor, and at the 2nd-floor atrium.
- No 36 Melantrich Building (1914), now home to Marks & Spencer; the balcony is where Havel and Dubček appeared to announce the end of communist rule in November 1989.
- No 34 Wiehl House (1896) is a gorgeous façade decorated with neo-Renaissance murals by top Czech artist Mikuláš Aleš and others; it's named after its designer, Antonín Wiehl.
- No 6 Baťa shoe store (1929) is a functionalist masterpiece, designed by Ludvík Kysela for Tomáš Baťa, art patron, progressive industrialist and founder of the worldwide shoe empire.
- No 4 Lindt Building (1927) was also designed by Ludvík Kysela, and is one of the republic's earliest Functionalist buildings.
- No 1 Koruna Palace (1914), an Art Nouveau design by Antonín Pfeiffer, has a tower topped with a crown of pearls; note its charming tiny façade around the corner on Na příkopě.

In contrast to the solemnity of this shrine, the square beyond it has become a monument to capitalism, a gaudy gallery of cafés, fast-food outlets, expensive shops, greedy cabbies and pricey hotels.

CHURCH OF OUR LADY OF THE SNOWS Map pp272-3
Kostel Panny Marie Sněžné; Jungmannovo náměstí 18; metro Můstek

The most sublime attraction in the neighbourhood is this Gothic church at the northern end of Wenceslas Square. It was begun in the 14th century by Charles IV but only the chancel was ever completed, which accounts for its proportions – seemingly taller than it is long. Charles had intended it to be the grandest church in Prague; the nave is higher than that of St Vitus Cathedral, and the altar is the city's tallest. It was a Hussite stronghold, ringing to the sermons of Jan Želivský, who led the 1419 defenestration that touched off the Hussite Wars.

The church is approached through an arch in the Austrian Cultural Institute on Jungmannovo náměstí. Beside the church is the Chapel of the Pasov Virgin, now a venue for temporary art exhibitions.

LUCERNA PALACE Map pp272-3
Palác Lucerna; Vodičkova 36; tram 3, 9, 14, 24

The most elegant of Nové Město's many shopping arcades runs beneath the Art Nouveau Lucerna Palace (1920) between Štěpánská and Vodičkova streets. The complex was designed by Václav Havel (grandfather of the ex-president), and is still partially owned by the family. It includes theatres, a cinema, shops, a rock club and several cafés and restaurants. In the marbled atrium hangs artist David Černý's sculpture *Horse,* a wryly amusing counterpart to the equestrian statue of St Wenceslas in Wenceslas Square. Here St Wenceslas sits astride a horse that is decidedly dead; Černý never comments on the meaning or symbolism of his works, but it's safe to assume that this Wenceslas (Václav in Czech) is a reference to Václav Klaus, former prime minister and now president of the Czech Republic.

The neighbouring **Novák Arcade**, connected to the Lucerna and riddled by a maze of passages, has one of Prague's finest Art Nouveau façades (overlooking Vodičkova), complete with mosaics of country life.

MUSEUM OF COMMUNISM Map pp268-9
Muzeum komunismu; ☎ 224 212 966; www.muzeum komunismu.cz; Na příkopě 10; adult/child 180/140Kč; ⏰ 9am-9pm; metro Můstek

It would be difficult to think of a more ironic site for a museum of communism – it occupies part of an 18th-century aristocrat's palace, stuck between a casino on one side and a McDonald's burger restaurant on the other. Put together by an American expat and his Czech partner, the museum tells the story of Czechoslovakia's years behind the Iron Curtain in photos, words and a fascinating and varied collection of…well, stuff. The empty shops, corruption, fear and double-speak of life in socialist Czechoslovakia are well conveyed, and there are rare photos of the Stalin monument that once stood on Letná terrace – and its spectacular destruction. Make sure to watch the video about protests leading up to the Velvet Revolution: you'll never think of it as a pushover again.

NA PŘÍKOPĚ

Na příkopě – meaning 'on the moat' – along with Revoluční (Revolution St), 28.října (28 October 1918; named for Czechoslovak Independence Day) and Národní třída (National Ave), follows the line of the moat that once ran along the foot of Staré Město's city walls (the moat was filled in at the end of the 18th century).

Na příkopě meets Wenceslas Square at **Na můstku** (On the Little Bridge; Map pp272–3). A small stone bridge once crossed the moat here – you can still see a remaining arch in the underground entrance to Můstek metro station, on the left just past the ticket machines.

In the 19th century this fashionable street was the haunt of Prague's German café society. Today it is (along with Wenceslas Square and Pařížská) the city's main upmarket shopping precinct, lined with banks, shopping malls and tourist cafés.

NATIONAL MUSEUM Map pp272-3

Národní muzeum; ☎ 224 497 111; www.nm.cz; adult/child 100/50Kč, admission free 1st Mon of each month; ☺ 10am-6pm May-Sep, 9am-5pm Oct-Apr, closed 1st Tue of month; metro Muzeum Looming above Wenceslas Square is the neo-Renaissance bulk of the National Museum, designed in the 1880s by Josef Schulz as an architectural symbol of the Czech National Revival.

The main displays of rocks, fossils and stuffed animals have a rather old-fashioned feel – serried ranks of glass display cabinets arranged on creaking parquet floors – but even if trilobites and taxidermy are not your thing it's still worth a visit just to enjoy the marbled splendour of the interior and the views down Wenceslas Square. The opulent main staircase is an extravaganza of polished limestone and serpentine, lined with paintings of Bohemian castles and medallions of kings and emperors. The domed pantheon, with four huge lunette

paintings of (strangely womanless) Czech legend and history by František Ženíšek and Václav Brožík, houses bronze busts and statues of the great and the good of Czech art and science.

The light-coloured areas on the façade of the museum are patched-up bullet holes. In 1968 Warsaw Pact troops apparently mistook the museum for the former National Assembly or the radio station, and raked it with gunfire. It's also here where you'll find a cross-shaped monument set into the pavement, to the left of the fountain in front of the museum, that marks the spot where Jan Palach fell (see the boxed text, p44).

NÁRODNÍ TŘÍDA

Národní třída (National Ave) is central Prague's 'high street', a stately row of mid-range shops and grand public buildings, notably the Národní divadlo at the Vltava River end.

Fronting Jungmannovo náměstí, at the eastern end, is an imitation Venetian palace known as the **Adria Palace**. Its distinctive, chunky architectural style, dating from the 1920s, is known as 'rondocubism'. Note how the alternating angular and rounded window pediments echo similar features in neoclassical baroque buildings such as the Černin Palace (p75).

Beneath it is the **Adria Theatre**, birthplace of Laterna Magika and meeting place of Civic Forum in the heady days of the Velvet Revolution. From here, Dubček and Havel walked to the Lucerna Palace and their 24 November 1989 appearance on the balcony of the Melantrich Building. Wander through the arcade for a look at the lovely marble, glass and brass decoration; the main atrium has a 1920s 24-hour clock flanked by sculptures depicting the signs of the zodiac, once the entrance to the offices of the Adriatica insurance company (hence the building's name).

Along the street, inside the arcade near No 16, is a **bronze plaque** on the wall with a cluster of hands making the peace sign and the date '17.11.89', in memory of students clubbed in the street by police on that date.

West of Voršilská, the lemon-yellow walls of the **Convent of St Ursula** (klášter sv Voršila) frame a pink church, which has a lush baroque interior that includes a battalion of Apostle statues. Out front is the figure of St John of Nepomuk, and in the façade's lower right niche is a statue of St Agatha holding her severed breasts – one of the more gruesome images in Catholic hagiography.

Across the road at No 7 is the Art Nouveau façade (by Osvald Polívka) of the **Viola Building**, former home of the Prague Insurance Co, with the huge letters 'PRAHA' entwined around five circular windows, and mosaics spelling out *život, kapitál, důchod, věno* and *pojišťuje* (life, capital, income, dowry and insurance). The building next door, a former publishing house, is also a Polívka design.

On the southern side at No 4, looking like it has been built out of used TV screens, is the **Nová Scéna** (1983), the 'New National Theatre' building, now home of Laterna Magika (see p173).

Finally, facing the Vltava near Smetanovo nábřeží is the **National Theatre** (Národní divadlo), neo-Renaissance flagship of the Czech National Revival and one of Prague's most impressive buildings. Funded entirely by private donations and decorated inside and out by a roll call of prominent Czech artists, architect Josef Zítek's masterpiece burned down within weeks of its 1881 opening but, incredibly, was funded again and restored under Josef Schulz in less than two years. It's now mainly used for ballet and opera performances (see p161).

Across from the theatre is the **Kavárna Slavia** (see boxed text, p153), known for its Art Deco interior and river views, once *the* place to be seen or to grab an after-theatre meal. Now renovated, it's once again the place to be seen – though mainly by other tourists.

PEČEK PALACE Map pp272-3
Pečkův palác; Politických vězňů 20; ☉ closed to the public; metro Muzeum

This gloomy neo-Renaissance palace served as the wartime headquarters of the Gestapo. A memorial on the corner of the building honours the many Czechs who were tortured and executed in the basement detention cells. Today, it is home to the Ministry of Trade & Industry.

ALONG THE RIVER
The Nové Město riverfront, stretching south from the National Theatre to Vyšehrad, is lined with some of Prague's grandest 19th- and early-20th-century architecture – it's a great place for an evening stroll (see p128).

Masarykovo nábřeží (Masaryk Embankment; Map pp272–3) sports a series of stunning Art Nouveau buildings. At No 32 is the duck-egg green **Goethe Institut**, once the East German embassy, while No 26 is a beautiful apartment building with owls perched in the decorative foliage that twines around the door, dogs peeking from the balconies on the 5th floor, and birds perched atop the balustrade.

No 16 is the **House of the Hlahol Choir**, built in 1906 by Josef Fanta for a patriotic choral society associated with the Czech National Revival. It's decorated with elaborate musical motifs topped by a giant mosaic depicting *Music* – the motto beneath translates as 'Let the song reach the heart; let the heart reach the homeland'.

At the next bridge is Jirásek Square (Jiráskovo náměstí), dedicated to writer Alois Jirásek (1851–1930), author of *Old Czech Legends* (studied by all Czech schoolchildren) and an influential figure in the drive towards Czechoslovak independence. His statue is overlooked by the famous Dancing Building.

A little further along the riverbank is **Rašínovo nábřeží 78**, an apartment building designed by the grandfather of ex-president Václav Havel – this was where Havel first chose to live (in preference to Prague Castle) after being elected as president in December 1989, surely the world's least pompous presidential residence.

Two blocks south, sitting on Palackého náměstí, is Stanislav Sucharda's extraordinary Art Nouveau **František Palacký Memorial** (Map pp272–3); a swarm of haunted bronze figures (allegories of the writer's imagination) swirling around a stodgy statue of the 19th-century historian and giant of the Czech National Revival.

DANCING BUILDING Map pp272-3
Tančící dům; Rašínovo nábřeží 80; tram 17, 21

The junction where Resslova meets the river at Rašínovo nábřeží is dominated by the Dancing Building, built in 1996 by architects Vlado Milunič and Frank O Gehry. The curved lines of the narrow-waisted glass tower clutched against its more upright and formal partner led to it being christened the 'Fred & Ginger Building', after legendary dancing duo Fred Astaire and Ginger Rogers. It's surprising how well it fits in with its ageing neighbours.

Dancing Building (p101)

MÁNES GALLERY Map pp272-3
Galerie Mánes; ☎ 224 930 754; Masarykovo nábřeží 1; adult/child 40/20Kč; ⏰ 10am-6pm Tue-Sun; tram 17, 21

Beneath the tower is the Mánes Building (1927–30), which houses an art gallery founded in the 1920s by a group of artists headed by painter Josef Mánes, as an alternative to the Czech Academy of Arts. It still has one of Prague's better displays of contemporary art, with changing exhibits. The building itself, designed by Oskar Novotný, is considered a masterpiece of Functionalist architecture.

SLAV ISLAND Map pp272-3
Slovanský ostrov; Masarykovo nábřeží; tram 17, 21

This island is a sleepy, dog-eared sandbank with pleasant gardens, river views and several boat-hire places. Its banks were reinforced with stone in 1784, and a spa and a dye works were built in the early part of the following century. Bohemia's first train had a demonstration run here in 1841, roaring down the island at 11km/h. In 1925 the island was named after the Slav conventions that had taken place here since 1848. In the middle is a 19th-century meeting hall and a restaurant. At the southern end is Šitovská věž, a 15th-century water tower (once part of a mill) with an 18th-century onion-dome roof.

CHARLES SQUARE & AROUND
At over seven hectares, Charles Square (Karlovo náměstí; Map pp272–3 and pp280–1) is the city's biggest square; it's more like a small park, really. Presiding over it is the Church of St Ignatius (kostel sv Ignáce), a 1660s baroque *tour de force* designed by Carlo Lurago for the Jesuits.

The baroque palace at the southern end of the square belongs to Charles University. It's known as Faust House (Faustův dům) because, according to a popular story, Mephisto took Dr Faust to hell through a hole in the ceiling here, and because of associations with Rudolf II's English court alchemist, Edward Kelley, who toiled here in the 16th century trying to convert lead to gold.

Resslova runs west from Karlovo náměstí to the river. Halfway along is the baroque Church of SS Cyril & Methodius, a 1730s work by Kilian Dientzenhofer (for more details on Dientzenhofer see the boxed text, p31) and Paul Bayer. The crypt now houses the moving National Memorial to the Victims of Post-Heydrich Terror.

On the other side of Resslova is the 14th-century Gothic Church of St Wenceslas in Zderaz, the former parish church of Zderaz, a village that predates Nové Město. On its western side are parts of a wall and windows from its 12th-century Romanesque predecessor.

The area to the east of Karlovo náměstí is occupied by Charles University's medical faculty, and is full of hospitals and clinics. Halfway between Žitná and Ječná is the 14th-century Church of St Stephen (kostel sv Štěpána). Behind it on Na Rybníčku II is one of Prague's three surviving Romanesque rotundas, the Rotunda of St Longinus (rotunda sv Longina), built in the early 12th century.

CHARLES UNIVERSITY BOTANICAL GARDEN Map pp280-1
Botanická zahrada Univerzity Karlovy; ☎ 221 953 142; Viničná 7; admission free; ⏰ 9am-6pm; tram 18, 24

Just south of Karlovo náměstí (entrances on Viničná and Vyšehradská) is Charles University's botanical garden. Founded in 1775 and moved from Smíchov to its present site in 1898, it's the country's oldest botanical garden. The steep, hillside garden concentrates on Central European flora and is especially pretty in spring.

CHURCH OF THE ASSUMPTION OF THE VIRGIN MARY & CHARLEMAGNE
Map pp280-1

Kostel Nanebevzetí Panny Marie a Karla Velikého; Ke Karlovu; metro IP Pavlova

At the southern end of Ke Karlovu is a little church with a big name, founded by Charles IV in 1350 and modelled on Charlemagne's burial chapel in Aachen. In the 16th century it acquired its fabulous ribbed vault, the revolutionary unsupported span of which was attributed by some to witchcraft.

From the terrace beyond the church you can see some of Nové Město's original fortifications, and look out towards ancient Vyšehrad and the modern **Nusle Bridge** (Nuselský most), which vaults across the valley of the Botič creek, with six lanes of traffic on top and the metro inside.

DVOŘÁK MUSEUM Map pp272-3
Muzeum Antonína Dvořáka; ☎ 224 918 013; Ke Karlovu 20; adult/child 50/25Kč; ☒ 10am-1.30pm & 2-5pm Tue-Sun Apr-Sep, from 9.30am Oct-Mar; metro IP Pavlova

The most striking building in the drab neighbourhood south of Ječná is the Vila Amerika, a 1720s, French-style summer house designed by (you guessed it) Kilian Dientzenhofer. It's one of the city's finest baroque buildings, and now houses a museum dedicated to the composer Antonín Dvořák. Special concerts of Dvořák's music are staged here.

EMMAUS MONASTERY Map pp280-1
Klášter Emauzy; Vyšehradská 49; ☒ 8am-6pm Mon-Fri, services noon Mon-Fri, 10am Sun; tram 18, 24

Founded for a Slavonic Benedictine order at the request of Charles IV, and originally called Na Slovanech, the Emmaus Monastery dates from 1372. During WWII the monastery was seized by the Gestapo and the monks were sent to Dachau concentration camp, then in February 1945 it was almost destroyed by a stray Allied firebomb. Some monks returned after the war, but the reprieve was short-lived: in 1950 the communists closed down the monastery, and tortured the prior to death. It was finally restored to the Benedictine order in 1990 and reconstruction has been going on ever since.

The monastery's Gothic **Church of Our Lady** (kostel Panny Marie), badly damaged by the 1945 bombing, reopened in 2003, though the swooping, twin spires were added back in the 1960s. The atmospheric Gothic cloisters have some fine, but faded, original frescoes dating from the 14th century, salted with bits of pagan symbolism.

Across Vyšehradská is the baroque **Church of St John of Nepomuk on the Rock** (kostel sv Jana Nepomuckého na Skalce), built in 1739, one of the city's most beautiful Dientzenhofer churches.

NATIONAL MEMORIAL TO THE VICTIMS OF POST-HEYDRICH TERROR Map pp272-3
Národní památník obětí heydrichiády; ☎ 224 920 686; Resslova 9; adult/child 50/20Kč; ☒ 10am-5pm Tue-Sun May-Sep, to 4pm Oct-Apr; metro Karlovo Náměstí

In 1942 seven Czech paratroopers that were involved in the assassination of Reichsprotektor Reinhardt Heydrich (see boxed text, p43) hid in the crypt of the Church of SS Cyril & Methodius for three weeks after the killing, until their hiding place was betrayed by the Czech traitor Karel Čurda. The Germans besieged the church, first attempting to smoke the paratroopers out and then flooding the church with fire hoses. Three paratroopers were killed in the ensuing fight; the other four took their own lives rather than surrender to the Germans. The crypt now houses a moving memorial to the men, with an exhibit and video about Nazi persecution of the Czechs. In the crypt itself you can still see the bullet marks and shrapnel scars on the walls, and signs of the paratroopers' last desperate efforts to dig an escape tunnel to the sewer under the street. On the Resslova side of the church the narrow gap in the wall of the crypt is still pitted with bullet marks.

NEW TOWN HALL Map pp272-3
Novoměstská radnice; ☎ 224 947 131; Karlovo náměstí 23; admission 30Kč; ☒ 10am-6pm Tue-Sun May-Sep; metro Karlovo Náměstí

The historical focus of Charles Square is the New Town Hall, built when the New Town was still new. From the window of the tower, two of Wenceslas IV's Catholic councillors were flung to their deaths in 1419 by followers of the Hussite preacher Jan

Želivský, giving 'defenestration' (throwing out of a window) a lasting political meaning, and sparking off the Hussite Wars. (This tactic was repeated at Prague Castle in 1618.) The 23m-tall tower was added to the building 35 years later. You can climb the 221 steps to the top, and visit the Gothic Hall of Justice, which was the site of the defenestration.

U KALICHA Map pp272-3
☎ 224 912 557; www.ukalicha.cz; Na bojišti 12;
⊙ 11am-11pm; metro IP Pavlova
A few blocks east of Karlovo náměstí is the pub U kalicha. This is where the eponymous antihero was arrested at the beginning of Jaroslav Hašek's comic novel of WWI, *The Good Soldier Švejk* (which Hašek cranked out in instalments from his own local pub). The pub is milking the connection for all it's worth. It's an essential port of call for Švejk fans, but the rest of us can find cheaper beer and dumplings elsewhere.

BEYOND THE CENTRE
Eating p144; Shopping p191; Sleeping p204
Clustered around the city's historic core are the ancient citadel of Vyšehrad and the suburbs of Holešovice, Bubeneč, Libeň, Žižkov, Karlín, Vinohrady, Smíchov and Dejvice. Also gathered together in this section are the various attractions that lie scattered around the outer fringes of the city; they are listed clockwise from Troja in the north, followed by Kobylisy, Kbely, Zbraslav, Barrandov, Střešovice and Břevnov.

VYŠEHRAD
Vyšehrad (High Castle) is regarded as Prague's mythical birthplace. According to legend the wise chieftain Krok built a castle

TRANSPORT - VYŠEHRAD
Metro Vyšehrad metro station on line C is five minutes' walk east of the citadel, past the Congress Centre (Kongresové centrum).
Tram Nos 17 and 21 run along the riverbank below the citadel; Nos 7, 18 and 24 run along the Nusle Valley to its east. From the tram stop on either line, it's a steep climb up to the citadel.

here in the 7th century. Libuše, the cleverest of his three daughters, prophesised that a great city would rise here. Taking as her king a ploughman named Přemysl, she founded the city of Prague and the Přemysl dynasty.

Archaeologists know that various early Slavonic tribes set up camp at Vyšehrad, a crag above the Vltava River south of the Nusle Valley. Vyšehrad may in fact have been permanently settled as early as the 9th century, and Boleslav II (r 972–99) may have lived here for a time. There was a fortified town by the mid-11th century. Vratislav II (r 1061–92) moved his court here from Hradčany, beefing up the walls and adding a castle, the Basilica of St Lawrence, Church of SS Peter & Paul and the Rotunda of St Martin. His successors stayed until 1140, when Vladislav II returned to Hradčany.

Vyšehrad then faded until Charles IV, aware of its symbolic importance, repaired the walls and joined them to those of his new town, Nové Město. He built a small palace, and decreed that the coronations of Bohemian kings should begin with a procession from here to Hradčany.

Nearly everything on the hilltop was wiped out during the Hussite Wars. The hill remained a ruin – except for a township of artisans and traders – until after the Thirty Years' War, when Leopold I refortified it.

The Czech National Revival generated new interest in Vyšehrad as a symbol of Czech history. Painters painted it, poets sang about the old days, Smetana set his opera *Libuše* here. Many fortifications were dismantled in 1866 and the parish graveyard was converted into a national memorial cemetery.

Vyšehrad retains a place in Czech hearts and is a popular destination for weekend family outings. Since the 1920s the old fortress has been a quiet park, with splendid panoramas of the Vltava Valley. Take along a picnic and find a quiet spot among the trees, or on the battlements with a view over the river.

CASEMATES Map pp280-1
Kasematy; Vratislavova; adult/child 30/20Kč;
⊙ 9.30am-6pm Apr-Oct, to 5pm Nov-Mar; metro Vyšehrad
At the 19th-century **Brick Gate** (Cihelná brána) on the northern side of the fortress is the

THE MISSING MONUMENTS

Prague witnessed several profound changes of political regime during the 20th century: from Habsburg Empire to independent Czechoslovak Republic in 1918; to Nazi Protectorate from 1938 to 1945; to communist state in 1948; and back to democratic republic in 1989.

Each change was accompanied by widespread renaming of city streets and squares to reflect the heroes of the new regime. The square in front of the Rudolfinum in Staré Město, for example, was known variously as Smetanovo náměstí (Smetana Square; 1918–39); Mozartplatz (Mozart Square; 1939–45); náměstí Krasnoarmějců (Red Army Square; 1948–89); and náměstí Jana Palacha (Jan Palach Square; 1989–present).

This renaming was often followed by the removal of monuments erected by the previous regime. Here are four of Prague's most prominent 'missing monuments'.

The Missing Virgin

If you look at the ground in Old Town Square (Staroměstské náměstí; Map pp268–9) about 50m south of the Jan Hus monument, you'll see a circular stone slab set among the cobblestones. This was the site of a Marian Column (a pillar bearing a statue of the Virgin Mary), erected in 1650 in celebration of the Habsburg victory over the Swedes in 1648. It was surrounded by figures of angels crushing and beating down demons – a rather unsubtle symbol of a resurgent Catholic Church defeating the Protestant Reformation.

The column was toppled by a mob – who saw it as a symbol of Habsburg repression – on 3 November 1918, five days after the declaration of Czechoslovak independence. Its remains can be seen in the Lapidárium at Výstaviště (p108).

The Missing General

A prominent victim of the change of regime in 1918 was the statue of Field Marshal Václav Radecký (1766–1858) – or Count Josef Radetzky, to give him his Austrian name – that once stood in the lower part of Malostranské náměstí (Map pp264–5); it is now in the Lapidárium. Although Radecký was a Czech, his fame derived from leading the Habsburg armies to victory against Napoleon and crushing the Italians at the battles of Custoza and Novara. (Composer Johann Strauss the Elder wrote the *Radetzky March* in his honour.) The restaurant Square (p136) was once called the Radetzky Café.

The Missing Dictator

If you stand on Old Town Square (Map pp268–9) and look north along the arrow-straight avenue of Pařížská you will see, on a huge terrace at the far side of Čechův most (Bohemia Bridge), a giant metronome. If the monumental setting seems out of scale that's because the terrace was designed to accommodate the world's biggest statue of Stalin. Unveiled in 1955 – two years after Stalin's death – the 30m-high, 14,000-tonne colossus showed Uncle Joe at the head of two lines of communist heroes, Czech on one side, Soviet on the other. Cynical Praguers used to constant food shortages quickly nicknamed it *fronta na maso* (the meat queue).

The monument was dynamited in 1962, in deference to Krushcev's attempt to airbrush Stalin out of history. The demolition crew was instructed: 'It must go quickly, there mustn't be much of a bang, and it should be seen by as few people as possible'. The Museum of Communism (p99) has a superb photo of the monument – and of its destruction.

The Missing Tank

Náměstí Kinských (Map pp270–1), at the southern edge of Malá Strana, was until 1989 known as náměstí Sovětských tankistů (Soviet Tank Crews Square), named in memory of the Soviet soldiers who 'liberated' Prague on 9 May 1945. For many years a Soviet T-34 tank – allegedly the first to enter the city – squatted menacingly atop a pedestal here (in fact it was a later Soviet 'gift').

In 1991 artist David Černý decided that the tank was an inappropriate monument to the Soviet soldiers and painted it bright pink. The authorities had it painted green again, and charged Černý with a crime against the state. This infuriated many parliamentarians, 12 of whom repainted the tank pink. Their parliamentary immunity saved them from arrest and secured Černý's release. For more on Černý see the boxed text, p24.

After complaints from the Soviet Union the tank was removed. Its former setting is now occupied by a circular fountain surrounded by park benches; the vast granite slab in the centre is split by a jagged fracture, perhaps symbolic of a break with the past. The tank still exists, and is still pink – it's at the Military Museum in Lešany, near Týnec nad Sázavou, 30km south of Prague.

entrance to the vaulted casemates (armoured compartments) beneath the ramparts. The chambers now house a museum exhibit explaining the history of Prague's fortifications.

Also buried deep in the ramparts, and entered via the Cihelná brána, is the barrel-vaulted Gorlice Hall (admission 10Kč), which served as an air-raid shelter and potato store during WWII. It now houses six of the original baroque statues from Charles Bridge, including *St Ludmila with the Young St Wenceslas* by Matthias Braun (the other originals are in the Lapidárium; see p108), as well as temporary art exhibitions in summer.

CHURCH OF SS PETER & PAUL
Map pp280-1

Kostel sv Petra a Pavla; ☎ 249 113 353; K rotundé 10; admission 20Kč; ☽ 9am-noon & 1-5pm Wed-Mon; metro Vyšehrad

Vratislav II's Church of SS Peter & Paul has been built and rebuilt over the centuries, culminating in a neogothic workover by Josef Mocker in the 1880s. The twin steeples, a distinctive feature of the Vyšehrad skyline, were added in 1903. The interior is a swirling acid trip of colourful Art Nouveau frescoes, painted in the 1920s by various Czech artists.

GOTHIC CELLAR Map pp280-1

Gotický sklep; Vyšehradský sady; adult/child 30/20Kč; ☽ 9.30am-6pm Apr-Oct, to 5pm Nov-Mar; metro Vyšehrad

The restored Gothic cellars that once lay beneath Charles IV's palace (now gone) house a new exhibition dedicated to the history of Vyšehrad. It is packed with archaeological finds and religious relics associated with life on the fortress from 3800 BC until the present day.

ROTUNDA OF ST MARTIN Map pp280-1

Rotunda sv Martina; V Pevnosti; ☽ closed to the public; metro Vyšehrad

Vratislav II's little chapel, the 11th-century Rotunda of St Martin, is Prague's oldest surviving building. In the 18th century it was used as a powder magazine. The door and frescoes date from a renovation made about 1880.

Nearby are a 1714 plague column and the baroque St Mary Chapel in the Ramparts (kaple Panny Marie v hradbách), dating

from about 1750, and behind them the remains of the 14th-century Church of the Beheading of St John the Baptist (kostelík Stětí sv Jana Křtitele).

VYŠEHRAD CITADEL Map pp280-1

☎ 241 410 348; www.praha-Vyšehrad.cz; V Pevnosti 5; admission free; ☽ grounds 24hr, information office 9.30am-6.30pm; metro Vyšehrad

The main entrance to the citadel is through the Tábor Gate (Táborská brána) at the southeastern end. On the other side of the brick ramparts and ditch are the scant remnants of the Gothic Peak Gate (Špička brána), a fragment of arch that is now part of the information office – all that remains of Charles IV's 14th-century fortifications. Beyond that lies the grand, 17th-century Leopold Gate (Leopoldova brána), the most elegant of the fortress gates.

It's possible to walk around most of the battlements, with grand views over the river and city. Beside the southwestern bastion are the foundations of a small royal palace built by Charles IV, but dismantled in 1655. Perched on the bastion itself is the Vyšehrad Gallery (galérie Vyšehrad; admission 10Kč; ☽ 9.30am-5.30pm Tue-Sun), which holds temporary exhibitions. Below the bastion are some ruined guard towers poetically named Libuše's Bath. You can also examine the foundations of the 11th-century Romanesque Basilica of St Lawrence (bazilika sv Vavřince; admission 10Kč; ☽ 11am-6pm). Ask for the key at the snack bar next door.

South of the Church of SS Peter & Paul lie the Vyšehrad Gardens (Vyšehradské sady), with four imposing statues by Josef Myslbek based on Czech legends. Prague's founders Libuše and Přemysl are in the northwestern corner; in the southeast are Šárka and Ctirad. On Sundays in May, June and August, open-air concerts are held here at 2.30pm, with anything from jazz to oompah to chamber music.

In the northwestern corner is the former New Provost's House (Nové probošství), built in 1874. In the adjacent park, Štulkovy sady, there is an open-air Summer Theatre (Letní scéna) where you can catch a concert or cultural show from 6pm on most Thursdays or the odd children's performance on Tuesday afternoon (usually around 2pm).

The information centre sells a map and guide to Vyšehrad's buildings in English, German, French and Italian.

VYŠEHRAD CEMETERY Map pp280-1

Vyšehradský hřbitov; ☎ 249 198 815; K rotundé 10; admission free; ⏱ 8am-4pm; metro Vyšehrad

For Czechs, the Vyšehrad Cemetery is the hill's main attraction. In the late 19th century the parish graveyard was made into a memorial cemetery for famous figures of Czech culture, with a graceful, neo-Renaissance arcade running along the northern and western sides. For the real heroes, an elaborate pantheon called the **Slavín** (loosely, Hall of Fame), designed by Antonín Wiehl, was added at the eastern end in 1894; its 50-odd occupants include painter Alfons Mucha, sculptor Josef Mýslbek and architect Josef Gočár. The motto reads 'AČ ZEMEŘELI JEŠTĚ MLUVÍ' (Though dead, they still speak).

The 600 or so graves in the rest of the cemetery include those of composers Smetana and Dvořák, and writers Karel Čapek, Jan Neruda and Božena Němcová; there's a directory of famous names at the entrance. One word that you will see all over the place is *rodina* – it means 'family'.

Many of the tombs and headstones are themselves works of art – Dvořák's is a sculpture by Vladislav Šaloun, the Art Nouveau sculptor who created the Jan Hus monument in Old Town Square. To find it from the gate beside the church, head straight across to the colonnade on the far side, and turn left; it's the fifth tomb on your right. To find Smetana's grave, go to the Slavín and stand facing the monument; it's the pale-grey obelisk to your right.

The Prague Spring music festival (see the boxed text, p161) kicks off every 12 May, the anniversary of Smetana's death, with a procession from his grave at Vyšehrad to the Municipal House (p93).

HOLEŠOVICE & BUBENEČ

The part of Prague that nestles inside the big bend of the Vltava River grew from two old settlements: the fishing village of Bubny, and the farming hamlet of Holešovice. Both remained small until the mid-19th century, when road and railway bridges linked them to the city centre, and industry began to develop. Close behind came a horse-drawn tram line, a river port and the exhibition grounds. The area was incorporated into Prague in 1884.

The vast exhibition grounds of **Výstaviště** (Map pp276–7) in the northern part of the

TRANSPORT - HOLEŠOVICE & BUBENEČ

Metro The Vltavská and Nádraží Holešovice metro stations on line C serve the southern and northern parts of Holešovice respectively.

Tram Nos 5, 12, 14, 15 and 17 run along Dukelských hrdinů, the main north–south street in Holešovice, while Nos 1, 8, 15, 25 and 26 run east–west on Milady Hořákové, serving both Holešovice and Bubeneč.

district grew up around the buildings erected for the 1891 Jubilee Exhibition. These include the **Prague Pavilion**(Map pp276–7) and the grand, Art Nouveau **Palace of Industry**.

Výstaviště was once the venue for the big spring and autumn trade fairs, but these are now held at the new **Prague Exhibition Centre** (Prazvský Veletržní areál; ☎ 225 291 611; www.pva.cz; Beranovych 667, Letňany; bus 758 from metro Českomoravská) at Letňany in the northeastern suburbs. Výstaviště still hosts smaller shows and exhibitions, and is home to a **Christmas Market** and the annual **St Matthew's Fair** (Matějská pouť), held in March, a traditional funfair full of roller-coasters, candyfloss, and half of Prague having fun.

ECOTECHNICAL MUSEUM Map p275

Ekotechnické muzeum; ☎ 233 325 500; www .ekotechnickemuzeum.cz; Papírenská 6, Bubeneč; adult/family 50/100Kč; ⏱ 10am-4.30pm Sat & Sun May-Oct; bus 131 from metro Hradčanská

Prague's former waste-water treatment plant was built between 1895 and 1906 following a design by English architect WH Lindley. Surprisingly as the plant was designed to service a city of 500,000 people, it remained in service until 1967, by which time Prague had a population of over a million. Several steam-powered engines are on display and more are being repaired; there are guided tours of the labyrinth of sewers beneath the building. Once a year, on a weekend in September, all the steam-driven machinery is demonstrated in full working order.

KŘIŽÍK FOUNTAIN Map pp276-7

Křižíkova fontána; ☎ 220 103 280; www.krizikova fontana.cz; U Výstaviště 1, Holešovice; shows around 200Kč; ⏱ performances hourly 8-11pm Mar-Oct; tram 5, 12, 14, 15, 17

Each evening from spring to autumn the musical Křižík Fountain performs its computer-controlled light-and-water dance. Performances range from classical music such as Dvořák's *New World* symphony to modern works by Jean Michel Jarre and Vangelis, rock music by Queen, and theme music from popular films. Call or check the website for details of what's on. The light show is best after sunset – from May to July go for the later shows.

LAPIDÁRIUM Map pp276-7
☎ 233 375 636; U Výstaviště 1, Holešovice; adult/child 20/10Kč; ⏱ noon-6pm Tue-Fri, 10am-6pm Sat & Sun; tram 5, 12, 14, 15, 17
An outlying branch of the National Museum, and an often-overlooked gem, the Lapidárium is a repository for some 400 sculptures from the 11th to the 19th centuries. The exhibits include the Lions of Kouřim (Bohemia's oldest surviving stone sculpture), parts of the Renaissance Krocín Fountain that once stood in Old Town Square, 10 of Charles Bridge's original statues, and many other superb sculptures. See also the boxed text, p105.

LETNÁ Map pp276-7
Letná is a vast open space between Milady Horáková and the river, with a parade ground to the north and a peaceful park, the Letná Gardens (Letenské sady), in the south, with picture-postcard views over the city and its bridges. In the summer you'll find an open-air beer garden (see boxed text, p157). In 1261 Přemysl Otakar II held his coronation celebrations here, and during communist times Letná was the site of Moscow-style May Day military parades. In 1989 around 750,000 people gathered here in support of the Velvet Revolution, and in 1990 Pope John Paul II gave an open-air Mass here to more than a million people.

In the southwestern corner is the charming neobaroque Hanavský Pavilón, built by Otto Prieser for the 1891 Jubilee Exposition (see p145).

LETNÁ TERÁSA Map pp268-9
The monumental, stepped terrace overlooking the river on the southern edge of Letná Gardens dates from the early 1950s, when a huge statue of Stalin, the world's biggest, was erected here by the Communist Party of Czechoslovakia, only to be blown up in 1962 by the same sycophants when Stalin was no longer flavour of the decade (see

the boxed text, p105). A giant metronome designed by artist David Černý – a symbolic reminder of the passing of time – has stood in its place since 1991.

MAROLDOVO PANORAMA Map pp276-7
☎ 220 103 210; U Výstaviště 1, Holešovice; adult/child 20/10Kč; ⏱ 2-5pm Tue-Fri, 10am-5pm Sat & Sun; tram 5, 12, 14, 15, 17
The Maroldovo Panorama is an impressive 360-degree diorama (11m high and 95m long) of the 1434 battle of Lipany, in which the Hussite Taborites lost to the Hussite Utraquists and Emperor Zikmund's forces. It was painted by Luděk Marold in 1898.

NATIONAL TECHNOLOGY MUSEUM
Map pp276-7
Národní technické muzeum; ☎ 220 399 111; www.ntm.cz; Kostelní 42, Holešovice; adult/child 70/30Kč; ⏱ 9am-5pm Tue-Fri, 10am-6pm Sat & Sun; tram 1, 8, 15, 25
This fun museum has a huge main hall full of vintage trains, planes and automobiles, including 1920s and '30s Škoda and Tatra cars and a couple of Bugattis. The motorcycle exhibit has a 1926 BSA 350-L in perfect nick, and among the vintage bicycles you'll find a 1921 predecessor of the 1970s Raleigh Chopper. Upstairs you can fool around with the cameras in a working TV studio, or head to the basement for a tour down a simulated mineshaft.

PRAGUE PLANETARIUM Map pp276-7
Planetárium Praha; ☎ 233 376 452; www.planetarium.cz; Královská obora 233, Holešovice; exhibition adult/child 10/5Kč, shows 40-120Kč; ⏱ 8.30am-noon & 1-8pm Mon-Thu, 9.30am-noon & 1-8pm Sat & Sun; tram 5, 12, 14, 15, 17
The Planetarium, in Stromovka park just west of Výstaviště, presents various slide and video presentations in addition to the star shows. Most shows are in Czech only, but one or two of the more popular ones provide a text summary in English. There's also an astronomical exhibition in the main hall.

STROMOVKA Map pp276-7
tram 5, 12, 14, 15, 17
Stromovka, west of Výstaviště, is Prague's largest park. In the Middle Ages it was a royal hunting preserve, which is why it's

sometimes called the Královská obora (Royal Deer Park). Rudolf II had rare trees planted here and several lakes created (fed from the Vltava River via a still-functioning canal). It's now the preserve of strollers, joggers, cyclists and in-line skaters (see p125).

VELETRŽNÍ PALACE Map pp276-7
Veletržní Palác; ☎ 224 301 111; www.ngprague.cz; Dukelských hrdinů 47, Holešovice; adult/child from 100/50Kč for any 1 floor to 250/120Kč for all 4 floors; ⏰ 10am-6pm Tue-Sun; tram 5, 12, 14, 15, 17

The huge, grimly Functionalist Veletržní palác (Trade Fair Palace), built in 1928 to house trade exhibitions, is now the home of the National Gallery's superb collection of 19th-, 20th- and 21st-century Czech and European art.

You could easily spend a whole day here – the collection is spread over four floors of the vast, ocean-liner-like building – but if you only have an hour to spare, head for the 3rd floor (Czech Art 1900–30, and 19th- and 20th-century French Art) to see the *Sunbeam Motorcyclist* sculpture by Otokar Sveč; the paintings of František Kupka, pioneer of abstract art; and the art, furniture and ceramics of the Czech Cubists. The French section includes some sculpture by Rodin, a few unexceptional Impressionist works, Gaugin's *Flight* and Van Gogh's *Green Wheat*.

Highlights of the 4th floor (19th-century Czech Art) include the Art Nouveau sculpture of Josef Myslbek, Stanislav Sucharda and Bohumil Kafka; the glowing portraits by Josef Mánes; and the forest landscapes by Július Mařák.

The 1st floor (20th-century Foreign Art) includes works by Picasso, Warhol and Lichtenstein, while the 2nd floor (Czech Art 1930 to present day) has early examples of kinetic art, some Socialist Realist stuff from the communist era and various amusing works by contemporary artists – check out the grotesque *Dog Family* by Karel Pauzer.

LIBEŇ
V HOLEŠOVIČKÁCH Map pp262-3
tram 10, 24

The spot in the suburb of Libeň where Reichsprotektor SS Obergruppenführer Reinhard Heydrich was assassinated (see the boxed text, p43) has changed considerably since 1942 – the tram tracks have gone and a modern road intersection has been built. It's near where the slip road exits north from V Holešovičkách to Zenklova, but as yet there is no marker to commemorate the event. Take tram No 10 or 24 to the Zenklova stop and walk south for a few minutes. The neighbouring streets, Gabčíkova and Kubišova, are named after the parachutists who carried out the attack.

The Army Museum in Žižkov (p110) has an exhibition detailing the assassination.

Sights

BEYOND THE CENTRE

Gardens and the Church of SS Peter & Paul (p106), Vyšehrad

ŽIŽKOV & KARLÍN

Named after the one-eyed Hussite hero, Jan Žižka, who defeated the Holy Roman Emperor Sigismund here in 1420, Žižkov has always been a rough-and-ready, working-class neighbourhood, full of revolutionary fizz well before 1948. Streets near the centre are slowly getting a face-lift but much of the district is still grimy and run-down. It's famous for its numerous bars and night-clubs, and the views from Vítkov and the futuristic TV Tower.

The famous battle of Vítkov – it was not renamed Žižkov Hill until much later – took place in July 1420 on the long, narrow ridge that separates the Žižkov and Karlín districts. A colossal statue of **Jan Žižka** (Map pp278–9), the Hussite general, was erected here in 1950, commanding superb views across Staré Město to Prague Castle. It's said to be the biggest equestrian statue in the world. Behind it is the National Monument.

The mostly residential suburb of Karlín lies north of Žižkov, squeezed between Žižkov Hill and the Vltava River.

ARMY MUSEUM Map pp278-9

Armádní muzeum; ☎ 220 204 924; www.military museum.cz; U Památníku 2; Žižkov; admission free; ⏰ 10am-6pm Tue-Sun; metro Florenc

On the way up Žižkov Hill you will find this grim-looking barracks of a museum, which displays a courtyard full of rusting tanks, and exhibits on the history of the Czechoslovak army and resistance movement from 1918 to 1945. There is also a fascinating exhibition on the 1942 assassination of Reinhard Heydrich (see boxed text, p43), with pride of place going to the Mercedes in which Heydrich was travelling when the attack took place.

JEWISH CEMETERY Map pp278-9

Židovské hřbitovy; Izraelská, Žižkov; admission free; ⏰ 9am-5pm Sun-Thu, to 2pm Fri Apr-Oct, to 4pm Sun-Thu & to 2pm Fri Nov-Mar, closed on Jewish hols; metro Želivského

Franz Kafka is buried in this cemetery, which opened around 1890 when the previous Jewish cemetery – now at the foot of the TV Tower – was closed. To find Kafka's grave, follow the main avenue east (sign-posted), turn right at row 21, then left at the wall; it's at the end of the 'block'. Fans

make a pilgrimage on 3 June, the anniversary of his death.

The entrance is beside Želivského metro station; men should cover their heads (yarmulkes are available at the gate). Last admission is 30 minutes before closing.

NATIONAL MONUMENT Map pp278-9

Národní památník; ☎ 222 781 676; U Památníku 1900, Žižkov; guided tour 30/20Kč; ⏰ 2pm on 1st Sat of each month Sep-Jun; metro Florenc

Although not, strictly speaking, a legacy of the communist era – it was completed in the 1930s – the huge monument atop Žižkov Hill is, in the minds of most Praguers over a certain age, inextricably linked with the Communist Party of Czechoslovakia, and in particular with Klement Gottwald, the country's first 'worker-president'.

Designed in the 1920s as a memorial to the 15th-century Hussite commander Jan Žižka, and to the soldiers who had fought for Czechoslovak independence, it was still under construction in the late 1930s. The occupation of Czechoslovakia by Nazi Germany in 1939 made the 'Monument to National Liberation', as it was called, seem like a sick joke.

After 1948 the Communist Party appropriated Jan Žižka and the Hussites for the purposes of propaganda, extolling them as shining examples of Czech peasant power. The communists completed the National Monument with the installation of the Tomb of the Unknown Soldier, and Bohumil Kafka's gargantuan bronze statue of Žižka. But they didn't stop there.

In 1953 the monument's mausoleum – originally intended for the remains of Tomáš Masaryk, Czechoslovakia's founding father – received the embalmed body of Klement Gottwald, displayed to the public in a refrigerated glass chamber, just like his more illustrious comrade Lenin in Moscow's Red Square. It soon became a compulsory outing for school groups and bus-loads of visiting Soviet-bloc tourists.

Gottwald's morticians, however, were not as adept as the Russians – by 1962 the body had decayed so badly that it had to be cremated. Since 1989 the monument has been closed to the public except on a few special occasions (although you can wander freely around the exterior). This is a pity; although the massive memorial building has all the elegance of the reactor house at

Sights BEYOND THE CENTRE

a nuclear power station, the interior here is a spectacular extravaganza of polished marble and gilt, and its memorials – Soviet as well as Czech – allow a glimpse into a period of Czech history that many would prefer to forget. You can visit the interior only on a prearranged tour; you can book through any PIS office (see p238 for contact details).

OLŠANY CEMETERY Map pp278-9
Olšanské hřbitovy; Vinohradská 153, Žižkov; admission free; ☻ 8am-7pm May-Sep, to 6pm Mar, Apr & Oct, 9am-4pm Nov-Feb; metro Flora
Huge and atmospheric, Prague's main burial ground was founded in 1680 during a plague epidemic; the oldest stones are in the northwestern corner, near the 17th-century St Roch Chapel (kaple sv Rocha). There are several entrances to the cemetery along Vinohradská, east of Flora metro station, and beside the chapel on Olšanská. Jan Palach, the student who set himself on fire in January 1969 in protest at the Soviet invasion (see the boxed text, p44), is buried here. To find his grave, enter the main gate (flanked by flower shops) on Vinohradská and turn right – it's about 50m along on the left of the path.

TV TOWER Map pp278-9
Televizní vysílač; ☎ 267 005 778; www.tower.cz; Mahlerovy sady 1, Žižkov; adult/child 150/30Kč; ☻ 10am-11pm; metro Jiřího z Poděbrad
Prague's tallest landmark – and, depending on your tastes, either its ugliest or its most futuristic – is the 216m-tall TV Tower, erected between 1985 and 1992. The viewing platforms, reached by high-speed lifts, have comprehensive information boards in English and French explaining what you can see. There is also a restaurant (at 63m; see p147 for details). But the most bizarre thing about it is the 10 giant crawling babies with coin-slots for faces that appear to be exploring the outside of the tower – an installation called *Miminka* (Mummy) by artist David Černý.

The tower is built on the site of a Jewish cemetery (admission 20Kč; ☻ 9am-1pm Tue & Thu). The cemetery was opened after the Old Jewish Cemetery in Josefov (see p91) was closed. This cemetery remained in use until the year 1890, when the Jewish Cemeteries (opposite) opened.

Jan Palach memorial (p89)

VINOHRADY
Vinohrady occupies a rounded hill above the valley of the Botič creek, east of Nové Město and south of Žižkov. The name means 'vineyards' and refers to the vines that were cultivated here in centuries past; as recently as 200 years ago there was little urbanisation. Today it is an upmarket residential district of elegant, early-20th-century apartment blocks and wooded parks.

Vinohrady's physical and commercial heart is Peace Square (náměstí Míru), dominated by the neogothic **Church of St Ludmilla** (kostel sv Ludmily). Right behind it is the neo-Renaissance **National House** (Národní dům), housing exhibition and concert halls. On the north side of the square is the **Vinohrady Theatre** (divadlo na Vinohradech), built in 1909, a popular drama venue.

The district is home to a few architectural curiosities, including Josef Gočár's constructivist **St Wenceslas Church** (kostel sv Václava; Map pp262–3; náměstí Svatopluka Čecha), built in 1930, and the Church of the Most Sacred Heart of Our Lord (below).

CHURCH OF THE MOST SACRED HEART OF OUR LORD Map pp278-9
Kostel Nejsvětějšího Srdce Páně; náměstí Jiřího z Poděbrad 19; ☻ services 8am & 6pm Mon-Sat, 7am, 9am, 11am & 6pm Sun; metro Jiřího z Poděbrad
This church was built in 1932 and is one of Prague's most original and unusual pieces of 20th-century architecture. It's the work of Jože Plečník, the Slovenian architect who

also raised a few eyebrows with his additions to Prague Castle. Inspired by Egyptian temples and early Christian basilicas, the glazed-brick building sports a massive, tombstone-like bell tower pierced by a circular glass clock-window.

SMÍCHOV

The suburb of Smíchov became part of Prague in 1838 and grew into an industrial quarter full of chimney stacks, railway yards and the sprawling Staropramen brewery. It is currently undergoing a wave of renovation and renewal, and is now home to the vast Nový Smíchov shopping centre (p191).

TRANSPORT - SMÍCHOV

Metro Metro line B has stations at Anděl, in the heart of Smíchov, and Smíchovské Nádraží in the south of the suburb.

Tram Nos 4, 7, 10 and 14 rumble across Palackého most from Karlovo náměstí to Smíchov; from Malá Strana take tram Nos 12 or 20 south from Malostranské náměstí or Újezd.

FUTURA GALLERY Map pp270-1
☎ 251 511 804; www.futuraprojekt.com; Holečkova 49; admission free; ☾ noon-7pm Wed-Sun; tram 4, 7, 9, 10

The Futura Gallery focuses on all aspects of contemporary art ranging from painting, photography and sculpture to video, installations and performance art. The gallery spaces, which include two floors of 'white cube' halls, a more intimate brick-vaulted cellar, and a garden with children's play area, host changing exhibitions by both Czech and international artists. The most notorious exhibit is in the garden, a permanent installation by David Černý (see the boxed text, p24). It consists of two huge, naked human figures, bent over at the waist with their heads buried in a blank wall. A ladder allows viewers to climb up and place their head – and there's really no polite way to say this – up the figure's arse, where they can watch a video of Czech president Václav Klaus and the director of Prague's National Gallery spooning mush into each other's mouths. Richly metaphorical, to say the least.

MOZART MUSEUM Map pp262-3
Vila Bertramka; ☎ 257 317 465; www.bertramka.com; Mozartova 169; adult/child 110/30Kč, concerts 390-450Kč; ☾ 9.30am-6pm Apr-Oct, to 5pm Nov-Mar; tram 4, 7, 9, 10

Mozart stayed at the elegant 17th-century Vila Bertramka during his visits to Prague in 1787 and 1791, as guest of composer František Dušek. Here he finished his opera *Don Giovanni*. Today the house is a modest Mozart museum. Regular concerts are held in the salon (see p161 for more details), and in the garden (April to October only).

DEJVICE

Dejvice, to the north of Hradčany, is a mix of university campuses and residential areas in the west, merging into the leafy backstreets of Prague's embassy district in the east. There's not too much to see out here, but there are some good restaurants and accommodation options.

Just north of Dejvice is the unusual 1930s villa suburb of **Baba**, a Functionalist project by a team of artists and designers that aimed to provide cheap, attractive, single-family houses. The **Hanspaulka** suburb to its southwest was a similar project, built between 1925 and 1930. Both are now highly desirable addresses.

BÍLEK VILLA Map pp264-5
Bílkova vila; ☎ 224 322 021; Mickiewiczova 1; adult/child 50/20Kč; ☾ 10am-6pm Tue-Sun; tram 18, 22, 23

In the south of Dejvice, near the northeastern edge of Hradčany, is the striking red-brick villa designed by sculptor František Bílek in 1911 as his own home. It houses a museum of his unconventional stone and wood reliefs, furniture and graphics.

DIVOKÁ ŠÁRKA Map pp262-3
Evropská; tram 20, 26

The valley of the Šárecký potok (Šárka Creek; Map pp262–3) is one of Prague's best-known and most popular nature parks. It's named after the legendary warrior Šárka, who is said to have thrown herself off a cliff here (see the boxed text, opposite). The most attractive area is nearby, among the rugged cliffs near the Džbán Reservoir. People sunbathe on the rocks, and you can swim in the Džbán Reservoir.

TRANSPORT - DEJVICE

Metro Metro station Dejvická is the northwestern terminus of line A; Hradčanská, the last stop but one, serves the southern part of the district.
Tram Nos 2, 8, 20 and 26 all pass through Vítézné náměstí in the centre of Dejvice.

From there it's a 7km walk northeast down the valley on a red-marked trail to the suburb of Podbaba, where the creek empties into the Vltava River. There's a bus stop by the Vltava at Podbaba, for the trip back to the centre, or you can walk south about 1.5km on Podbabská to the northern terminus of tram No 8, opposite the Hotel Crowne Plaza in Dejvice (below). Bus No 116 to Dejvice runs along the lower half of the Šárka Valley, should you want to cut your walk short.

HOTEL CROWNE PLAZA Map p275
☎ 224 393 111; www.crowneplaza.cz; Koulova 15; tram 8
The silhouette of this huge Stalinist building in northern Dejvice will be familiar to anyone who has visited the Russian capital. Originally called the Hotel International, it was built in the 1950s to a design inspired by the tower of Moscow University, right down to the Soviet-style star on top of the spire (though this one is green, not red).

Nip into the gleamingly restored, marble-clad lobby bar (to the right), and take a look at the large tapestry hanging on the wall in the far left-hand corner. Entitled *Praga Regina Musicae* (Prague, Queen of Music), and created by Cyril Bouda around 1956, it shows an exaggerated aerial view of central Prague. Bang in the centre is the former Stalin Monument on Letná terása, and at the bottom edge you can spot the now-departed Soviet Tank memorial (see the boxed text p105). For a review of the hotel see p208.

TROJA
Troja is a mostly residential suburb on the south-facing hillside overlooking the Vltava River north of Holešovice.

TRANSPORT - TROJA

Boat Take a boat trip (see p58) from the city centre to the Troja landing.
Bus Take bus No 112 from Nádraží Holešovice metro station to the end of the line.
On Foot Walk from Výstaviště to Troja through Stromovka (see p125).

PRAGUE ZOO Map pp262-3
Zoo Praha; ☎ 296 112 111; U Trojského zámku 120; adult/child 90/60Kč Apr-Sep, 70/40Kč Oct-Mar; ⌚ 9am-7pm Jun-Aug, to 6pm Apr, May, Sep & Oct, to 5pm Mar, to 4pm Nov-Feb; bus 112 from metro Nádraží Holešovice
Prague's attractive zoo is set in 60 hectares of wooded grounds on the banks of the river. Pride of place, at the top of the hill, goes to a herd of Przewalski's horses, little steppe-dwellers that still survive in the wilds of Mongolia and are successfully bred in captivity here.

TROJA CHATEAU Map pp262-3
Trojský zámek; ☎ 283 851 614; U Trojského zámku 1; adult/child 100/50Kč; ⌚ 10am-6pm Tue-Sun; bus 112 from metro Nádraží Holešovice
Troja Chateau is a 17th-century baroque palace that now houses the Prague City Gallery's collection of 19th-century Czech art, and modern Czech sculpture (1900–70); the cellars contain an exhibition on the history of wine-making in the Czech lands. There's free admission to the palace grounds, where you can wander in the beautiful French gardens, watched by a gang of baroque stone giants on the balustrade outside the southern door.

Sights
BEYOND THE CENTRE

LOVE HURTS

According to Czech legend Šárka was one of a renegade army of warrior women who fled across the Vltava River after the death of Libuše, mother of the Přemysl line. She was chosen as a decoy to trap Ctirad, captain of the men's army. Unfortunately she fell in love with him, and when her fellow amazons killed him she threw herself into the Šárka Valley in remorse. The women were slaughtered by the men of Hradčany in a final battle.

There are monumental statues of Šárka and Ctirad in the Vyšehrad Gardens (see p104).

National Museum (p100)

KOBYLISY

KOBYLISY ANTI-FASCIST RESISTANCE MEMORIAL

Památník protifašistického odboje v Kobylisích; Žernosecká; admission free; ⏰ 24hr; tram 10, 17, 24

This grassy quadrangle of earthen embankments, ringed by trees and overlooked by apartment blocks, was once the Kobylisy Rifle Range. More than a hundred Czechs were executed here by firing squads during WWII. Today it's the site of a national memorial; a huge bronze plaque lists all the names of the dead, and – such was Nazi bureaucracy – the dates and times of their executions. Take tram No 10, 17 or 24 to the terminal at Ďáblická, then walk west for 10 minutes along Žernosecká.

KBELY

AIRCRAFT MUSEUM

Letecké muzeum; ☎ 220 207 504; Mladoboleslavská; admission free; ⏰ 10am-6pm Tue-Sun May-Oct; bus 185 or 259 from metro Českomoravská

The Kbely airfield in northeastern Prague is home to this aircraft museum where you can have a close look at Russian MiG fighter planes and a host of exhibits on aeronautics and space flight. The impressive collection amounts to no less than 275 aircraft.

ZBRASLAV

This small town on the western bank of the Vltava, 10km south of the centre, was only recently incorporated into Greater Prague.

ZBRASLAV CHATEAU

Zámek zbraslav; ☎ 257 921 638; Bartoňova 2; adult/child 80/40Kč; ⏰ 10am-6pm Tue-Sun; bus 129, 241 or 243 from metro Smíchovské Nádraží

As early as 1268 Přemysl Otakar II built a hunting lodge and a chapel here, later rebuilt as a Cistercian monastery. In 1784 it was converted into a baroque chateau that now houses the National Gallery's permanent collection of Asian art, with copies of well-known Czech sculptures in the gardens.

BARRANDOV

The southern suburb of Barrandov, on the western bank of the Vltava River, was developed in the 1930s by Václav Havel, the father of ex-president Havel. It is famous for the Barrandov Studios, the film studios founded by Miloš Havel (the ex-president's uncle) in 1931, and increasingly popular today with Hollywood producers – *Amadeus* (1984), *Mission Impossible* (1996), *Blade II* (2002), *The League of Extraordinary Gentlemen* (2003) and *Doom* (2005) were all shot here.

The suburb was named after the 19th-century French geologist, Joachim Barrande, who studied the fossils in the contorted limestone of the **Barrandov Cliffs** (Barrandovské skály; Map pp262–3) – hundreds of them are on display in the National Museum.

STŘEŠOVICE

Střešovice is a largely residential suburb stretching to the west of Hradčany.

TRANSPORT - STŘEŠOVICE

Tram Nos 1, 2 and 18 run along Střešovická, the main street.

PUBLIC TRANSPORT MUSEUM

Map pp264–5

Muzeum MHD; ☎ 296 124 900; Patočkova 4; adult/child 40/20Kč; ☼ 9am-5pm Sat, Sun & hols Apr-Oct; tram 1, 2, 18

The museum at the Střešovice tram depot has a large collection of trams and buses, from an 1886 horse-drawn tram to present-day vehicles. It's great for kids as they can climb into some of the vehicles.

VILLA MÜLLER Map pp262–3

Müllerova vila; ☎ 224 312 012; www.mullerovavila .cz; Nad hradním vodojemem 14; guided tours in Czech 300/200Kč, in English or German 400/300Kč; ☼ 9am-6pm Tue, Thu, Sat & Sun Apr-Oct, 10am-5pm Tue, Thu, Sat & Sun Nov-Mar; tram 1, 2, 18

Fans of Functionalist architecture will enjoy this masterpiece of domestic design. It was built in 1930 for construction entrepreneur František Müller, and designed by the Viennese architect Adolf Loos, whose clean-cut, ultramodernist exterior contrasts with the polished wood, leather and oriental rugs of the classically decorated interior. The villa can be visited only by guided tour, which must be booked in advance.

BŘEVNOV

Břevnov, a sprawling, low-density residential suburb that consists mostly of open green space, takes its name from the 1000-year-old Břevnov Monastery.

TRANSPORT - BŘEVNOV

Tram Nos 15, 22 and 25 run along Patočkova and Bělohorská, the main drag. No 15 terminates at the Vypich stop, 22 and 25 continue to Bílá Hora.

BŘEVNOV MONASTERY Map pp262–3

Břevnovský klášter; ☎ 220 406 111; Patočková 72; gardens admission free, guided tour of church, crypt & monastery 50Kč; ☼ gardens 10am-6pm Sun, tours 10am, 2pm & 4pm Sat & Sun; tram 15, 22, 25

Břevnov Monastery is the Czech Republic's oldest Benedictine monastery, founded in 993 by Boleslav II and Bishop Vojtěch Slavníkovec (later to be canonised as St Adalbert). The two men, from powerful and opposing families intent on dominating Bohemia, met at Vojtěška spring, each having had a dream that this was the place where they should found a monastery. Its name comes from *břevno* (beam), after the beam laid across the spring where they met.

The present baroque monastery building and the nearby **Basilica of St Margaret** (bazilika sv Markéty) were completed in 1720 by Kristof Dientzenhofer. During the communist era the monastery housed a secret-police archive; Jan Patočka (1907–77), a leading figure of the Charta 77 movement, who died after interrogation by the secret police, is buried in the cemetery behind the monastery. In 1993 (the 1000th anniversary of the monastery's founding) the restored 1st floor, with its fine ceiling frescoes, and the Romanesque crypt, with the original foundations and a few skeletons, were opened to the public for the first time.

TOP FIVE FOR KIDS

- Boat trips (p58).
- Children's Island (p82) is a leafy riverside retreat with swings and sandpit.
- Mirror Maze (p84) is a fun maze on Petřín hill where kids can distort their facial features with no lasting consequences.
- The National Technology Museum (p107) is stuffed with vintage trains, planes and automobiles, many of which kids can clamber aboard.
- Various theatres put on traditional puppet shows (p173) aimed at children.

The church, crypt and monastery can be only be visited by guided tour, but you can wander the gardens at your leisure.

STAR SUMMER PALACE Map pp264-5
Letohrádek hvězda; ☎ 235 357 938; Obora Hvězda, entrances on Libocká & Bělohorská; adult/child 30/15Kč; ⊗ 10am-6pm Tue-Sun May-Sep, to 5pm Tue-Sun Apr & Oct; tram 15, 22, 25

The Letohrádek Hvězda is a Renaissance summer palace in the shape of a six-pointed star built in 1556 for Archduke Ferdinand of Tyrol. It sits at the end of a long avenue through the lovely wooded park of Obora Hvězda, a hunting reserve established by Ferdinand I in 1530. The palace houses a small museum about its history, and an exhibit on the battle of White Mountain (see right).

From the Vypich tram stop, bear right across open parkland to the white archway in the wall; the avenue on the far side leads to the palace (a 15-minute walk from the tram).

WHITE MOUNTAIN Map pp262-3
Bílá hora; access from Karlovarská; tram 22, 25

The 381m-high White Mountain – more of a gentle hillock, actually – on the western outskirts of Prague was the site of the 1620 collapse of Protestant military forces that ended Czech independence for almost 300 years. The only reminder of the battle is a small memorial cairn located on a mound in the middle of a field, with the roof of the Star Summer Palace (left) poking above the forest to the northeast.

Take the tram to the end of the line, then continue west past the **Church of Our Lady Victorious** (kostel Panny Maria Vítězná; Map pp264–5), an early-18th-century celebration of the Habsburg victory at White Mountain, and turn right; the field is visible up ahead.

Walking Tours

Walking Tours

MALÁ STRANA GARDENS

This walk will lead you through some of the hidden green corners of Malá Strana, visiting the various gardens that once belonged to the quarter's 18th-century aristocratic residents. Begin at the **lookout 1** just outside the eastern entrance to Prague Castle, which offers a fine view over Malá Strana.

Go through the gate into the Garden on the Ramparts (Zahrada na valech; p75) and find the top entrance of the **Palace Gardens beneath Prague Castle 2** (Palácové zahrady pod Pražským hradem; p81). Note that this entrance is only accessible from April to October; in winter, begin the walk from Malostranská metro station, and walk southwest along Valdštejnská to the main gate of the Palace Gardens).

Having explored these lovely terraced gardens, exit via the main gate on Valdštejnská and turn right. On your left is the **Wallenstein Palace 3** (Valdštejnský palác; p81); when you reach Wallenstein Square (Valdštejnské náměstí), turn left into the palace's main entrance, and go through the courtyard and into the peace of the **Wallenstein Garden 4** (Valdštejnská zahrada; p81).

WALK FACTS

Start Prague Castle, tram 22, 23 or metro Malostranská

End Petřín Hill, tram 12, 20, 22, 23 or funicular

Distance 4km

Duration Two hours

Fuel Stops Hergetova Cihelna (p135); El Centro (p134)

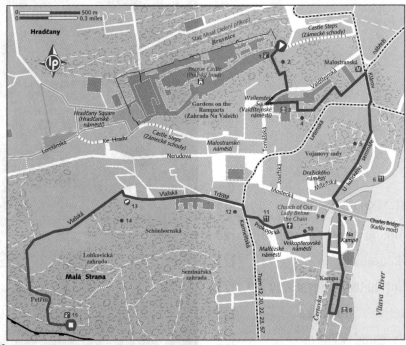

Mirror Maze, Petřín hill (p84)

Head for the northeastern corner, to the right of the big fishpond, and leave through the gate beside Malostranská metro station (if it's closed, go back along the southern wall and exit through the gate on Letenská).

Turn right on Klárov, and go straight across the junction with the tram line, continuing along U lužického semináře. Just past the Černý Orel restaurant, a gate on the right gives access to the **Vojan Gardens 5** (Vojanovy sady), the poor relation of Malá Strana's many parks. Less manicured but more peaceful than the others, it's a public park where local folk take a breather with the kids, or sit in the sun on the park benches. If you're feeling hungry, the riverside terrace of **Hergetova Cihelna 6** (p135) is a great place for lunch.

Continue along U lužického semináře, and when the street narrows bear left across the little bridge over the Čertovka (Devil's Stream) onto Kampa island (p82). Pass under Charles Bridge and emerge into the picturesque little square of Na Kampě. To your left, at about waist height on the wall to the left of the little gallery under the stairs, is a small **metal plaque 7** that reads 'Výska vody 4.žáří 1890' (height of waters, 4 September 1890), marking the level reached by the floodwaters of 1890. Directly above it – above head height – is another marking the height of the 2002 floods. (There are several similar plaques around Kampa.) By the way, fans of the film *Mission Impossible,* starring Tom Cruise, might recognise this little square – many of the night scenes in the movie were shot here.

Head on through the square and into the leafy riverside park known simply as Kampa (from the Latin campus, meaning 'field'), one of the city's favourite chill-out zones, usually littered with lounging bodies in summer. If the mood strikes, go for a wander through the modern art collections of the **Kampa Museum 8** (p82), housed in a restored mill complex on the edge of the river.

Return north but, as soon as you reach the cobblestones before Na Kampě, bear left along Hroznová, a backstreet that leads to a little bridge over the Čertovka beside Prague's most photographed **water wheel 9**. The bridge leads onto a tiny cobbled square with the **John Lennon Wall 10** (p82) on one side, and the baroque palace that houses the French embassy on the other. The far end of the square curves right, past the severe Gothic towers of the Church of Our Lady Below the Chain (kostel Panny Marie pod řetězem; p82). Just beyond the church, on the right, is the embassy of the Knights of Malta, which featured in the movie *Amadeus* as the house of Salieri.

Turn left opposite the church and bear right along Prokopská; if you fancy a drink, and you may well do by now, **El Centro 11** (p134) is on your right. At the end of Prokopská, cross busy Karmelitská and turn right. Just past U malého Glena pub is the alley that leads to the **Vrtbov Garden 12** (Vrtbovská zahrada; p83), one of Malá Strana's least visited but most beautiful gardens. After visiting the garden, turn left along Tržiště and its continuation Vlašská, passing in turn the Irish, US and **German embassy 13**.

A few hundred metres beyond the German embassy there's a little **park 14** and playground on the left; leave the street and turn left along the dirt track beyond the wall at the far end of the playground, and you'll be able to peek into the back garden of the German embassy to see David Černý's famous sculpture *Quo Vadis,* a Trabant car perched on four human legs. It's a memorial to the East German asylum seekers who sought refuge here in 1989, during the final death throes of the communist era (for more on David Černý, see the boxed texts on p24 and p84).

Follow Vlašská to its end and climb the steps that lead up to the top of Petřín Hill and finish your walk at the **Petřín Lookout Tower 15** (Petřínská rozhledna; p84). From here you can take the funicular railway (20Kč; every 10 to 20 minutes from 9.15am to 8.45pm) back down to Újezd or slowly wander down one of the many footpaths. Halfway down the funicular is Restaurant Nebozízek (p135), which is a great spot for a snack with a view after your stroll through the gardens.

AROUND WENCESLAS SQUARE

Start at the steps in front of the neo-Renaissance **National Museum 1** (Národní muzeum; p100), which dominates the upper end of Wenceslas Square (Václavské náměstí). From the steps you have a grand view down the square, a focal point of Czech history since the 19th century. At the foot of the steps is a pavement memorial to student Jan Palach (see the boxed text, p44).

Cross the busy traffic artery of Mezibranská to Prague's famous landmark, the equestrian **statue of St Wenceslas 2** (sv Václav), the 10th-century 'Good King Wenceslas' of Christmas carol fame. Below the statue is a modest **memorial 3** to those who died for their resistance to communism.

Wander down the middle of the square, admiring the grand buildings on either side. The finest is the 1906 Art Nouveau **Grand Hotel Evropa 4** (p201) at No 25, about halfway down on the right. Across the street at No 36 is the **Melantrich Building 5**, from whose balcony the death

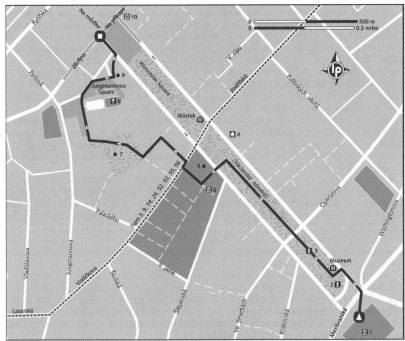

WALK FACTS

Start National Museum, metro Muzeum

End Na můstku, metro Můstek

Distance 1.5km

Duration 30 minutes

Fuel stop Any of the Wenceslas Square cafés

of Czech communism was pronounced by Alexander Dubček and Václav Havel on 24 November 1989 (it now houses a Marks & Spencer store).

Turn left into Pasáz Rokoko, a shopping arcade directly across the street from the Grand Hotel Evropa. It leads to the central atrium of the **Lucerna Palace 6**, dominated by David Černý's *Horse*, an ironic twist on the St Wenceslas statue in the square outside (it helps to know that the first prime minister of the Czech Republic was also a Václav). For more on David Černý, see the boxed texts on p24 and p84.

Turn right beneath the dead horse (you'll see when you get here), and follow the passage to Vodičkova. Bear right across the street and enter the Světozor arcade. Up ahead you'll see a stained-glass window dating from the late 1940s – it's actually an advertisement for Tesla Radio, an old Czech electronics company.

At the far end of the Světozor arcade, turn left into the **Franciscan Garden 7** (Františkánská zahrada), a hidden oasis of peace and greenery. Make your way to the far northern corner of the garden, diagonally opposite to where you came in, and you'll find an exit to Jungmannovo Square. Go past the arch leading to the **Church of Our Lady of the Snows 8** (kostel Panny Marie Sněžné; p99) and turn right.

Keep to the right of the Lancôme shop, and you will come to what must be the only **Cubist lamppost 9** in the entire world, dating from 1915. Turn left here and then duck right through the short Lindt arcade that returns you to Wenceslas Square. Look up and to the left and you will see the corner tower of the Art Nouveau **Koruna Palace 10**, complete with its crown of pearls.

You can now head right along Na příkopě to the Municipal House and the beginning of the Not Quite the Royal Way walking tour (p123), or retire to one of the many nearby bars and cafés.

HRADČANY

Although Prague Castle is usually crammed with crowds of tourists, there are many peaceful corners in the surrounding Hradčany district. This walk explores these quiet backstreets.

As you leave the top of the escalators in Hradčanská metro station, turn right and head for the stairway in the right-hand corner marked 'Pražský hrad'. At street level turn right, and then go right again through the gap in the building opposite the railway level crossing on the other side of the street. This leads to the street called K Brusce – head for the stone gateway of the **Písek Gate 1** (Písecká brána) that you'll see straight ahead. The baroque gateway, decorated with carved military emblems, was built by Giovanni Battisti for Charles VI in 1721 as part of Prague's new fortifications; the streets on either side still follow the outlines of the bastions of sv Jiří (St George) to the right, and sv Ludmila to the left. A century later, in 1821, the gate became the terminus of Prague's first horse-drawn railway.

Romantik Hotel U Raka (p195), alongside the castle moat wall

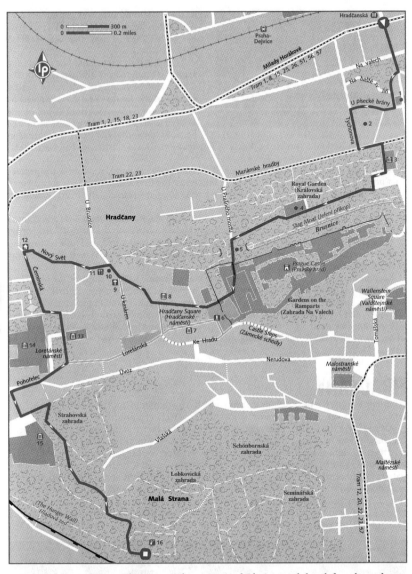

Bear right past the gate, then turn right on U písecké brány, and then left at the end onto Tychonova. Here you will pass two attractive **Cubist houses** 2 designed by Josef Gočár. When you reach Mariánské hradby (the street with the tram lines), cross it and enter the Royal Garden (Královská zahrada; p71) beside the beautiful, Renaissance **Summer Palace** 3 (Letohrádek). The gardens are open from April to October only; at other times of the year you'll have to go right along Mariánské hradby and enter the castle via U Prašného mostu.

Turn right beyond the Letohrádek, continuing past the equally stunning **Ball-Game House** 4 (Míčovna), and follow the upper rim of the Stag Moat to the western end of the gardens. Go through the gate and turn left to enter the Second Courtyard of Prague Castle via the **Powder Bridge** 5 (Prašná most); that's powder as in gunpowder, not a reference to poor-quality

WALK FACTS

Start Hradčanská metro station
End Petřín Hill, tram 12, 20, 22, 23 or funicular
Distance 2.5km
Duration One hour
Fuel stop U zlaté hrušky (p134)

construction. Visit the castle if you wish, but for the moment we'll leave the courtyard via the first gate on the right, which leads past a window giving a glimpse into the ruins of a Romanesque chapel, and into Hradčany Square (Hradčanské náměstí).

This square, now watched over by a **statue of TG Masaryk 6**, the first president of Czechoslovakia, was once the social heart of the aristocratic quarter of Hradčany; in the wake of the Thirty Years' War, many Catholic nobles built their palaces here to be close to the power centre of the castle. On the southern side of the square is the extravagant Renaissance status symbol of the **Schwarzenberg Palace 7** (Schwarzenberský palác; p75), while on the northern side you can see the rococo Archbishop's Palace (Arcibiskupský palác) and the *sgrafitto*-covered **Martinic Palace 8** (Martinický palác), which served as Hradčany's town hall. More recently the palace was used as Mozart's house in the film *Amadeus*.

At the far end of the square, bear right down the narrow cobbled street of Kanovnická, and pass the pretty little **Church of St John Nepomuk 9** (kostel sv Jan Nepomucký), built in 1729 by the king of Prague baroque, Kilian Dientzenhofer (see the boxed text p31). Take the first lane on the left downhill from the church. This is called Nový Svět (New World) and is a picturesque cluster of little cottages once inhabited by court artisans and tradesmen, a far cry from the fancy palaces at the top of the hill. **No 1 Nový Svět 10** was the humble home of court astronomer Tycho Brahe and, after 1600, his successor Johannes Kepler. The atmospheric restaurant **U zlaté hrušky 11** (p134), serving a selection of traditional Czech dishes, is just next door.

Continue downhill to where Nový Svět ends in a leafy hollow occupied by the **Romantik Hotel U Raka 12** (p195). Turn left and climb slowly up Černínská to the pretty square in front of the extravagantly baroque **Loreta 13** (p76), a shrine to the Virgin Mary and a hugely popular place of pilgrimage for Roman Catholics. Facing it is the imposing 150m-long façade of the **Černín Palace 14** (Černínský palác; p75), which dates from 1692.

At the southern end of the square turn right into Pohořelec and continue to the far western side. A little alley at No 9 leads into the courtyard of **Strahov Monastery 15** (Strahovský klášter; p76), where you can visit the library before exiting the eastern end of the courtyard into the gardens above Malá Strana. Turn right on the footpath here (signposted) and finish the walk with a stroll along to the **Petřín Lookout Tower 16** (p84).

NOT QUITE THE ROYAL WAY

The Royal Way (Královská cesta; p92) is an ancient processional route from the Powder Gate to the castle via Charles Bridge. In Staré Město it leads along Celetná to Old Town Square, and then on by Karlova to the bridge, but the only procession that makes its way along these streets today is the daily crush of tourists shouldering their way through a gauntlet of gaudy souvenir shops and bored-looking leaflet touts. This walk follows the general direction of the Royal Way, but dodges the main route – and the crowds – at every opportunity.

At the starting point, Republic Square (náměstí Republiky), three ages of Prague architecture face each other across the intersection of Na příkopě and Celetená – the sooty Gothic tracery of the **Powder Gate 1** (Prašná brána), the elegant Art Nouveau convolutions of the Municipal House (Obecní dům; p93), and the stern Functionalist façades of the Czech National Bank (Česká národní banka) and the Commercial Bank (Komerční banka). As you look west along Celetná you'll see the tower of the Old Town Hall framed in the end of the street like a target in a gunsight; set off towards it.

As well as the many souvenir shops, Celetná is lined with many interesting buildings, but as you reach the open space of Ovocný trh you'll see an unusual, origami-like façade on the left. It belongs to the **House of the Black Madonna 2** (dům U černé Matky Boží), one of Prague's finest examples of Cubist architecture, and home of the Museum of Czech Cubism (p94).

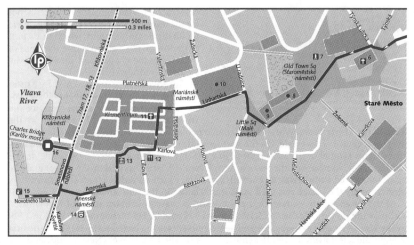

A little further along Celetná, turn right into the passage at No 17, which leads to a peaceful little courtyard beside the **Celetná Theatre 3** (divadlo v Celetné; p173). Head up the stairs to Café Gaspar Kasper (p155) if you fancy a coffee or a cold beer. The passage on the far side of the courtyard leads out onto Štupartská; go straight ahead along Malá Štupartská for a look at the baroque sculptures adorning the façade of the **Church of St James 4** (kostel sv Jakuba; p87), and if it's open, go inside for a peek at its gloomy, gilded splendour and the grisly exhibit hanging next to the door.

WALK FACTS

Start Republic Square (náměstí Republiky), metro Náměstí Republiky
End Charles Bridge, tram 17, 18
Distance 1.5km
Duration 45 minutes
Fuel stops Café Gaspar Kasper (p155); Reykjavík (p141)

Retrace your steps for a few metres and turn right through the cobbled passage just beyond Big Ben Bookshop, to enter the **Týn Courtyard 5** (Týnský dvůr). This lovely little courtyard is lined with posh shops, good restaurants and a Renaissance loggia, and has a fine view of the twin steeples of the **Church of Our Lady Before Týn 6** (kostel Panny Marie před Týnem; p86). Exit at the western end and go around to the right of the church, stopping to look up at the semicircular tympanum above the northern door, decorated with a superb Gothic relief of the Last Judgment (this is actually a copy – the original is in the Lapidárium; p108).

A narrow alley continues along the northern side of the church and spits you out into the melee of Old Town Square (Staroměstské náměstí; p85), dominated by the brooding statue of Jan Hus **7** and the Gothic tower of the **Old Town Hall 8** (Staroměstská Radnice; p88). If you've timed it right, you'll be able to join the crowd at the foot of the tower to watch a performance by the Astronomical Clock (see the boxed text, p86). Beyond the clock, keep right and enter the Gothic arcade at the foot of the *sgraffito*-clad **House at the Minute 9** (dům U minuty), and follow it around to the right into the neighbouring square of Little Square (Malé náměstí). You'll see the main tourist throng bearing left into Karlova, but head for the opposite end of the square and then turn left into Linhartská.

This leads to the quieter space of Virgin Mary Square (Mariánské náměstí), dominated by **City Hall 10**, (Pražské radnice), where the façade is framed by brooding Art Nouveau statues by Ladislav Šaloun, the same chap who created the Jan Hus Monument in Old Town Square. Facing City Hall across the square is the main gate of the Klementinum (p92). Go through the gate into the courtyard and turn left; on your right is the entrance to the **Chapel of Mirrors 11** (Zrcadlová kaple), where classical concerts are held daily at around 5pm. Continue past the chapel and through the arch, and head for the doorway straight ahead. This leads out into the heaving crowds of Karlova; if it's lunchtime, the old-fashioned,

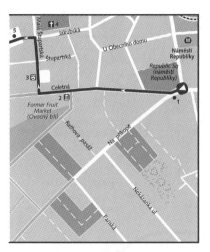

bar-like dining room of **Reykjavík 12** (p141) is just across the street.

Allow the flow of the crowd to pull you west along narrow Karlova as far as the **Museum of Marionettes 13** (muzeum Loutek; p93), then duck left into the museum entrance passage which leads to a courtyard. Another passage at the far side of the courtyard (bear right) leads out onto Anenská; turn right and you'll find yourself in the near-deserted St Anne's Square (Anenské náměstí), a hundred metres and a million miles away from crowded Karlova. At the far side of the square is the **Theatre on the Balustrade 14** (divadlo Na Zábradlí; p174), where ex-president Havel spent his formative years as a playwright.

Continue along Anenská and cross the busy traffic artery of Smetanovo nabřeží, and walk out to the end of the café-fringed terrace called Novotného lávka, where you'll find a **viewpoint 15** with a picture-postcard view of Charles Bridge and the castle. Retrace your steps and turn left into the gaudy arcade that leads north to Křížovnické náměstí, at the eastern end of Charles Bridge. End your walk by climbing up the **Old Town Bridge Tower 16** (Staroměstská mostecká věž; p88) for a view over Prague's most famous bridge.

LETNÁ & STROMOVKA

This is a long walk through some of the leafiest parts of Prague; make a half-day or even a full-day expedition out of it. Instead of taking the bus and metro from Troja back to the city centre, you could time it so as to catch a boat trip back (see p58).

Watching the Astronomical Clock (p86)

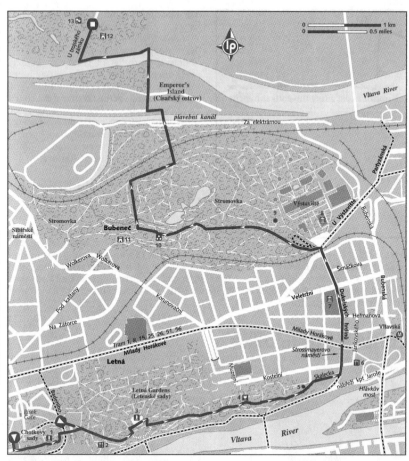

Begin at the Summer Palace (Leto-hrádek) at the eastern end of the Royal Garden (Královská zahrada; p71), north of Prague Castle. A path at the southern end of the Summer Palace leads east into the neighbouring park of Chotkovy sady; in the centre of the park you'll find a little **stone grotto** 1 dedicated to the historical novelist Josef Zeyer and, nearby, a park bench with a superb view over the river and Staré Město. Doing this part of the route is only

WALK FACTS

Start Summer Palace, tram 22, 23 (Letohrádek stop)
End Troja, bus 112 to metro Nádraží Holešovice
Distance 6km
Duration Two to three hours
Fuel stops Hanavský pavilón (p145); La Crêperie (p145)

possible from April to October, as the Royal Garden is closed in winter. An alternative start involves taking tram No 18 to the Chotkova stop, and following Gogolova east into Letná Gardens (Letenské sady). You can visit Chotkovy sady by doubling back across the bridge at the eastern end of the gardens.

A footbridge at the eastern end of the gardens leads across Chotkova and into the huge Letná Gardens, crossing a broad grassy ditch lined with red-brick walls that once formed part of Prague's fortifications. Follow the main path which bears right from the park entrance, but detour further right to visit the **Hanavský pavilón 2** (p145), where you can enjoy a superb panorama and, perhaps, a little lunch.

The path continues along the top of a bluff directly above the Vltava, with great views over the river and the eastern and southern parts of the city, before arriving at a monumental stepped terrace topped by a giant, creaking **metronome 3**. Designed by artist David Černý, the metronome sits on a spot once occupied by a giant statue of Stalin (for more on David Černý, see the boxed texts on p24 and p84).

Continue east along the path at metronome level and you will eventually arrive at Letná's popular **beer garden 4** (see the boxed text, p157), where it's almost compulsory to stop for a cold one. Beyond the beer garden, the path slopes down through pretty flower gardens and along an avenue of plane trees, past the futuristic **Expo 58 Restaurant 5**. Built for the Brussels World Exposition of 1958, and later re-erected here, it is no longer a restaurant but has been beautifully renovated and now houses some fortunate office workers. If the Hanavský Pavilón didn't tempt you into a lunch stop, perhaps cosy **La Crêperie 6** (p145) on nearby Janovského will.

Leave the park and continue downhill on Skalecka, then turn left along busy Dukelských hrdinů. Follow this street north for 400m – stopping to visit the **Veletržní Palace 7** (p109), Prague's premier collection of modern art, if you wish – to the entrance of the Výstaviště exhibition grounds; if you don't fancy walking this section, hop on a tram for a couple of stops (No 5, 12 or 17 will do).

If the Veletržní Palace has whetted your appetite for cultural attractions (or maybe it's just started raining), you might like to detour into the **Lapidárium 8** (p108) for a wander among some of the city's finest sculptures. Otherwise, bear left at the entrance to Výstaviště and follow the path just to the left of the No 5 tram line's terminal loop, passing the dome of the **Prague Planetarium 9** (Planetárium Praha; p108) on your right as you enter the former royal hunting ground, Stromovka (p108).

Follow your nose as the path curves to the left, past people playing *boules* on the gravel verge, and a rundown 1960s 'space-age' children's playground, then bear right towards the pond. Turn left when you reach a broad main path (signposted Dejvice & Bubeneč), which leads between a series of artificial lakes on the right, and a once-grand but now ruined **old restaurant 10** and bandstand on the left. Beyond this you'll see the Renaissance **Místodržitelský Summer Palace 11** perched on a hill to the left, where Bohemian royals used to hang out on their hunting trips to Stromovka. It was remodelled in neogothic style in the early 19th century.

National Theatre (p101)

At the T-junction below the palace, go right (signposted Troja) along an avenue of trees, and follow the path as it curves around to the right. Take the first path on the left, continue through the short tunnel under the railway line, and go up the steps ahead in the distance. Cross the bridge and go left, then right (signposted Zoo; if you're planning on taking the boat back into town, this is where it leaves from). You are now on Emperor's Island (Císařský ostrov); the road leads to a sweeping pedestrian bridge over the main branch of the Vltava, with a canoe slalom course visible upstream (if there's a competition on, you can guarantee there'll be a beer tent there also). At the far end of the pedestrian bridge go left along the riverbank path, and in about 300m you'll reach a parking area; turn right, and the road will lead you to the No 112 bus terminus. On one side of the bus terminus is **Troja Chateau 12** (Trojský zámek; p113), with a museum of wine-making in the cellar; and on the other is the entrance to **Prague Zoo 13** (p113). Take your pick.

VYŠEHRAD & VLTAVA

This walk begins at the ancient citadel of Vyšehrad (p104), and ends with an easy riverside stroll past some of Nové Město's grandest buildings. It's especially nice in the late afternoon or early evening, when the setting sun gilds the grand façades along the Vltava.

You exit from the metro station into a concrete plaza, a favourite haunt of local skaters, beneath the concrete façade of the **Congress Centre 1** (Kongresové centrum). Set off with the centre on your left and a view towards the twin spires of the Church of SS Peter & Paul off to your right. At the far end of the plaza go down the steps and follow Na Bučance left towards the Vyšehrad battlements. Go past the first bastion you come to and turn right to enter the fortress through the **Tábor Gate 2** (Táborská brána). It's soon followed by the scant remains of the **Peak Gate 3** (Špička brána), with the brick-and-stone-lined ditches of the 17th-century fortifications in between. You then pass through the much more impressive **Leopold Gate 4** (Leopoldova brána), which film buffs will recognise from its appearance at the end of the movie *Amadeus,* after Mozart's funeral.

Just beyond the Leopold Gate, take the first path on the left. This leads up to the citadel's southern battlements. Turn right and follow the wall around to the point of the next bastion, where there are park benches with an excellent **view 5** south along the river; this is a good spot for a picnic lunch. Descend from the battlements towards the **Church of SS Peter & Paul 6** (kostel sv Petra a Pavla), and take a turn around the neighbouring Vyšehrad cemetery (Vyšehradský hřbitov; p107), then follow the street, Štulcová, which passes between the church and the restaurant opposite. Go through the gate in the brick wall on the left side of the road, and descend the long staircase towards the river. Turn left along the cobbled lane at its foot, which leads around to the main road next to a **Cubist villa 7** at Rašínovo nábřeží 6–10. Go along the pavement past the villa to a pedestrian crossing just before the tunnel, then cross the road and double back along the far side of the river for a proper view of the Cubist façade.

The rest of the walk follows the river embankment all the way back into the city centre. Just before you pass under the railway bridge, you can admire another fine Cubist house, the **Villa Libušina 8**, on the right.

The embankment to the north of the railway bridge is lined with crumbling Art Nouveau apartment blocks, and a huge Functionalist apartment block with some Cubist-influenced features. As you continue further north the buildings become grander still, and are more likely to have been renovated. Opposite the next bridge is the open space of Palacký Square (Palackého náměstí), backed by the swooping twin spires of Emmaus Monastery (klášter Emauzy; p103), and dominated by the huge, swirlingly romantic **František Palacký Memorial 9**, a monument to the country's best-known historical writer.

WALK FACTS

Start Vyšehrad metro station
End National Theatre, tram 6, 9, 18, 21, 22, 23
Distance 3km
Duration One hour
Fuel stops Na Rybárne (p144); Kavárna Slavia (boxed text p153)

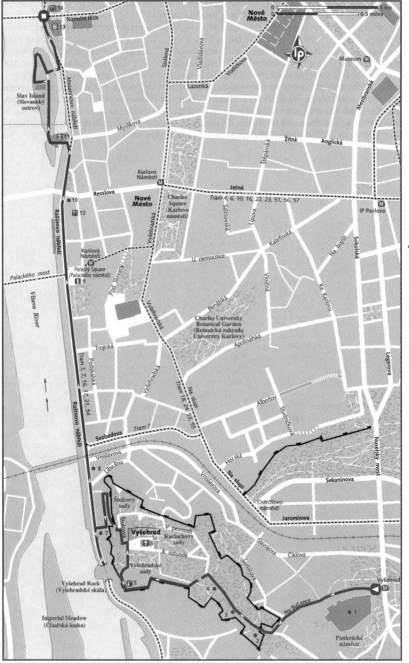

North of the square you pass by ever-grander apartment blocks (see p101 for a detailed description), with the attention-grabbing **Dancing Building** 10 (Tančící dům; p101) in the middle of them all. This is another spot similar to Republic Square where many different ages of Prague architecture come face to face – facing the Dancing Building are grandiose neo-Renaissance and neobaroque apartment buildings and just beyond them, a Gothic water tower and the 1920s **Mánes Gallery** 11 (Galerie Mánes; p102). If you're feeling hungry, the excellent fish restaurant **Na Rybárne** 12 (p144) is just a block east of the Dancing Building.

Go left along the terrace outside the Mánes Gallery, and down the stairs at the western end for a stroll along wooded Slav Island (Slovanský ostrov; p102), before rejoining the mainland via the bridge at the northern end of the island. From here, a few more paces lead to the **National Theatre** 13 (Národní divadlo; p101) and the **Kavárna Slavia** 14 (see the boxed text, p153), its chilled display shelves groaning with cakes.

Eating

Eating

Since the Czech Republic joined the EU in 2004, the steady increase in the number, quality and variety of Prague's restaurants has, if anything, accelerated. You can now enjoy a wide range of international cuisine, from Afghan to Argentinean, Korean to Cantonese, and even – miracle of miracles – expect service with a smile in the majority of eating places.

However, don't let this kaleidoscope of cuisines blind you to the pleasures of good old-fashioned Czech grub. The city's many pubs dish up tasty pork and dumplings, often at very low prices, and a lot of the more upmarket restaurants offer gourmet versions of classic Bohemian dishes such as pork knuckle or roast duck.

Opening Hours

In general, lunch is served from noon to 3pm, and dinner from 6pm to 9pm. Most Prague restaurants, however, are open all day, from 10am or noon to 10pm or 11pm, allowing a laid-back approach to meal times. Cafés are usually open from 8am; see the boxed text on p148 for breakfast recommendations.

How Much?

On average, you can expect to pay around 250Kč to 500Kč per person for a meal in a midrange restaurant, not including drinks. In the more upmarket places you can double that, and in the very best restaurants the bill will be in the area of 1500Kč per person before drinks.

On the other hand, it's possible to eat well for very little. You can fill up in a pub or café for less than 200Kč per person – and that includes a glass of beer.

PRICE GUIDE	
Average cost of dinner for two including a bottle of wine:	
€€€€	more than 2000Kč
€€€	1200Kč to 2000Kč
€€	600Kč to 1199Kč
€	less than 600Kč

Unless otherwise indicated, price ranges quoted in this chapter's restaurant reviews are for main courses at dinner; prices for main courses at lunch are often cheaper.

Booking Tables

It's always a good idea to reserve a table at upmarket restaurants, especially during the high season; almost without fail the phone will be answered by someone who speaks English. That said, we spent months researching in Prague and we mostly did just fine without making any reservations at all.

Tipping

It's pretty much unheard-of for Prague restaurants to include a service charge on your bill (check, though; a few do). In most tourist-area places the helpful message 'Tips Not Included', in English (hint, hint), is printed on the bill. The normal rate for tipping is 10% of the total.

Normal practice in pubs, cafés and midrange restaurants is to round up the bill to the next 10Kč (or the next 20Kč if it's over 200Kč). The usual protocol is for the staff to hand you the bill and for you, as you hand over the money, to tell them the total amount you want to pay with the tip included.

Change is usually counted out starting with the big notes, on down to the smallest coins. If you say *děkuji* (thank you) during this process the staff will stop and assume the rest is a tip.

Self-Catering

There is a wide variety of self-catering options available with *potraviny* (grocery or food shops) and supermarkets everywhere, the best-stocked and priciest being in flashy department stores near the centre. Note that some perishable supermarket food items bear a date of manufacture *(datum výroby)* plus a 'consume-within…' *(spotřebujte do…)* period, whereas others (such as long-life milk) have a stated minimum shelf-life *(minimální trvanlivost)* date, after which the freshness of the product is not guaranteed.

For supermarket supplies, head to the basement of **Kotva** (Map pp268–9; náměstí Republiky; 9am-8pm Mon-Fri, to 6pm Sat, 10am-6pm Sun; metro Náměstí Republiky) or **Tesco** (Map pp272–3; Národní třída 26; 8am-9pm Mon-Fri, 9am-8pm Sat, 10am-8pm Sun; metro Národní Třída). In Malá Strana you'll find the handy **Vacek Bio-Market** (Map pp264–5; Mostecká 3; 7am-10pm Mon-Sat, 10am-10pm Sun), a well-stocked minisupermarket.

The city has several open-air produce markets. The biggest one in the city centre is the tourist-oriented **open-air market** (Map pp268–9; Havelská; 8am-6pm) south of the Old Town Square. More authentic neighbourhood markets – mainly open in the mornings only and closed on Sundays – include the open-air market (Map p275) on Dejvická, near Hradčanská metro station in Dejvice.

In Staré Město, **Bakeshop Praha** (Map pp268–9; Kozí 1; 7am-7pm) is a fantastic bakery that sells some of the best bread in the city, along with pastries, cakes and takeaway sandwiches, salads and quiche. Another good bakery near Old Town Square is **Michelské pekářství** (Map pp268–9; Dlouhá 1; 6.30am-6pm Mon-Fri, 11am-6pm Sun), which sells a wide range of freshly baked breads and freshly prepared sandwiches.

Delicatessens that are good for stocking up on picnic supplies include **Fruits de France** (Map pp272–3; Jindřišská 9, Nové Město; 9.30am-6.30pm Mon-Fri, to 1pm Sat; metro Můstek) which sells French wine, cheese, pastries and more. Next door is the similar **Paris-Praha** (Map pp272–3; Jindřišská 7, Nové Město; 7am-6.30pm Mon-Fri; metro Můstek).

Cellarius (Map pp272–3; Lucerna pasáž, Václavské náměstí 36, Nové Město; 9.30am-9pm Mon-Sat, 3-9pm Sun; metro Můstek) is the place to head if you're looking for Czech and imported wines.

HRADČANY

Most of the restaurants in the castle district are aimed squarely at the tourist crowds, and the whole area becomes pretty quiet in the evenings after the castle closes. The following places, which are a cut above the usual tourist eateries regarding character and cuisine, are worth seeking out – Peklo and U zlaté hrušky for Czech food with some atmosphere, Saté and Malý Buddha for authentic Asian cooking.

MALÝ BUDDHA Map pp264-5   Asian €

220 513 894; Úvoz 46; mains 60-120Kč; noon-10.30pm Tue-Sun; tram 22, 23

Candlelight, incense and a Buddhist shrine characterise this intimate, vaulted restaurant which tries to capture the atmosphere of an oriental tearoom. The menu is a mix of Asian influences, with authentic Thai, Chinese and Vietnamese dishes, many of them vegetarian, and a drinks list that includes ginseng wine, Chinese rose liqueur and all kinds of tea. Credit cards are not accepted.

RESTAURANT PEKLO

Map pp264-5   Modern Czech €€-€€€

220 516 652; Strahovské nádvoří 1/132; mains 300-550Kč; noon-11pm; tram 22, 23

Peklo is an eerily atmospheric restaurant set in a stone-and-brick vaulted wine cellar beneath the grounds of Strahov Monastery (p76) – it was named Peklo (hell) because the gardens above are called 'Paradise'. The menu of Czech and international cuisine is heavy on grilled and roast meat and filled with infernal puns, from filet mignon diavolo (flambéed steak with potato dumplings) to chicken à la Mefisto (roast chicken with caramelised onions and sour cherry sauce).

SATÉ Map pp264-5   Indonesian/Malaysian €

220 514 552; Pohořelec 3; mains 80-125Kč; 11am-10pm; tram 22, 23

Saté is one of Prague's longest-serving Asian restaurants, a no-frills place just five minutes' walk west of the castle serving inexpensive Indonesian and Malaysian

Eating

HRADČANY

dishes such as *nasi goreng* (fried rice with veggies, prawns and egg), beef rendang (coconut-based curry), Javanese beefsteak and a string of tasty vegetarian dishes.

U ZLATÉ HRUŠKY Map pp264-5   Czech €€€€

☎ 220 514 778; Nový svět 3; mains 600-800Kč; ⏰ 11.30am-3pm & 6.30pm-midnight; tram 22, 23

'At The Golden Pear' is a cosy, wood-panelled gourmet's corner, serving beautifully prepared Czech fish, fowl and game dishes. It's frequented as much by locals as by tourists and visiting dignitaries (the Czech foreign ministry is just up the road). In summer you can opt for a table in its leafy *zahradní restaurace* (garden restaurant) across the street.

MALÁ STRANA

You'll be spoilt for choice looking for somewhere to eat in Malá Strana. The tourist crowds are swelled by hungry office workers from the district's many embassies and government offices, and this well-heeled clientele means that there are lots of quality restaurants offering a wide range of cuisines. Many of the best restaurants take advantage of a riverside location, or are perched on a hillside with a view over the city.

BAR BAR Map pp270-1   International €

☎ 257 312 246; Všehrdova 17; mains 90-155Kč; ⏰ noon-midnight Sun-Thu, to 2am Fri & Sat; tram 12, 20, 22, 23

A cosy cellar bar decked with posters and works by local artists, Bar Bar serves up Slovak *halušky* (cheese dumplings with bacon), giant salads and a zillion kinds of tasty crepes, ranging from savoury pancakes stuffed with smoked bacon, sauerkraut and cheese to sweet ones filled with ice cream, walnuts and maple syrup. The food stops at midnight, but drinks go on till 2am on Friday and Saturday.

BOHEMIA BAGEL Map pp270-1   Café €-€€

☎ 257 310 694; Újezd 18; snacks 90-270Kč; ⏰ 7am-midnight Mon-Fri, 8am-midnight Sat & Sun; tram 6, 9, 12, 20, 22, 23

A backpackers' favourite, this internet café offers bagels, quiches, soups, salads and all-you-can-drink soft drinks and coffee, as well as a range of all-American breakfast offerings that includes pancakes and maple

syrup, biscuits and gravy, and bacon, egg and hash browns. There's another branch in Staré Město (p138).

CANTINA Map pp270-1   Mexican €€

☎ 257 317 173; Újezd 38; mains 120-300Kč; ⏰ noon-midnight; tram 6, 9, 12, 20, 22, 23

This homely hacienda, decked out in bleached pine and Brazilian coffee sacks, serves up the most authentic margaritas in Prague – perhaps a little light on the tequila, but nicely iced and with a good zing of fresh lime. The menu is as good as Tex-Mex gets in this town, with big portions of burrito, chimichanga, quesadilla and fajitas with both meat and vegetarian fillings; if the salsa isn't hot enough for you, there are bottles of chilli sauce on the table to add a bit of bite. This place is popular, so get there early, book a table, or be prepared to wait.

COWBOYS Map pp264-5   International €€-€€€

☎ 296 826 107; Nerudova 40; mains 200-500Kč; ⏰ noon-2am; tram 12, 20, 22, 23

Another success from the Kampa Park stable, this sophisticated steakhouse and cocktail bar inhabits a stylishly uplit cavern of red-brick vaults with so-tacky-they're-cool cowhide-patterned banquettes and efficient staff sporting jeans, cowboy hats and smiles the size of Texas. The menu offers meltingly tender steaks and burgers, but also caters for vegetarians with dishes such as Portobello mushroom burgers with cheese, spinach and grilled tomato. There's also an outdoor terrace for those long, sunny, summer afternoons.

EL CENTRO Map pp264-5   Spanish €€

☎ 257 533 343; Maltézské náměstí 9; mains 150-375Kč, tapas 80-200Kč; ⏰ noon-midnight; tram 12, 20, 22, 23

Bright colours, chunky wooden furniture and Spanish-speaking staff lend an authentic air to this classic tapas bar. Here you can

TOP FIVE MALÁ STRANA

- Cantina (above)
- Hergetova Cihelna (opposite)
- Kampa Park (opposite)
- U Maltézských rytířů (p136)
- U Zlaté studně (p137)

nibble on snackettes of chorizo, calamari and *gambas pil-pil* (prawns in garlic) over a bottle of Rioja, or splash out on a full meal of steak, grilled chicken or paella washed down with a jug of sangria. (We can recommend the vegetarian paella.)

HERGETOVA CIHELNA

Map pp264-5   International €€-€€€

☎ 257 535 534; Cihelná 2b; mains 225-550Kč;
⏲ 9am-2am; metro Malostranská

Housed in a converted 18th-century *cihelná* (brickworks), this place enjoys one of Prague's hottest locations with a riverside terrace offering sweeping views of Charles Bridge and the Old Town waterfront. The menu is as sweeping as the view – choose from tempura-fried tuna, chicken fajitas, Czech dishes, burgers and stir-fries, washed down with a bottle of local wine (the Sonberg Rýnský Ryzlink is an excellent Moravian white). Note that there are two wine lists, one reasonably priced, the other eye-poppingly expensive.

KAMPA PARK Map pp264-5   International €€€€

☎ 257 532 685; Na Kampě 8b; mains 600-800Kč;
⏲ 11.30am-1am; tram 12, 20, 22, 23

Kampa Park was a pioneer of Prague's fine-dining scene, opened back in 1994. Since then it has attracted celebrity visitors like moths around a flame – Mick Jagger, Johnny Depp, Lauren Bacall, Robbie Williams and Bill and Hillary Clinton have all overtipped the staff here. The cuisine is as famous as the clientele, from the grilled octopus with roasted broccoli, raisins and capers, to the filet mignon with glazed sweetbread and chanterelles. There's a stylish dining room and roof terrace, but for a really romantic dinner reserve a candlelit table on the cobblestoned terrace, draped in fairy lights, right beside the river, with the lights of Charles Bridge glittering on the water.

LA BASTILLE Map pp270-1   French €€

☎ 257 312 830; Újezd 26; mains 130-400Kč;
⏲ noon-1am; tram 6, 9, 12, 20, 22, 23

Rustic red brick, broad pine floorboards, dark wood tables and timber beams make a cosy setting for this relaxing French-style restaurant and cocktail bar. The menu includes French classics such as onion soup, ratatouille, chicken Provençal and a per-

Diners at Ariana (p137)

fectly cooked trout with almonds, as well as a handful of Czech dishes. Wine, both Czech and French, is available by the glass at reasonable prices.

PÁLFFY PALÁC

Map pp264-5   French/International €€€-€€€€

☎ 257 530 522; Valdštejnská 14; mains 550-750Kč;
⏲ 11am-11pm; metro Malostranská

Housed in the same neobaroque palace as the Prague Conservatoire (music school), the Pálffy is a local institution patronised at lunchtime by staff from the nearby embassies and government offices. The food is good, but the main attraction is the faded grandeur of the setting and the 1st-floor terrace with views of the palace gardens. There are good-value set menus at lunch, offering dishes like baked fillet of trout with herb butter, and pork tenderloin marinated in mustard and honey, available on weekdays only and ranging in price from 350Kč to 700Kč.

RESTAURANT NEBOZÍZEK

Map pp270-1   Czech €€-€€€

☎ 257 315 329; Petřínské sady 411; mains 260-560Kč; ⏲ 11am-11pm; tram 12, 20, 22 or 23, then Petřín funicular

Set in a 17th-century summerhouse halfway up Petřín hill (p83), Nebozízek serves traditional Bohemian dishes, including roast rabbit with tomatoes, potatoes and dumplings, fish dishes such as roast fillet of cod with herb butter and pine nuts, and tasty vegetarian salads in a flower-bedecked conservatory and terrace that enjoys panoramic views across the Vltava River to the Old Town.

RYBÁŘSKÝ KLUB Map pp270-1   Czech €€

☎ 257 534 200; U sovových mlýnů 1; mains 250-420Kč; ☽ noon-11pm; tram 6, 9, 12, 20, 22, 23
If you're looking for riverside dining that doesn't break the bank, Český rybářský svaz, the old Fishermen's Guild, offers a peaceful setting at the southern end of Kampa island, with rustic wooden chairs and benches indoors and a handful of outdoor tables beside the river. The menu specialises in freshwater fish including carp, trout and catfish; try the delicious roasted *candát* (pikeperch) with wild mushroom sauce, or grilled pike with herb butter.

SQUARE Map pp264-5   Mediterranean €€-€€€

☎ 257 532 109; Malostranské náměstí 5; mains 200-500Kč; ☽ 8am-1am; tram 12, 20, 22, 23
This stylish restaurant and cocktail bar occupies the premises of the old Café Radetzky (later renamed Malostranská kavárna), established in 1874 and frequented by Czech literary lions such as Jan Neruda and Franz Kafka. Its latest incarnation specialises in tapas, pasta and seafood, serving dishes such as sea bass ceviche, wild mushroom and *taleggio* lasagne, and crisp battered fish and chips. The cocktail bar mixes a mean *mojito*, too.

SUSHI BAR Map pp270-1   Japanese €€€-€€€€

☎ 603 244 882; Zborovská 49; mains 290-680Kč, sushi boxes 440-680Kč; ☽ noon-10pm; tram 6, 9, 22, 23
This dinky little sushi bar is as compact and neatly ordered as, well…a plate of sushi. The menu includes sashimi (raw fish thinly sliced and elegantly arranged), *maki sushi*

(raw fish and rice rolled in a thin sheet of crisp seaweed) and *nigiri sushi* (a piece of fish or other seafood pressed onto a pad of vinegared rice, with soy sauce for dipping), with sake (rice wine), *mogi-shochu* (Japanese spirit) and Kirin beer to wash it down. It's run by a seafood importer – there's a fresh-fish shop next door – so the sushi is always superbly fresh.

U MALÍŘŮ Map pp264-5   French €€€€

☎ 257 530 000; Maltézské náměstí 11; mains 800-1100Kč; ☽ 11.30am-midnight; tram 12, 20, 22, 23
'The Painter's House' is an opulent shrine to *haute cuisine*, all starched linen, shiny silverware and stiff-backed waiters, set in a vaulted 15th-century dining room filled with colourful frescoes (the painted decoration dates only from the 1930s). Opinions vary as to whether the standard of the food is as consistently high as the prices – the lobster served with scallops and Béarnaise sauce (2400Kč per person) is going to be a big letdown if it's the head chef's night off – but when it's good it's very, very good.

U MALTÉZSKÝCH RYTÍŘŮ

Map pp264-5   Czech/International €€
☎ 257 530 075; Prokopská 10; mains 250-350Kč; ☽ 1-11pm; tram 12, 20 22, 23
'At the Maltese Knights' is a cosy and romantic olde-worlde restaurant, with candle-lit tables tucked into niches in the Gothic vaults downstairs (the ground-floor tables are much less atmospheric). Typical dishes include roast wild boar with rosehip sauce, and grilled fillet of pikeperch rolled in vine leaves with caper sauce; it's a popular spot, so book well ahead.

U MODRÉ KACHNIČKY

Map pp270-1   Czech €€€
☎ 257 320 308; Nebovidská 6; mains 385-580Kč; ☽ noon-4pm & 6.30-11.30pm; tram 12, 20, 22, 23
A chintzy, baroque hunting lodge hidden away on a quiet side street, 'At the Blue Duckling' is a plush, old-fashioned place with quiet, candlelit nooks perfect for a romantic dinner. The menu is heavy on traditional Bohemian duck, game and fish dishes, with selections such as roast duck with walnut stuffing and potato dumplings, or rump of venison with rosehip sauce and potato pancakes.

TOP FIVE ROMANTIC RESTAURANTS

- Kampa Park (p135)
- La Provence (p140)
- U Maltézských rytířů (right)
- U modré kachničky (right)
- U zlaté hrušky (opposite)

U ZLATÉ STUDNĚ

Map pp264-5   International €€€€

☎ 257 533 322; U Zlaté studně 4; mains 620-980Kč;
🕑 noon-4pm & 6-11pm; metro Malostranská

Perched atop a Renaissance mansion within a champagne-cork's pop of the castle, 'At the Golden Well' enjoys one of finest settings in Prague. Weather will dictate whether you sit in the red-and-gold dining room, or head upstairs to the outdoor terrace – both command a stunning panorama across the red-tiled rooftops of Malá Strana. The menu, which has French, Mediterranean and Asian influences, includes dishes such as sushi-style marinated tuna, grilled sea bass with braised fennel and rocket, and confit of duck with braised red cabbage.

STARÉ MĚSTO

The Old Town is littered with tourist traps, especially around Old Town Square, but there are also plenty of excellent restaurants to discover. The maze of streets leading away from Old Town Square contains many hidden gems, while the swanky strip of Pařížská boasts a more obvious string of stylish, upmarket eateries. The classic Staré Město dining room is in a brick-lined cellar – you'll soon become a connoisseur of subterranean décor.

AMBIENTE PASTA FRESCA

Map pp268-9 Italian €€

☎ 224 230 244; Celetná 11; mains 180-350Kč;
🕑 11am-midnight; metro Náměstí Republiky

Slick styling and service with a smile complement an extensive menu at this busy Italian restaurant. Choose from dishes such as melt-in-the-mouth *carpaccio* of beef, piquant spaghetti *aglio-olio* with chilli and crisp pancetta, and rich creamy risotto with *porcini*, along with a wide range of Italian and Czech wines. There's a long, narrow, café at street level, but you'll find a more formal, intimate cellar restaurant located down below.

AMBIENTE PIZZA NUOVA

Map pp268-9   Italian €€

☎ 221 803 308; Revoluční 1; mains 220Kč;
🕑 11.30am-11.30pm; metro Náměstí Republiky

The latest idea from the Ambiente team is this cool 1st-floor space next door to the

TOP FIVE STARÉ MĚSTO

- Bodeguita del Medio (p138)
- Danico (p139)
- Orange Moon (p140)
- U Zavoje (p141)
- V zátiší (p141)

Kotva shopping centre, filled with big tables and banquettes with picture windows overlooking náměstí Republiky. For a fixed price (220Kč) you get an all-you-can-eat deal – either help yourself from the salad and antipasti buffet, or choose from the hot pasta dishes and pizzas offered up by a band of wandering waiters (buffet and pizza-pasta combined costs 370Kč). Wine by the glass is around 65Kč.

ARIANA Map pp268-9   Afghan €-€€

☎ 222 323 438; Rámová 6; mains 110-250Kč;
🕑 11am-11pm; tram 5, 8, 14

Ariana is a welcoming little place decked out with Persian rugs and photos of Kabul, with Asian music wailing in the background. It serves a range of unusual Afghani dishes, including *ashak* (a sort of ravioli containing chopped leeks, with a rich sauce of minced lamb and yogurt), various lamb and chicken kebabs and tasty vegetarian specialities, served with light, fluffy *nan-i-dashi* (hot bread) on the side.

AU GOURMAND Map pp268-9   Café €

☎ 222 329 060; Dlouhá 10; snacks 60-120Kč;
🕑 7am-7pm Mon-Fri, 8.30am-7pm Sat, 9am-7pm Sun; metro Staroměstská

Au Gourmand is a French-style patisserie and café gaily decked out in colourful 19th-century tiles and wrought-iron furniture. It offers baguettes, pastries and a joyously bewildering array of cakes, and its *caffe latte* is among the best in town.

BEAS VEGETARIAN DHABA

Map pp268-9   Vegetarian/Indian €

☎ 603 035 727; Týnská 19; mains 80-100Kč;
🕑 10am-8pm Mon-Sat, to 6pm Sun; metro Náměstí Republiky

Tucked away in a courtyard off Týnská, this friendly and informal little restaurant offers vegetarian curries (cooked by chefs from North India) served with rice, salad, chutneys and raita; an extra 20Kč gets you a drink and dessert. It's tasty, good value, and a great place to meet Czechs of an alternative bent.

BELLEVUE Map pp272-3 — French €€€€
☎ 224 221 443; Smetanovo nábřeží 18; mains 600-900Kč; ⏰ noon-3pm & 5.30-11pm Mon-Sat, 11am-3.30pm & 7-11pm Sun; tram 17, 21
Snappy service, crisp linen and the clink of crystal accompany top-notch *nouvelle cuisine* at this long-standing French favourite, famed for its outdoor terrace tables with a majestic view of the river, Charles Bridge and the castle. Sunday features a champagne brunch (895Kč) with live jazz from 11am to 3.30pm; make sure you book a table.

BODEGUITA DEL MEDIO
Map pp268-9 — Cuban €€-€€€
☎ 224 813 922; Kaprova 5; mains 300-550Kč; ⏰ 10am-2am; metro Staroměstská
The Prague incarnation of the Havana cocktail-bar and restaurant chain brings a whiff of Hemingway to the Old Town streets, with chunky wooden tables, ceiling fans and cigars. And, of course, classic *mojito* cocktails (well, it did invent them, after all). The seafood is excellent, especially the zingy *gambas Punta Arenas* (prawns with chilli, lime and ginger), the cappuccinos are froth-topped caffeine bombs, and the pavement tables catch the sun at lunchtime…perfecto.

BOHEMIA BAGEL Map pp268-9 — Café €-€€
☎ 224 81 25 60; Masná 2; mains 90-270Kč; ⏰ 7am-midnight Mon-Fri, 8am-midnight Sat & Sun; metro Náměstí Republiky
The second branch of the popular café in Malá Strana (p134) is a big, bustling place with friendly staff, diner-style booths and a tiny courtyard with outdoor tables, and offers a range of bagels, sandwiches, grills and breakfasts washed down with American-style filter coffee (complete with free refills). Place your order at the counter.

CAFÉ-RESTAURANT METAMORPHIS
Map pp268-9 Italian/Czech €-€€
☎ 221 771 068; Týnský dvůr, Malá Štupartská 5; mains 100-250Kč; ⏰ 9am-1am; metro Náměstí Republiky
Metamorphis is the place to go if you want romantic outdoor dining (April to October)

TOP FIVE VEGETARIAN RESTAURANTS

- Albio (p142)
- Beas Vegetarian Dhaba (p137)
- Café FX (p147)
- Country Life (below)
- Restaurace Akropolis (p146)

with a view of the Týn Church spires, but without the crowds and inflated prices of places on Old Town Square. The menu is mainly Italian, including good pizzas and pasta dishes, and gorgeous ice-cream sundaes. The more formal restaurant (mains 150Kč to 400Kč) in the atmospheric Romanesque cellar downstairs offers crisp linen, candlelight and attentive service.

CHEZ MARCEL Map pp268-9 — French €€
☎ 222 315 676; Haštalská 12; mains 150-350Kč; ⏰ 8am-1am Mon-Fri, 9am-1am Sat & Sun; tram 5, 8, 14
There's an authentic French bistro atmosphere at this peaceful backstreet café-bar, from the blue haze of cigarette smoke hanging over the dark wood tables to the copies of *Le Monde* and *Le Figaro* and the *escargots* on the menu. Stick to the simple dishes – steak au poivre, grilled chicken, quiche lorraine, the daily specials – and you won't be disappointed.

COUNTRY LIFE Map pp268-9 — Vegetarian €
☎ 224 213 366; Melantrichova 15; mains 75-150Kč; ⏰ 9am-8.30pm Mon-Thu, to 6pm Fri, 11am-8.30pm Sun; metro Můstek
Prague's first-ever health-food shop, opened in 1991, Country Life is an all-vegan cafeteria and sandwich bar offering inexpensive salads, sandwiches, pizzas, vegetarian goulash, sunflower-seed burgers, soy drinks etc. There is plenty of seating in the courtyard out back, but it gets crowded at lunchtime, so go early or buy sandwiches to go.

DAHAB
Map pp268-9 — North African/Middle Eastern €€
☎ 224 827 375; Dlouhá 33; mains 200-400Kč; ⏰ noon-1am; tram 5, 8, 14
Dahab is a dimly lit North African *souq* scattered with oriental rugs and cushions

where you can lounge on a divan and sip Moroccan mint tea to an oriental-jazz-ragga soundtrack. The menu ranges from baklava and other sweet snacks to more substantial couscous, *tajine* (meat and vegetable stew), lamb and chicken dishes, and there are teas from India, China and Turkey. Or just kick back with a hookah (hubble-bubble pipe); 175Kč gets you a chunk of perfumed baccy that'll last around 45 minutes.

DANICO Map pp268-9   Italian €€
☎ 222 311 807; Dlouhá 21; mains 150-400Kč; ⏱ 11am-1am; tram 5, 8, 14

Soon after it opened in 2005 DaNico was being touted as the best Italian restaurant in Prague, and it's easy to see why – fresh produce and ingredients imported from Italy, classic Mediterranean dishes such as carpaccio of smoked swordfish, risotto with fresh clams and zucchini, fillet of veal in a herb crust, and homemade tiramisu, a range of regional Italian wines (expensive!), and a warm, welcoming atmosphere. Bookings necessary for Friday and Saturday evenings.

DINITZ Map pp268-9   International €€
☎ 222 313 308; Bílkova 12; mains 150-350Kč; ⏱ 11am-11pm; tram 17

Only five minutes' walk north of Old Town Square, but feeling way off the beaten tourist track, Dinitz is a hidden treasure, a cellar sandwich bar and restaurant with a hint of Art Deco design and some of the best-value food in the Old Town. As well as Prague's best roast-beef sandwich (with mustard, aioli, rocket and roast peppers), the menu

offers inventive salads, jui[...] pasta, and the Israeli chef a[...] Eastern flavour with dishes [...] kebabs with tahini, hummus [...] ised onion, pistachios and hor[...] bread, and Lebanese salad.

DIVINIS Map pp268-9   Italian €€€
☎ 224 808 318; Týnská 19; mains 300-600Kč; ⏱ 4pm-2am; metro Náměstí Republiky

This designer wine bar has an engaging décor in shades of cream enlivened with candlelight and splashes of crimson, pale wood tables with chairs zipped into neat linen covers, and a homely clutter of shelves stacked with wine bottles, kitchen implements and chunky wooden sculptures. The uncomplicated menu offers a choice of a dozen starters and main courses, from prosciutto with rocket and parmesan to grilled sea bass with tomato and basil, while the wine list extends to more than 200 labels.

EBEL COFFEE HOUSE Map pp268-9   Café €
☎ 224 895 788; Týn 2; mains 100-165Kč; ⏱ 9am-10pm; metro Náměstí Republiky

If you can't face the watery instant coffee served up with your hotel breakfast, head to Ebel for a jolt of full-fat, 98-octane arabica. Munchies on offer include yummy toasted bagels with herby cream cheese, quiches, carrot cake and chocolate brownies. Only a few minutes' walk from Old Town Square, this branch is in a top people-watching spot in a corner of the Týn courtyard (p86); there are several other branches across the city.

Goods for sale at Country Life (opposite)

pp268-9   French €€€€

☎ 222 002 770; Obecní dům, náměstí Republiky 5; mains 700-950Kč; ⏲ noon-4pm & 6-11pm; metro Náměstí Republiky

The French Restaurant in the Municipal House (p93) is a stunning Art Nouveau dining room offering gourmet cuisine, from caviar and foie gras to lobster bisque and saddle of veal. It's hugely popular with visitors, so book to avoid disappointment. The à la carte menu is complemented by a two-/three-course set lunch menu for 1050/1150Kč. Next door is an equally opulent café, Kavárna Obecní Dům (see the boxed text, p153).

KÁVA KÁVA KÁVA Map pp272-3   Café €

☎ 224 228 862; Platýz pasáž, Národní třída 37; snacks 30-110Kč; ⏲ 7am-10pm Mon-Fri, 9am-10pm Sat & Sun; metro Národní Třída

Tucked away in the peaceful Platýz courtyard, this American-owned café has some of the best coffee in town – the *grande cappuccino* is big enough to bathe in – and a selection of bagels, croissants, chocolate brownies, carrot cake and other goodies. There's also internet access via desktop computers and a wi-fi hotspot. You can find a second branch in Smíchov (p148).

KLUB ARCHITEKTŮ

Map pp272-3   International €€

☎ 224 401 214; Betlémské náměstí 5; mains 150-300Kč; ⏲ 11.30am-11.30pm; metro Národní Třída

Trust an architects' society to combine a candlelit 12th-century cellar with exposed industrial ducting and modern metalwork… whatever, they're doing something right, as this place is always busy. The extensive menu caters for vegetarians and vegans as well as carnivores but, as in any place with a big menu, we recommend you go for the daily specials. The garlic soup is wicked.

KOLKOVNA Map pp268-9   Czech €€

☎ 224 819 701; V Kolkovně 8; mains 160-400Kč; ⏲ 9am-midnight; metro Staroměstská

Owned and operated by the Pilsner Urquell brewery, Kolkovna is a stylish, modern take on the traditional Prague beer hall, with décor by top Czech designers and posh (but hearty) versions of classic Czech dishes such as goulash, roast duck and roast pork, including the Czech favourite pork and dumplings (the dish of the day is only 95Kč). All washed down with exquisite Urquell beer, of course.

LA PROVENCE Map pp268-9   French €€€-€€€€

☎ 257 535 050; Štupartská 9; mains 400-800Kč; ⏲ noon-midnight; metro Náměstí Republiky

With its dark-wood beams, cushion-strewn benches, dim yellow lighting and shelves crammed with cooking implements, La Provence makes a good fist of passing itself off as a French country kitchen. The menu matches the décor, ranging from *fricassée d'escargots* to *cassoulet du Midi*. In the evening, when candlelight and soft piano music add to the atmosphere, it's an ideal spot for a romantic *tête-à-tête*.

LARY FARY Map pp268-9   International €€-€€€

☎ 222 320 154; Dlouhá 30; mains 200-500Kč; ⏲ 11am-midnight; tram 5, 8, 14

This intriguing restaurant boasts several sections with different décor, from the sushi bar to the brick-vaulted cellar by way of the 'romantic' room (decadent red and deep chocolate brown set off with Moroccan mirrors, candlelight and textile lampshades). The menu wanders around the globe, with Asian, Czech and Mediterranean dishes as well as hearty steaks and salads, but the speciality is the 'skewer', a giant kebab served rather theatrically on a dagger dangling from a wrought-iron stand – choose from chicken, pork, beef, fish or veggie.

LES MOULES Map pp268-9   Belgian €€-€€€

☎ 222 315 022; Pařížská 19; mains 300-500Kč; ⏲ 8.30am-midnight Mon-Fri, 9am-midnight Sat & Sun; tram 17

This impressive, wood-panelled, Belgian-style brasserie serves up steaming pans of mussels in a range of sauces, from traditional *marinière* (white wine, cream and garlic) to Thai-style curry, as well as steaks, pork ribs, *boeuf bourguignon* and lobster fresh from the *vivier* (live tank). The bar offers a selection of Belgian beers, including Leffe and Hoegaarden on tap.

ORANGE MOON Map pp268-9   Asian €€

☎ 222 325 119; Rámová 5; mains 165-230Kč; ⏲ 11.30am-11.30pm; tram 5, 8, 14

Buddhist statues, Eastern carved-wood panels, paper lanterns and warm, sunny colours make for a welcoming combination at this popular Asian restaurant. The menu is mostly Thai, with authentically spicy *tom yum kai* (hot and sour chicken broth) laden with smouldering chillis, crispy *pow pyet* (spring rolls) and fragrant *kaeng phed kai* (chicken in red curry). There are also some Indonesian, Burmese and Indian dishes, and bottles of Singha beer to take the edge off that chilli burn.

RASOI Map pp268-9   Indian €€-€€€
☎ 222 328 400; Dlouhá 13; mains 200-500Kč;
🕑 4-11pm; tram 5, 8, 14
Relax with a Singapore Sling in the Bombay cocktail bar, then head down to Rasoi, a posh Indian restaurant with a refined, semi-formal atmosphere, in a cellar that's been tarted up to look like a maharajah's mansion. The cuisine is certainly good enough for royalty, though you're more likely to be sharing with an appreciative crowd of expat Brits hankering after authentic tandoori chicken, *rogan josh* and chicken jalfrezi.

RED, HOT & BLUES
Map pp268-9   American/Tex-Mex €€
☎ 222 314 639; Jakubská 12; mains 180-480Kč;
🕑 9am-11pm; metro Náměstí Republiky
This long-established New Orleans–style restaurant pulls in the crowds with great nachos, burgers, burritos and shrimp creole, plus some wicked desserts. It also serves a range of Western breakfasts, including pancakes and maple syrup, and a full British fry-up; the 'Home Run Special' (bacon, eggs, hash browns, pancakes and toast) will soak up the heaviest hangover, and lay a firm foundation for further debauchery.

REYKJAVÍK
Map pp268-9   Seafood/International €€-€€€
☎ 222 221 218; Karlova 20; mains 200-550Kč;
🕑 11am-midnight; metro Staroměstská
Reykjavík has an appealingly old-fashioned dining room, all dark wood, gleaming brass, dim globes and candlelight, with musical instruments hung all over the place. Though billed as an Icelandic restaurant the menu is not noticeably Scandinavian (except for the salted cod) – as well as seafood specialities such as deep-fried cod and chips, and grilled salmon with rice pilaf, there's succulent seared tuna, barbecue ribs, and a selection of steaks and burgers.

SIAM-I-SAN Map pp268-9   Thai €€€
☎ 224 814 099; Valentínská 11; mains 350-550Kč;
🕑 10am-midnight; metro Staroměstská
This unusual little restaurant is tucked away at the back of the glassware boutique Arzenal (p184), in a colourful room created by the local architect and designer Boris Šípek – it has a dramatically uplit bar, grey, orange and yellow décor, colourful print tablecloths, and arty glass *objets* from the neighbouring shop. Even the coffee cups have a designer touch, with an asymmetric sway reminiscent of the Dancing Building. The cuisine is authentic Thai – some of the best Thai food in Prague – with a wide range of dishes, including many vegetarian ones.

U ZAVOJE Map pp268-9   French €€-€€€
☎ 226 006 120; Havelská 25; mains 350-500Kč;
🕑 11am-midnight; metro Můstek
This gourmet complex, set in a beautiful old passageway between Havelská and Kožná streets, includes a wine bar, restaurant, coffee house and delicatessen, all dedicated to fine food and French and Czech wines. The menu concentrates on fresh seasonal produce, with springtime offerings including exquisite creamed pea soup with San Daniele prosciutto and baby carrots, and tender, juicy grilled chicken with vivid green fava beans and a velvety red pepper sauce.

V ZÁTIŠÍ
Map pp272-3   International/Modern Czech €€€€
☎ 222 221 155, Liliová 1; mains 500-800Kč;
🕑 noon-3pm & 5.30-11pm; tram 17, 18
'Still Life' is one Prague's top restaurants, famed for the quality of its cuisine. There are two dining rooms, one classically decorated in shades of ochre, with wrought-iron chairs and lamp fittings, the other more modern, with a dark wood floor and bold stripes of red and orange. Of the dozen or so main courses on offer, four are seafood and three are vegetarian; there are also gourmet versions of traditional Czech dishes – the crispy roast duckling with red cabbage and herb dumplings is superb. There's a two-course lunch menu, including one drink (695Kč), or you can lash out on the five-course degustation menu (1575Kč; plus 875Kč extra for wines to match the dishes).

Eating

STARÉ MĚSTO

NOVÉ MĚSTO

The New Town has an eclectic collection of eating places, with cafés and traditional Czech pubs as well as a range of international restaurants. The main eating streets are Wenceslas Square and Na příkopě, lined with restaurants offering cuisines that cross the world from Italy to India and Argentina to Japan; there are also lots of less obvious eateries hidden in the back streets between Wenceslas Square and the river.

TOP FIVE NOVÉ MĚSTO

- Dinitz Café (right)
- El Gaucho (right)
- Kogo (opposite)
- La Perle de Prague (opposite)
- Suterén (p144)

ALBIO Map pp268-9 Vegetarian €-€€

☎ 222 325 414; Truhlářská 18; mains 100-260Kč; ⊗ 11am-10pm; metro Náměstí Republiky

This family-friendly wholefood restaurant is as bright and fresh as an Alpine morning, decked out in blonde wood and rustic timber set off with salmon-pink tablecloths and seat-cushions. It sources all its food from local organic farmers and operates its own on-site bakery, shop and advice counter offering tips on organic food and healthy eating. The menu includes fish, vegetarian and vegan dishes, such as vegetable tempura with horseradish dip, and buckwheat pancakes filled with onion mash and grilled zucchini, and there are organic wines and unpasteurised beer so you can work up a wholesome hangover.

BRANICKÝ SKLÍPEK Map pp272-3 Czech €-€€

U Purkmistra; ☎ 224 237 103; Vodičkova 2; mains 70-270Kč; ⊗ 9am-11pm Mon-Fri, 11am-11pm Sat & Sun; metro Můstek

This is one of the few rough-and-ready, old-fashioned beer halls left in central Prague, serving meaty, good-value Czech dishes washed down with cheap beer. Menus and staff are Czech only, which puts off most tourists, but persevere – this is the real deal, and serves up the finest pork, dumplings and sauerkraut in town (look for *purk-mistrová mísa* on the menu). Nonsmokers, beware – the atmosphere is smoky enough to kipper a truckload of herring.

BUFFALO BILL'S Map pp272-3 Tex-Mex €€

☎ 224 948 624; Vodičkova 9; mains 150-390Kč; ⊗ noon-midnight; tram 3, 9, 14, 24

Mosey on down to Bill's saloon for a touch of the Old West – dark wood panelling and brass rails, tall bar stools and bentwood chairs, wagon wheels, John Wayne posters and photos of Native Americans. The menu bulges with Tex-Mex classics, from nachos and enchiladas to barbecue ribs and fajitas (not quite authentic, but pretty good by Prague standards), with jugs of frozen margaritas to slake that midsummer thirst.

COUNTRY LIFE Map pp272-3 Vegetarian €

☎ 224 247 280; Jungmannova 1; mains 75-150Kč; ⊗ 9.30am-6.30pm Mon-Thu, 9am-6pm Fri; tram 3, 9, 14, 24

Country Life is a cafeteria-style health-food restaurant with all-vegan food and buffet service – load up your plate, and pay by weight (that's right! you weigh in at the till). There are only four tables at this branch, which caters mainly to the takeaway trade – if you want a better chance of a seat, head for the branch in Staré Město (p138).

DINITZ CAFÉ Map pp268-9 International €€

☎ 222 313 308; Na poříčí 12; mains 200-400Kč; ⊗ 9am-3am; metro Náměstí Republiky

This cool, Art Deco coffee house – a branch of the original Dinitz restaurant (p139) – harks back to the sophisticated café society of the 1920s, with fine food and drink served from breakfast till 2am, and live music every night from 9pm – try to get a table on mezzanine overlooking the stage. The menu focuses on fresh food, simply prepared, with influences ranging from Mediterranean to Middle Eastern by way of British – don't miss the city's finest fish and chips, fried in crisp beer-and-parsley batter with crunchy, golden fries and delicious herb aioli.

EL GAUCHO Map pp272-3 Argentinean €€€-€€€€

☎ 221 629 410; Václavské náměstí 11; mains 450-950Kč; ⊗ 11.30am-midnight; metro Můstek

El Gaucho is carnivore heaven – a big, rustic, rug-draped basement serving a range of charcoal-grilled steaks with *chimichuri* sauce (oil, garlic and herbs), and probably the most succulent and tasty hamburgers in town, with side orders of crisp, perfectly cooked French fries. The service is cheerful

Outdoor dining, Nové Město

and a good range of wines is available by the glass. On summer evenings, tables filled with conversation and candlelight spill over into the leafy courtyard.

LA PERLE DE PRAGUE
Map pp272-3   French €€€-€€€€

☎ 221 984 160; Rašínovo nábřeží 80; mains 500-750Kč; ⏰ noon-2pm & 7-10.30pm Tue-Sat, 7-10.30pm Mon; metro Karlovo Náměstí

Located on the 7th floor of the spectacular Dancing Building (p101), La Perle de Prague's dining room and outdoor terrace offer stunning views across the river to Malá Strana and Prague Castle. The cuisine is French, with the accent on seafood and meat dishes – nothing for veggies here – and the atmosphere is crisply formal. Some visitors feel the dinner menu is overpriced, but the two-course business lunch (490Kč) is good value.

MILLHOUSE SUSHI
Map pp268-9   Japanese €€€

☎ 222 716 003; Slovanský dům, Na příkopě 22; portions 80-420Kč; ⏰ 11am-11pm; metro Náměstí Republiky

A chef who earned his stripes working at a five-star hotel in China supplies the conveyor belt with beautifully arranged *nigiri*, *maki* and *temaki* sushi and sashimi in this bright and appealing little sushi bar. Keep an eye on the number of dishes piling up if you don't want to break the bank, or come along between 11am and 5pm on Sunday when they do an all-you-can-eat deal for 680Kč.

MIYABI
Map pp272-3   Japanese €€

☎ 296 233 102; Navrátilova 10; mains 160-420Kč; ⏰ 11am-11pm Mon-Fri, noon-11pm Sat & Sun; tram 3, 9, 14

Miyabi is a relaxed, café-style Japanese restaurant with minimalist décor and modern art on the walls – a refreshing change from more formal Japanese places. There's a small sushi menu, and main courses that include tempura (prawns and pieces of vegetables dipped in batter and deep-fried), *sakana no amiyaki* (grilled salmon marinated in saki) and *karaage* (grilled chicken marinated with ginger). The good-value set Japanese lunch is served from 11am to 2pm Monday to Friday.

and efficient, but watch out when the waiter asks if you'd like a large beer – large here means a whole litre.

HOT
Map pp272-3   Asian/International €€€

☎ 222 247 240; Václavské náměstí 45; mains 360-650Kč; ⏰ 7am-1am; metro Muzeum

To use an Australian expression, this place is up itself. But with good reason. It looks fantastic – an old Art Deco space has been transformed with the use of stainless steel, polished marble and leather, the neutral tones spiced up with touches of zingy red that hold the whole thing together. It has a great location – halfway up Wenceslas Square. And the food is top notch – an inventive mix of Asian and European dishes (the honey and soy glazed salmon with wasabi mayonnaise is superb). If only the staff could stop checking themselves in the mirror long enough to take your order…

KOGO
Map pp268-9   Italian €€

☎ 221 451 259; Slovanský dům, Na příkopě 10; pizzas 150-250Kč, mains 200-450Kč; ⏰ 9am-midnight; metro Náměstí Republiky

Chic and businesslike, but also relaxed and child-friendly (highchairs provided), Kogo is a stylish restaurant serving top-notch pizza, pasta, steak and seafood – the rich, tomatoey *zuppa di pesce* (fish soup) is delicious –

NA RYBÁRNĚ Map pp272-3   Fish & Seafood €€

☎ 224 918 885; Gorazdova 17; mains 100-400Kč;
🕑 9.30am-11pm; tram 17, 21

This unassuming little fish restaurant has been around for almost a century and has seen more than a few celebrity diners, ranging from writer Karel Čapek to ex-president Václav Havel, Rolling Stone Mick Jagger and former US secretary of state Madeleine Albright. The menu here offers everything from salmon and tuna to cuttlefish and tiger prawns, but the best dishes are the simplest and most traditional – trout with herb butter, and daily specials such as baked carp or grilled eel with lemon butter.

PIZZERIA KMOTRA Map pp272-3   Pizza €

☎ 224 934 100; V jirchářích 12; pizza 85-130Kč;
🕑 11am-midnight; metro Národní Třída

One of Prague's oldest and best pizzerias, 'The Godmother' can rustle up more than two dozen varieties of pizza, from margherita to marinara, cooked in a genuine wood-fired pizza oven. Sit beside the bar upstairs, or head down to the basement where you can watch the chef slinging pizza dough in the open kitchen. It gets busy here after 8pm, so try to snag a table before then.

SIAM ORCHID Map pp268-9   Thai €€

☎ 222 319 410; Na poříčí 21; mains 160-280Kč;
🕑 10am-10pm; tram 3, 8, 24, 26

The setting – a scatter of plastic tables and chairs on a 1st-floor balcony hidden up a passage beside a department store – looks none too promising, but this tiny restaurant, tucked away beside a Thai massage studio, offers some of the city's most authentic Thai cuisine. From the crisp, grease-free po-pia thot (spring rolls with pork and black mushrooms) and succulent kai sa-te (chicken satay) to the fiery kaeng khiao wan kai (chicken in green curry with basil), pretty much everything on the menu is a delight.

SUTERÉN Map pp272-3   International €€€

☎ 224 933 657; Masarykovo nábřeží 26; mains 350-500Kč; 🕑 11.30am-midnight Mon-Sat; tram 17, 21

'The Basement' is a beautiful cellar space, where the modern detailing complements the old red-brick and wooden beams

perfectly – cream linen chairs, set at gleaming black tables with a single, deep-pink rose in the middle of each one, are ranked around a circular glass bar with a colourful marine aquarium along one wall. The Suterén menu leans toward seafood, beef and game, and the signature dishes take their inspiration from cocktails – the 'salmon mojito', for example, has the fish marinated in rum and lime juice, served with tart lime jam and sweet rum-and-mint sauce.

TAJ MAHAL Map pp272-3   Indian €€

☎ 224 225 566; Škrétova 10; mains 200-300Kč;
🕑 noon-11pm Mon-Fri, 1-11pm Sat & Sun; metro Muzeum

Hidden away behind the National Museum (p100), the Taj Mahal is one of the city's best Indian restaurants, complete with the live sitar-twanging in the evenings. There are separate smoking and nonsmoking dining rooms, and although the food here is delicious the atmosphere can occasionally be a little formal and restrained. Cobra and Kingfisher beers from India are available, and there is a sampler menu (495Kč for seven dishes) that changes daily.

BEYOND THE CENTRE

Eateries in the outer suburbs are for the most part less touristy and less expensive than their city-centre counterparts, catering to a clientele of local residents and expats. You'll find some great-value dining here, and have more chance of mixing with real Praguers.

Vyšehrad

JAMES COOK Map pp280-1   International €-€€

☎ 224 936 652; Oldřichova 14; mains 120-260Kč;
🕑 11am-11pm Mon-Fri, noon-11pm Sat & Sun; tram 7, 18, 24

Terracotta tiles, earth-toned walls and timber beams draped with fishing nets and nautical knick-knacks lend a vaguely exotic air to this unassuming place in the shadow of Vyšehrad's citadel. The menu ranges across the globe, promising kangaroo steaks and roast shark as well as more familiar Asian, American and European dishes. There are no less than eight vegetarian options.

RIO'S VYŠEHRAD

Map pp280-1   International €€-€€€

☎ 224 922 156; Štulcova 2; mains 200-500Kč; ☾ 11am-midnight; metro Vyšehrad

Located opposite the Church of SS Peter & Paul in the Vyšehrad fortress, this is an attractive modern restaurant set in an ancient building. There's a nautical theme indoors, with jaunty blue and yellow tables and chairs, and model ships and lifebelts all over the place. But the main attraction is the garden, a lovely spot for an outdoor lunch or dinner. The menu is mostly steak and chicken, but unusually there's an entire section devoted to tartare and *carpaccio* (both made with raw ingredients) – from classic beef *carpaccio* with fresh basil and parmesan, to tuna *carpaccio* with wasabi.

U NEKLANA Map pp280-1   Czech €-€€

☎ 224 916 051; Neklanova 30; mains 100-200Kč; ☾ 11am-midnight; tram 7, 18, 24

U Neklana is a welcoming local pub nestled in the corner of one of Prague's coolest apartment buildings, a Cubist classic dating from 1915. Decked out in the cheerful red colours of the Budvar brewery, it dishes up hearty Czech fare such as potato and mushroom soup served in a scooped-out loaf of rye bread (the menu is in English and German as well as Czech), and there's a hits-of-the-'80s jukebox providing a suitably retro soundtrack.

Holešovice & Bubeneč
HANAVSKÝ PAVILÓN

Map pp268-9   Czech/International €€€€

☎ 233 323 641; Letenské sady, Bubeneč; mains 600-900Kč; ☾ 11am-1am, terrace till 11pm; tram 18

Perched on a terrace high above the river, this ornate, neobaroque pavilion dating from 1891 houses a smart restaurant with a postcard-perfect view of the Vltava bridges – from April to September you can dine on the outdoor terrace. There's a three-course set menu (from 520Kč) of Czech classics.

HONG KONG Map pp276-7   Chinese €€

☎ 233 376 209; Letenské náměstí 5, Holešovice; mains 150-300Kč; ☾ 10.30am-11pm; tram 1, 8, 15, 25, 26

Impressively gaudy décor, with ornately carved wooden panels, an illuminated,

TOP FIVE RIVERSIDE RESTAURANTS

- Bellevue (p138)
- Hergetova Cihelna (p135)
- Kampa Park (p135)
- La Perle de Prague (p143)
- Rybářský klub (p136)

painted-glass ceiling and red silk seat-cushions, Cantonese pop on the music system and a clientele that includes local Chinese families; it all smacks of authenticity. And that extends to the mostly Cantonese menu which, along with favourites such as dim sum, soy-sauce duck and salt-and-pepper shrimp, has more adventurous options such as 'cold sliced pork tongue with soy sauce', 'chicken with strange tastes' and 'chicken with five smells'.

LA BODEGA FLAMENCA

Map pp276-7   Spanish €

☎ 233 374 075; Šmeralová 5, Holešovice; tapas 40-80Kč, mains 100-150Kč; ☾ 4pm-1am Sun-Thu, to 3am Fri & Sat; tram 1, 8, 15, 25, 26

La Bodega is an atmospheric, red-brick cellar painted and plastered to look like an adobe shack. It has Latin music turned down low, a low buzz of conversation, flickering candlelight and an authentically Spanish menu – the list of delicious tapas includes *tortilla español, chorizo al vino tinto* (chorizo sausage stewed in red wine) and *gambas pil-pil* (prawns in garlic and chilli). You can order a paella for four (800Kč), and the drinks list includes a good selection of Spanish wines and Mexican beers.

LA CRÊPERIE Map pp276-7   French €

☎ 220 878 040; Janovského 6, Holešovice; mains 50-100Kč; ☾ 9am-11pm Mon-Sat, to 10pm Sun; metro Vltavska

A cosy little basement with old pine tables and creaky wooden chairs, this place sports the Breton flag on the walls and authentic *galettes* (savoury pancakes) and nicely chilled Breton cider on the menu. It's quiet in the afternoons – curl up with a good book and excellent coffee on the old sofa hidden under the stair – but it livens up later with a young and mostly local crowd.

Eating

BEYOND THE CENTRE

Sampling Czech beer (p50) in the Old Town Square

RESTAURANT CORSO

Map pp276-7   International €-€€

☎ 220 806 541; Dukelských hrdinů 7, Holešovice; mains 125-350Kč; ☼ 10am-10pm; tram 5, 12, 17

The Corso has 'interesting' décor – something like a cross between abstract Asian design and Art Deco on acid, with lots of painted glass, pierced wooden screens and chunky glass cubes (though you have to feel sorry for the lugubrious giant gourami trapped in a fishtank barely twice its length). The food is excellent value – traditional Czech cuisine, steaks and pasta dishes, including delicious cream of onion soup and homemade apple strudel, and a wine list that offers more than 20 different Czech wines. The great-value three-course set lunch (300Kč) includes a beer and a Bechorovka.

Žižkov

HANIL Map pp278-9   Japanese/Korean €€-€€€

☎ 222 715 867; Slavíkova 24; mains 300-500Kč; ☼ 11am-2.30pm & 5.30-11pm Mon-Sat, 5.30-11pm Sun; metro Jiří z Poděbrad

White walls, blond-wood lattice screens, paper lanterns and polished granite tables create a relaxed and informal setting where a mixed crowd of businesspeople, locals and expats enjoys authentic Japanese and Korean cuisine without the fuss and formality of more expensive restaurants. Tuck into a hot bowl of tasty *pibimbap* (rice topped with meat and pickled vegetables and spiced with hot pepper paste), or order a sashimi platter.

MAILSI Map pp278-9   Pakistani €€

☎ 222 717 783; Lipanská 1; mains 160-425Kč; ☼ noon-3pm & 6-11pm; tram 5, 9, 26

Mailsi was Prague's first Pakistani restaurant, and is still one of the city's best for authentic curry cuisine. The outside is inconspicuous, and it's only the qawwali music that guides you into the attractively decorated green and terracotta dining room with its tropical fishtank. Service is courteous, the food delicioius and prices modest for a speciality restaurant – though helpings are often small. Dishes with prawns are more expensive (up to 500Kč).

RESTAURACE AKROPOLIS

Map pp278-9   International €-€€

☎ 296 330 913; Kubelíkova 27; mains 80-180Kč; ☼ 11.30am-1am Mon- Sat; tram 5, 9, 26

More than a decade old now, the café in the famous Palác Akropolis club (p175) is a Žižkov institution, with its eccentric combination of marble panels, quirky metalwork light fittings and weird fishtank installations designed by local artist František Skála. The menu has a good selection of vegetarian dishes, from nachos to gnocchi, plus great garlic soup, searingly hot buffalo wings and steak tartare. Kids are welcome – you'll find toys and colouring books (though it can get a bit smoky) – and so are dogs, who can choose from their own menu of biscuits and chew toys.

TV TOWER RESTAURANT
Map pp278-9   Czech/International €€

☎ 242 418 778; Mahlerovy sady 1; mains 200-450Kč; ✆ 10am-11pm; metro Jiřího z Poděbrad

This restaurant sits 63m above ground level, halfway up the TV Tower in Žižkov (p111). It serves decent Czech and international dishes – from prawn cocktail to tournedos of beef with Parma ham – at modest prices, but the main attraction is the view. You have to pay the normal admission fee for the tower's sightseeing deck, but this gets you 5% off the menu prices.

Vinohrady

AMBIENTE
Map pp280-1   International €€

☎ 222 727 851; Mánesova 59; mains 200-400Kč; ✆ 11am-midnight Mon-Fri, noon-midnight Sat & Sun; metro Jiřího z Poděbrad

'Ambiente' means atmosphere, and the warm yellow walls, bottle-green banquettes, bamboo-and-basketwork chairs and rich mahogany woodwork make for a relaxing one in this popular Vinohrady restaurant, a pioneer of Prague's new wave of welcoming, well-run, service-with-a-smile eateries. The American-themed menu offers a huge range of salads (including Caesar, goat's cheese, roast veggies, avocado), tasty pasta dishes, barbecue ribs, fajitas, steaks and chicken wings, and there are excellent house wines for around 90Kč a glass.

AROMI
Map pp280-1   Italian €€

☎ 222 713 222; Mánesova 78; mains 160-425Kč; ✆ noon-10pm Sun-Thu, to 11pm Fri & Sat; metro Jiřího z Poděbrad

Red brick, polished wood, country-style furniture and sprigs of fresh rosemary and thyme on each table create a pleasantly rustic atmosphere in this gourmet Italian restaurant. Brisk and businesslike at lunchtime, romantic in the evenings, Aromi has a reputation for authentic Italian cuisine, from the *zuppa di cannellini* (cannellini bean soup) to the *branzino al guazzetto* (sea bass baked in a sea-salt crust; seafood is a speciality).

TOP FIVE TABLES WITH A VIEW
- Hanavský pavilón (p145)
- La Perle de Prague (p143)
- Restaurant Nebozízek (p135)
- TV Tower (left)
- U Zlaté studně (p137)

CAFÉ FX
Map pp272-3   Vegetarian €-€€

☎ 224 254 776; Bělehradská 120; mains 100-200Kč; ✆ 11.30am-2am; metro IP Pavlova

Café FX offers some of the best food in Prague in its price range – and it's all vegetarian. This hippy-chic restaurant at the entrance to the nightclub Radost FX (p175) – looking like a faded bordello with its draped chiffon, tasselled lampshades and distressed walls – comes up with imaginative dishes ranging from spinach ravioli stuffed with hazelnut pesto and cheese, to sage and mushroom 'meatballs' with mashed potatoes and creamy mushroom sauce.

CHEERS
Map pp272-3   International €-€€

☎ 222 513 108; cnr Náměstí Míru & Belgická; mains 100-200Kč; ✆ 11am-1am; metro Náměstí Míru

Cheers is a modern take on the traditional Czech pub, with bright and breezy colours, lots of stainless steel and a splash or two of contemporary art. The theory behind the menu seems to be to include one favourite dish from a dozen or so cuisines around the world, so you can choose nachos or *nigiri* sushi, *carpaccio* or cheeseburgers, fresh hummus or fish and chips. There's a great range of beers available too, including Budvar, Hoegaarden and Guinness on tap, and Leffe and Corona in bottles.

MODRÁ ŘEKA
Map pp272-3   Yugoslavian €-€€

☎ 222 251 601; Mánesova 13; mains 100-200Kč; ✆ 3-11pm Mon-Fri, 5-11pm Sat & Sun; tram 11

The 'Blue River' is a homely Yugoslav restaurant run by a couple who fled to Prague from Sarajevo in 1992. The dining room is tiny, with space for around 20 diners, and the deliciously spicy menu includes Balkan classics such as *čevapčiči* (minced-meat kebabs) with *adžvar* (roasted red-pepper puree), *sudjuk* (spicy sausage) and *gibanica* (a rich cake filled with fruit, nuts and poppy seeds).

Eating

BEYOND THE CENTRE

TIGER TIGER Map pp280-1   Thai €€

☎ 222 512 048; Anny Letenské 5; mains 190-280Kč; ⏱ 11.30am-11pm Mon-Fri, 5-11pm Sat & Sun; metro Náměstí Míru

Tiger Tiger has a dapper little dining room dressed in cheerful yellow with smart navy upholstery, a restrained and elegant setting for some of the city's best Thai cuisine. Authentic specialities include *tom yam kung* (hot and sour prawn soup), *som tam* (spicy carrot salad) and *kaeng ped gai* (chicken in red curry sauce); symbols on the menu rate the chilli levels.

WINGS CLUB Map pp278-9   International €-€€

☎ 222 713 151; Lucemburská 11; mains 130-300Kč; ⏱ 11.30am-11pm; metro Jiřího z Poděbrad

Owned by three pilots, this is half restaurant, half museum, filled with fascinating memorabilia of WWII Czech aviation ranging from photographs and uniforms to a gleaming, full-sized propeller. The menu is solid, good-quality Czech pub grub, from smoked pork with sauerkraut and dumplings to pork kebabs marinated in mustard to stir-fried beef, and there are half a dozen vegetarian dishes too, including deep-fried jalapeño peppers stuffed with cheese, and baked aubergine with Parmesan.

Smíchov

KÁVA KÁVA KÁVA Map pp270-1   Café €

☎ 257 314 277; Lidická 42; mains 70-120Kč; ⏱ 7am-10pm; metro Anděl

The Smíchov branch of the popular internet café in Staré Město (above) is bigger and brighter than the original, with Etruscan orange walls, terracotta floor tiles and modern art on the walls, and a more extensive

menu too – you can snack on salads, sandwiches, quiche or nachos, or tuck into more substantial chicken gyros, Mexican chilli or home-made soup of the day. There's free wi-fi access too (provided you spend at least 50Kč).

MEDUZZY Map pp270-1   Greek/Italian €-€€

☎ 251 510 557; Mělnická 13; mains 100-250Kč; ⏱ 11.30am-11pm; tram 6, 9, 12, 20

Meduzzy goes for a Mediterranean vibe, with blonde wood and terracotta, and windmill and Medusa motifs. Service is friendly, and the food is fairly authentic – *choriatiki* salad (feta cheese, olives, tomato and cucumber), freshly made pitta bread, and *tsatziki* (yogurt, cucumber and garlic dip) with enough raw garlic in it to stun a horse.

NA VERANDÁCH Map pp262-3   Czech €-€€

☎ 257 191 200; Nádražní 84; mains 100-200Kč; ⏱ 11am-midnight Mon-Thu, to 1am Fri & Sat, to 11pm Sun; metro Anděl

Bustling green-aproned waiters bearing trays of foaming Staropramen dodge among crowds of local drinkers, business people and tourists in this big, brassy, modern bar and restaurant. It's part of the Staropramen Brewery (p112), so there's no shortage of quality beer (there are seven varieties on tap) to wash down traditional Czech pub grub such as *utopenec* (pickled sausage), *pivní chilli guláš* (beer and chilli goulash) and *vepřové koleno* (pork knuckle).

NAGOYA Map pp262-3   Japanese €€

☎ 251 511 724; Stroupežnického 21; mains 150-400Kč; ⏱ 6-11pm Mon-Sat; metro Anděl

Nagoya, hidden away down an escalator in a passage next to Anděl's Hotel (p207),

---

TOP FIVE BREAKFASTS

- From scrambled eggs and full English fry-up to US-style biscuits and gravy, and pancakes and maple syrup, go to **Bohemia Bagel** (p134 and p138; ⏱ breakfast served till 2pm).
- You can get classic bacon-and-egg brekkie and strawberry muesli, as well as more unusual stuff such as guacamole crostini, at **Dinitz Café** (p142; ⏱ breakfast served all day).
- Have some of the best coffee in town, accompanied by bagels, croissants, cakes and pastries, at **Káva Káva Káva** (p140 & above; ⏱ breakfast served all day).
- A range of cooked breakfasts, from full British fry-up to pancakes with maple syrup to huevos rancheros, are served at **Red Hot & Blues** (p141; ⏱ breakfast served till 11.30am Mon-Fri, till 4pm Sat & Sun).
- It's a sophisticated start to the day at **Square** (p136; ⏱ breakfast served till 4pm), with scrambled egg and chives, eggs Benedict with smoked salmon, or croissants with butter and jam.

French pastries at Au Gourmand (p137)

is one of the few truly authentic Japanese restaurants in Prague. It has crisp, minimalist décor, with paper screens, globe lampshades and bamboo plants; most of the seating is at ordinary tables, but there are also some low tables with tatami mats if you want to take off your shoes and get the genuine Japanese dining experience. The menu ticks all the usual boxes – sushi, sashimi, teriyaki, *yakitori*, *tempura* and miso soup – but also includes *sakana,* small savoury snacks a bit like Japanese tapas, which are great if you want to try a range of flavours.

PIZZERIA CORLEONE

Map pp262-3   Italian €-€€

☎ 251 511 244; Na Bělidle 42; mains 120-280Kč; 🕑 11am-11pm; metro Anděl

Ask Prague expats where to find the best pizza in town, and most of them will point you towards this popular and lively neighbourhood restaurant, where the wood-fired pizza oven turns out all the classics, from *margherita* to *moscardina*, and also allows you to choose your own toppings. The dining room shows a taste for the art of Jack Vettriano, whose paintings are reproduced in several large murals. There's a no-smoking area in the basement.

WIGWAM Map pp270-1   International €-€€

☎ 257 311 707; Zborovská 54; mains 100-200Kč; 🕑 10am-1am; tram 6, 9, 12, 20

This appealing café-bar has clean-cut modern lines set off with rustic brick, tile and weathered wood, enlivened with African masks and wooden idols and framed art and photography. The menu veers from Mexican to Asia by way of Europe, with a selection of Thai dishes alongside nachos, steak with jalapeños and roast tomatoes, and house speciality Chicken Wigwam (grilled chicken breast marinated in ginger, garlic, chilli and lemon juice).

Dejvice

HAVELI Map p275   Indian €€

☎ 233 344 800; Dejvická 6; mains 230-330Kč; 🕑 11am-midnight; metro Hradčanská

Indian music and a waft of incense will guide you towards this popular and authentic curry restaurant with tables split between an informal street-level bar and a cosy red-brick and whitewash cellar. The onion *bhaji* is light and crisp, the naan bread soft and buttery, and the curry dishes nicely spiced; there's a good selection of vegetarian dishes, including a very tasty *channa pindi* (chick peas and white cheese

149

in a tangy sauce rich in cumin and fresh coriander).

PIZZERIA GROSSETO Map p275   Italian €

☎ 233 342 694; Jugoslávských partyzánů 8; mains 100-155Kč; ⊗ 11.30am-11pm; metro Dejvická

This is a lively and friendly pizzeria that pulls in crowds of students from the nearby university campus with its genuine, wood-fired pizza oven and Moravian Radegast beer. As well as a huge choice of tasty pizza varieties, the menu also offers salads, pastas, risotto, roast chicken, steak and grilled salmon. The main dining room, where you can watch the pizza chefs twirling their

dough, is complemented by an attractive timber-decked conservatory out back.

RESTAURANT U CEDRU

Map p275   Lebanese €€

☎ 233 342 974; Národní obrany 27; mains 200-400Kč; ⊗ 11am-11pm; metro Dejvická

'At the Cedar' is a welcoming Lebanese restaurant with tasty *mezzes* (appetisers) such as *baba ganoush* (smoky aubergine and garlic puree), tabouleh salad and stuffed vine leaves. Rather than agonise over the menu, you can order a spread of 10 *mezzes* (795Kč), which the chef will select for you – a great start to dinner, or a lunch in itself.

Drinking

Drinking

Bars in Prague go in and out of fashion with alarming speed, and trend-spotters are forever flocking to the latest 'in' place only to desert it as soon as it becomes mainstream. The best areas to go looking for good drinking dens include Vinohrady, Žižkov, Smíchov, Holešovice and 'SoNa' (the area south of Národní třída in Nové Město).

Most pubs serve beer snacks; some of the most popular are *utopenci* (sliced sausage pickled in vinegar with onion), *topinky* (fried toast) and, of course, the famous *Pražská šunka* (Prague ham) with gherkin. Many of the places listed here also serve more substantial meals.

If you want to avoid bumping into stag parties, stay away from Irish and English pubs in the city centre, and the sports bars on and around Ve Smečkách in the New Town.

CAFÉS & TEAROOMS

MALÁ STRANA

KAFÍČKO Map pp264-5

☎ 724 151 795; Míšenská 10; ⏰ 10am-10pm; tram 12, 20, 22, 23

This smoke-free, family-friendly little café, with its cream walls, bentwood chairs, fresh flowers and arty photographs, is an unexpected setting for some of Prague's finest tea and coffee. Choose from a wide range of quality roasted beans from all over the world, and have them freshly ground and made into espresso, cappuccino or latte (37Kč to 50Kč); the espresso is served, as it should be, with a glass of water.

U ZELENÉHO ČAJE Map pp264-5

☎ 257 530 027; Nerudova 19; ⏰ 11am-10pm; tram 12, 20, 22, 23

'At the Green Tea' is a charming little olde-worlde tea house on the way up to the castle. The menu offers around a hundred different kinds of tea (32Kč to 80Kč a pot) from all over the world, ranging from classic green and black teas from China and India to fruit-flavoured teas and herbal infusions, as well as tempting cakes and tasty sandwiches.

NOVÉ MĚSTO

CAFÉ LOUVRE Map pp272-3

☎ 224 930 949; 1st fl, Národní třída 2; ⏰ 8am-11.30pm Mon-Fri, 9am-11.30pm Sat & Sun; metro Národní Třída

Established in 1902, the Louvre is an elegant, French-style café with smart apron-and-waistcoated staff serving reasonably priced coffee, beer and wine. It sports a billiard hall, art gallery and summer terrace, and has an extensive breakfast menu that offers Czech, British, French and American options.

DOBRÁ ČAJOVNA Map pp272-3

☎ 224 231 480; Václavské náměstí 14; ⏰ 10am-9.30pm Mon-Fri, 3-9.30pm Sat & Sun; metro Můstek

This tearoom, tucked up a passage off Wenceslas Square, is a little haven of warm orange walls, oriental rugs and cushions hidden away from the heaving crowds on the nearby street. They take their tea seriously here, and you can choose from a wide range of Chinese, Indian, Sri Lankan, Japanese and Turkish leaves. There are also cakes and vegetarian snacks such as hummus and pitta bread.

INSTITUT FRANÇAIS Map pp272-3

☎ 224 216 630; Štěpánská 35; ⏰ 8.30am-7pm Mon-Fri, 10am-3pm Sat; tram 3, 9, 14, 24

Prague's French cultural institute has a nice little café at the back (go in the main entrance and bear right), frequented by French expats but open to all, where you can read the latest issues of *Le Monde* and *Le Figaro* over *café au lait* and a croissant or *pain au chocolat*.

VINOHRADY

KAVÁRNA MEDÚZA Map pp280-1

☎ 222 515 107; Belgická 17; ⏰ 10am-1am Mon-Fri, noon-1am Sat & Sun; metro Náměstí Míru

The perfect Prague coffee house, Medúza is an oasis of old, worn furniture, dark

GRAND CAFÉS

Prague's café society flourished from the late 19th century until the 1930s, when the city's coffee houses provided a meeting place for artists, writers, journalists, activists and political dissidents. Many fell into disrepair following WWII, but a half-dozen or so have survived or been restored to their former glory.

Café Savoy (Map pp270–1; ☎ 257 311 562; Vítězná 5, Malá Strana; ☾ 8am-10.30pm Mon-Fri, 9am-10.30pm Sat & Sun; tram 6, 9, 22, 23) Established in 1893 and restored in 2004, the Savoy fairly glows with belle-époque splendour, its colourful, ornately decorated ceiling decked with crystal chandeliers (grab a table on the mezzanine for a closer view) and its waiting staff dressed in matching red waistcoats and ties. Great coffee and hot chocolate, and a decent wine list too.

Grand Café Orient (Map pp268–9; ☎ 224 224 240; Ovocný trh 19, Staré Město; ☾ 9am-10pm Mon-Fri, 10am-10pm Sat & Sun; metro Náměstí Republiky) Prague's only Cubist café, the Orient was designed by Josef Gočár and is Cubist down to the smallest detail, including the lampshades and coat-hooks. It was restored and reopened in 2005, having lain closed since 1920. Decent coffee and inexpensive cocktails.

Kavárna Lucerna (Map pp272–3; ☎ 224 215 495; Palác Lucerna, Štěpánská 61, Nové Město; ☾ 10am-1am Mon-Sat, to 11pm Sun; tram 3, 9, 14, 24) The least touristy of the cafés listed here, the Lucerna is part of an Art Nouveau shopping arcade designed by the grandfather of ex-president Václav Havel. Filled with faux marble, ornamental metalwork and glittering crystal lanterns (*lucerna* is Czech for lantern), this 1920s gem has arched windows overlooking David Cerný's famous *Horse* sculpture hanging beneath the glass-domed atrium.

Kavárna Obecní dům (Map pp268–9; ☎ 222 002 763; náměstí Republiky 5, Staré Město; ☾ 7.30am-11pm; metro Náměstí Republiky) The spectacular café in Prague's opulent Municipal House (Obecní dům) offers the opportunity to sip your cappuccino amid an orgy of Art Nouveau splendour. Also worth a look is the neat little American Bar in the basement of the building, all polished wood, stained glass and gleaming copper.

Kavárna Evropa (Map pp272–3; ☎ 224 228 117; Václavské náměstí 25, Nové Město; ☾ 9.30am-11pm; metro Můstek) The Grand Hotel Evropa sports the most atmospheric café on Wenceslas Square, a fading museum of over-the-top Art Nouveau. Sadly, it has long since become a tourist trap, with second-rate cakes and coffee and rip-off prices (89Kč for a cappuccino), but it's still well worth a look inside.

Kavárna Slavia (Map pp272–3; ☎ 224 220 957; Národní třída 1, Nové Město; ☾ 8am-midnight Mon-Fri, 9am-midnight Sat & Sun; metro Národní Třída) The Slavia is the most famous of Prague's old cafés, a cherrywood and onyx shrine to Art Deco elegance, with polished limestone-topped tables and big windows overlooking the river. It has been a celebrated literary meeting place since the early 20th century – Rainer Maria Rilke and Franz Kafka hung out here, and it was frequented by Václav Havel and other dissidents in the 1970s and '80s.

wood, creaking armchairs and local artworks, with an antique sugar bowl on every table and an atmosphere that invites you to sink into a novel or indulge in a conversation on the nature of self. Coffee, tea, hot chocolate, beer, wine and non-alcoholic cocktails are all on the menu, along with pancakes, nachos and banana splits.

BARS & PUBS

HRADČANY

PIVNICE U ČERNÉHO VOLA Map pp264-5

☎ 220 513 481; Loretánské náměstí 1; ☾ 10am-10pm; tram 22, 23

Many religious people make a pilgrimage to the Loreta, but just across the road is a shrine that pulls in pilgrims of a different kind – the 'Black Ox'. This surprisingly inexpensive beer hall is visited by real-ale aficionados for its authentic atmosphere and lip-smackingly delicious draught beer, Velkopopovický Kozel (24.50Kč for 0.5L), which comes from a small town southeast of Prague.

MALÁ STRANA

BLUE LIGHT Map pp264-5

☎ 257 533 126; Josefská 1; ☾ 6pm-3am; tram 12, 20, 22, 23

The Blue Light is an appropriately dark and atmospheric jazz cavern, as popular with locals as with tourists, where you can enjoy a relaxed cocktail as you cast an eye over the vintage posters, records and graffiti that deck the walls. The background jazz is recorded rather than live, but on a quality sound system that never overpowers your conversation.

HOSTINEC U KOCOURA Map pp264-5

☎ 257 530 107; Nerudova 2; ⏰ 11am-11pm; tram 12, 20, 22, 23

'The Tomcat' is a long-established traditional pub, still enjoying its reputation as a former favourite of ex-president Havel, and still managing to pull in a mostly Czech crowd despite being in the heart of touristville (maybe it's the ever-present pall of cigarette smoke). It has relatively inexpensive beer for this part of town – 26Kč for 0.5L of draught Budvar or Pilsner Urquell.

KLUB ÚJEZD Map pp270-1

☎ 257 316 537; Újezd 18; ⏰ 2pm-4am; tram 6, 9, 12, 20, 22, 23

Klub Újezd is one of Prague's many 'alternative' bars, spread over three floors (DJs in the cellar, and a café upstairs) and filled with a fascinating collection of handmade furniture and fittings, original art and weird wrought-iron sculptures. Clamber onto a two-tonne bar stool in the agreeably grungy street-level bar, and sip on a beer while you watch a thick rope of herbal-scented smoke uncoil across the ceiling beside the scaly, fire-breathing sea-monster that dangles over your head. Trippy.

ST NICHOLAS CAFÉ Map pp264-5

☎ 257 530 205; Tržiště 7; ⏰ noon-1am Mon-Fri, 4pm-1am Sat & Sun; tram 12, 20, 22, 23

Descend from the bustle of Malá Strana into this dark and peaceful Gothic cellar, a favourite midday refuge in the heart of

the tourist zone. Dimly lit alcoves, flickering candlelight and worn wooden tables make an appealing setting for a few quiet beers or a bottle of wine; later in the evening it gets busier and develops a cool, jazzy atmosphere.

U ZAVĚŠENÉHO KAFE Map pp264-5

☎ 605 294 595; Úvoz 6; ⏰ 11am-midnight; tram 12, 20, 22, 23

This is a superb little drinking den barely five minutes' walk from the castle. Head for the cosy, wood-panelled back room, quirkily decorated with weird art and mechanical curiosities by local artist Kuba Krejci (all for sale), and an ancient jukebox crammed with Beatles, Stones and Czech rock. Foaming Gambrinus is only 20Kč a half-litre, and the coffee is damn fine too.

STARÉ MĚSTO

ALOHA WAVE LOUNGE Map pp268-9

☎ 724 055 704; Dušní 11; ⏰ 6pm-2am Sun-Tue, to 4am Wed-Sat; metro Staroměstská

The cocktail menu at this popular Hawaiian surf-themed bar is heavy on drinks involving rum, coconut, pineapple and banana, while the décor tends towards palm fronds and 1950s surf-dude posters. Head for the candlelit downstairs lounge, with its leather sofas and laid-back sounds (Latin Monday and Tuesday, beach hits Wednesday, live bands Thursday and dance parties Friday and Saturday).

BAR & BOOKS Map pp268-9

☎ 731 184 123; Týnská 19; ⏰ 2pm-4am Mon-Fri, 6pm-4am Sat, to 3am Sun; metro Náměstí Republiky

The walls are indeed lined with books at this branch of the famous Manhattan cocktail bar, but the well-heeled clients are more likely to be reading the labels on the vast range of single malts, bourbons, brandies and vintage ports on offer, along with Cuban and Dominican cigars. The black-waistcoated staff are unerringly polite and efficient, and mix a mean martini, margarita or champagne cocktail.

BLATOUCH Map pp268-9

☎ 222 328 643; Vězeňská 4; ⏰ 11am-1am Mon-Thu, 1am-3am Fri, 2pm-3am Sat, 1pm-midnight Sun; metro Staroměstská

Pouring drinks at Blue Light (p153)

SMALL IS BEAUTIFUL

While big multinational brewing companies have been busy taking over traditional Czech breweries, a growing number of enthusiasts have been setting up microbreweries that stay true to the origins of Bohemian beer, serving tasty, unpasteurised brews in atmospheric brewery-pubs. Here are six in the capital:

Klášterní pivovar Strahov (Strahov Monastery Brewery; Map pp264–5; ☎ 233 353 155; Strahovské nádvoří 301, Hradčany; ☺ 10am-10pm; tram 22, 23) Dominated by two polished copper brewing kettles, this convivial little pub serves up two varieties of its St Norbert beer – *tmavý* (dark), a rich, tarry brew with a creamy head, and *polotmavý* (amber), a full-bodied, hoppy lager, both 49Kč per 0.4L.

Novoměstský pivovar (New Town Brewery; Map pp272–3; ☎ 224 232 448; Vodičkova 20, Nové Město; 8am-11.30pm Mon-Fri, 11.30am-11.30pm Sat, noon-10pm Sun; tram 3, 9, 14, 24) Like U Fleků (below), the 'New Town Brewery' has largely been taken over by coach-party invasions, but it's considerably cheaper (42Kč for 0.5L), and the food is not only edible but actually rather good. If you haven't booked, you'll be lucky to get a table.

Pivovar u Bulovky (Bulovka Brewery; Map pp262–3; ☎ 284 840 650; Bulovka 17, Libeň; ☺ 11am-11pm Mon-Thu, to midnight Fri, noon-midnight Sat; tram 10, 15, 24, 25) Opened in 2004, this is a genuine neighbourhood bar out in the suburbs, a homely wood-panelled room with quirky metalwork, much of it home-built by the owner. The delicious house *ležák* (lager; 28Kč for 0.5L) is a yeast beer, cloudy in appearance, and crisp, citrusy and refreshing in flavour. Well worth the tram trip, but don't expect the staff to speak English!

Pivovarský Dům (Brewery House; Map pp272–3; ☎ 296 216 666; cnr Ječná & Lipová, Nové Město; ☺ 11am-11.30pm; tram 4, 6, 10, 16, 22, 23) While the tourists flock to U Fleků (below), locals gather here to sample the classic Czech lager (in light, dark and mixed varieties; 33Kč per 0.5L) that is produced on the premises, as well as wheat beer and a range of flavoured beers (including coffee, banana and cherry, 33Kč per 0.3L). The pub itself is a pleasant place to linger, decked out with polished copper vats and brewing implements and smelling faintly of malt and hops.

U Fleků (Map pp272–3; ☎ 224 934 019; Křemencová 11, Nové Město; ☺ 9am-11pm; metro Karlovo Náměstí) A festive warren of drinking and dining rooms, U Fleků is a Prague institution, though usually clogged with tour groups high on oompah music and the tavern's home-brewed, 13-degree black beer (59Kč for 0.4L), known as Flek. Purists grumble but go along anyway because the beer is good, though tourist prices have nudged out many locals. You might still find an empty seat at 7pm on a weekday, but probably not.

U Medvídků (At the Little Bear; Map pp272–3; ☎ 224 211 916; Na Perštýně 7, Staré Město; ☺ beer hall 11.30am-11pm, museum noon-10pm; metro Národní třída) The most micro of Prague's microbreweries, with a capacity of only 250L, U Medvídků only started producing its own beer in 2005, though its beer hall has been around for many years. What it lacks in size, it makes up for in strength – the dark lager produced here, marketed as X-Beer, is the strongest in the country, with an alcohol content of 11.8% (as strong as many wines). Available in bottles only (48Kč for 0.33L), it's a malty, bitter-sweet brew with a powerful punch; handle with caution!

A pleasantly relaxed literary hangout, with a long, narrow bar lined with antique bookcases and Edward Hopper prints, and a tiny garden courtyard at the back. It serves coffee, tea and snacks as well as alcoholic drinks – the perfect place to read the papers over an afternoon glass of wine.

CAFÉ BAMBUS Map pp268-9

☎ 224 828 110; Benediktská 12; ☺ 9am-2am Mon-Fri, 11am-2am Sat, to midnight Sun; metro Náměstí Republiky

Bambus is a dimly lit and often-smoky café-bar sporting potted bamboo plants, a pleasantly laid-back atmosphere, and a good cocktail menu. It pulls in a mixed crowd of young locals plus occasional backpackers who have found their way from nearby hostels.

CAFÉ GASPAR KASPER Map pp268-9

☎ 222 326 843; Celetná 17; ☺ 9am-midnight; metro Náměstí Republiky

A convivial, nonsmoking café-bar in an L-shaped nook overlooking the courtyard at the Celetná Theatre, hidden away from the tourist crowds. Its arty credentials include lots of theatrical literature lying around for your perusal, and a naked scarlet lady with green nipples perched above the bar. The inexpensive snack menu includes sandwiches, potato pancakes and cheeseburgers.

CHATEAU L'ENFER ROUGE Map pp268-9

☎ 222 316 328; Jakubská 2; ☺ noon-3am Mon-Thu, to 4am Fri, 4pm-4am Sat & Sun; metro Náměstí Republiky

Chateau is a raucous, late-night party pub where the cheap(ish) beer, table football, pinball machines and dance-club cellar never fail to pull in a huge, mixed crowd of tourists, stag parties, expats and slumming Praguers – by midevening it's often standing-room only. Everything in this self-consciously cool bar is backlit, including the smiles of the clientele.

FRIENDS Map pp272-3

☎ 224 211 920; Bartolomějská 11; ☽ 8pm-6am; metro Národní Třída

Friends is a welcoming gay music-and-video bar serving excellent coffee, cocktails and wine. It's a good spot to sit back with a drink and check out the crowd, or join in the party spirit on assorted theme nights, which range from Czech pop music and movies to cowboy parties. DJs add their own spin from 10pm on Friday and Saturdays.

KONVIKT PUB Map pp272-3

☎ 224 231 971; Bartolomějská 11; ☽ 9am-midnight Mon-Fri, 11am-midnight Sat & Sun; metro Národní Třída

The Konvikt – so named because it's set on a street filled with police offices, off the beaten tourist trail – is a traditional, down-to-earth Czech bar and café serving good Pilsner Urquell (27.50Kč a half-litre) and solid Bohemian fare, such as smoked pork, sauerkraut and dumplings – excellent value.

KOZIČKA Map pp268-9

☎ 224 818 308; Kozí 1; ☽ noon-4am Mon-Fri, 6pm-4am Sat, 6pm-3am Sun; metro Staroměstská

The 'Little Goat' is a buzzing, red-brick basement bar decorated with cute steel goat sculptures, serving Krušovice on tap at 35Kč for 0.5L (though watch out, the bartenders will sling you a 1L glass if they think you're a tourist). It fills up later in the evening with a mostly Czech crowd, and is a very civilised setting for a late-night session.

TOP FIVE TRADITIONAL PUBS

- Hostinec U kocoura (p154)
- Pivnice U Černého vola (p153)
- Pivovarský dům (boxed text, p155)
- U Vystřeleného oka (p158)
- U Zlatého Tygra (right)

MOLLY MALONE'S Map pp268-9

☎ 224 818 851; U obecního dvora 4; ☽ 9am-1am; metro Náměstí Republiky

Molly's is the most relaxed and convivial of Prague's many Irish bar, a wood-panelled haven of peace on a quiet backstreet, serving not only draught Guinness (88Kč for 0.4L) but also an excellent menu of high-cholesterol comfort food – this is the place to come for a great bacon sandwich, bangers and mash, or a bacon-and-egg fry-up, even at midnight.

U ZLATÉHO TYGRA Map pp268-9

☎ 222 221 111; Husova 17; ☽ 3-11pm; metro Staroměstská

The 'Golden Tiger' is one of the few old-town drinking holes that has hung on to its soul – and its low prices (26Kč per 0.5L of Pilsner Urquell), considering its location. It was novelist Bohumil Hrabal's favourite hostelry – there are photos of him on the walls – and the place that Václav Havel took fellow president Bill Clinton in 1994 to show him a real Czech pub.

NOVÉ MĚSTO

JÁGR'S SPORT BAR Map pp272-3

☎ 224 032 481; Palác Blaník, Václavské náměstí 56; ☽ 11am-midnight; metro Muzeum

Owned by NHL ice-hockey superstar Jaromír Jágr – mainstay of the Pittsburgh Penguins in the '90s, and winner of Olympic gold with the Czech national team in '98 – this cavernous sports bar offers fans four large projection screens and no fewer than 40 TVs, so you needn't miss a moment of that important match. Better priced than other sports bars (37Kč per 0.5L of Pilsner Urquell), but get in early – it fills up quickly before big events.

JÁMA Map pp272-3

☎ 224 222 383; V jámě 7; ☽ 11am-1am; metro Muzeum

The Hollow, southeast off Vodičkova, is a popular American expat bar and restaurant, with a leafy little beer garden out back shaded by lime and walnut trees. The clientele is a mix of expats, tourists and young Praguers, and there's Pilsner Urquell, Gambrinus and Velkopopvický Kozel on draught. The food menu includes good burgers, steaks, ribs and chicken wings.

BEER GARDENS

On a hot summer day, what could be finer than sitting outdoors with a chilled glass of Bohemia's finest beer, admiring a view over river or city. Many of Prague's pubs have small beer gardens or courtyards, but the following summer-only spots are truly out in the open air. Opening times are weather-dependent, but typically noon to midnight June to September; expect to pay around 25Kč a half-litre for beer.

Letná Gardens (Map pp276–7; Letenské sady, Bubeneč) A slew of rickety benches and tables spread along a dusty scarp beneath the trees at the eastern end of Letná Gardens enjoys one of the city's most stunning views, looking across the river to the spires of Staré Město, and southwest to Malá Strana. Gambrinus on tap.

Letní bar (Map pp270–1; Střelecký ostrov, Malá Strana) Basically a shack serving Budvar in plastic cups, this is the place to pick up a beer before hitting the little beach at the northern end of the island.

Park Café (Map pp278–9; Riegrovy sady, Vinohrady) Perched on top of precipitous Riegrovy Park, this bustling beer garden has awesome night-time views of the castle, a big screen showing sport and the opportunity to play table football and table hockey with half of Prague. Pilsner Urquell and Gambrinus.

VELRYBA Map pp272-3

☎ 224 912 484; Opatovická 24; ⏲ 11am-midnight Sat-Thu, to 2am Fri; metro Národní Třída

The 'Whale' is an arty café-bar – usually quiet enough to have a real conversation – with vegetarian-friendly snacks, a smoky back room and a basement art gallery. A clientele of Czech students, local office workers and foreign backpackers attracted by the low prices keep the place jumping.

HOLEŠOVICE & BUBENEČ

LE TRAM Map pp276-7

☎ 233 370 359; Šmeralová 12, Bubeneč; ⏲ 8pm-6am; tram 1, 8, 15, 25, 25, 26

There are several good neighbourhood bars on this side street, but Le Tram stands out. Looking like it's been furnished from a Prague public transport closing-down sale – it's filled with plastic seats, benches and other accoutrements salvaged from decommissioned trams, as well as other 1970s *objets trouvés* – this pleasantly scruffy French-owned bar pulls in a truly international crowd with cheap beer, lively conversation and cool tunes.

ŽIŽKOV

HAPU Map pp278-9

☎ 222 720 158; Orlická 8; ⏲ 6pm-2am; metro Jiřího z Poděbrad

Low-ceilinged, dimly lit and immensely cool, Hapu is almost in Vinohrady – geographically and socially on the opposite side of Žižkov from U Vystřeleného oka. It's a tiny, smoky cocktail lounge with shabby-chic décor and expert staff who really know how to mix a mean cocktail – not only that, but every drop of fruit juice is freshly squeezed.

PIANO BAR Map pp278-9

☎ 222 727 496; Milešovská 10; ⏲ 5pm-midnight or later; metro Jiřího z Poděbrad

The Piano Bar is a homely little cellar bar cluttered with junk and bric-a-brac, and yes, there is a piano where you can play chopsticks until someone raps a pool cue across your knuckles. It's a stalwart of the Prague gay scene, frequented mainly by locals, a good spot for a quiet drink and a chat.

Interior, Dobrá Čajovna (p152)

Drinking

BARS & PUBS

U RADNICE Map pp278-9

☎ 222 782 713; Havlíčkovo náměstí 7; ☯ 11am-11pm Mon-Fri, to 10pm Sat & Sun; tram 5, 9, 26
'At the Town Hall' is a cheerful neighbourhood *pivnice* (which has its own six- to 10-person sauna, no less!) with plain wooden tables and a band of loyal regulars, where you can sample excellent Podkováň beer from the Kokořín region north of Mělník (17Kč a half-litre). (The sauna needs to be booked in advance, by the way.)

U VYSTŘELENÉHO OKA Map pp278-9

☎ 226 278 714; U Božích bojovníků 3; ☯ 4.30pm-1am Mon-Sat; bus 133, 207
You've got to love a pub that has vinyl pads on the wall above the gents' urinals to rest your forehead on. 'The Shot-Out Eye' – the name pays homage to the one-eyed Hussite hero atop the hill behind the pub (see p110) – is a bohemian (with a small 'b') hostelry with a raucous beer garden where the cheap food and beer pulls in a typically heterogeneous Žižkov crowd, ranging from art students and writers to lost backpackers and tattooed bikers.

VINOHRADY

CAFFÉ KAABA Map pp278-9

☎ 222 254 021; Mánesova 20; ☯ 8am-10pm; tram 11
Caffé Kaaba is a stylish little architect-designed café-bar with retro furniture and pastel-coloured décor that comes straight out of the 1959 Ideal Homes Exhibition. It serves up excellent coffee (made with freshly ground imported beans), offers an extensive list of Czech and imported wines (the house wine is only 30Kč a glass), and also has an in-house news and tobacco counter.

CLUB STELLA Map pp280-1

☎ 224 257 869; Lužická 10; ☯ 8pm-5am; tram 4, 22, 23
Club Stella is an intimate, candlelit café-bar that seems to be the first place everyone recommends when you ask about gay and lesbian bars in Prague. There's a long narrow bar where you can just squeeze onto a bar stool, an armchair-filled lounge that looks like somebody's living room, and a welcoming crowd of locals. Ring the doorbell to get in.

ZVONAŘKÁ Map pp280-1

☎ 224 251 990; Šafaříkova 1; ☯ 11am-11pm Mon-Thu, noon-midnight Fri & Sat, to 11pm Sun; metro IP Pavlova
Sitting at the far end of a quiet residential street where Vinohrady spills over into the Nusle valley, Zvonařka has a stylish, minimalist interior, but its biggest attraction is outdoors – a broad, tree-shaded terrace overhanging a steep hill, with expansive views across the valley to Vyšehrad, a great place for a beer on a summer evening.

Entertainment

Entertainment

Across the spectrum, from ballet to blues, jazz to rock, theatre to tennis, there's a bewildering range of entertainment on offer in this eclectic city. Prague is now as much a European centre for jazz, rock and hip hop as it is for classical music. The biggest draw, however, is still the Prague Spring festival of classical music and opera.

For reviews, day-by-day listings and a directory of venues, consult the 'Night & Day' section of the weekly *Prague Post* (www.praguepost.cz). Monthly listings booklets include *Culture in Prague* and the Czech-language *Přehled,* available from PIS offices (see p238 for contact details); there are listings on the PIS website (www.pis.cz) too.

Look out for *Provokátor* (www.provokator.org), a free monthly magazine that is dedicated to art, music, culture and politics; the website has listings of upcoming cultural events. You can pick up the print magazine in clubs, cafés, arthouse cinemas and backpacker hostels. There is also *Metropolis,* a free weekly booklet with film, theatre and music listings, available in cinemas, pubs and clubs (it's in Czech only, but the listings are easily deciphered).

For web-based entertainment listings, check out www.prague.tv and www.heartofeurope .cz, or download the twice-monthly Prague Podcast (www.praguepodcast.libsyn.com), which features tracks from bands that will be playing live in Prague in the following few weeks.

Tickets & Reservations

For classical music, opera, ballet, theatre and some rock concerts – even with the most thoroughly 'sold-out' events – you can often find a ticket or two on sale at the theatre's box office a half-hour or so before show time.

If you want to be sure of a seat, Prague is awash with ticket agencies (see the boxed text, below). Their advantage is convenience: most are computerised, fast, and accept credit cards. Their drawback is a probable 8% to 15% mark-up.

Many venues have discounts for students and sometimes for the disabled. Most performances have a certain number of tickets set aside for foreigners. For rock and jazz clubs you can turn up at the door, but advance bookings are recommended for big names.

BUYING TICKETS

The 'wholesalers' with the largest agency networks are Bohemia Ticket International (BTI), FOK and Ticketpro; the others probably get their tickets from them.

Bohemia Ticket International (BTI; Map pp268–9; ☎ 224 227 832; www.ticketsbti.cz; Malé náměstí 13, Staré Město; ⏰ 9am-5pm Mon-Fri, 9am-1pm Sat) BTI provides tickets for all kinds of events. There's another **branch** (Map pp268–9; ☎ 224 227 832; Na příkopě 16, Nové Město; ⏰ 10am-7pm Mon-Fri, to 5pm Sat, to 3pm Sun) near the Municipal House.

FOK Box Office (Map pp268–9; ☎ 222 002 336; U obecního domu 2, Staré Město; ⏰ 10am-6pm Mon-Fri) Prague Symphony Orchestra box office, for classical concert tickets; also open for one hour before performance begins.

Ticketcentrum (Map pp268–9; ☎ 296 333 333; Rytířská 31, Staré Město; ⏰ 9am-12.30pm & 1-5pm Mon-Fri) Walk-in centre for all kinds of tickets; branch of Ticketpro.

Ticketpro (Map pp272–3; ☎ 296 333 333; www.ticketpro.cz; pasáž Lucerna, Štěpánská 61, Nové Město; ⏰ 9am-1pm & 11.30-5.30pm Mon-Fri) Tickets are available here for all kinds of events. There Ticketpro branches in PIS offices (see p238) and many other places.

Ticketstream (www.ticketstream.cz) Internet-based booking agency that covers events in Prague and all over the Czech Republic.

MUSIC
CLASSICAL MUSIC, OPERA & BALLET

There are half-a-dozen concerts of one kind or another almost every day during the summer, making a fine soundtrack to accompany the city's visual delights. Many of these are chamber concerts performed by aspiring musicians in the city's churches – gorgeous but chilly (take an extra layer, even on a summer day) and not always with the finest of acoustics. However, a good number of concerts, especially those promoted by people handing out flyers in the street, are second-rate, despite the premium prices that foreigners pay. If you want to be sure of quality, go for a performance by one of the city's professional orchestras.

In addition to the hours indicated here in the individual reviews, box offices are also open from 30 minutes to one hour before the start of a performance. For opera and ballet listings, check out www.czechopera.cz.

DVOŘÁK HALL Map pp268-9
Dvořákova Síň; ☎ 227 059 352; www.rudolfinum.cz; náměstí Jana Palacha 1, Staré Město; tickets 200-600Kč; ⏰ box office 10am-12.30pm & 1.30-6pm Mon-Fri; metro Staroměstská
The Dvořák Hall in the neo-Renaissance Rudolfinum is home to the world-renowned Czech Philharmonic Orchestra (Česká filharmonie). Sit back and be impressed by some of the best classical musicians in Prague.

DVOŘÁK MUSEUM Map pp272-3
Muzeum Antonína Dvořáka; ☎ 224 918 013; Ke Karlovu 20, Nové Město; tickets 545Kč; ⏰ concerts 8pm Tue & Fri Apr-Oct; metro IP Pavlova
The pretty little Vila Amerika was built in 1717 as a count's immodest summer retreat. These days it's home to the Dvořák Museum (p103), and stages performances of Dvořák's vocal and instrumental works by the Original Music Theatre of Prague, complete with period costume. Tickets are available through BTI (see the boxed text, opposite).

ESTATES THEATRE Map pp268-9
Stavovské divadlo; ☎ 224 902 322; www.narodni-divadlo.cz; Ovocný trh 1, Staré Město; tickets 100-2000Kč; ⏰ box office 10am-6pm; metro Můstek

The Estates Theatre (also see p95) is the oldest theatre in Prague, famed as the place where Mozart conducted the premiere of *Don Giovanni* on 29 October 1787. A touristy version is staged here by the Opera Mozart company each summer; the rest of the year sees various opera, ballet and drama productions. The theatre is equipped for the hearing-impaired and has wheelchair access (wheelchair bookings can be made up to five days in advance); the box office is around the corner in the Kolowrat Palace.

MOZART MUSEUM Map pp262-3
Muzeum Mozarta; ☎ 257 317 465; www.bertramka.com; Vila Bertramka, Mozartova 169, Smíchov; tickets 390-450Kč; tram 4, 7, 9, 10
Mozart stayed in the Vila Bertramka during his visits to Prague. It now houses a museum (p112) which serves as a charming venue for classical concerts held in the salon and garden from April to October. You can buy tickets at the museum cash desk, or through BTI or Ticketpro.

NATIONAL THEATRE Map pp272-3
Národní divadlo; ☎ 224 901 377; www.narodni-divadlo.cz; Národní třída 2, Nové Město; tickets 100-2000Kč; ⏰ box office 10am-6pm; metro Národní Třída
The glorious, golden-roofed centrepiece of the Czech National Revival, the National Theatre provided a stage for the re-emergence of Czech culture in the late 19th and

Prague State Opera (below)

early 20th century. Today traditional opera, drama and ballet by the likes of Smetana, Shakespeare and Tchaikovsky share the programme with more modern works by composers and playwrights such as Philip Glass and John Osborne.

PRAGUE STATE OPERA Map pp272-3
Státní opera Praha; ☎ 224 227 266; www.opera .cz; Wilsonova 4, Nové Město; opera tickets 100-1200Kč, ballet tickets 100-900Kč; ☯ box office 10am-5.30pm Mon-Fri, to noon & 1-5.30pm Sat & Sun; metro Muzeum
The impressive neo-rococo home of the Prague State Opera provides a glorious setting for performances of opera and ballet. An annual Verdi festival takes place here in August and September, and less conventional shows, such as Leoncavallo's rarely staged version of *La Bohème,* are also performed here.

SMETANA HALL Map pp268-9
Smetanova Síň; ☎ 220 002 101; www.obecnidum .cz; náměstí Republiky 5, Staré Město; tickets 250-600Kč; ☯ box office 10am-6pm; metro Náměstí Republiky
Smetana Hall, centrepiece of the stunning Municipal House (Obecní dům; p93), is the city's largest concert hall with seating for 1200. This is the home venue of the Prague Symphony Orchestra (Symfonický orchestr hlavního města Prahy), and also stages performances of folk dance and music.

JAZZ & BLUES
Prague has lots of good jazz clubs, many of which have been around for decades. Unless otherwise indicated, most have a cover charge of around 200Kč.

AGHARTA JAZZ CENTRUM Map pp268-9
☎ 222 211 275; www.agharta.cz; Železná 16, Staré Město; ☯ 7pm-1am, music 9pm-midnight; metro Můstek
Agharta has been staging top-notch modern Czech jazz, blues, funk and fusion since 1991, but only moved into this very central Old Town venue in 2004. A typical jazz cellar with red-brick vaults and a cosy bar and café, the centre also has a music shop (open 7pm to midnight), which sells CDs, T-shirts and coffee mugs. As well as hosting local musicians, the centre occasionally stages gigs by leading international artists.

METROPOLITAN JAZZ CLUB Map pp272-3
☎ 224 947 777; Jungmannova 14, Nové Město; ☯ 7pm-1am, music 9pm-12.30am; metro Národní Třída
A basement jazz haunt with an easily digestible menu of traditional Dixieland, ragtime and swing, the Met shows a similar preference for substance over style in its choice of décor, with a plain tiled floor, a few musical instruments and posters on the walls, and a general lack of adornment that focuses attention on the solid, dependable, evergreen music.

DINITZ CAFÉ Map pp268-9
☎ 222 313 308; www.dinitz.cz; Na poříčí 12, Nové Město; admission free Sat-Thu, 150Kč Fri; ☯ 9am-3am, music 9pm-midnight; metro Náměstí Republiky
Dinitz is a relatively new bar and restaurant (see p142) that has swiftly gained a reputation for excellent live jazz, blues, Latin and funk, including a regular Tuesday-night session by Prague blues legend Stan the Man. If you want to brush up your dance steps, there are salsa lessons on Wednesday (6.30pm) and Friday (7pm).

REDUTA JAZZ CLUB Map pp272-3
☎ 224 933 487; www.redutajazzclub.cz; Národní třída 20, Nové Město; admission 300Kč; ☯ 9pm-3am; metro Národní Třída
The Reduta is Prague's oldest jazz club, founded in 1958 during the communist era – it was here in 1994 that former US president Bill Clinton famously jammed on a new saxophone presented to him by Václav Havel. It has an intimate setting,

(Continued on page 171)

1 *Mosaic above the entrance of Municipal House (Obecní dům; p93)* **2** *Grand Hotel Evropa (p201), on Wenceslas Square* **3** *Art Nouveau façade, Elišky Krásnohorské, Josefov (p88)* **4** *Art Nouveau detail, Maiselova, Josefov (p88)*

previous page *The lavish interior of one of Prague's many grand cafés (p153)*

1 *Façade of the Hotel Paříž (p200)*
2 *Municipal House (Obecní dům; p93)* **3** *Stained-glass windows, St Vitus Cathedral (p71)*

1 Cellar dining at Klub architektů (p140) 2 A traditional pub, Hostinec U ko... (p154) 3 Nightlife in Staré Město (p154)

1 *Bar with a view across to the St Nicholas Church (p80)* **2** *Velryba (p157): a café, bar and gallery* **3** *Inside Prague's most famous old café, Kavárna Slavia (p153)*

EDUARD ČAPEK

ŽELEZÁŘSTVÍ · POTŘEBY DO DOMÁCNOSTI

EDUARD ČAPEK
OTEVŘENO Po-Pá 10-18

VYKUPUJEME

OSTŘÍM
Nože
nůžky
sekáče a.j.

1 *Eduard Čapek outside the shop (p184) that has been in his family since 1911* 2 *The 15th-century Church of Our Lady Before Týn (p86)* 3 *La Provence restaurant (p140)* 4 *Hand-painting Easter eggs for traditional Easter celebrations (p9)*

1 *Herbal lotions for sale in Botanicus (p184)* **2** *Christmas market on Wenceslas Square (p98)*
3 *Art Nouveau window display on U Obecního domu, Staré Město (p85)* **4** *Open-air market in front of the Church of St Gall (p94)*

with smartly dressed patrons squeezing into tiered seats and lounges to soak up the big-band, swing and Dixieland atmosphere. Book a few hours ahead at the box office (open from 5pm Monday to Friday and from 7pm Saturday and Sunday), or through Ticketpro.

U MALÉHO GLENA Map pp264-5

☎ 257 531 717; www.malyglen.cz; Karmelitská 23, Malá Strana; ☻ 10am-2am, music from 9.30pm Sun-Thu, from 10pm Fri & Sat; tram 12, 20, 22, 23

'Little Glen's' is a lively American-owned bar and restaurant where hard-swinging local jazz or blues bands play in the stone-vaulted cellar every night'. There are regular jam sessions where amateurs are welcome

---

OTHER CONCERT VENUES

Numerous churches and baroque palaces also serve as concert venues, staging anything from choral performances and organ recitals to string quartets, brass ensembles and occasionally full orchestras. You can get comprehensive details of these concerts from PIS offices (see p238). We've listed here a selection of the more popular venues around town.

Hradčany & Malá Strana

Basilica of St George (Bazilika sv Jiří; Map p70; Náměstí u s Jiří, Prague Castle) The Czech Republic's best-preserved Romanesque church.

Liechtenstein Palace (Lichtenštejnský palác; Map pp264–5; Malostranské náměstí, Malá Strana; tram 12, 20, 22, 23) Home to the Music Faculty of the Prague Academy of Performing Arts (Hudební fakulta AMU; www.hamu.cz).

St Nicholas Church (Kostel sv Mikuláše; Map pp264–5; Malostranská náměstí 38, Malá Strana; metro Malostranská) Mozart himself tickled the ivories on the 2500-pipe organ here in 1787.

St Vitus Cathedral (Chrám sv Víta; Map p70; 3rd Courtyard, Prague Castle, Hradčany; metro Malostranská) The nave of Prague's cathedral is flooded with colour from beautiful stained-glass windows.

Strahov Monastery (Strahovský klášter; Map pp264–5; Strahovské nádvoří 1, Hradčany; tram 22, 23) Mozart is said to have played the organ here.

Staré Město

Bethlehem Chapel (Betlémská kaple; Map pp268–9; Betlémské náměstí 1; tram 6, 9, 18, 21, 22, 23) This 14th-century chapel was torn down during the 18th century and painstakingly reconstructed between 1948 and 1954.

Chapel of Mirrors (Zrcadlová kaple; Map pp268–9; Klementinum, Mariánské náměstí; tram 17, 18, 53) Ornately decorated chapel dating from the 1720s.

Church of St Francis (Kostel sv Františka; Map pp268–9; Křížovnické náměstí; tram 5, 8, 14) Alongside the complex of the Convent of St Agnes.

Church of St Nicholas (Kostel sv Mikuláše; Map pp268–9; Staroměstské náměstí; metro Staroměstská) Built in the 1730s by Kilian Dientzenhofer.

Convent of St Agnes (Klášter sv Anežky; Map pp268–9; U milosrdných 17; tram 5, 8, 14) Prague's oldest surviving Gothic building.

Nové Město

National Museum (Národní muzeum; Map pp272–3; Václavské náměstí 68; metro Muzeum) Chamber music and operatic duets performed on the grand staircase in the museum's main hall at 6pm most evenings.

Take care when buying tickets through people who hand out flyers in the street – some of these concerts are OK, but some may turn out to be a disappointment. Make sure you know exactly where the concert will be held – if you are told just 'the Municipal House', don't expect the magnificent Smetana Hall, as it may well be in one of the smaller concert halls.

(as long as you're good!). It's a small venue, so get here early.

USP JAZZ LOUNGE Map pp268-9

☎ 603 551 680; www.jazzlounge.cz; Michalská 9, Staré Město; ☺ 7pm-2am, music 9pm-midnight; metro Můstek

Located in the basement of the Hotel U Staré paní (see p200), this long-established jazz club caters to all levels of musical appreciation. There's a varied programme of modern jazz, soul, blues and latin rhythms, and a nightly DJ spot from midnight onwards.

ROCK

Prague has a high-energy live-music scene, with rock, metal, punk, hip-hop and newer sounds at a score of DJ and live-music venues. Most have a cover charge of around 50Kč to 200Kč. As well as the venues listed here, clubs such as Futurum, Klub 007 Strahov, Palác Akropolis and Roxy (see under Clubbing, p174) also host live rock bands.

For current listings and reviews check out the media noted on p160 – and watch the posters around town.

BATALION Map pp272-3

☎ 220 108 147; www.batalion.cz; 28.října 3, Staré Město; ☺ bar 24hr, music from 9pm; metro Můstek

Batalion is a delightfully grungy bar with a basement music club offering anything from rock and jazz to punk and death metal performed by up-and-coming Czech bands (plus DJs on Fridays and Saturdays). Despite a location in the midst of the tourist hordes, it pulls in a young, mainly local crowd.

KLUB DELTA

☎ 233 311 398; www.noise.cz/delta; Vlastina 887, Na Dědině; ☺ from 7pm, music from 8pm; bus 218

Klub Delta is a big theatre and exhibition venue that hosts mainly alternative and underground Czech bands such as Kolektivní Halucinace (Collective Hallucination), who describe themselves as 'psychedelic punk folk rock'! It's almost at the airport – take bus No 218 from Dejvická metro station to the Sídliště Na Dědině stop.

LUCERNA MUSIC BAR Map pp272-3

☎ 224 217 108; http://musicbar.iquest.cz; Vodičkova 36, Nové Město; ☺ 8pm-4am; metro Můstek

Nostalgia reigns supreme at this atmospheric old theatre, now looking a little dog-eared, with anything from Beatles tribute bands to mainly Czech artists playing jazz, blues, pop, rock and more on midweek nights. But the most popular event is the regular 1980s and '90s video party held every Friday and Saturday night, which pulls in huge crowds of young locals bopping along to Duran Duran and Gary Numan.

MALOSTRANSKÁ BESEDA Map pp264-5

☎ 257 532 092; Malostranské náměstí 21, Malá Strana; ☺ bar 5pm-1am, music from 8.30pm; tram 12, 20, 22, 23

Malá Strana's former town hall now houses a large café-bar that hosts anything from hard rock to bluegrass via jazz and folk, playing to a young and mostly Czech crowd. It packs out early, particularly on weekends.

ROCK CAFÉ Map pp272-3

☎ 224 914 416; www.rockcafé.cz; Národní třída 20, Nové Město; ☺ 10am-2.30am Mon-Fri, 5pm-2.30am Sat, to 1am Sun, music from 7.30pm; metro Národní Třída

Not to be confused with the Hard Rock Café, this is a multilevel club next door to the Reduta Jazz Club with an auditorium for DJs and live rock (being rebuilt at the time of research), with a café-bar downstairs, a cinema and an art gallery. Live bands are mostly local, ranging from nu-metal to folk-rock to Doors and Sex Pistols tribute bands.

THEATRE

Most Czech drama is, not surprisingly, performed in Czech, which rather diminishes its appeal to non-Czech-speakers. However, there are some English-language productions, and many predominantly visual shows where language is not a barrier.

Prague is famous for its black-light theatre – occasionally called just 'black theatre' – a hybrid of mime, drama, dance and special effects where live actors wearing fluorescent costumes do their thing in front of a black backdrop lit only by ultraviolet light (it's a growth industry in Prague, with at least half a dozen venues). An even older Czech tradition is puppetry, and the city has several marionette shows on offer.

Entertainment

THEATRE

Live music at Reduta Jazz Club (p162)

CELETNÁ THEATRE Map pp268-9
Divadlo v Celetné; ☎ 222 326 843; www.divadlov
celetne.cz; Celetná 17, Staré Město; tickets 50-290Kč;
⊙ box office 10am-7.30pm Mon-Fri, 2-7.30pm Sat &
Sun; metro Náměstí Republiky

The Divadlo v Celetné, in a courtyard
between Celetná and Štupartská, stages
mainly Czech drama, both old and new,
some foreign plays (including Shakespeare
and Tom Stoppard) translated into Czech,
and the occasional opera production by the
students of the Prague Conservatory.

MINOR THEATRE Map pp272-3
Divadlo Minor; ☎ 222 231 351; www.minor.cz;
Vodičkova 6, Nové Město; ⊙ box office 10am-
1.30pm & 2.30-8pm Mon-Fri, 11am-6pm Sat & Sun;
metro Karlovo Náměstí

Divadlo Minor is a wheelchair-accessible
children's theatre that offers a fun mix of
puppets, clown shows and pantomime.
There are performances (in Czech) at
9.30am Monday to Friday and at 6pm or
7.30pm Tuesday to Thursday, and you can
usually get a ticket at the door before the
show.

IMAGE THEATRE Map pp268-9
Divadlo Image; ☎ 222 314 448; www.imagetheatre
.cz; Pařížská 4, Staré Město; tickets 400Kč; ⊙ box
office 9am-8pm; metro Staroměstská

Founded in 1989, this company uses creative black-light theatre along with pantomime, modern dance and video – not to
mention liberal doses of slapstick – to tell
its stories. The staging can be very effective,
but the atmosphere is often dictated by
audience reaction.

LATERNA MAGIKA Map pp272-3
☎ 224 931 482; www.laterna.cz; Nová Scéna,
Národní třída 4, Nové Město; tickets 680Kč; ⊙ box
office 10am-8pm Mon-Sat; metro Národní Třída

Laterna Magika has been wowing audiences, both at home and abroad, ever since
its first cutting-edge multimedia show
caused a stir at the 1958 Brussels World
Fair. Its imaginative blend of live dance,
opera, music and projected images continues to pull in the crowds. Nová Scéna,
the futuristic glass-block building next to
the National Theatre, has been home to
Laterna Magika since it moved here from
its birthplace in the basement of the Adria
Palace in the mid-1970s. Some agencies
(which charge 735Kč a ticket) may tell you
it's booked out, but you can often bag a
leftover seat at the box office on the day
before a performance, or a no-show seat
half an hour before the show starts.

NATIONAL MARIONETTE THEATRE
Map pp268-9
Národní divadlo marionet; ☎ 224 819 323; www
.mozart.cz; Žatecká 1, Staré Město; tickets 490Kč;
⊙ box office 10am-8pm; metro Staroměstská

Loudly touted as the longest-running classical marionette show in the city – it has been

Entertainment

THEATRE

performed almost continuousy since 1991 – *Don Giovanni* is a life-sized puppet version of the Mozart opera that has spawned several imitations around town. Younger kids' attention might begin to wander fairly early on during this two-hour show.

REDUTA THEATRE Map pp272-3

Divadlo Reduta; ☎ 257 921 835; www.blacktheatre srnec.cz; Národní třída 20, Nové Město; tickets 490Kč; ⓨ box office 3-7pm Mon-Fri; metro Národní Třída
The Reduta Theatre is home to the Black Theatre of Jiří Srnec, who was a founding member of Prague's original black-light theatre back in the early 1960s. Today the company's productions include versions of *Alice in Wonderland* and *Peter Pan,* and a compilation of the best of black theatre from the early days.

SPEJBL & HURVÍNEK THEATRE Map p275

Divadlo Spejbla a Hurvínka; ☎ 224 316 784; www .spejbl-hurvinek.cz; Dejvická 38, Dejvice; tickets 50-90Kč; ⓨ box office 10am-2pm & 3-6pm Tue-Fri, 1-5pm Sat & Sun; metro Dejvická
Created in 1930 by puppeteer Josef Skupa, Spejbl and Hurvinek are the Czech marionette equivalents of Punch and Judy, although they are father and son rather than husband and wife. Most shows are in Czech, a few are in German, but most can be followed whatever language you speak.

TA FANTASTIKA Map pp268-9

☎ 222 221 366; www.tafanstastika.cz; Karlova 8, Staré Město; tickets 200-600Kč; ⓨ box office 11am-9.30pm; metro Staroměstská
Established in New York in 1981 by Czech émigré Petr Kratochvil, Ta Fantastika moved to Prague in 1989. The theatre produces black-light theatre based on classic literature and legends such as *Alice in Wonderland, Excalibur, The Picture of Dorian Gray* and *Joan of Arc.*

THEATRE ON THE BALUSTRADE

Map pp268-9
Divadlo Na Zábradlí; ☎ 222 868 868; www.nazabradli .cz; Anenské náměstí 5, Staré Město; tickets 90-250Kč; ⓨ box office 2-4pm & 4.30-7pm Mon-Fri, 2hr before show starts Sat & Sun; tram 17, 18
The theatre where Václav Havel honed his skills as a playwright four decades ago is now the city's main venue for serious Czech-language drama, including works by a range of foreign playwrights translated into Czech.

CLUBBING

Prague's club scene is nothing to rave about. With few exceptions, the city's dance clubs cater to crowds of partying teenagers and tourists weaned on MTV Europe – if you want to dance to anything other than '80s hits or happy house, you'll have to look long and hard. Prague's main strengths are its alternative-music clubs, DJ bars and 'experimental' venues such as Klub 007 Strahov, Palác Akropolis and the Roxy.

Refreshingly, dress codes don't seem to have reached Prague yet, and it's unlikely you'll be knocked back anywhere unless you're stark naked. Check www.prague.tv, www.techno.cz/party or www.hip-hop.cz for up-to-date club listings.

ANGEL CLUB Map pp270-1

☎ 776 668 632; www.angel-club.info; Kmochova 8, Smíchov; admission free-70Kč; ⓨ 7pm-6am Fri & Sat; tram 4, 7, 9, 10
The Angel Club – formerly the dark and throbbing heart of Prague's gay dance-club scene – has had a complete makeover, reopening at the start of 2006 with sleek designer décor. Sensuous Italian sofas, smooth white styling and clever lighting set off the rough brick and concrete walls, while the atmosphere has been transformed from sweaty to sophisticated. The clientele is now mixed, with DJs on Friday nights playing dance music to a mostly straight crowd, while Saturdays are billed as '(Almost) Boys Only'.

FUTURUM Map pp270-1

☎ 257 328 571; www.musicbar.cz; Zborovská 7, Smíchov; admission 100Kč; ⓨ 9pm-3am; tram 7, 9, 12, 14
Futurum is a weird cross-fertilisation of alternative and mainstream, with an equally

---

TOP FIVE CLUBS

- Palác Akropolis (opposite)
- Radost FX (opposite)
- Roxy (opposite)
- Sedm Vlků (p176)
- Wakata (p176)

weird décor that looks like a cross between an Art Deco ballroom and Flash Gordon's spaceship. Midweek nights see a mix of live jazz and soul, indie bands, record launches and film screenings, but what really pulls in the crowds is the regular Friday and Saturday night '80s and '90s Video Party, with local DJs blasting out everthing from REM and Nirvana to Bon Jovi and Village People, complete with cringeworthy videos.

KARLOVY LÁZNĚ Map pp268-9

☎ 222 220 502; www.karlovylazne.cz; Novotného lávka 1, Staré Město; admission 50-120Kč; ☺ 9pm-5am; tram 17, 18
Billed as the biggest club in central Europe, KL is a vast, steaming hive of heaving bodies, awash with alcohol and teenage pheromones. That said, it's a fascinating venue in a labyrinthine medieval building with old murals, mosaics and partly preserved Roman-style baths (now dance floors); a single cover charge admits you to four floors – from the Music Café (black music) on the ground floor, up through Discotheque (classic disco sounds) and Kaleidoskop ('60s, '70s and '80s revival) to Paradogs (dance, house, techno, drum'n'bass etc).

KLUB 007 STRAHOV Map pp270-1

☎ 257 211 439; www.klub007strahov.cz; Block 7, Chaloupeckého 7; admission 50-250Kč; ☺ 7pm-1am Sun-Thu, to 2am Fri & Sat; bus 143, 176, 217
Klub 007 is one of several grungy student clubs in the basements of the big dormitory blocks in Strahov. The legendary 007 has been around since 1987, when it was a focus for underground music, and is now famed for its devotion to hardcore, punk, ska, ragga, jungle, ambient and other alternative sounds. On Saturday nights it hosts a regular hip-hop party.

M1 SECRET LOUNGE Map pp268-9

☎ 227 195 235; Masna 1, Staré Město; admission free; ☺ 6pm-4am; tram 5, 8, 14
An American-owned, industrial-chic cocktail den where concrete and exposed air-con ducts contrast with candlelight and plush sofas, M1 attracts lots of English-speaking expats, well-heeled locals and the occasional visiting celebrity (absolutely no stag parties). Wednesday nights are best, when a more studenty crowd comes in to enjoy a mix of indie rock, Britpop and electro (from 10pm).

MECCA Map pp276-7

☎ 283 870 522; www.mecca.cz; U Průhonu 3, Holešovice; admission 90-390Kč Fri & Sat, free Wed & Thu; ☺ 10pm-6am Wed-Sat; tram 5, 12, 15
This former warehouse in Holešovice is home to an ultrafashionable dance club, its industrial red brick and right angles softened by rounded shapes, floaty drapes, and futuristic curvy couches. Mecca is a magnet for models, film stars and fashionistas who hang out in the stylish restaurant, and the legion of Ibiza-bred clubbers who come for the huge, DJ-dominated dance floor and pumping sound system.

PALÁC AKROPOLIS Map pp278-9

☎ 296 330 911; www.palacakropolis.cz; Kubelíkova 27, Žižkov; admission free-30Kč; ☺ club 7pm-5am; tram 5, 9, 26
The Akropolis is a Prague institution, a labyrinthine, sticky-floored shrine to alternative music and drama. Its various performance spaces host a smorgasbord of musical and cultural events, from DJs to string quartets to Macedonian Roma bands to local rock gods to visiting talent – Marianne Faithfull, the Flaming Lips and the Strokes have all played here. DJs do their stuff in the Theatre Bar (Divadelní Bar) and Small Hall (Malá Scéna), spinning everything from house to hip-hop, reggae to breakbeat.

RADOST FX Map pp272-3

☎ 224 254 776; www.radostfx.cz; Bělehradská 120, Vinohrady; admission 100-250Kč; ☺ 10pm-6am; metro IP Pavlova
Though not quite as hot as it once was, Prague's slickest, shiniest and most self-assured club is still capable of pulling in the crowds, especially for its Thursday hip-hop night, FXbounce (www.fxbounce.com). The place has a chilled-out, bohemian atmosphere, with Moroccan-boudoir-meets-Moulin-Rouge décor, and there's an excellent lounge-cum-vegetarian restaurant that keeps serving into the small hours.

ROXY Map pp268-9

☎ 224 826 296; www.roxy.cz; Dlouhá 33, Staré Město; admission 100-250Kč Fri & Sat; ☺ 7pm-midnight Mon-Thu, 7pm-6am Fri & Sat; tram 5, 8, 14
Set in the ramshackle shell of an Art Deco cinema (now extensively restored after severe flood damage in 2002), the Roxy has

nurtured the more independent and innovative end of Prague's club spectrum since 1987 – this is the place to check out the Czech Republic's top DJs. On the 1st floor is NoD, an 'experimental space' that stages drama, dance, preformance art, cinema and live music; events here usually begin earlier in the evening before the nightclub kicks off.

SEDM VLKŮ Map pp278-9

☎ 222 711 725; www.sedmvlku.cz; Vlkova 7, Žižkov; ⏰ 5pm-3am Mon-Sat; tram 5, 9, 26
'Seven Wolves' is a cool, two-level, art-studenty café-bar and club – at street level there's candlelight, friendly staff, weird wrought-iron work and funky murals, and the music's low enough to have a conversation; down in the darkened cellar, DJs pump out techno, breakbeat, drum'n'bass and ragga from 9pm on Friday and Saturday nights.

TERMIX Map pp280-1

☎ 222 710 462; www.club-termix.cz; Třebízckého 4a, Vinohrady; admission free; ⏰ 8pm-5am Wed-Sun; metro Jiřího z Poděbrad
Termix is one of Prague's most popular gay and lesbian dance clubs, with an industrial/high-tech vibe (lots of shiny steel and glass, plush sofas and a car sticking out of one wall), cute bar staff and a young crowd that contains as many tourists as locals. The smallish dance floor fills up fast during Thursday's techno party, when you'll probably have to queue to get in.

WAKATA Map pp276-7

☎ 233 370 518; www.wakata.cz; Malířská 14, Bubenec; admission free; ⏰ 5pm-3am Mon-Thu, to 5am Fri & Sat, 6pm-3am Sun; tram 1, 8, 25, 26
No designer chic or style statements in this small, unpretentious, laid-back DJ lounge, a house-free zone where you can enjoy

Cinema posters

inexpensive beers and cocktails among the scuffed and mismatched furniture while you bop along to a soundtrack of funk, Latin, dub, ambient, jungle, reggae or hip-hop. The real McCoy.

CINEMA

Prague has more than 30 cinemas, some showing first-run Western films, some showing Czech films, and several excellent arthouse cinemas. For cinema listings check the 'Night & Day' section of the *Prague Post*, or www.prague.tv.

Most films are screened in their original language with Czech subtitles (*české titulky*), but Hollywood blockbusters are often dubbed into Czech (*dabing*); look for the labels 'tit.' or 'dab.' on cinema listings. Czech-language films with English subtitles are listed as having *anglický titulky*.

KINO AERO Map pp262-3

☎ 271 771 349; www.kinoaero.cz; Biskupcova 31, Žižkov; tickets 80-90Kč; tram 5, 9, 10, 16, 19
The Aero is Prague's best-loved arthouse cinema, with themed programmes, retrospectives and unusual films, often in English or with English subtitles. This is the place to catch reruns of classics from *Smrt v Benátkách* (Death in Venice) to *Život Briana* (The Life of Brian). The same managers run a similar venue in the city centre, Kino Světozor (opposite).

Entertainment
CINEMA

KINO MAT Map pp272-3

☎ 224 915 765; www.mat.cz; Karlovo náměstí 19, Nové Město; tickets 99Kč; metro Karlovo Náměstí

Kino Mat is a former film and TV studio's private screening room (there are only 40 seats) turned hip, arthouse cinema, where film buffs sip espressos in the celluloid-decorated downstairs bar while discussing the use of visual metaphor in *Citizen Kane*. The programme includes the latest Czech films (with English subtitles), and the latest European films (with Czech ones).

KINO PERŠTÝN Map pp272-3

☎ 221 668 559; Na Perstýně 6, Staré Město; tickets 85-90Kč; metro Národní Třída

This film-clubbish cinema forgoes those boring old rows of seats for a sociable scattering of tables and chairs, and screens mostly English- and foreign-language films with Czech subtitles. You can bring drinks into the cinema, but smoking is confined to the next-door bar.

KINO SVĚTOZOR Map pp272-3

☎ 224 946 824; www.kinosvetozor.cz; Vodičkova 41, Nové Město; tickets 80-100Kč; metro Můstek

The Světozor is under the same management as Kino Aero but is more central, and has the same emphasis on classic cinema and arthouse films screened in their original language – everything from *Battleship Potemkin* and *Casablanca* to *Annie Hall* and *Motorcycle Diaries*.

PALACE CINEMAS Map pp268-9

☎ 257 181 212; www.palacecinemas.cz; Slovanský dům, Na příkopě 22, Nové Město; tickets 159Kč; metro Náměstí Republiky

Housed in the posh Slovanský dům shopping centre, this is central Prague's main popcorn palace – a modern 10-screen multiplex showing first-run Hollywood films (mostly in English). There's also a 12-screen multiplex (Map pp270–1; Plzeňská 8, Smíchov; metro Anděl) on the top floor of the huge Nový Smíchov shopping centre.

ACTIVITIES
FITNESS CENTRES

You can use the *posilovna* (weights room) at the Sportcentrum YMCA (p179) for 90Kč

per hour. The weights room at the Sportcentrum Hotel Čechie (p179) charges 100Kč to 120Kč for up to three hours. Guests of the hotel can use the pool for free. There's also the centrally located Fitness Týn (Map pp268–9; ☎ 224 808 295; Týnská 21, Staré Město; casual workout 95Kč; ⏰ 7am-9pm Mon-Fri, 10am-8pm Sat & Sun). The luxurious Cybex Health Club & Spa (Map pp278–9; ☎ 224 842 375; www.cybexprg.cz; Pobřežní 1, Nové Město; ⏰ 6am-10pm Mon-Fri, 7am-10pm Sat & Sun; metro Florenc) in the Hotel Hilton charges 900Kč for a day pass, which gives access to the gym, pool, sauna, Jacuzzi and steam room.

FOOTBALL (SOCCER)

Prague's two big football clubs, Slavia Praha and Sparta Praha, are both leading contenders in the national *fotbal* (football) league. Two other Prague-based teams are FC Bohemians (Map pp262–3; ☎ 271 721 459; www.fc-bohemians.cz; Vršovická 31, Vinohrady; tram 4, 22) and FK Viktoria Žižkov (Map pp278–9; ☎ 221 423 427; www.fkvz .cz; Seifertova, Žižkov; tram 5, 9, 26). The season runs from August to December and February to June, and matches are mostly played on Wednesday, Saturday and Sunday afternoons.

AC SPARTA PRAHA STADIUM
Map pp276-7

Toyota Arena; ☎ 296 111 400; www.sparta.cz; Milady Horákové 98, Bubeneč; tickets 50-230Kč; tram 1, 8, 15, 25, 26

The all-seater Toyota Arena, with a capacity of 20,854, is the home ground of Sparta Praha – winners of the Czech football league in 2000, 2001, 2003 and 2005, and of the Czech National Cup in 2004 – and is also used by the Czech national football team for big international matches. The club was founded in 1893.

SK SLAVIA PRAHA STADIUM Map pp262-3

Stadión Evžena Rošického; ☎ 257 213 290; www .slavia.cz; Diskařská 100, Strahov; tickets 50-200Kč; bus 176

Founded in 1892, SK Slavia Praha is one of the oldest sporting clubs in continental Europe and an honorary member of England's Football Association. Czech National Cup winner in 1997, 1999 and 2002, it holds an unusual record – the design of its distinctive red-and-white strip has remained unchanged since 1896.

GOLF

GOLF CLUB PRAHA Map pp262-3

☎ 257 216 584; Plzeňská 401/2, Motol; green fees (nine holes) 400-500Kč Mon-Fri, 600Kč Sat, Sun & hols; tram 7, 9 or 10

Prague has one nine-hole golf course, the Golf Club Praha behind the Hotel Golf in the western suburbs. Here you can hire a set of clubs for 500Kč. Take tram No 7, 9 or 10 west to the Hotel Golf stop.

GOLF & COUNTRY CLUB

☎ 244 460 435; www.hodkovicky.cz; Vltavanů 982, Hodkovičky; green fees (nine holes) 400-600Kč, driving range per 50 balls 75Kč; 8am-9pm May-Oct, 10am-4pm Nov-Apr; tram 3, 17 or 21

The Golf & Country Club, on the southern edge of the city, has a nine-hole course, a driving range and chipping and putting greens. Take tram No 3, 17 or 21 south to the Černý kůň stop, and walk west towards the river on V náklích (follow the signs for Hostel Boathouse) for 100m, then turn first right immediately after passing under the railway bridge.

KARLŠTEJN GOLF COURSE

☎ 311 604 999; www.karlstejn-golf.cz; Běleč 280, Líteň; green fees 2000Kč Mon-Fri, 3000Kč Sat, Sun & hols

The closest 18-hole course to Prague is the prestigious Karlštejn Golf Course overlooking Karlštejn Castle, southwest of the city (see p211). It's several kilometres from Karlštejn village, on the southern bank of the Berounka River.

HORSE RACING

PRAGUE RACECOURSE

Velká Chuchle závodiště Praha; ☎ 257 941 431; www.velka-chuchle.cz; Radotínská 69, Velká Chuchle; admission adult/child under 15 70Kč/free; bus 129, 172, 243, 244, 255

Check out the *dostihy* (horse racing) scene at Prague Racecourse on the southern edge of the city. There are races every Sunday from April to October – the website has details of the racing calendar. You can reach the racecourse by taking the bus from Smíchovské Nádraží metro station.

An ice-hockey match (opposite)

ICE HOCKEY

The Czech national ice-hockey (*lední hokej*) team has won the world championship 11 times (most recently in 2005) and took Olympic gold at the winter Olympics in Nagano in 1998. HC Sparta Praha and HC Slavia Praha are Prague's two big teams. The season runs from September to early April.

SAZKA ARENA Map pp262-3

☎ 266 212 111; www.sazkaarena.com, www.hc-slavia.cz; Ocelářská 2, Vysočany; metro Českomoravská
Completed in time to host the 2004 Ice Hockey World Championship, the Sazka Arena is Prague's biggest multipurpose venue, and home rink of HC Slavia Praha. It can accommodate up to 18,000 spectators, and is used to host sporting events, rock concerts, exhibitions and other major events as well as hockey games.

T-MOBILE ARÉNA Map pp276-7

☎ 266 727 443; www.hcsparta.cz; Za elektrámou 419, Výstaviště, Holešovice; tickets 40-160Kč; tram 5, 12, 14, 15, 17
You can see HC Sparta Praha – Czech Extraleague champions 2005-06 – play at the 13,000-capacity T-Mobile Arena beside the Exhibition Grounds in Holešovice.

RUNNING

PRAGUE INTERNATIONAL MARATHON

☎ 224 919 209; www.pim.cz; Záhořanského 3, 120 00 Praha 2
The Prague International Marathon (Pražský Mezinárodní maraton), established 1989, is now an annual event (normally held mid- to late May), attracting more foreign runners than Czechs. There's also a half-marathon, held in late March. If you'd like to compete, you can register online or obtain entry forms from the website. Registration fee is €60, and entries must be received at least 10 days before the race.

SKATING

The Czechs are skate-mad. In summer, Prague's parks are filled with inline skaters, and in winter, when the mercury drops below zero, sections of parks are sprayed with water and turned into ice rinks. There are also plenty of indoor ice rinks and roller rinks.

INLINE PŮJČOVNA Map pp276-7

Inline Skate Rental; ☎ 739 046 040; Nad štolou 1, Holešovice; ☒ noon-10pm Mon-Fri, 10am-10pm Sat & Sun; tram 1, 8, 15, 25, 26
You can rent inline skates from this place (they speak a bit of English), which is close to the extensive skating trails in Letná Gardens.

ŠTVANICE STADIUM Map pp268-9

Zimní stadión Štvanice; ☎ 233 378 327; Ostrov Štvanice 1125, Holešovice; adult/child under seven 50/20Kč; ☒ public skating 9-11am & 3-5pm; tram 3, 26
This is the oldest ice-hockey stadium in Central Europe – Czechoslovakia's first ice-hockey match on artificial ice was played here in 1931. It provides public skating sessions as well as hosting ice-hockey and roller-hockey games in season.

SWIMMING

PODOLÍ SWIMMING POOL Map pp262-3

Plavecký stadión Podolí; ☎ 241 433 952; Podolská 74, Podolí; admission 80/125Kč per 1½/3hr, child under 13 half-price; ☒ 6am-9.45pm; tram 3, 16, 17, 21
This huge swimming complex has Olympic-sized pools, both indoor and outdoor, with plenty of sunbathing space (best to bring footwear for the grotty showers, though). To get there, take the tram to the Kublov stop; from there it's a further five-minute walk.

SPORTCENTRUM HOTEL ČECHIE
Map pp262-3

☎ 266 194 100; U Sluncové 618, Karlín; ☒ 4-11pm Mon, 1-11pm Tue-Fri, 10am-11pm Sat & Sun; metro Invalidovna
The pool and sauna at the Sportcentrum Hotel Čechie are open to the public, and cost 200/100Kč for an adult/child under 15 for up to three hours.

SPORTCENTRUM YMCA Map pp268-9

☎ 224 875 811; www.scymca.cz; Na poříčí 12; admission 90Kč per hr; ☒ 6.30am-9.30pm Mon-Fri, 10am-8.30pm Sat & Sun; metro Náměstí Republiky
There is a 25m pool at the Sportcentrum YMCA. The pool is not available to the public at all times; you should check the

Entertainment

ACTIVITIES

website (follow the link Služby/Bázen for the relevant information) – the sessions that are blocked out in green and marked 'veřejnost' are open to the public.

TENNIS & SQUASH

CZECH LAWN TENNIS CLUB Map pp278-9
Český Lawn-Tennis Klub; ☎ 222 316 317; www.cltk.cz; Ostrov Štvanice 38, Holešovice; match tickets 90Kč; tram 3, 26

Founded in 1893, this is the oldest and most prestigious tennis club in the country (despite the name, all its courts are clay!), and it was here that Ivan Lendl and Martina Navratilova cut their teeth. The 8000-seat centre court hosts the annual Prague Open (www.pragueopen.cz) tournament in May.

ESQUO SQUASHCENTRUM Map pp270-1
☎ 233 109 301; www.squashstrahov.cz; Vaníčkova 2b, Strahov; ☾ 7am-11pm Mon-Fri, 8am-11pm Sat & Sun

You can rent squash courts at Esquo for 140Kč to 350Kč per hour, depending on the time of day.

SPORTCENTRUM HOTEL ČECHIE
Map pp262-3
☎ 266 194 100; U Sluncové 618, Karlín; ☾ 7am-11pm Mon-Fri, 8am-11pm Sat & Sun; metro Invalidovna

The Čechie has six outdoor clay courts which you can rent for 100Kč to 200Kč per hour, and indoor courts for 300Kč to 650Kč per hour. It also offers squash courts for 200Kč to 350Kč per hour.

Shopping ▶

Shopping

In the last decade or so Prague's shopping scene has changed beyond recognition. A massive influx of global brand names and a wave of glitzy new malls crammed with designer outlets, smart cafés and big Western brand names has left the city's main shopping streets looking very much like those of any other European capital.

Imported goods often carry Western European prices, but Czech products remain affordable for Czechs and cheap for Westerners. While tourist gift shops outside Prague (eg in Karlštejn or Mělník; see p211) have smaller selections, prices are significantly lower. If you're hunting for bargains, the word *'sleva'* means 'discount'.

Shopping Areas

The city centre's single biggest – and most exhausting – retail zone is around **Wenceslas Square** (Václavské náměstí), its pavements jammed with browsing visitors and locals making beelines for their favourite stores. You can find pretty much everything here, from high fashion and music megastores to run-of-the-mill department stores and gigantic book emporia. Many of the more interesting shops are hidden away in arcades and passages, such as the **Palác Lucerna** (Map pp272–3).

The other main shopping drag intersects with the lower end of Wenceslas Square, comprising **Na příkopě** (Map pp268–9), **28.října** (Map pp272–3) and **Národní třída** (Map pp272–3). Most of the big stores and malls are concentrated on Na příkopě, with the biggest of them all – the shiny new **Palladium Praha Shopping Centre** – at its northeast end, opposite the Municipal House.

In Staré Město, the elegant avenue of **Pařížská** (Map pp268–9) is lined with international designer boutiques including Dior, Boss, Armani and Louis Vuitton, while the winding lanes between the Old Town Square and Charles Bridge are thronged with tacky souvenir shops flaunting puppets, Russian dolls and 'Czech This Out' T-shirts.

In recent years many new shops have opened up outside the centre, notably in **Vinohrady** (Map pp280–1 and pp278–9), which is good for antiques and designer furniture, **Smíchov** (Map pp270–1), dominated by the huge Nový Smíchov mall, and in the suburb of Zlíčin on the far western edge of the city, which has a vast shopping centre anchored around Tesco and IKEA.

Anagram bookshop (opposite)

Opening Hours

Prague shops usually open anywhere between 8am and 10am, and close between 5pm and 7pm on Monday to Friday; major shops, departments stores and tourist businesses open on weekends, too, but more local shops may be closed on Saturday afternoon and Sunday.

Consumer Taxes

Value-added tax (VAT, or DPH in Czech) is applied at 5% on food, hotel rooms and restaurant meals, but 22% on luxury items (including alcohol). This tax is included in the marked price and not added at the cash register.

It is possible to claim VAT refunds of up to 14% of the purchase price for purchases totalling more than 2000Kč that are made in shops displaying the 'Tax Free Shopping' sticker. They will give you a Tax Free Shopping voucher, which you then need to present to customs for validation when you leave the country (which must be within three months from the date of purchase). You can then claim your refund either at a duty-free shop in the airport (after passing through passport control), or from a cash-refund office back home (within six weeks of the purchase date). For more information see www.global refund.com.

HRADČANY

ANTIQUE MUSIC INSTRUMENTS

Map pp264-5   Antiques

☎ 233 353 779; Pohořelec 9; ⏰ 9am-6pm; tram 22, 23

It may not get the prize for most inventive shop name, but this place is a real treasure-trove of vintage stringed instruments. You'll find an interesting stock of antique violins, violas and cellos dating from the 18th century to the mid-20th century, as well as bows, cases and other musical accessories.

ICONS GALLERY Map pp264-5   Antiques

☎ 233 353 777; Pohořelec 9; ⏰ 9am-6pm; tram 22, 23

In the same building as Antique Music Instruments, this cluttered little shop has a luminous collection of Russian and Eastern European religious icons, as well as lots of other decorative *objets d'art,* watches, porcelain and Art Nouveau glassware.

MALÁ STRANA

CAPRICCIO Map pp270-1   Music

☎ 257 320 165; Újezd 15; ⏰ 10am-6pm Mon-Fri; tram 6, 9, 12, 20

Pick up the score for Mozart's *Don Giovanni* or Dvořák's *New World Symphony* at this eclectic sheet-music shop, and hum away to yourself at the in-store café. Or you might enjoy the books of country-music favourites – who wouldn't want to learn how to sing *Rhinestone Cowboy* in Czech?

SHAKESPEARE & SONS Map pp264-5   Books

☎ 257 531 894; U Lužickéo seminaře 10; ⏰ 11am-7pm; tram 12, 20, 22, 23

This is a newer and smaller branch of the famous English-language secondhand bookshop of the same name in Vinohrady (see p191).

VETEŠNICTVI Map pp270-1   Antiques

☎ 257 530 624; Vítezná 16; ⏰ 10am-5pm Mon-Fri, 10am-noon Sat; tram 6, 9, 12, 20, 22, 23

This is an Aladdin's cave of secondhand goods, bric-a-brac and junk with, in all likelihood, some genuine antiques for those who know what they're looking for. There's affordable stuff for everyone, from communist-era lapel pins, medals, postcards, old beer mugs and toys to crystal, shot glasses, porcelain, china, pipes and spa cups, all presided over by a bust of Lenin.

STARÉ MĚSTO

ANAGRAM Map p266-7   Books

☎ 224 895 737; Týn 4; ⏰ 10am-8pm Mon-Sat, 10am-7pm Sun; metro Náměstí Republiky

An excellent English-language bookshop, Anagram offers a vast range of fiction and nonfiction, with an especially good selection on European history, philosophy, religion, art and travel, as well as Czech works in translation and children's books. Seek out the remainders section for some bargain new books as well as secondhand offerings on various topics.

ART DECO GALERIE Map pp268-9 Antiques

☎ 224 223 076; Michalská 21; ⏰ 2-7pm Mon-Fri; metro Můstek

Specialising in early-20th-century items, this shop has a wide range of 1920s and '30s stuff including clothes, handbags, jewellery, glassware and ceramics, along with knick-knacks such as the kind of cigarette case you might imagine Dorothy Parker pulling from her purse.

ART DÉCORATIF Map pp268-9 Arts & Crafts

☎ 224 222 283; Melantrichova 5; ⏰ 10am-8pm; metro Můstek

This is a beautiful shop dealing in Czech-made reproductions of fine Art Nouveau and Art Deco glassware, jewellery and fabrics, including some stunning vases and bowls. It's also an outlet for the gorgeously delicate creations of Jarmila Plockova, granddaughter of Alfons Mucha, who uses elements of his paintings in her work.

ARZENAL Map pp268-9 Glassware

☎ 224 814 099; Valentinská 11; ⏰ 10am-midnight; metro Staroměstská

Arzenal is a design salon and showroom for the striking and colourful glassware of Bořek Šípek, one of the Czech Republic's leading architects and designers. Unusually, it is also home to one of the city's best Thai restaurants, Siam-I-San (p141).

BIG BEN Map pp268-9 Books

☎ 224 826 565; Malá Štupartská 5; ⏰ 9am-6.30pm Mon-Fri, 10am-5pm Sat, noon-5pm Sun; metro Náměstí Republiky

Big Ben is a small but well-stocked English-language bookshop, with shelves devoted to Czech and European history, books on Prague, travel (including Lonely Planet guides), science fiction, children's books, poetry, and all the latest fiction bestsellers. There are also English-language newspapers and magazines at the counter.

BOHÈME Map pp268-9 Fashion

☎ 224 813 840; Dušní 8; ⏰ 11am-8pm Mon-Fri, to 5pm Sat; metro Staroměstská

This trendy fashion store showcases the designs of Hana Stocklassa and her associates, with collections of knitwear, leather and suede clothes for women. Sweaters, turtlenecks, suede skirts, linen blouses, knit

dresses and stretch denim suits seem to be the stock in trade, and there's a range of jewellery to choose from as well.

BOTANICUS Map pp268-9 Cosmetics

☎ 224 895 445; Týn 3; ⏰ 10am-8pm; metro Náměstí Republiky

Prepare for olfactory overload in this always-busy outlet for natural health and beauty products. The scented soaps, herbal bath oils and shampoos, fruit cordials and handmade paper products are made using herbs and plants grown on an organic farm at Ostrá, east of Prague.

BRÍC Á BRAC Map pp268-9 Antiques

☎ 224 815 763; Týnská 7; ⏰ 10am-6pm; metro Náměstí Republiky

Hidden up a narrow lane behind the Týn church, this is a wonderfully cluttered cave of old household items and glassware and toys and apothecary jars and 1940s leather jackets and cigar boxes and typewriters and stringed instruments and… Despite the junky look of the place, the knick-knacks are surprisingly expensive; there are two 'showrooms', a small one on Týnská, and a larger one in a nearby courtyard (follow the signs), and the affable Serbian owner can give you a guided tour around every piece in his extensive collection.

DEVACO Map pp268-9 Jewellery

☎ 222 323 639; Pařížská 15; ⏰ 10am-8pm; metro Staroměstská

This gorgeously stocked jewellery boutique includes the trademark Easter egg pendants created by Fabergé, jewellers to the Russian royal family, as well as a sparkly array of rings, cufflinks, brooches, bracelets and necklaces.

EDUARD ČAPEK Map pp268-9 Bric-a-Brac

Dlouhá 32; ⏰ 10am-6pm Mon-Fri; metro Náměstí Republiky

The Čapek clan has lovingly operated its bric-a-brac shop since 1911 – it is supposedly the only shop to have continued in private ownership right through the communist era – and nothing has ever been thrown away, including the dust. Rolls of recycled electrical wire, rusty tools, dog-eared magazines and battered handbags are among the many, er…treasures awaiting your perusal.

FREY WILLE Map pp268-9 · Jewellery
☎ 272 142 228; Havířská 3; ⊗ 10am-6pm; metro Můstek

An Austrian jewellery maker famed for its enamel work, Frey Wille produces a distinctive range of highly decorative pieces. Its traditional Paisley and Egyptian designs have now been complemented by a range of Art Nouveau designs based on the works of Alfons Mucha.

GALERIE VLASTA Map pp268-9 · Jewellery
☎ 222 318 119; Staroměstské náměstí 5; ⊗ 10am-6pm Mon-Fri, to 1pm Sat; metro Staroměstská

This small boutique showcases the delicate creations in gold and silver wire of award-winning contemporary Czech designer Vlasta Wasserbauerová, including a range of highly distinctive netlike brooches, necklaces and earrings.

GRANÁT TURNOV Map pp268-9 · Jewellery
☎ 222 315 612; Dlouhá 28-30; ⊗ 10am-6pm Mon-Sat, to 1pm Sun; metro Náměstí Republiky

Part of the country's biggest jewellery chain and specialising in Bohemian garnet, Granát Turnov stocks a huge range of gold and silver rings, brooches, cufflinks and necklaces showing off these small, dark blood-red stones. It also has pearl and diamond jewellery, as well as less expensive pieces set with the dark green semiprecious stone known in Czech as *vltavín* (moldavite).

IVANA FOLLOVÁ ART & FASHION GALLERY Map pp268-9 · Fashion
☎ 224 895 460; Týn 1; ⊗ 10.30am-7pm; metro Náměstí Republiky

Prague designer Ivana Follová specialises in handpainted silk dresses, many of which can be seen at this chic boutique. Only natural materials are used in her colourful creations. The shop also has accessories, including handmade glass beads, and some excellent, if pricey, locally produced paintings, jewellery and sculpture.

KERAMIKA V UNGELTU
Map pp268-9 · Arts & Crafts
Týn 7; ⊗ 10am-6pm; metro Náměstí Republiky

This little shop in a corner of the Týnský dvůr is a good place to look for both traditional Bohemian pottery and modern blue-and-white wares, as well as wooden toys and marionettes, with prices up to 25% lower than at many other outlets in Staré Město.

KLARA NADEMLÝNSKÁ
Map pp268-9 · Fashion
☎ 224 818 769; Dlouhá 3; ⊗ 10am-7pm Mon-Fri, 11am-6pm Sat; metro Staroměstská

Klara Nademlýnská is one of the Czech Republic's top fashion designers, having trained in Prague and worked for almost a decade in Paris. Her clothes are characterised by clean lines, simple styling and quality materials, making for a very wearable range that covers the spectrum from swimwear to evening wear via jeans, halter tops, colourful blouses and sharply styled suits.

KOTVA Map pp268-9 · Department Store
☎ 224 801 111; náměstí Republiky 8; ⊗ 9am-8pm Mon-Fri, 10am-7pm Sat, to 6pm Sun; metro Náměstí Republiky

This huge, ugly brown mall has five floors of varied goods, from stationery, mobile-phone accessories and cosmetics on the ground floor, through furniture, china, glass kitchenware toys and sports equipment, to electronics and electrical goods on the top floor. There's also a pharmacy and tax-free shopping service on the ground floor, including a supermarket in the basement.

KUBISTA Map pp268-9 · Arts & Crafts
☎ 224 236 378; Ovocný trh 19; ⊗ 10am-6pm; metro Náměstí Republiky

Appropriately located in the Museum of Czech Cubism (p94) in Prague's finest Cubist building, this shop specialises in limited-edition reproductions of distinctive Cubist furniture and ceramics, and designs by masters of the form such as Josef Gočár and Pavel Janák. It also has a few original pieces for serious collectors with serious cash to spend.

LE PATIO LIFESTYLE Map pp268-9 · Homewares
☎ 222 320 260; Pařížská 20; ⊗ 10am-7pm Mon-Sat, 11am-7pm Sun; metro Staroměstská

There are lots of high-quality household accessories here, from wrought-iron chairs and lamps forged by Bohemian blacksmiths to scented wooden chests made by Indian carpenters. Plus you'll find funky earthenware plant pots, chunky crystal wineglasses in contemporary designs, and many more tempting items that you just *know* will fit into your already crammed suitcase…

MANUFAKTURA Map pp268-9   Arts & Crafts

☎ 221 632 48; Melantrichova 17; ⏰ 10am-7.30pm; metro Můstek

This is the biggest of six shops of the same name scattered between Prague Castle and Old Town Square, all stocked with quality wooden toys, scented soaps, beeswax candles, ceramics, linen and ironwork – handmade in traditional styles and/or using traditional materials. Things to look out for include painted Easter eggs, wooden kitchen utensils, colourful ceramics with traditional designs and Bohemian lacework.

MAXIMUM UNDERGROUND

Map pp268-9   Music

☎ 222 541 333; Jílská 22; ⏰ 11am-7pm Mon-Sat, 1-7pm Sun; metro Můstek

On the 1st floor in an arcade just off Jílská, this place is stocked with CDs and LPs of indie, punk, hip-hop, techno and other contemporary genres. It also has a selection of new and secondhand street and club wear for those after that Central European grunge look.

MODERNISTA Map pp272-3   Furniture

☎ 602 305 633; Betlemské náměstí 5a; ⏰ 2-6pm Mon-Fri, noon-4pm Sat; metro Národní Třída

Located at the back of the Fraktaly architectural bookshop, Modernista is an elegant gallery specialising in reproduction 20th-century furniture in classic styles ranging from Art Deco and Cubist to functionalist and Bauhaus. Its collection includes those sensuously curved chairs by Jindřich Halabala and an unusual chaise lounge by Adolf Loos, a copy of the one you can see in the drawing room of the Villa Müller (p115).

PHILHARMONIA Map pp272-3   Music

☎ 224 247 291; Pasáž Alfa, Václavské náměstí 28; ⏰ 10am-7pm Mon-Fri, 11am-6pm Sat & Sun; metro Můstek

You can sample entire collections of classics at this superbly stocked store where you'll find the works of top Czech composers including Dvořák, Smetana and Janáček. You will also find jazz, Czech folk music and

Jewish music and an eclectic selection of 'marginal genres' including rockabilly, blues and other random offerings.

ROTT CRYSTAL Map pp268-9   Glassware

☎ 224 229 529; Malé náměstí 3; ⏰ 10am-8pm; metro Staroměstská

This place is housed in a beautifully restored neo-Renaissance building (originally an ironmongers) with 1890s wall paintings on the façade. Rott now has four floors of glassware, jewellery and ceramics, but it's best known for its stock of fine-quality Bohemian and imported crystal.

SANU-BABU Map pp268-9   Speciality

☎ 221 632 401; Michalská 20; ⏰ 10.30am-7.30pm Mon-Sat, 11.30am-7.30pm Sun; metro Můstek

This Old Town hideaway is a sandalwood-scented hippie heaven filled with all manner of New Age essentials including incense sticks and holders, bongs, handmade Nepalese paper, wooden carvings and a colourful range of Nepalese clothes.

SPARKYS Map pp268-9   Toys

☎ 224 239 309; Havířská 2; ⏰ 10am-7pm Mon-Sat, to 6pm Sun; metro Můstek

Sparkys is an inviting toy store spread across four floors with lots of stuffed animals ranging from tiny to ultrahuge, as well as teddy bears, traditional Czech toys and marionettes, model cars, radio-controlled planes, computer games, board games and cartoon videos and DVDs.

STAROŽITNOSTI ALMA

Map pp268-9   Antiques

☎ 222 325 865; Valentinská 7; ⏰ 10am-6pm; metro Staroměstská

Alma specialises in Art Nouveau and Art Deco antiques, and also has a wide selection of rather twee porcelain and lacy items, rather stuffy furniture and glassware, and a veritable army of scary-looking dolls.

TOP FIVE DESIGNER BOUTIQUES

- Bohéme (p184)
- Helena Fejková Gallery (p188)
- Ivana Follová Art & Fashion Gallery (p185)
- Klara Nademlýnská (p185)
- TEG (opposite)

Traditional Easter eggs at Manufaktura (opposite)

STAROŽITNOSTI V. ANDRLE

Map pp268-9   Antiques

☎ 222 311 625; Křížovnická 1; ⏰ 10am-7pm Mon-Sat, to 6pm Sun; metro Staroměstská

Mr Andrle's shop is a little treasure house of antique gold, jewellery, clocks, watches, glassware and ceramics from all over Central Europe, and is a regular port of call for serious collectors from around the world.

TEG Map pp268-9   Fashion

☎ 222 327 358; V kolkovně 6; ⏰ 10am-7pm Mon-Fri, to 5pm Sat; metro Staroměstská

TEG (Timoure et Group) is the design team created by Alexandra Pavalová and Ivana Šafránková, two of Prague's most respected fashion designers. This boutique showcases their quarterly collections, which feature a sharp, imaginative look that adds zest and sophistication to everyday, wearable clothes.

TUPESY LIDOVÁ KERAMIKA

Map pp268-9   Ceramics

☎ 224 210 728; Havelská 21; ⏰ 10am-6pm; metro Můstek

Tupesy Lidová Keramika stocks a good selection of folk ceramics in traditional blue, green and yellow patterns that come from the Slovácko region of Moravia and the Chodsko region of Bohemia.

U ČESKÉ ORLICE Map pp268-9   Jewellery

☎ 224 228 544; Celetná 30; ⏰ 10am-8pm; metro Náměstí Republiky

'At the Bohemian Eagle' – the symbol of the Czech nation – houses a range of elegant traditional Czech jewellery including lots of elaborate garnet and chunky amber, as well as more restrained pieces in gold and silver. Exquisite handpainted porcelain and other *objets d'art* fill out the shop.

NOVÉ MĚSTO

ABRAM KELLY Map pp268-9   Gifts

☎ 224 233 282; Senovážné náměstí 16; ⏰ 10am-7pm Mon-Fri; tram 3, 9, 14, 24

This little workshop and studio produces handmade paper using traditional techniques, and sells it in the form of greeting cards, business cards, stationery, calligraphy, antique map prints and photographic prints.

BAŤA Map pp272-3   Shoes

☎ 224 218 133; Václavské náměstí 6; ⏰ 9am-9pm Mon-Fri, 9am-7pm Sat, 10am-6pm Sun; metro Můstek

Established by Tomáš Baťa in 1894, the Baťa footwear empire is still in family hands and is one of the Czech Republic's most successful companies. The flagship store on Wenceslas Square, built in the 1920s, is

Shopping

NOVÉ MĚSTO

187

considered a masterpiece of modern architecture, and houses six floors of shoes (including international brands such as Nike, Salomon and Cat, as well as Baťa's own), handbags, luggage and leather goods.

BAZAR Map pp272-3 — Music
☎ 602 313 730; Krakovská 4; ☻ 10am-6pm Mon-Sat; metro Muzeum

There's a vast selection of secondhand CDs, LPs and videos to browse through here at Bazar, representing a wide range of genres. Czech and Western pop jostle with jazz, blues, heavy metal, country and world music, though with CDs costing around 300Kč to 400Kč this place is not exactly what you'd call a bargain basement.

BELDA JEWELLERY Map pp272-3 — Jewellery
☎ 224 910 476; Mikulandská 10; ☻ 10am-6pm Mon-Thu, 10am-5pm Fri; metro Národní Třída

Belda & Co is a long-established Czech firm dating from 1922. Nationalised in 1948, it was revived by the founder's son and grandson, and continues to create gold and silver jewellery of a very high standard. Its range includes its own angular, contemporary designs, as well as reproductions based on Art Nouveau designs by Alfons Mucha.

BONTONLAND Map pp272-3 — Music
☎ 224 473 080; Václavské náměstí 1-3; ☻ 9am-8pm Mon-Sat, 10am-7pm Sun; metro Můstek

Supposedly the biggest music megastore in the Czech Republic, with pretty much everything including Western chart music, classical, jazz, dance and heavy metal, as well as an extensive collection of Czech pop. It also sells videos and DVDs, and has a large Playstation arena and internet café.

FOTO ŠKODA Map pp272-3 — Photography
☎ 222 929 029; Vodičkova 37; ☻ 8.30am-8pm Mon-Fri, 9am-6pm Sat; metro Můstek

One of Prague's biggest camera shops, Foto Škoda stocks a wide range of digital

---

TOP FIVE JEWELLERY SHOPS

- Belda Jewellery (above)
- Devaco (p184)
- Frey Wille (p185)
- Galerie Vlasta (p185)
- U České orlice (p187)

---

and film cameras, video cameras, film (professional as well as amateur) and photographic accessories. It also sells used cameras, and offers a camera-repair service.

FRUITS DE FRANCE Map pp272-3 — Delicatessen
☎ 224 220 304; Jindřišská 9; ☻ 9.30am-6.30pm Mon-Fri, 9.30am-1pm Sat; metro Můstek

Francophile foodies will make a beeline for this delectable deli and its range of fine French wines, cheeses, pastries and all manner of fresh, canned and bottled French fare.

GALERIE ČESKÉ PLASTIKY
Map pp268-9 — Art

Czech Sculpture Gallery; ☎ 222 310 684; Revoluční 20; ☻ 11.30am-7.30pm Mon-Sat; tram 5, 8, 14

This commercial gallery is a treasure house of 19th- and 20th-century and contemporary Czech sculpture, paintings, prints and photography. There are regular themed exhibitions, and all items are for sale, with prices ranging from 2000Kč to 2 million Kč.

GIGASPORT Map pp268-9 — Sporting goods
☎ 224 233 552; Myslbek Bldg, Na příkopě 19-21; ☻ 9.30am-7.30pm; metro Můstek

This sports superstore in the Myslbek Shopping Centre has three floors of sportswear and equipment, covering just about all the activities and big-name brands that you might want. You're not allowed to take large bags into the store – use the lockers just inside the door.

GLOBE BOOKSHOP & CAFÉ
Map pp272-3 — Books

☎ 224 934 203; Pštrossova 6; ☻ 10am-10pm; metro Karlovo Náměstí

A popular hangout for book-hunting backpackers, the Globe is a cosy English-language bookshop with a quiet café-bar in which to peruse your purchases, and internet access (1Kč a minute). There's a good range of new fiction and nonfiction, as well as a big selection of secondhand novels.

HELENA FEJKOVÁ GALLERY
Map pp272-3 — Fashion

☎ 224 211 514; Lucerna Pasáž, Štěpánská 61; ☻ 10am-7pm Mon-Fri, to 3pm Sat; metro Muzeum

Kit yourself out in the latest Czech fashions at this chic boutique and showroom. Contemporary men's and women's fashion and accessories by Prague designer Helena Fejková and others are on display, and private fashion shows can be arranged.

HUDY SPORT Map pp268-9   Outdoor Sports

☎ 224 813 010; Havlíčkova 11; ⌚ 9am-7.30pm Mon-Fri, 10am-6pm Sat, 1am-4pm Sun; metro Náměstí Republiky

One of the half-dozen branches of this nationwide chain of stores, Hudy Sport provides reasonably priced equipment for hiking, climbing, camping and other outdoor activities and pursuits. There is a good selection of boots, backpacks, sleeping bags, tents, waterproofs and the like, as well as more specialist gear such as crampons, ice axes and climbing ropes. There are seven branches in the city, including another central one at Na Perštýné 14 (Map pp272–3).

JAN PAZDERA Map pp272-3   Photography

☎ 224 216 197; Vodičkova 28; ⌚ 10am-6pm Mon-Sat; tram 3, 9, 14, 24

The friendly and knowledgeable staff members at this long-standing shop are happy to show you around their impressive stock of secondhand cameras, darkroom gear, lenses, binoculars and telescopes. Models range from the basic but unbreakable Russian-made Zenit to expensive Leicas.

KANZELSBERGER Map pp272-3   Books & Maps

☎ 224 219 214; Václavské náměstí 4; ⌚ 9am-7pm; metro Můstek

Housed in the tall, glass-fronted Lindt building at the foot of Wenceslas Square, Kanzelsberger has five floors of bookshelves, with a café on the 1st floor overlooking the square. You'll probably want the top floor, where there's a selection of books in English, German and French, plus hiking and city maps covering the whole of the Czech Republic.

KIWI Map pp272-3   Books & Maps

☎ 224 948 455; Jungmannova 23; ⌚ 9am-6.30pm Mon-Fri, to 2pm Sat; metro Národní Třída

This small specialist travel bookshop stocks a huge range of maps covering not only the Czech Republic but many other countries. It also has an extensive selection of Lonely Planet guidebooks.

> ## TOP FIVE ENGLISH-LANGUAGE BOOKSHOPS
>
> - Anagram (p183)
> - Big Ben (p184)
> - Globe Bookshop & Café (opposite)
> - Palác Knih Neo Luxor (below)
> - Shakespeare & Sons (p183)

MARKS & SPENCER

Map pp272-3   Department Store

☎ 224 237 503; Melantrich Bldg, Václavské náměstí 36; ⌚ 9.30am-8.30pm Mon-Fri, 10am-8pm Sat & Sun; metro Náměstí Republiky

British high-street fashion comes to Prague, with four floors of men's and women's clothing in M&S's traditional smart-casual style, as well as children's clothes, cosmetics, toiletries, household goods and a selection of M&S luxury groceries.

MOSER Map pp268-9   Glassware

☎ 224 211 293; Na příkopě 12; ⌚ 10am-8pm Mon-Fri, to 7pm Sat & Sun; metro Můstek

One of the most exclusive and highly respected of Bohemian glass makers, Moser was founded in Karlovy Vary in 1857 and is famous for its rich and flamboyant designs. The shop on Na příkopě is worth a browse as much for the décor as the goods – it's in a magnificently decorated, originally Gothic building called the dům U černé růže (House of the Black Rose).

MOTHERCARE Map pp268-9   Babycare

☎ 222 240 008; Myslbek Bldg, Na příkopě 19-21; ⌚ 9am-8pm Mon-Fri, 9am-7pm Sat, 11am-7pm Sun; metro Náměstí Republiky or Můstek

If you're travelling with a baby or toddler, you'll find pretty much everything you need to meet their nonedible demands in this bright and modern babycare shop on the first floor of the Myslbek mall – toys, clothes, accessories and all manner of other goods for mother and child.

PALÁC KNIH NEO LUXOR

Map pp272-3   Books

☎ 221 111 336; Václavské náměstí 41; ⌚ 8am-8pm Mon-Fri, 9am-7pm Sat, 10am-7pm Sun; metro Muzeum

Palác Knih Neo Luxor is Prague's biggest bookshop – head for the basement to find

Shopping

NOVÉ MĚSTO

189

a wide selection of fiction and nonfiction in English, German, French and Russian, including Czech authors in translation. You'll also find internet access (1Kč per minute), a café and a good selection of international newspapers and magazines.

SLOVANSKÝ DŮM

Map pp268-9   Shopping Centre

☎ 221 451 400; Na příkopě 22; ⏰ shops 10am-8pm; metro Náměstí Republiky

This is Prague's glitziest shopping mall, at least in terms of its shops if not its appearance, housing numerous upmarket fashion boutiques, a 10-screen multiplex cinema, a nightclub, and a handful of chic restaurants. There's a pleasant tree-lined courtyard at the back with a beer garden for tired and thirsty shoppers.

STAROŽITNOSTI Z. KRIŽEK

Map pp272-3   Antiques

Žitna 3; ⏰ 10am-noon & 1-5pm Mon-Fri; metro Karlovo Náměstí

This is a dusty treasure-trove of antique furniture, porcelain toilet bowls, old postcards and photographs, vintage newspapers and magazines, and art books.

TESCO Map pp272-3   Department Store

☎ 222 003 111; Národní třída 26; ⏰ 8am-9pm Mon-Fri, 9am-8pm Sat, 10am-7pm Sun; metro Národní Třída

This bustling multistorey maze of consumerism will leave even the hardiest shopaholic feeling dazed and confused. The ground floor minimarket here seems constantly occupied by a shuffling queue of shoppers, but beyond spreads a smorgasbord of quality coffee, chocolates, wine and spirits, stationery and cosmetics. The floors above are crammed with everything from low-priced electrical goods to baby wear, while Tesco's basement houses a huge and well-stocked supermarket (open 7am to 10pm Monday to Friday, 8am to 8pm Saturday, 9am to 8pm Sunday).

ZERBA Map pp268-9   Toys

☎ 221 024 616; 1st fl, Černa Růže Shopping Centre, Na příkopě 12; ⏰ 9am-7pm Mon-Fri, to 6pm Sat, to 5pm Sun; metro Můstek

This place is a paradise for model-railway enthusiasts of all ages, with a huge range of track and rolling stock in N- and OO-gauge, as well as a good selection of Scalextric racing sets and Matchbox model cars.

Wooden toys at Sparkys toy shop (p186)

BEYOND THE CENTRE
Holešovice

PIVNÍ GALERIE Map pp276-7   Beer
☎ 220 870 613; U Průhonu 9; ◷ 11am-8pm Mon-Fri; tram 1, 3, 5, 25

If you think that Czech beer begins and ends with Pilsner Urquell, a visit to the tasting room at Pivní Galerie (The Beer Gallery) will soon lift the scales from your eyes. Here you can sample and purchase a huge range of Bohemian and Moravian beers – more than 180 varieties from 34 different breweries – with expert advice from the owner, who speaks both English and Swedish.

PRAŽSKÁ TRŽNICE Map pp276-7   Market
Prague Market Hall; ☎ 220 800 945; Bubenské nábřeží 306; ◷ 7am-7pm Mon-Fri, to 2pm Sat; tram 1, 3, 5, 25

Almost a suburb in itself, Prague's sprawling city market includes a large open-air area selling fresh fruit, vegetables and flowers, large covered halls housing supermarkets, electrical goods and car accessories, and dozens of stalls selling everything from cheap clothes to garden gnomes. In the eastern part of the market are several antiques warehouses, some of which look like they have emptied a baroque palace or two.

Vinohrady

KAREL VÁVRA Map pp272-3   Musical Instruments
☎ 222 518 114; Lublaňská 65; ◷ 9am-5pm Mon-Fri; metro IP Pavlova

Handmade fiddles decorate the interior of this old-fashioned violin workshop where Karel and his assistants beaver away making and repairing these instruments in time-honoured fashion. Even if you are not in search of a custom-made violin, it's worth a look just for the time-warp atmosphere.

ORIENTÁLNÍ KOBERCE PALÁCKA
Map pp280-1   Carpets
☎ 541 214 620; Vinohradská 42; ◷ 10am-7pm Mon-Fri, to 2pm Sat; metro Náměstí Míru

The 'Oriental Carpet Palace' is a sumptuous showroom stocked with handmade carpets, rugs and wall-hangings from Iran and other Central Asian states. The colourful pieces come in all sizes and prices, in intricate traditional designs, and the knowledgeable staff will be happy to help you make an informed purchase.

PALÁC FLÓRA Map pp278-9   Shopping Centre
☎ 255 741 712; Vinohradská 151; ◷ 8am-midnight; metro Flóra

You could be anywhere in the capitalist world in this shiny, glittering shrine to consumerism. Slick cafés share floor space with girly emporia of tiny T-shirts, sparkly make-up and globalised brand names – Hilfiger, Sergio Tacchini, Nokia, Puma, Lacoste, Guess, Diesel, Apple; a branch of the Thai restaurant Orange Moon (p140), an eight-screen multiplex and an IMAX cinema keep the crowds coming in the evenings.

SHAKESPEARE & SONS
Map pp280-1   Books
☎ 271 740 839; Krymská 12; ◷ 10am-7pm; tram 4, 22, 23

Though its shelves groan with a formidable range of literature in English, both new and secondhand, Shakes is more than a bookshop – it's a congenial literary hangout, with a café (open till midnight) that regularly hosts poetry readings, author events and live jazz, and where you can buy magazines, such as the *New York Review of Books*, *Harpers* and *Atlantic Monthly*, and settle down for a read over coffee and cakes.

VINOHRADSKÝ PAVILON
Map pp280-1   Shopping Centre
☎ 222 097 111; Vinohradská 50; ◷ 9.30am-9pm Mon-Sat, noon-8pm Sun; metro Jiřího z Poděbrad

Housed in a lovingly restored 1902 market pavilion, this small but searingly trendy mall – completely refurbished in 2006 – has three floors of brand-name boutiques (including Tommy Hilfiger, Sergio Tacchini, La Perla), Sony electronics, jewellery, shoes and household goods. Oh, and it has that obligatory adjunct to all Prague shopping malls – there's a supermarket in the basement.

Smíchov

MAPIS Map pp270-1   Maps
☎ 257 315 459; Štefánikova 63; ◷ 9am-6.30pm Mon-Fri; tram 6, 9, 12, 20

Mapis is a specialist map shop with a wide selection of local, national and international maps, including hiking maps and city plans covering not just the city but the whole of the Czech Republic.

NOVÝ SMÍCHOV Map pp270-1 Shopping Centre
☎ 251 511 151; Plzeňská 8; 🕑 9am-9pm; metro Anděl

Nový Smíchov is a vast shopping mall that occupies an area the size of several city blocks. It is an airy, well-designed space with lots of fashion boutiques and niche stores – for example you could check out Profimed, which has all the dental-care products you never knew you needed. There's a big computer store, a food court, a virtual games hall, a 12-screen multiplex cinema; and it also includes a huge and well-stocked Carrefour hypermarket (open 7am to midnight).

Dejvice
ANTIKVITA Map p275 Antiques
☎ 233 336 601; Na hutích 9; 🕑 10am-5pm Mon-Fri; metro Dejvická

This antique shop is a collector's delight, crammed with cases and cabinets overflowing with vintage toys, model trains, dolls, coins, medals, jewellery, clocks, watches, militaria, postcards, porcelain figures, glassware and much, much more. If you have something to sell, Antikvita holds buying sessions on Wednesday and Thursday (from 10am till noon and 2pm till 5pm).

Sleeping ■

Sleeping

Accommodation Styles

Prague offers a wide range of accommodation options, from cosy, romantic hotels set in historic town houses to luxurious international chain hotels, and from budget hostels and pensions to a new generation of sharply styled boutique hotels. Most midrange and top-end hotels have rooms with private bathrooms, but some older midrange places and many budget hotels (especially those outside the centre) still offer cheaper rooms with shared facilities. Note that a *hotel garni* denotes a hotel that does not have a restaurant.

An increasing number of Prague hotels provide specially adapted rooms and facilities for wheelchair users; we have noted these facilities in the individual listings.

Price Ranges

A double room in a midrange hotel in central Prague will cost around 4000Kč to 5000Kč; outside the centre, this might fall to around 3500Kč. Top-range hotels cost from 6000Kč. The 'cheap sleeps' options listed in this chapter charge 2000Kč or less for a double room. Note that some midrange and top-end hotels quote rates in euros, and a few quote in US dollars. At these hotels you can pay cash in Czech crowns if you like,

PRICE GUIDE
Average cost of double room:
€€€€   more than 6500Kč (€200)
€€€   4000Kč to 6499Kč (€150-199)
€€   2000Kč to 3999Kč (€70-149)
€   less than 2000Kč (€70)

but the price will depend on the exchange rate on the day you settle the bill.

The rates quoted in this chapter are for the high season, which generally covers April to June, September and October, and the Christmas/New Year holidays. July and August are midseason, and the rest of the year is low season.

Even high-season rates can be inflated by up to 15% on certain dates, notably at New Year, Easter and at weekends (Thursday to Sunday) in May, June and September. On the other hand, you can often find much lower rates from January to March and there are often good internet booking deals from June to August.

Most hostel, pension and budget-hotel rates do not include breakfast; most midrange and top-end hotel rates do. If only a double-room rate is quoted, then that's what you'll pay for single use too.

Reservations

Booking your accommodation in advance is strongly recommended (especially if you want to stay in or near the centre), and there are dozens of agencies that will help you find a place to stay; some are better than others. The places listed on p229 are reliable, and even if you turn up in peak period without a booking, these agencies should be able to find you a bed.

Hotels usually require you to check out on the day of departure between 10am and noon. As to check-in times, there are no hard-and-fast rules, but if you're going to arrive late in the evening, it's best to mention this when you book your room.

Longer-Term Rentals

More and more travellers are discovering the pleasures of renting an apartment in Prague. Before you scoff at the idea, consider that the extra cost of a very basic self-catering flat near the centre means minimal transportation costs, access to cheap local food, and the freedom to come and go as you like.

Many Prague agencies will find a flat for you (see p229). Typical rates for a modern two-person apartment with living room/ bedroom, bathroom, TV and kitchenette range from around 1200/6000/15,000Kč per night/week/month for a place in the outer suburbs, to around 2500/15,000/35,000Kč for a flat near Old Town Square. All short-term rental apartments are fully furnished and serviced, meaning that utilities (gas, water, electricity) and bed linen are in-cluded in the price, and staff will clean up and change the beds at least weekly.

The real-estate section of the weekly *Prague Post* (www.praguepost.cz) newspa-per also lists agencies and private individu-als with apartments to rent by the month.

HRADČANY

Stay in Hradčany and you're only a few minutes from the castle. It's a mostly peaceful district, as the crowds drain away at the day's end leaving the streets almost deserted.

DOMUS HENRICI Map pp264-5   Hotel €€€
☎ 220 511 369; www.domus-henrici.cz; Loretán-ská 11; s/d from €155/170; tram 22, 23;
This historic building in a quiet corner of Hradčany is intentionally nondescript out front, hinting that peace and privacy are top priorities here. There are eight spacious and stylish rooms, half with private fax, scanner/copier and internet access, and all with polished wood floors, large bathrooms, comfy beds and fluffy bathrobes. Service is impeccable, and there's an attractive guest lounge as well as a sunny outdoor terrace with gorgeous views over the city.

HOTEL SAVOY Map pp264-5   Hotel €€€€
☎ 224 302 430; www.hotel-savoy.cz; Keplerova 6; d from €365; tram 22, 23
Built in 1911 in Art Nouveau style, the Savoy is a calm oasis of understated elegance. The

TOP FIVE ROMANTIC HOTELS
- Hotel 16 U Sv Kateřiny (p201)
- Hotel Casa Marcello (p198)
- Hotel U Krále Karla (p196)
- Le Palais Hotel (p206)
- Romantik Hotel U Raka (right)

Hotel U Zlaté studně (p197)

spacious bedrooms have plush blue carpets and big marble bathrooms, and all are large enough to have a sitting area. The public areas include a library with leather arm-chairs and sofas, and leather-topped tables (with a log fire in winter), formal restaurant and roof terrace, and in-house pampering extends to fitness trainers, hairdressers, sauna, spa and gym. Previous celebrity guests have included David Bowie, Tina Turner, Princess Caroline of Monaco and the entire Ajax Amsterdam football team.

ROMANTIK HOTEL U RAKA
Map pp264-5   Hotel €€€
☎ 220 511 100; www.romantikhotels.com; Černínská 10; s/d from €160/180; tram 22, 23
Concealed in a manicured rock garden in a quiet corner of Hradčany, the historic Hotel U Raka is an atmospheric, late-18th-century timber cottage with just six ele-gant, low-ceilinged doubles, complete with timber beams, wooden floors and red-brick fireplaces. With its cosy bedrooms, atten-tive staff, artistic décor and farmhouse kitchen–style breakfast room, it's ideal for a romantic getaway, and the castle is less than 10 minutes' walk away. Be sure to book at least a few months ahead.

MALÁ STRANA

Lots of Malá Strana's lovely old Renaissance and baroque buildings have been converted into hotels and apartments, making this a good district to stay in if you're looking for a romantic atmosphere. You'll also be within walking distance of Charles Bridge, ideal for atmospheric evening strolls.

CASTLE STEPS Map pp264-5   Apartments €-€€
☎ 257 532 921; www.castlesteps.com; Nerudova 10; r €37-78, apt €62-168; tram 12, 20, 22, 23
The name applies to a collection of suites and apartments spread across three buildings on Nerudova street and one a little further uphill on Úvoz. Management is laid back, helpful and gay friendly, and decidedly informal – don't expect porters and room service! (By the way, there are no lifts either.) The various 16th- and 17th-century buildings have been converted into apartments and suites sleeping from two to eight, and offer remarkable value in a great location. All have been beautifully renovated and equipped to a high standard, and are furnished with antiques and pot plants. The reception office is at Nerudova 10 (ring the buzzer on the street, and wait for someone to come down and meet you).

HOTEL ARIA Map pp264-5   Boutique Hotel €€€€
☎ 225 334 111; www.ariahotel.net; Tržíště 9; d from €250; tram 12, 20, 22, 23; (P) (回)
The Aria offers five-star luxury with a musical theme – each of the four floors is dedicated to a musical genre (jazz, opera, classical and contemporary), and each room celebrates a particular artist or musician and contains a selection of their music that you can enjoy on the in-room hi-fi system. Service is professional and efficient, and the rooms are furnished with crisp bed linen, plump continental quilts, Molton Brown toiletries and complimentary chocolates. Other facilities include a music and movie library, screening room, fitness

TOP FIVE LUXURY HOTELS

- Hotel Aria (above)
- Hotel Carlo IV (p202)
- Hotel Praha (p208)
- Le Palais Hotel (p206)
- Radisson SAS Alcron Hotel (p203)

centre and steam room. The location is very central, a few minutes' walk from Charles Bridge, and just around the corner from a major tram stop.

HOTEL NERUDA
Map pp264-5   Boutique Hotel €€€€
☎ 257 535 557; www.hotelneruda-praha.cz; Nerudova 44; s/d €260/300; tram 12, 20, 22, 23; (回)
Set in a tastefully renovated Gothic house dating from 1348 and recently extended into the neighbouring building, the Neruda offers a refreshingly modern and stylish alternative to the sometimes-tacky so-called 'historic' hotels, which are all too common in Malá Strana. The décor is chic and minimalist in shades of chocolate and cream, with a lovely glass-roofed atrium that houses the hotel café, and a sunny roof terrace. The comfortable bedrooms share the modern, minimalist décor and are mostly reasonably sized, but be aware that some of the rooms in the top of the building are a bit on the cramped side – ask for one on the 1st or 2nd floor. The staff are friendly and unfailingly helpful, and the breakfasts are excellent (and served until 11am if you fancy a long lie-in).

HOTEL SAX Map pp264-5   Hotel €€€
☎ 257 531 268; www.hotelsax.cz; Jánský vršek 3; s/d 4100/4400Kč; tram 12, 20, 22, 23
Set in a quiet corner of Malá Strana, amid embassies and monastery gardens, the Sax is refreshingly low key and unpretentious. The building is 18th century on the outside but modern on the inside – the interior has been completely remodelled, with a dramatic glass-roofed atrium where the courtyard used to be, sleek designer furniture and colourful paintings of giant fruit. The tidy, uncluttered bedrooms are comfortable, though nothing special, but the rates are very reasonable considering its quiet, central location – less than 10 minutes' walk from the castle's main gate.

HOTEL U KRÁLE KARLA
Map pp264-5   Hotel €€€
☎ 257 532 869; www.romantichotels.cz; Úvoz 4; s/d from 5000/5500Kč; tram 12, 20 22, 23; (P)
The 'King Charles' is a cosy, romantic hotel set in a lovely 'baroquefied' Gothic building with rooms set on landings around an impressive central atrium with a stained-

glass ceiling. The atmosphere leans towards medieval/fairytale, with studded wood-and-leather antique furniture, painted timber ceilings, murals, stained-glass windows and statues of Czech kings and queens (though in places they have been a bit heavy-handed with the pastel-pink paint). The rooms are filled with dark polished wood, Persian rugs, swagged crimson drapes and ostentatious fireplaces – charming, if you like that sort of thing – while the bathrooms, though reasonably sized, are beige and forgettable. The hotel vies with Hotel Neruda (opposite) for the title of closest hotel to the castle, as it's just a few minutes' walk from the main gate.

HOTEL U TŘÍ PŠTROSŮ

Map pp264-5   Hotel €€€€

☎ 257 532 410; www.upstrosu.cz; Dražického náměstí 12; s/d 4900/6900Kč; tram 12, 20, 22, 23; Ⓟ 🖳

'At the Three Ostriches' is a grand old merchant's house at the foot of the Malá Strana bridge tower on Charles Bridge. According to local legend, the name was bestowed in honour of a group of foreign diplomats who stayed here one night, bringing with them three ostriches as a gift for Emperor Charles IV. More likely, though, is that it was the home of a wealthy merchant who dealt in ostrich feathers. Dating from the 15th century, it's filled with interesting historic details, including Renaissance frescoes and painted wooden ceilings. It enjoys an unbeatable location, and many rooms have splendid views across Charles Bridge.

HOTEL U ZLATÉ STUDNĚ

Map pp264-5   Hotel €€€€

☎ 257 011 213; www.zlatastudna.cz; U Zlaté studně 4 d from €200, ste from €250; metro Malostranská; 🖳

'At the Golden Well' is one of Malá Strana's hidden secrets, tucked away at the end of a cobbled cul-de-sac – a Renaissance house that once belonged to Emperor Rudolf II (and was once inhabited by astronomer Tycho Brahe), with an unbeatable location perched on the southern slope of the castle hill. The rooms (five twins, 12 doubles and three luxury suites) are quiet and spacious, with polished wood floors, reproduction period furniture, and blue-and-white bathrooms with underfloor heating and

whirlpool baths; many have views over the Palace Gardens below. The hotel has an excellent restaurant (see p137) and a terrace with superb outlook over the city.

HOTEL WILLIAM Map pp270-1   Hotel €€€

☎ 257 320 242; www.euroagentur.cz; Hellichova 5; s/d from €135/150; tram 12, 20 22, 23; Ⓟ ✕ 🖳

The William has a great location only five minutes' walk from Charles Bridge. Depending on your tastes, the décor in the public areas is either wonderfully 'fairytale' or just plain twee – lots of swagged curtains, frills and flounces – but the rooms are much plainer, and rather basic (no bedside lamps). The lift is tiny and starts on the 1st floor (!), so you'll still have to haul your bags up at least one flight of stairs. Try to get a room overlooking the garden rather than the street, as the noise from the trams can be a nuisance.

TRAVELLERS HOSTEL ISLAND

Map pp270-1   Hostel

☎ 224 932 991; www.travellers.cz; Strelecký ostrov 36; dm 300Kč; ⊙ mid-Jun–mid-Sep; tram 6, 9, 22, 23

Set on the island beneath Legions Bridge (Legii most), and occupying a 19th-century building which has clearly seen better days, this hostel has a couple of huge single-sex dorms containing between 20 and 50 beds, so if it's peace and privacy you're looking for, look elsewhere. Having said that, it's a friendly and sociable place, and the young, international backpacking crowd that inhabits it during the summer months seems to enjoy the casual communal atmosphere. The dorms are pretty basic affairs, but it's the location that's the big draw here. 'Marksmen's Island' is a green, leafy space where locals have picnics and walk their dogs, where the occasional drunk sprawls in the grass, and where the views upriver are fantastic.

STARÉ MĚSTO

Staré Město offers a wide range of accommodation, from backpacker hostels to some of the city's most luxurious hotels, with everything in between. Be aware that a lot of pensions and midrange hotels have been squeezed into historic old buildings with no room for a lift – be prepared for a bit of stair climbing.

Lobby at Hotel Josef (opposite)

APOSTOLIC RESIDENCE

Map pp268-9   Apartments €€€€

☎ 221 632 222; www.prague-residence.cz; Staroměstské náměstí 26; s/d from 4600/5700Kč, apt from 7000Kč; metro Staroměstská; 🖳

This lovely old building on Old Town Square has been converted into a luxury hotel with 30 large and well-appointed rooms filled with heavy antique furniture and rugs, paintings, wooden floors and chandeliers; some have the additional charm of painted wooden-beamed ceilings (the attic apartment, with its spiral staircase and massive timber beams, is our favourite). The unique selling point, though, is its location – you can hang out your window and watch the Astronomical Clock do its thing. You'll pay extra for a room with a view of Old Town Square, but for this level of quality, it's still reasonable value compared to many top-end hotels around town.

DŮM U KRÁLE JIŘÍHO

Map pp268-9   Pension €€

☎ 221 466 100; www.kinggeorge.cz; Liliová 10; s/d 2250/3550Kč; metro Staroměstská

'King George's House' is an appealing pension with smallish rooms that have been given a crisp, modern makeover; the attic rooms, with exposed, head-bumping wooden beams, are the most attractive. Antique-style furniture graces the cosy rooms, which come in different shapes and sizes although some are rather small. Interior design revolves around stark white walls and the odd framed print. Mod

cons include minibars and TVs, and the well-equipped bathrooms are bright and spotless. It's within lurching distance of Old Town Square, although the bar is so comfortable you may not bother venturing outside. There's no lift, only steep stairs.

HOSTEL TÝN Map pp268-9   Hostel €

☎ 224 808 333; www.tyn.prague-hostels.cz; Týnská 19; dm/s/d 400/1200/1200Kč; metro Náměstí Republiky; 🗙

If all you want is a cheap place to lay your weary head at night, you couldn't do much better than this sparkling little hostel. It's the most central budget accommodation in Prague, a couple of minutes' walk from Old Town Square and within sight of the soaring spires of historic Týn Church. The 14 rooms themselves are basic and unadorned and all have shared bathrooms, but they're spotlessly clean and comfortable, and are often booked up well ahead during busy times of year. The hostel is located at the back of a courtyard off Týnska, so it's fairly secluded and avoids most of the noise you'd expect in this area. Also in this courtyard are some rather unexpected, but very welcome, facilities including a sauna, gym, Jacuzzi and vegetarian restaurant (see p137).

HOTEL ANTIK Map pp268-9   Hotel €€

☎ 222 322 288; www.hotelantik.cz; Dlouhá 22; s/d 3590/3990Kč; metro Náměstí Republiky

As the name suggests, this place has a passion for bric-a-brac, with an antique shop on the ground floor and various pieces scattered elsewhere throughout the building. The location is ideal, right in the heart of the Old Town and close to lots of good restaurants and bars. The 12 cosy rooms have been thoroughly modernised and are perfectly comfortable though a little lacking in character – ask for one with a balcony overlooking the garden, to avoid any noise from night-time revellers in the street. Breakfast is served in the lovely garden courtyard out back.

HOTEL CASA MARCELLO

Map pp268-9   Hotel €€-€€€

☎ 222 310 260; www.casa-marcello.cz; Řásnovka 783; d from €130, ste from €185, apt from €215; tram 5, 8, 14; 🖳

A former aristocratic residence housed in two medieval buildings that were once part of the nearby Convent of St Agnes. Beautifully furnished with a mixture of antique furniture and modern artworks, its small size, intimate atmosphere and attentive service make it an ideal romantic hideaway in the heart of Staré Město; room 104, with king-size bed and preserved medieval archway, is our favourite. It's in a very quiet part of town, but only a short walk from Old Town Square; added attractions include a sunny garden courtyard where you can enjoy a drink or a snack, and a sauna.

HOTEL CLEMENTIN Map pp268-9   Hotel €€€
☎ 222 221 798; www.clementin.cz; Seminářská 4; s/d 4250/5250Kč; metro Staroměstská

This is a pretty little place with nine cosy rooms squeezed into a 14th-century town house that is probably the narrowest building in Prague; a façade just two windows wide. This sliver of a Gothic building, originally built around 1360 and squeezed between two much heftier places, is certainly one of the more eye-catching structures in this part of the Old Town, aided in no small part by its pistachio-green façade. Space isn't in great supply here so 'compact and bijou' could best describe the sleeping arrangements. Having said that, the rooms are stylishly furnished and decorated in warm tones, creating a cosy, homely feel. The bathrooms are small as well, though they do have both bathtubs and showers. It's on a narrow alley just off the tourist thoroughfare of Karlova, halfway between Charles Bridge and Old Town Square.

HOTEL CLOISTER INN Map pp272-3   Hotel €€
☎ 224 211 020; www.cloister-inn.cz; Konviktská 14; s/d €122/130; metro Národní Třída; P 🖳

The Cloister Inn's refurbished convent rooms were once part of the still-operational St Bartholomew Church. While some architectural touches remain from the convent, they're a little overwhelmed by the hotel's resolutely modern décor and warm brown-and-yellow colour scheme. Rooms are comfortable and spotlessly clean, with great power showers; if you can snag one of the top-floor executive rooms you'll also get in-room fax, internet access and minibar.

HOTEL ČERNÝ SLON Map pp268-9   Hotel €€
☎ 222 321 521; www.hotelcernyslon.cz; Týnská ulička 1; s/d 3200/3900Kč; metro Náměstí Republiky

Set in a lovely historic building barely 30 paces from Old Town Square, the 'Black Elephant' has 16 mostly smallish but comfortable rooms, a Gothic-vaulted dining room and a tiny courtyard garden. Although it has undergone a complete renovation, it has retained much of its historic charm, with exposed wooden beams in some of the rooms and wonderful Gothic vaulting in the dining room. The brightly polished bathrooms are all thoroughly modern, and most have both tubs and showers. Try to book the attic room, which is the largest, prettiest and quietest, with a forest of steeply pitched roof beams and a window overlooking the small square in front of the hotel.

HOTEL JOSEF
Map pp268-9   Boutique Hotel €€€-€€€€
☎ 221 700 111; www.hoteljosef.cz; Rybná 20; s/d from €149/173; metro Náměstí Republiky; P ☒ 🖳

Designed by London-based Czech architect Eva Jiřičná, the Josef is one of Prague's most stylish contemporary hotels. As soon as you step through the doors into the stark, white, minimalist lobby, with its glass spiral staircase, you get the impression that they're eager to impress you with how exceedingly cool and trendy it all is. But it's tastefully done, and staff are welcoming and helpful. The minimalist design is continued in the bedrooms, where things are kept clean and simple, with plenty of white and subtle neutral tones in the bed linen and furniture. The glass-walled en suites are especially attractive, boasting extra-large 'rainfall' shower heads and modish glass bowl basins. There are two wheelchair-accessible rooms, and a stylish bar and business lounge.

HOTEL MEJSTŘÍK
Map pp268-9   Boutique Hotel €€€-€€€€
☎ 224 800 055; www.hotelmejstrik.cz; Jakubská 5; s/d €178/203; metro Náměstí Republiky; P 🖳

Established back in 1924 (by the father of the present owner), this place got an impressive Art Deco face-lift in 2000 and is now one of Staré Město's more impressive small hotels. From the lobby lined with pale-green marble, to the stained-glass windows and crystal chandeliers in the restaurant, the public areas provide an authentic Deco atmosphere. The bedrooms are much plainer, but well sized and with very comfortable beds. The location is good, on a reasonably quiet back street just around the corner from the Municipal House, close to a metro station and only five minutes' walk from Old Town Square.

HOTEL PAŘÍŽ Map pp268-9   Hotel €€€

☎ 222 195 195; www.hotel-pariz.cz; U Obecního domu 1; d from €155; metro Náměstí Republiky; P ✕ ▣

Built in 1904 in a mix of neogothic and Art Nouveau, the stately Paříž remains a bastion of belle époque style in the centre of the city. It has 86 individually designed rooms and suites, many of which are strikingly modern in design, while public areas form a showcase of early-20th-century glamour. It's an unashamedly exuberant memorial to the heady days of Alfons Mucha and Gustav Klimt (who, incidentally, have plush suites named in their honour); the public areas have stunning mosaic walls, wood panelling, artistic plasterwork and unmistakably Art Nouveau chandeliers and paintings. The 'deluxe' and slightly pricier 'executive' rooms are spacious and sunny, furnished largely in contemporary style, with the occasional piece of early-1900s-inspired art to remind you where you are. The shiny bathrooms have everything you need, including that nice extra touch: heated floors.

HOTEL U KLENOTNÍKA

Map pp272-3   Hotel €€

☎ 224 211 699; www.uklenotnika.cz; Rytířská 3; s/d 2500/3800Kč; metro Můstek

A friendly, central hotel with 10 plain-but-comfy rooms decorated with unique art and a stylish restaurant adorned with surreal painted glass. The location, roughly halfway between Old Town Square and Wenceslas Square, is ideal for sightseeing: close enough to most of the big sights, but far enough away to avoid the noise and ceaseless tourist traffic that characterise the main tour-group hubs. The name, 'At the Jeweller's', comes from one of its previous incarnations as an upmarket jewellery shop in the first half of the 20th century. The ground floor's snazzy gilt ceilings covered with jewel motifs are a reminder of the property's former life. The rooms (two singles and eight doubles) are simple, clean and unfussy, and there's a good restaurant and bar downstairs.

HOTEL U STARÉ PANÍ Map pp268-9   Hotel €€

☎ 224 228 090; www.ustarepani.cz; Michalská 9; s/d 3250/3950Kč; metro Můstek

Like many midrange hotels in the Old Town, the curiously named 'At the Old Lady' sells itself on its location – just a few minutes' stroll from Old Town Square – rather than on the sumptuousness of its rooms, which, to be honest, are fairly plain and ordinary. Having said that, they're all perfectly clean and well maintained, and the small bathrooms have everything you need. The hotel is spread over four floors – note that there's no lift here (building regulations are very strict when it comes to these historic structures), so it's not really suitable for anyone with mobility problems. The jazz club of the same name (p172) occupies the cellar, with live bands playing into the wee hours, making this an ideal spot for night owls and jazz aficionados. It's well soundproofed, so there shouldn't be too much sax wafting up to the hotel rooms.

HOTEL U ZLATÉHO STROMU

Map pp268-9   Hotel €€€

☎ 222 220 441; www.zlatystrom.cz; Karlova 6; s/d 3850/4050Kč; tram 17

The 22-room 'At the Golden Tree' has a pleasingly historical atmosphere with period features and many timber-ceilinged rooms. You'll be right in the thick of tourist town here, with all its crowds, noise, buskers, souvenir shops and countless other distractions. The building dates back to the 13th century, and has been completely renovated to accommodate a four-star hotel, nightclub, 24-hour restaurant and coffee bar. Suites are large and furnished in a bright, contemporary style, and the 'regular' rooms are smart, functional and fitted with the usual facilities such as minibars and satellite TVs. But you're really paying for the central location. Unless you're in a party mood, try to get a room on the upper floors – this is a very noisy location, and the club in the hotel often rages till 6am. Reception is up a narrow flight of stairs from ground level, and there's no lift.

PENSION U LILIE Map pp268-9   Pension €€

☎ 222 220 432; www.pensionulilie.cz; Liliová 15; s/d 2000/3050Kč; metro Staroměstská

Location, location, location – this place has it in spades, five minutes' walk from Charles

Bridge and almost close enough to Old Town Square to hear the astronomical clock chiming. The rooms at 'The Lily' are plain but pleasant with en suite bathroom and TV, and excellent value – our favourite is the timber-lined attic room (No 14). There is a downside to central location – street noise and a seedy club across the road – but ask for a room at the back of the hotel and you'll be fine.

PENSION U MEDVÍDKŮ

Map pp272-3   Pension €€

☎ 224 211 916; www.umedvidku.cz; Na Perštýně 7; s/d from 2300/3500Kč; metro Národní Třída

Cosy and centrally located, 'At the Little Bear' is a traditional beer hall (see the boxed text, p155) on the southern edge of the Old Town, about 10 minutes' walk from Old Town Square. The rooms have polished hardwood floors and dark wooden furniture, with good-sized bathrooms (and good water pressure in the showers). Some of the 1st-floor rooms have Renaissance painted wooden ceilings, and a few are almost big enough to be called a suite (the 'historic' rooms, which have a bit of character, cost 10% more than the ordinary ones, which have less atmosphere but are similar in size). For a romantic splurge, choose one of the attic rooms – No 33 is the best in the house, spacious and atmospheric, with a big pine bed and huge exposed roof beams.

PENSION UNITAS & ART PRISON HOSTEL Map pp272-3   Pension/Hostel €

☎ 224 211 020; www.unitas.cz; Bartolomějská 9; dm per person 350-510Kč, s/d 1280/1580Kč; metro Národní Třída; Ⓟ ✕

This former convent is an interesting place to stay – many of its cramped rooms were once prison cells (ex-president Havel once did time here, in what is now room No P6) – with shared bathrooms and a generous breakfast included. The rooms in the basement, where political prisoners were once imprisoned, are tiny and basic and retain their forbidding iron doors, but for sheer atmosphere they're hard to beat! If all this seems a bit too grim, the larger 'pension' rooms on the ground floor and 1st floor provide more comfort, with brightly painted walls, flowery curtains, pot plants and prints. All rooms have shared bathrooms, and the building is 100% nonsmoking.

NOVÉ MĚSTO

Although there are one or two grand old luxury hotels here, Nové Město's accommodation is mostly in modern chain hotels and upgraded 1930s establishments. What they might lack in historical atmosphere and romantic appeal, they make up for in spaciousness and facilities. Those on Wenceslas Square are right in the thick of things, but there are quiet corners to be found as well, especially in southern Nové Město (ie Charles Square and its surrounds).

GRAND HOTEL EVROPA

Map pp272-3   Hotel €€

☎ 224 228 117; www.hotelevropa.cz; Václavské náměstí 25; s/d from 1600/2600Kč; metro Můstek

The Evropa's gorgeous Art Nouveau façade conceals a musty warren of ill-lit corridors and mostly shabby, run-down 1950s rooms. The original Art Nouveau décor in the café, bar, staircases and mezzanine is beautiful, but it doesn't carry over into the bedrooms. These days the place is trading solely on its fame; it is often full of noisy parties, and the atmosphere gets distinctly seedy at night.

HOSTEL U MELOUNU Map pp280-1   Hostel €

☎ 224 918 322; www.hostelumelounu.cz; Ke Karlovu 7; dm 390Kč, s/d from 700/1000Kč; metro IP Pavlova; Ⓟ 🖳

One of the prettier hostels in town, 'At the Watermelon' is set in a historic building on a quiet backstreet, a short walk from Vinohrady's restaurants and bars (it's a 10-minute walk south of IP Pavlova metro station). A variety of rooms, all on the ground floor, range from basic dorms to self-contained apartments radiating off a large central garden, giving the place a peaceful, cottagey feel. Dorms, sleeping between six and 10 people in bunk beds, are the basic, functional spaces you would expect, but they are spotlessly clean and have lockers, and there's the added attraction of that peaceful, sunny garden complete with barbecue.

HOTEL 16 U SV KATEŘINY

Map pp272-3   Boutique Hotel €€

☎ 224 920 636; www.hotel16.cz; Kateřinská 16; s/d from 2800/3500Kč; metro Karlovo Náměstí; Ⓟ 🖳

Near the Botanic Gardens and about five minutes' walk from Karlovo Náměstí metro station, the 'St Catherine' Hotel is a friendly family-run little place with just 14 rooms, tucked away in a very quiet corner of town where you're more likely to hear birdsong than trundling traffic. The rooms vary in size and are simply but smartly furnished; the best ones are those at the back with views onto the peaceful terraced garden. Buffet breakfast is included in the price, and the hotel is fitted with a lift.

HOTEL ADRIA Map pp272-3   Hotel €€€

☎ 221 081 111; www.hoteladria.cz; Václavské náměstí 26; s/d from €165/195; metro Můstek
Conveniently located in the busiest part of town, the Adria has a yellow baroque façade that is Wenceslas Square's oldest surviving building (late 18th century). Its 88 rooms (including two wheelchair-accessible doubles), however, are entirely modern; the superb location explains the somewhat high rates for what is essentially a fairly straightforward, unfussy business hotel. Green is the colour of choice in the smart, restful rooms and there are certainly no complaints when it comes to comfort. Be sure to check out the hotel's restaurant (dating from 1912), a bizarre but atmospheric blend of baroque stalactite grotto and Art Nouveau salon.

HOTEL CARLO IV Map pp268-9   Hotel €€€-€€€€

☎ 224 593 111; www.boscolohotels.com; Senovázné náměstí 13; d/ste from €180/600; metro Hlavní Nádraží; Ⓟ ☒ ▢ ☎
Housed in a neo-Renaissance palace that was once a banking headquarters, the five-star Carlo IV is a monument to designer decadence – the height of elegance, or just over-the-top ostentation, depending on your taste. Acres of marble, glass, leather, wood, silk and linen will have you trailing your fingers across every surface, and the luxurious rooms are the sort that make you think, Do we *have* to go sightseeing? Let's just stay here… While health-conscious guests slip into the wonderfully atmospheric swimming pool (in the style of an antique spa), the more decadent will be sloping off to the Cigar Bar to savour some hand-rolled Havanas.

HOTEL ESPLANADE Map pp272-3   Hotel €€€

☎ 224 501 172; www.esplanade.cz; Washingtonova 19; d from €149; metro Muzeum; Ⓟ
The Esplanade is one of the city's older luxury hotels, dating from 1927, with a classy location opposite the Prague State Opera

and close to Wenceslas Square. The soaring marble lobby gives the impression you're in for something special – those who can upgrade to an apartment will get the full luxury treatment. Otherwise, expect clean and comfortable rooms that match fussily with the original neobaroque décor, all glitteringly lit by a mass of crystal chandeliers.

HOTEL GREEN GARDEN

Map pp280-1   Hotel €€
☎ 224 261 181; www.greengarden.cz in Czech; Fügnerovo náměstí 4; s/d €100/116, apt €150; metro IP Pavlova; Ⓟ
Although it's sandwiched between the raging traffic of Legerova and Sokolská, the Green Garden has friendly staff, bags of old-fashioned character, and a lovely glass-roofed 'winter garden' sitting area. It's a stylish place with 55 good-sized rooms furnished in an elegant, contemporary style, with lots of cream and brown tones, colourful prints and curious glass lamps. The bathrooms, though, are pretty small and no more than functional. All have showers only, apart from the five apartments, which also have bathtubs. One of the rooms is fitted for disabled access. Go for a room on the top floor – it's quieter, and there are great views towards the castle.

Hotel Pařiž (p200)

HOTEL ROKOKO Map pp272-3   Hotel €€
☎ 271 751 045; www.rokokohotelprague.com;
Václavské náměstí 38; s/d from €100/120; metro
Můstek; P 🖳

The Rokoko occupies a prime piece of real
estate bang in the middle of Wenceslas
Square. Housed in an Art Deco building that
dates from the 1920s, it offers great-value
accommodation for such a central location,
provided you don't mind the noise and
bustle of the city's main square. Deco details
survive in the staircases and in some of
the furniture and light fittings in the public
areas, but the rooms, while perfectly pleasant, are in the 'intercontinental bland' style.
Possible moans might include the lack of air-
conditioning (rooms on upper floors can be
rather hot in midsummer), and the absence
of shower curtains in the over-bath showers.

HOTEL TCHAIKOVSKY
Map pp272-3   Boutique Hotel €€
☎ 224 912 121; www.hoteltchaikovsky.com; Ke
Karlovu 19; s/d €107/126; metro IP Pavlova

Lurking down a quiet side street off busy
Ječná, this neat little hotel has 19 restful
rooms ranged around a balcony overlooking a peaceful courtyard; they all offer the
possibility of adding an extra bed (at an
extra charge) if desired. The vaguely 19th-
century style is maintained throughout,
with rich drapery, floral fabrics and antique-
style furnishings, while amenities such as
satellite TVs and minibars are welcome
modern comforts. The attractively tiled
bathrooms (tubs and showers provided) are
bright, well equipped and spotless.

HOTEL YASMIN
Map pp272-3   Boutique Hotel €€€€
☎ 234 100 100; www.hotel-yasmin.cz; Politických
věžňů 12; d from €260; metro Můstek; ✕

This brand-new hotel a block east of Wenceslas Square is very cutting edge, a blend
of Space Age and organic – the public areas
are covered in motifs in the shape of jas-
mine blossoms, from small white petals on
the black granite floors to giant leaf prints
on the walls, and decorated with birch-twig
arrangements and chrome balls (we're not
sure what the orange, furry sculptures in the
breakfast room are meant to be – triffids?).
The spacious bedrooms have a neutral
palette of white, beige and tan, the clean
lines set off by plants, flowers or a curved

edge here and there; the bathrooms are in
black tile and chrome. The hotel is entirely
nonsmoking.

MISS SOPHIE'S Map pp272-3   Hostel €
☎ 296 303 530; www.miss-sophies.com;
Melounova 3; dm 440Kč, s/d from 1500/1700Kč,
apt from 2100Kč; metro IP Pavlova; ✕ 🖳

This hostel in a converted apartment
building on the southern edge of the New
Town makes a pleasant change from the
usual characterless backpacker hive. There's
a touch of contemporary style here, with
oak-veneer floors and stark, minimalist
décor – the main motif is 'distressed' concrete, along with neutral colours and black
metal-framed beds. The place is famous for
its 'designer' showers, with autographed
glass screens and huge 'rainfall' shower
heads. There is a very cool lounge in the
basement, with red-brick vaults and black
leather sofas, and reception (open 24
hours) is staffed by a young, multilingual
crew who are always eager to help.

PENSION BŘEZINA Map pp272-3   Pension €
☎ 296 188 888; www.brezina.cz; Legerova 39-41;
s/d economy 1100/1300Kč, luxury 2000/2200Kč;
metro IP Pavlova; 🖳

The Březina is a welcoming pension in a
converted Art Nouveau apartment block
with a small garden out back, where you
can sit and have a drink in summer. There
are three categories of rooms, ranging from
basic, with shared bathroom, to the comfortable 'lux' rooms. Most are reasonably
spacious and although rather plain, they're
spotlessly clean and well maintained; the
attic rooms, with exposed wooden beams
and slanted ceilings, have a bit more character. Cheapest are the two 'economy'
rooms, which share a bathroom and a
kitchen. They are located on the ground
floor, looking out onto the courtyard, and
are a real bargain for budget travellers. Ask
for a room at the back as those facing the
street can be pretty noisy.

RADISSON SAS ALCRON HOTEL
Map pp272-3   Hotel €€€€
☎ 222 820 000; www.radissonsas.com; Štěpánská
40; d from €200; metro Můstek; P 🖳

Located just a few minutes' walk from Wenceslas Square, the five-star Radisson is the
modern reincarnation of the 1930s Alcron

Hotel, and has long been favoured by celebrities and diplomats. Many of the original Art Deco marble-and-glass fittings have been preserved, and the 211 rooms have been far more tastefully renovated than in many other refurbished Prague hotels. The rooms have pleasant, soft furnishings, retro prints and chic marble bathrooms, while mod cons such as wi-fi access, video games and mini-bars add to the comfort and convenience. There are also wheelchair-accessible rooms for disabled guests.

BEYOND THE CENTRE

You'll find a wide range of accommodation options in the outer suburbs, from the budget hostels and pensions of Žižkov and Holešovice (often more appealing than their city-centre counterparts) to the small family-run hotels of Vinohrady and Smíchov. These options offer the chance to save some money on accommodation in return for a 15- to 20-minute tram or metro trip from the centre.

Vyšehrad

HOTEL AMADEUS Map pp280-1   Hotel €€

☎ 224 937 572; www.dhotels.cz; Slavojova 8; s/d/ste 3050/3250/4750Kč; metro Vyšehrad; Ⓟ

This good-value hotel is located on a quiet street below the Vyšehrad citadel. Rooms in the front block are spacious and elegant, decorated in shades of pale yellow, dark blue and tan; those at the back are a little more cramped, but overlook a peaceful courtyard. The four suites at the top of the building are on two levels – a large sitting room with sofa, chairs and writing desk, with stairs leading up to a mezzanine sleeping area. The city centre is just 10 minutes away by tram.

HOTEL UNION Map pp280-1   Hotel €€

☎ 261 214 812; www.hotelunion.cz; Ostrčilovo náměstí 4; s/d from €98/120; tram 7, 16, 24; Ⓟ

The Union is a grand old hotel that dates from 1906; nationalised by the communists in 1958, it was returned to the grandson of the former owner in 1991. It is still family run, and the staff take great pride in looking after their guests properly. Comfortably renovated, with a few period touches left intact, the hotel is at the foot of the hill below the Vyšehrad fortress; Charles Bridge

is just 10 minutes away on tram No 18. The bedrooms are plain but pleasant, and the double glazing helps to cut down on street noise; ask for one of the deluxe corner rooms (from €142 a double), which are huge and have bay windows with a view of either Vyšehrad or the distant castle.

Holešovice & Bubeneč

ART HOTEL Map pp276-7   Boutique Hotel €€

☎ 233 101 331; www.arthotel.cz; Nad Kralovskou oborou 53, Bubeneč; s/d from €100/110; tram 1, 8, 15, 25, 26; Ⓟ ✕ ▯

There are lots of word-of-mouth recommendations for this small hotel hidden away in the peaceful embassy district. It has sleek modern styling with a display of contemporary Czech art in the lobby, and art photography on the walls of the bedrooms. Room No 203 is the best in the house, with a balcony and a view of the sunset; rooms 102 and 104 also have balconies. It may look out of the way on the map, but it's only a few minutes' walk from a tram that will take you to the city centre in 10 minutes.

HOTEL BELVEDERE Map pp276-7   Hotel €€

☎ 220 106 111; www.europehotels.cz; Milady Horákové 19; s/d from €95/128; tram 1, 8, 15, 25, 26; Ⓟ

The Belvedere is an old communist-era hotel that has been completely refurbished, and now provides good-value accommodation within easy reach of the city centre. The standard rooms are nothing special, but they're comfortable and spotlessly clean. The 'executive' rooms (doubles €147) on the 2nd floor are much more spacious, with soundproofed windows, smart crimson drapes and bedspreads, and huge, white, marble-lined bathrooms. The large breakfast room has a slightly institutional feel, but the food is good and there's plenty of it. There's a tram stop right outside the front door, and it's only five minutes to Náměstí Republiky metro station on tram No 8.

HOTEL EXTOL INN Map pp276-7   Hotel €-€€

☎ 220 876 541; www.extolinn.cz; Přístavní 2, Holešovice; s/d from 790/1350Kč; tram 1, 3, 5, 25; Ⓟ ✕

A favourite with visiting Czech and Polish businesspeople, the bright and modern Extol Inn provides budget accommodation in an up-and-coming neighbourhood within easy reach of the city centre. The cheapest rooms (on the upper floors) are basic, no-frills affairs with shared bathrooms; these are often occupied by large groups of school-children, so if you value your peace and quiet it might be worth paying a bit extra for the more expensive three-star rooms (doubles from 2260Kč), which have private bathroom, TV, minibar and free use of the hotel sauna and spa. The hotel is entirely nonsmoking and wheelchair-accessible. There's a tram stop 100m away, from which it's a 10-minute ride to the city centre.

SIR TOBY'S HOSTEL Map pp276-7   Hostel €

☎ 283 870 635; www.sirtobys.com; Dělnická 24, Holešovice; dm 340-400Kč; s/d 1000/1350Kč; tram 1, 3, 5, 25; P X 🖵

Set in a quiet, nicely refurbished apartment building with spacious kitchen and com-mon room, and run by friendly, cheerful staff, Sir Toby's is only 10 minutes north of the city centre by tram. The dorms have between four and eight bunks, and the bigger dorms are probably the cheapest in Prague. The private rooms, meanwhile, are fitted with metal-framed single beds. All rooms are light, clean and spacious, but don't expect anything fancy. The mat-tresses are a little on the thin side, too, but all sheets and blankets are provided at no extra cost. There's a communal kitchen for self-caterers to do their thing, a lounge and a relaxing little garden where you can sit back and chat.

Žižkov & Karlín

CLOWN & BARD HOSTEL
Map pp278-9   Hostel €

☎ 222 716 453; www.clownandbard.com; Bořivojova 102, Žižkov; dm 300-380Kč; d 1000Kč; apt 2400Kč; tram 5, 9, 26; P 🖵

Set in the heart of Žižkov's pub district, the Clown & Bard is a full-on party place – don't

---

come here looking for peace and quiet. This ever-popular hostel has a café (with all-you-can-eat breakfast till 1pm), a bar, friendly, knowledgeable staff and good tours. As well as dorms and doubles, there are six-person self-catering flats in the attic. The party crowd gravitates towards the thumping basement bar that stays open till midnight and features regular live acts and DJ nights. Rooms are fairly basic, but very clean and perfectly comfortable. The self-catering flats are perfect for those travelling in larger groups, and come with a modern, fully fitted kitchen and bathroom, offering a fair degree of seclusion and independence.

HOSTEL ELF Map pp278-9   Hostel €

☎ 222 540 963; www.hostelelf.com; Husitská 11, Žižkov; dm 320-360Kč; s/d 1000/1200Kč; metro Florenc; 🖵

Young, hip and sociable, Hostel Elf wel-comes a steady stream of party-hearty backpackers from across the globe to its well-maintained dorms, and many end up staying longer than they originally planned. The dorms, sleeping up to 11 people, are kept immaculately clean and are brightly decorated with graffiti art or the odd mural. Some doubles have their own bathrooms, but even the shared bathrooms allow a lot of privacy. There's a little beer-garden terrace and cosy lounge, with free tea and coffee and cheap beer, and Žižkov with its many pubs is right on the doorstep; the downside is the noisy train line that runs close by. The hostel is less than 10 minutes' walk from Florenc bus station.

HOTEL GOLDEN CITY GARNI
Map pp278-9   Hotel €€

☎ 222 711 008; www.goldencity.cz; Táboritská 3, Žižkov; s/d/tr 1900/2700/2900Kč; tram 5, 9, 26; P X 🖵

This is a converted 19th-century apartment block with crisp, clean, no-frills rooms, good buffet breakfasts and friendly, helpful staff. The owners have put a lot of money and effort into renovating the building over the last 10 years, with many period details on the exterior now lovingly restored, and in redesigning and redecorating the rooms to create comfortable, modern accommo-dation. The main train station is just two tram stops away, and Wenceslas Square is four stops.

TOP FIVE BOUTIQUE HOTELS

- Anděl's Hotel (p207)
- Art Hotel (opposite)
- Hotel Josef (p199)
- Hotel Neruda (p196)
- Hotel Yasmin (p203)

HOTEL U TŘÍ KORUNEK

Map pp278-9   Hotel €€

☎ 222 781 112; www.3korunky.cz; Cimburkova 28, Žižkov; s/d from 2480/3380Kč; tram 5, 9, 26; P

Spread across three buildings in a peaceful corner of Žižkov, the 'Three Crowns' has 78 comfortable, spotless rooms, four of which are wheelchair accessible. Most are spacious, with room for a table and a couple of armchairs, but it's worth shelling out for one of the 'superior' rooms (300Kč extra), which are rather more stylish, with wood veneer floors, designer furniture, flat-screen TVs and huge walk-in showers. Don't be put off by the slightly run-down-looking neighbourhood; it's quiet and safe, and the city centre is only a few tram stops away.

Vinohrady

HOTEL ANNA Map pp280-1   Hotel €€

☎ 222 513 111; www.hotelanna.cz; Budečská 17; s/d from €70/90, ste from €100; metro Náměstí Míru

The Hotel Anna is small and friendly, with helpful and knowledgeable staff who speak both English and German. The late-19th-century building retains many of its Art Nouveau period features, and the bedrooms are bright and cheerful with floral bedspreads and arty black-and-white photos of Prague buildings on the walls. There are two small suites on the top floor, one of which has a great view towards the castle. The hotel is tucked away on a quiet backstreet but close to the metro and lots of good restaurants and bars; you can walk to the top end of Wenceslas Square in 10 minutes.

Radisson SAS Alcron Hotel (p203)

HOTEL SIEBER Map pp278-9   Boutique Hotel €€€

☎ 224 250 025; www.sieber.cz; Slezská 55; s/d/ste 4480/4780/5480Kč; metro Jiřího z Poděbrad; ✗ 💻

Popular with business travellers, the Sieber is a small luxury hotel with 13 rooms and seven suites, set in a grand 19th-century apartment building. Stylish décor and attentive service are accompanied by thoughtful little touches such as bathrobes and fresh flowers. The building dates from 1889 and has been restored to its former grandeur after suffering years of neglect under the communist regime, and the rooms are decorated in restful, neutral tones (lots of cream and light wood). Service can't be faulted, and staff are courteous and very helpful.

LE PALAIS HOTEL Map pp280-1   Hotel €€€€

☎ 234 634 111; www.palaishotel.cz; U Zvonařky 1; s/d €335/370, ste from €680; tram 6, 11; P ✗ 💻

Le Palais is housed in a gorgeous *belle époque* building dating from the end of the 19th century that was once home to Czech artist Luděk Marold (1865–98; his former apartment is now rooms 407 to 412). It has been beautifully restored, complete with original floor mosaics, period fireplaces, marble staircases, wrought-iron balustrades, frescoes, painted ceilings and delicate stuccowork. The luxury bedrooms are decorated in warm shades of yellow, pink and ochre, while the various suites – some located in the corner tower, some with a south-facing balcony – make the most of the hotel's superb location perched on top of a bluff with views of Vyšehrad fortress.

PENSION ARCO

Map pp280-1   Pension/Apartments €-€€

☎ 271 742 908; www.arco-guesthouse.cz; Voroněžská 21; d/apt from 1200/1900Kč; tram 4, 22, 23; 💻

The Arco is a gay-owned pension and café-bar offering clean and comfortably furnished pension rooms, as well as several two- to four-person apartments in nearby buildings. The apartments are good value – bright and clean with laminate floors and IKEA furniture, and close to a tram line that will take you all the way to the castle, while Vinohrady's restaurants, pubs and clubs are just a few blocks away.

NEAR THE AIRPORT

The following places all lie at the western edge of the city and are the best options for staying within easy reach of the airport.

Hotel Elegant (☎ 235 300 521; www.hotelelegant.cz; Ruzyňská 197, Ruzyně; s/d 3400/3800Kč; bus 225; Ⓟ) A stylish 1930s Functionalist building that has been converted into a boutique hotel. Only five minutes from the airport by car, or seven minutes on bus No 225; get off at the Ruzyňská škola stop.

Hotel Tranzit (☎ 236 161 111; www.hoteltranzit.cz; Aviatická; d from €110; bus 100, 119, 179; Ⓟ 🖳) Modern hotel with bright, attractive rooms just five minutes' walk from the airport terminal, with some wheelchair-accessible rooms.

Pension Věterný Mlyn (☎ 235 301 686; www.pensionmlyn.cz; Ruzyňská 3/96, Ruzyně; s/d 1000/1600Kč; bus 225; Ⓟ) The 'Windmill' is a friendly, family-run pension where all rooms have TV and en suite shower. It's just across the street from Hotel Elegant (above).

Ramada Airport Hotel (☎ 220 111 250; www.euroagentur.cz; Terminal Jih, K letišti 25a, Ruzyně; s/d €130/150; Ⓟ) The Ramada is at the southern terminal of Ruzyně airport, four stops on bus No 100, 119, 179 or 225 from the main terminal.

PENSION BEETLE Map pp280-1 Pension €-€€

☎ 222 515 093; www.beetle-tour.cz; Šmilovského 10; d from 1800Kč, ste from 3200Kč; tram 4, 22, 23

The Beetle occupies a lovely 1910 apartment building in a leafy backstreet, far from the tourist throng. The cheaper rooms are plain but functional, while the larger rooms and 'suites' (like two-room apartments) are more stylishly decorated and furnished with antique and stripped pine furniture, and are equipped with bedside lamps, minibar, table and chairs. A continental breakfast, with all the coffee you can drink, is included in the price.

Smíchov

ADMIRÁL BOTEL Map pp280-1 Hotel €€

☎ 257 321 302; www.admiral-botel.cz; Hořejší nábřeží 57; s/d 2980/3130Kč, ste 5400Kč; metro Anděl; Ⓟ

If you've ever harboured a desire to sleep in a ship's cabin but would rather do without the seasickness, then climb aboard the Admiral, a permanently berthed riverboat floating quietly off the west bank of the Vltava. The reception area, with its plush leather seating and polished wood and brass, has a smart nautical feel, with narrow corridors leading towards the rooms. These cabins are what you might expect: simple, compact and functional rather than luxurious, with tiny en suite shower rooms; those facing the river have an attractive outlook, and you can feed the swans from your window.

ANDĚL'S HOTEL PRAGUE

Map pp262-3 Boutique Hotel €€€€

☎ 296 889 688; www.andelshotel.com; Stroupežnického 21; s/d from €235/255; metro Anděl; Ⓟ ✗ 🖳

Nowhere sums up the new Smíchov quite like Anděl's. This sleek designer hotel, all stark contemporary style in beige, black and red, has floor-to-ceiling windows, DVD and CD players, internet access, and modern abstract art in every room, while the bathrooms are a wonderland of polished chrome and frosted glass. Superior 'club rooms' come with pleasurable perks such as bathrobes and slippers, newspapers delivered to your room and free room-service breakfast.

HOTEL JULIAN Map pp270-1 Hotel €€€

☎ 257 311 150; www.julian.cz; Elišky Peškové 11; s/d/ste 3680/3980/4800Kč; tram 6, 9, 12, 20; Ⓟ ✗ 🖳

A deservedly popular small hotel with helpful staff and a quiet location just south of Malá Strana. The smart, well-kept bedrooms are decorated with relaxing pastel shades and pine-topped furniture, and the public areas include a clubbish drawing room with a library, comfy armchairs and an open fire; smokers get their breakfast here (served till 11am at weekends), and the main breakfast room is smoke-free. If you're travelling with kids or in a group, there is a family room (two adults and two children) and three suites (sleeping three to six adults), and there's one wheelchair-accessible room.

Dejvice

HOTEL CROWNE PLAZA

Map p275   Hotel €€-€€€

☎ 296 537 111; www.crowneplaza.cz; Koulova 15; d from €125; tram 8; ℗ ⊠ ▥

Originally called the Hotel International, this place was built in the 1950s in the style of Moscow University, complete with Soviet star atop the tower. Now modernised, it is comfortable and quiet, tucked away at the end of the tram line. Come here for the décor rather than anything else – although the rooms here are standard chain-hotel style, with all the necessities but not too many luxuries, the building itself is really something special, covered in polished marble, bas reliefs and frescoes of the noble worker. The deluxe rooms, on the 9th floor and above, are more spacious and have good views over the city.

HOTEL PRAHA Map pp262-3   Hotel €€€€

☎ 224 341 111; www.htlpraha.cz; Sušická 20; d €280; taxi; ℗ ⓢ

The Hotel Praha is one of Prague's more interesting hotels – hidden away on a hill in Dejvice, surrounded by several hectares of private grounds that were once protected by an electric fence, it's a luxury complex that was built in 1981 for the Communist Party elite. The public areas of the hotel are an intriguing mix of 1970s futuristic (sweeping curves and stainless steel) and 1950s Soviet splendour (polished marble and cut-glass chandeliers). The bedrooms are very spacious, with all the luxury you'd expect from a five-star establishment, and many are accessible to wheelchair users. But the hotel's biggest drawcard is the fact that each of its 124 rooms has its own private balcony – the entire southern face of the hotel is a sloping grandstand of stacked balconies, all draped with greenery and commanding a superb view of Prague Castle. Before 1989, such Soviet-era stalwarts as Nicolae Ceaușescu, Erich Honecker and Eduard Shevardnadze all hung their hats here; in recent years, the clientele has shifted from heads of state to Hollywood, with stars such as Tom Cruise, Johnny Depp, Alanis Morissette, Kris Kristofferson and Paul Simon ringing room service in the small hours.

OTHER SUBURBS

SANS SOUCI HOTEL Map pp262-3   Pension €€

☎ 244 461 225; www.hotelsanssouci.cz; V podhájí 12, Podolí; s/d 2200/2600Kč, ste 4000Kč; tram 3, 17; ℗ ⊠

The nine-room Sans Souci is a quiet and charming family-friendly pension in a restored 19th-century villa in the southern suburbs. The recently redecorated rooms are bright and appealing, with white walls and polished wood furniture, and breakfast is served in a parquet-floored, timber-beamed dining room that opens onto the garden. The suite can sleep a family of five, and has a fully fitted kitchen. To get there, take tram No 3 or 17 to the Dvorce stop, walk up Jeremenkova street on the left and turn through the underpass just beyond the shops at No 14. At the top of the stairs, walk right on Na Zvoničce for a few minutes until you see the hotel up on the right. By car, follow the signs from Jeremenkova.

HOSTEL BOATHOUSE   Hostel €

☎ 241 770 051; www.aa.cz/boathouse; Lodnická 1, Braník; dm 350-420Kč; tram 3, 17, 21; ℗ ▥

Travellers rave about the Boathouse, a friendly and popular hostel with a peaceful riverbank setting, run by the vivacious and unstinting crew of Vera and Helena. Accommodation is in three- to nine-bed rooms, with separate bathroom facilities for men and women, and there's a sunny, outdoor deck in front. A continental breakfast is provided free (you can get a cooked breakfast for 40Kč) and extras available include bike and boat hire, a minishop and laundry service. Take tram No 3, 17 or 21 to the Černý kůň stop, and follow the hostel signs west to the river (it's a five-minute walk).

VILLA VOYTA   Boutique Hotel €€€

☎ 261 711 307; www.villavoyta.cz; K Novému dvoru 124/54, Lhotka; s/d €165/185; bus 113, 171, 189, 215; ℗

The Villa Voyta is a beautiful Art Nouveau hotel dating from 1912. Rebuilt in the 1990s when a new 'wing' was added across the road, the Villa Voyta is now a small and executive-friendly hotel with 20 chintzy, elegant rooms, free parking and an excellent gourmet French restaurant. Take bus No 113, 171, 189 or 215 south from Kačerov metro station to the Zálesí stop, and walk three blocks west along Na Větrově.

Excursions

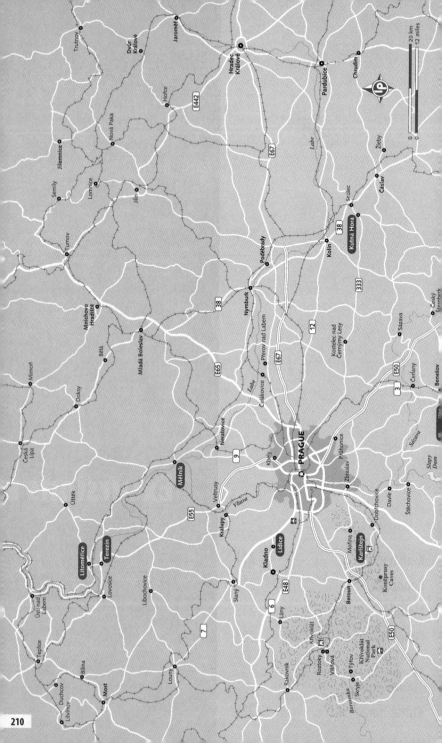

Excursions

The Central Bohemian countryside, most of it within an hour's train or bus ride from Prague, is rich in rural landscapes, attractive towns and historic sights. This chapter lists a selection of day trips and potential overnight visits that can be made easily using public transport. Top of the list are photogenic Karlštejn Castle, the appealing silver-mining town of Kutná Hora and the harrowing former concentration camp, Terezín. Be prepared for huge summer crowds at Karlštejn and Konopiště castles.

Central Bohemia is rich in castles and chateaux, the former country seats of kings and aristocrats, within easy reach of the capital city. Popular castles include Karlštejn (below), a fairytale fortress built to house Charles IV's royal treasury; Konopiště (p212), the country retreat of the ill-fated Archduke Franz Ferdinand, whose assassination kicked off WWI; and the Lobkowicz family's chateau at Mělník (p213), with its tiny but historic vineyard overlooking the confluence of the Labe and Vltava rivers.

There are many interesting medieval towns in the region surrounding Prague; they provide an escape from the crowds that churn though the capital's narrow streets. Litoměřice (p218) has a picture-postcard town square lined with lovely Gothic and Renaissance houses, while the tiny old town of Mělník (p213) has peaceful backstreets and a stunning view over the Bohemian countryside. Most impressive of all is Kutná Hora (p219), with its lovely cathedral, baroque statues and hilltop setting.

The region to the north of Prague contains two deeply moving monuments to the suffering of the Czech people in WWII – the village of Lidice (p215), destroyed by the Nazis as an act of vengeance for the assassination of Reichsprotektor Reinhard Heydrich, and Terezín (p215), a former concentration camp through which 150,000 Czech Jews passed on their way to the gas chambers.

There's also a number of sights around Prague that are decidedly out of the ordinary. The Trophy Corridor and Chamois Room in Konopiště Chateau (p212), crammed with the antlers, skulls and stuffed heads of thousands of animals, stand as bizarre witness to the hunting obsession of Archduke Franz Ferdinand, and Kutná Hora's Czech Silver Museum (p219) offers the chance to don a miner's helmet and lamp and explore the claustrophobic tunnels of a medieval silver mine beneath the town. Most extraordinary of all is the Sedlec Ossuary (p219) at Kutná Hora, where the bones of 40,000 people have been fashioned into a series of weird and wonderful decorations.

KARLŠTEJN

Karlštejn Castle, rising above the village of Karlštejn southwest of Prague, is in such good shape these days that it wouldn't look out of place on Disney's Main St. The crowds come in theme-park proportions as well (it is best to book ahead for the guided tours), but the peaceful surrounding countryside offers views of Karlštejn's stunning exterior that rival anything you'll see on the inside.

Perched high on a crag that overlooks the Berounka River, and sporting a spotless new paint job, this cluster of turrets, high walls and looming towers is as immaculately maintained as it is powerfully evocative. It's rightly one of the top attractions of the Czech Republic, and the only drawback is its overwhelming popularity: in the summer months it is literally mobbed with visitors, ice-cream vendors and souvenir stalls.

TRANSPORT

Distance from Prague 30km
Direction Southwest
Travel time One hour
Train Trains to Beroun from Praha-Hlavní Nádraží and Praha-Smíchovské stop at Karlštejn (46Kč, 45 minutes, hourly).

Karlštejn was born of a grand pedigree, starting life in 1348 as a hideaway for the crown jewels and treasury of the Holy Roman Emperor, Charles IV. Run by an appointed Burgrave, the castle was surrounded by a network of landowning knight vassals, who came to the castle's aid whenever enemies moved against it.

Karlštejn again sheltered the Bohemian and Imperial crown jewels during the Hussite wars, but fell into disrepair as its defences became outmoded. Considerable restoration work, not least by Josef Mocker in the late 19th century, has returned the castle to its former glory.

There are two tours through the castle. Tour I (50 minutes) passes through the **Knight's Hall**, still daubed with the coats-of-arms and names of the knight vassals, **Charles IV's Bedchamber**, the **Audience Hall** and the **Jewel House**, which includes treasures from the Chapel of the Holy Cross and a replica of the St Wenceslas Crown.

Tour II (70 minutes) must be booked in advance and takes in the **Great Tower**, the highest point of the castle, which includes a museum on Mocker's restoration work, the **Marian Tower** and the exquisite **Chapel of the Holy Cross**, with its decorative ceiling.

Sights & Information

Karlštejn Castle (☎ 274 008 154; www.hradkarlstejn.cz; Karlštejn; ☼ 9am-6pm Tue-Sun Jul & Aug; to 5pm May, Jun & Sep; to 4pm Apr & Oct; to 3pm Nov-Mar) Tour I adult/concession 220/120Kč, Tour II adult/concession 300/100Kč.

Eating & Sleeping

Pension & Restaurant U Janů (☎ 311 681 210; info@ujanu.cz; d 1000Kč, apt 1200Kč) On the road up to the castle, this atmospheric place has a decent dollop of authentic charm; there are three apartments and one double room.

Penzión U královny Dagmar (☎ 311 681 378; www.penziondagmara.cz; d/tr 1150/1350Kč, apt 1550Kč) Close to the castle and a rung up the price ladder, this slick place has all the creature comforts and a top-notch eatery.

Karlštejn Castle (left)

KONOPIŠTĚ

Archduke Franz Ferdinand d'Este, heir to the Austro-Hungarian throne, is famous for being dead – it was his assassination in 1914 that sparked off WWI. But the archduke was an enigmatic figure who avoided the intrigues of the Vienna court, and for the last 20 years of his life he hid away in what became his ideal country retreat, **Konopiště Chateau**.

Konopiště, lying amid extensive grounds 2km west of the town of Benešov, is a testament to the archduke's twin obsessions – hunting and St George. Having renovated the massive Gothic and Renaissance building in the 1890s, and installed all the latest technology – including electricity, central heating, flush toilets, showers and a luxurious lift – Franz Ferdinand decorated his home with his hunting trophies. His game books record that he shot about 300,000 creatures in his lifetime, from foxes and deer to elephants and tigers. About 100,000 of them adorn the walls, each marked with the date and place it met its end – the crowded **Trophy Corridor** (Tour I and III), with a forest of mounted animal heads, and the antler-clad **Chamois Room** (Tour III), with its 'chandelier' fashioned from a stuffed condor, are truly bizarre sights.

There are three guided tours available. Tour III is the most interesting, visiting the private apartments used by the archduke and his family, which have remained unchanged since the state took possession of the chateau in 1921. Tour II takes in the **Great Armoury**, one of the largest and most impressive collections in Europe.

The archduke's collection of art and artefacts relating to St George is no less impressive, amounting to 3750 items, many of which are on show in the **St George Museum** beneath the terrace at the front of the castle.

TRANSPORT

Distance from Prague 50km
Direction South
Travel time 1¼ hours
Bus There are buses from Prague's Roztyly metro station to Benešov (37Kč, 40 minutes, twice hourly) – their final destination is usually Pelhřimov or Jihlava. There are also buses to Benešov from Prague's Florenc bus station (44Kč, 40 minutes, eight daily).
Train There are frequent direct trains from Prague's Hlavní Nádraží to Benešov u Prahy (64Kč, 1¼ hours, hourly). Konopiště is 2km west of Benešov. Local bus No 2 (7Kč, six minutes, hourly) runs from a stop on Dukelská, 400m north of the train station (turn left out of the station, then first right on Tyršova and first left) to the castle car park. Otherwise it's a 30-minute walk. Turn left out of the train station, go left across the bridge over the railway, and follow Konopištská street west for 2km.

Sights & Information

Konopiště Chateau (☎ 317 721 366; Benešov; ☯ 9am-5pm Tue-Sun May-Aug; to 4pm Tue-Fri, to 5pm Sat & Sun Sep; to 3pm Tue-Fri, to 4pm Sat & Sun Apr & Oct; to 3pm Sat & Sun Nov; closed noon-1pm year-round) Tour I or Tour II in English adult/child 180/100Kč; Tour III in English 300/200Kč.

St George Museum (Muzeum sv Jiří; adult/child 25/10Kč; ☯ same hr as chateau)

Eating & Sleeping

Hostinec U zlaté hvězdy (☎ 317 723 921; Masarykovo náměstí 2, Benešov; mains 80-150Kč; ☯ 11am-11pm) Enjoy Bohemian pub grub at this snug central *pivnice* (beer hall).

Hotel Atlas (☎ 317 724 771; www.hotel-atlas.cz; Tyršova 2063, Benešov; s/d 742/864Kč) This place is bland and functional, but the rooms are spotless and comfortable. Benešov is located just 2km east of the Konopiště Chateau.

Hotel Nová Myslivna (☎ 317 722 496; www.hotelmyslivna .zde.cz; Konopiště; d/tr 550/825Kč; Ⓟ) The sweeping angular roof of this chalet-style hotel clashes somewhat with the softer lines of the castle, but the hotel's location by the Konopiště Chateau car park is unbeatable.

Konopiště Chateau (left)

MĚLNÍK

Pretty Mělník, an hour's drive north of Prague, sprawls over a rocky promontory surrounded by the flat sweep of Bohemia's modest wine-growing region. Staunchly Hussite in its sympathies, the town was flattened by Swedish troops in the Thirty Years' War, but the castle was rebuilt as a prettier, less threatening chateau and the centre retains a strong historical identity. Modernity has caught up with the town's trailing edge, bringing a clutch of factories to its outskirts, but views from the castle side are untouched and Mělník remains a good place for a spot of wine-tasting far from the bustle of the capital.

Mělník Chateau (below)

The Renaissance **Mělník Chateau** (zámek Mělník) was acquired by the Lobkowicz family in 1739; the family opened it to the public in 1990. You can wander through the former living quarters, which are crowded with a rich collection of baroque furniture and 17th- and 18th-century paintings. Additional rooms have changing exhibits of modern works and a fabulous collection of 17th-century maps detailing Europe's great cities. A separate tour descends to the 14th-century wine cellars where you can taste the chateau's wines; a shop in the courtyard sells the chateau's own label.

Next to the chateau is the 15th-century Gothic **Church of SS Peter & Paul** (kostel sv Petra a Pavla), with its baroque furnishings and tower. Remnants of its Romanesque predecessor have been incorporated into the rear of the building. The old crypt is now an **ossuary**, packed with the bones of some 10,000 people dug up to make room for 16th-century plague victims, and arranged in macabre patterns.

The path between chateau and church leads to a **terrace** with superb views across the river and the central Bohemian countryside. The steep slopes below the terrace are planted with vines – supposedly descendants of the first vines to be introduced to Bohemia, by Charles IV, back in the 14th century.

Sights & Information

Mělník Chateau (Zámek Mělník; ☎ 315 622 121; adult/ concession 70/50Kč; ☉ castle 10am-6pm, wine cellar to 5pm) Self-guided tour with English text. Wine-tasting 70Kč to 350Kč.

Ossuary (adult/child 25/15Kč; ☉ 9.30am-12.30pm & 1.15-4pm Tue-Fri, 10am-12.30pm & 1.15-4pm Sat & Sun)

Tourist Information Centre (☎ 315 627 503; infocentrum@melnik.cz; náměstí Míru 11; ☉ 9am-5pm May-Sep, Mon-Fri only Oct-Apr) Sells maps and historical guides, and can help with accommodation.

Eating & Sleeping

Hotel U Rytířů (☎ 315 621 440; www.urytiru.cz; Svatová-clavská 17; d 1900-2500Kč) Located conveniently right next to the castle, this opulent little place has plush, apartment-style rooms with all the trimmings, and a garden restaurant (mains 100Kč to 250Kč, open 8am to 11pm).

Penzión V podzámčí (☎ 315 622 889; www .penzionvpodzamci.cz; Seiferta 167; s/d incl breakfast

650/1300Kč) This reasonably central place (it's three blocks from náměstí Míru, to the left as you face the chateau) has some modest, modern rooms above a Bohemia crystal shop.

Restaurace sv Václav (☎ 315 622 126; Svatováclavská 22; mains 90-180Kč; ☉ 11am-11pm) Dark wood décor, cigar humidors, red leather seats and an outdoor terrace that's a lunchtime sun-trap conspire to make this one of Mělník's most appealing restaurants.

LIDICE, TEREZÍN & LITOMĚŘICE

The Bohemian countryside to the north of Prague contains two villages that provide a sobering reminder of the horrors inflicted on the Czech people during WWII. If you're driving, Lidice and Terezín can be combined in one day; if you want to spend the night, head for the attractive town of Litoměřice, 3km north of Terezín. Using public transport, you'll have to choose; it's only practical to do one or the other in a single day.

LIDICE

When British-trained Czechoslovak paratroops assassinated Reichsprotektor Reinhard Heydrich in June 1942 (see the boxed text, p43), the Nazis took a savage revenge. Picking – apparently at random – the mining and foundry village of **Lidice**, 18km northwest of Prague, they proceeded on 10 June to obliterate it from the face of the earth. All its men were shot, the women and the older children were shipped to the Ravensbrück concentration camp, and the younger children were farmed out to German foster homes. The village was systematically burned and bulldozed so that no trace remained. Of its 500 inhabitants, 192 men, 60 women and 88 children eventually died. The atrocity caused shock around the world and triggered a campaign to preserve the village's memory. The site is now a green field, eloquent in its silence, dotted with a few memorials and the reconstructed foundations of a farm where most of the men were murdered. The onsite **Muzeum Lidice** recreates the village in photographs and text, and also screens chilling SS film footage of its destruction.

TRANSPORT

Distance from Prague 60km (to Terezín)
Direction North
Travel time 1½ hours
Bus Direct buses from Prague to Litoměřice (61Kč, 1¼ hours, hourly), stopping at Terezín, depart from stance No 17 at Florenc bus station (final destination Ústí nad Labem). There are also frequent buses between Litoměřice bus station and Terezín (8Kč, 10 minutes, at least hourly). Buses from Prague to Lidice (21Kč, 30 minutes, hourly) depart from the bus stop on Evropa, opposite the Hotel Diplomat, just west of Dejvická metro station.

TEREZÍN

A bulwark of stone and earth, the immense fortress of **Terezín** (Theresienstadt in German) was built in 1780 by Emperor Joseph II with a single purpose in mind: to keep the enemy out. Ironically, it is more notorious for keeping people in – it served as a prison in the later days of the Habsburg Empire, and Gavrilo Princip, the assassin who killed Archduke Franz Ferdinand was incarcerated here during WWI – and when the Germans took control during WWII, the fortress became a grim holding pen for Jews bound for the extermination camps. In contrast to the colourful, baroque face of many Czech towns, Terezín is a stark but profoundly evocative monument to a darker aspect of Europe's past.

The bleakest phase of Terezín's history began in 1940 when the Gestapo established a prison in the Lesser Fortress. Evicting the inhabitants from the Main Fortress the following year, the Nazis transformed the town into a transit camp, through which some 150,000 people eventually passed en route to extermination camps. For most, conditions were appalling. Between April and September 1942 the ghetto's population increased from 12,968 to 58,491, leaving each prisoner with only 1.65 sq m of space and causing disease and starvation on a terrifying scale. In the same period, there was a 15-fold increase in the number of deaths within the prison walls.

Terezín later became the centrepiece of one of Nazism's more extraordinary public-relations coups. Official visitors to the fortress, including representatives of the Red Cross, saw a town that was billed as a kind of Jewish 'refuge', with a Jewish administration, banks, shops, cafés, schools and a thriving cultural life – it even had a jazz band – in a charade that twice completely fooled international observers. The reality was a relentlessly increasing concentration of prisoners, regular trains departing for the gas chambers of Auschwitz, and the death by starvation, disease or suicide of some 35,000 people.

TEREZÍN

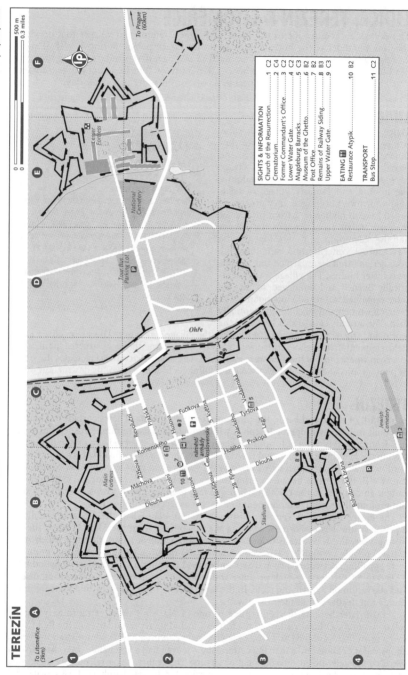

To Litoměřice (3km)

To Prague (60km)

Main Fortress

Lesser Fortress

National Cemetery

Tour Bus Parking Lot

Ohře

Jewish Cemetery

náměstí armády

Stadium

500 m
0.3 miles

Streets labeled: Revoluční, Pražská, Husova, Fučíkova, Komenského, Máchova, Žižkova, Školní, Dlouhá, B Němcové, Havlíčkova, Cestoslovenské, 28 října, Holého, 5 května, Palackého, Prokopa, Vodárenská, Tyršova, Dlouhá, Leží, Bohušovická brána

From the ground, the sheer scale of the maze of walls and moats that surrounds the **Main Fortress** (hlavní pevnost) is impossible to fathom – mainly because the town is actually inside them. In fact, when you first arrive by bus or car you may be left thinking that the central square looks no different to 101 other small town centres. Take a peek at the aerial photograph in the Museum of the Ghetto, or wander past the walls en route to the Lesser Fortress, however, and a very different picture begins to emerge. At the heart of the Main Fortress is the neat grid of streets that makes up the town of Terezín. There's little to look at except the chunky, 19th-century **Church of the Resurrection**, the arcaded commandant's office, the neoclassical administrative buildings on the square and the surrounding grid of houses with their awful secrets. South of the square are the anonymous remains of a **railway siding**, built by prisoners, on which loads of further prisoners arrived – and departed.

The main attraction here is the absorbing **Museum of the Ghetto** (Muzeum ghetta), which has two branches. The main branch explores the rise of Nazism and life in the Terezín ghetto, using the period bric-a-brac to startling and evocative effect. Erected in the 19th century to house the local school, the museum building was later used by the Nazis to accommodate the camp's 10- to 15-year-old boys. The haunting images painted by these children still decorate the walls. A newer branch is housed in the former **Magdeburg Barracks** (Magdeburská kasárna), which served as the seat of the Jewish 'town council'. Here you can visit a reconstructed dormitory, and look at exhibits on the extraordinarily rich cultural life – music, theatre, fine arts and literature – that somehow flourished against this backdrop of fear. There is also a small exhibit in the grim **Crematorium** (Krematorium; ☯ 10am-5pm Sun-Fri Mar-Nov) in the Jewish Cemetery just off Bohušovická brána, about 750m south of the main square.

You can take a self-guided tour of the **Lesser Fortress** (Malá pevnost) through the prison barracks, isolation cells, workshops and morgues, past execution grounds and former mass graves. It would be hard to invent a more menacing location, and it is only while wandering through the seemingly endless tunnels beneath the walls that you begin to appreciate fully the vast dimensions of the fort. The Nazis' mocking concentration-camp slogan, Arbeit Macht Frei (Work Makes You Free) hangs above the gate. In front of the fortress is a National Cemetery, established in 1945 for those exhumed from the Nazis' mass graves.

Terezín's Lesser Fortress (above)

LITOMĚŘICE

After gritting your teeth through the horrors of Terezín, **Litoměřice** is your chance to exhale. Although only a few kilometres to the north of the infamous fortress, this quaint riverside town is a million miles away in atmosphere. Pastel-hued façades and intricate gables jostle for dominance on the main square, and the town's lively bars and restaurants play host to some vibrant after-hours action. Once stridently Hussite, much of the Gothic face of Litoměřice was levelled during the Thirty Years' War and today the town's unassuming castle plays second fiddle to a clutch of effete Renaissance houses and impressive churches (many by esteemed 18th-century architect Ottavio Broggio).

Dominating Mírové náměstí, the town's attractive main square, is the Gothic tower of **All Saints Church** (kostel Všech svatých), built in the 13th century and 'Broggio-ised' in 1718. Beside it, with multiple gables, pointy arches and a copper-topped tower, is the handsome, Gothic **Old Town Hall** (Stará radnice), with a small town museum. Most striking is the 1560 Renaissance **House at the Black Eagle** (dům U Černého orla), covered in *sgraffito* biblical scenes and housing the Hotel Salva Guarda. A few doors down is the present town hall, in the 1539 **House at the Chalice** (dům U Kalicha), with a massive Hussite chalice on the roof. This building also houses the tourist information office. The thin slice of baroque wedding cake at the uphill end of the square is the **House of Ottavio Broggio**.

Along Michalská at the southwest corner of the square you'll find another house where Broggio left his mark, the excellent **North Bohemia Fine Arts Gallery** with the priceless Renaissance panels of the Litoměřice Altarpiece.

Turn left at the end of Michalská and follow Domská towards grassy, tree-lined Domské náměstí on Cathedral Hill, passing pretty **St Wenceslas Church**, a true baroque gem, along a side street to the right. At the top of the hill is the town's oldest church, **St Stephen Cathedral**, dating from the 11th century.

Go through the arch to the left of the cathedral and descend a steep cobbled lane called Máchova. At the foot of the hill turn left then first right, up the zigzag steps to the **old town walls**. You can follow the walls to the right as far as the next street, Jezuitská, where a left turn leads back to the square.

Sights & Information

Lesser Fortress (Malá pevnost; ☎ 416 782 576; www .pamatnik-terezin.cz; Terezín; adult/child 160/130Kč; ☼ 8am-6pm Apr-Oct, to 4.30pm Nov-Mar) Combined ticket for Muzeum Ghetta and Malá pevnost is 180/140Kč.

Lidice Museum (Muzeum Lidice; www.lidice-memorial.cz; Lidice; adult/concession 80/40Kč; ☼ 9am-6pm Apr-Sep, to 5pm Oct & Mar, to 4pm Nov-Feb)

Litoměřice Tourist Information Office (☎ 416 732 440; www.litomerice.cz; Mírové náměstí 15, Litoměřice; ☼ 8am-6pm Mon-Fri, 8am-5.30pm Sat, 9.30am-4pm Sun May-Sep; 8am-5pm Mon & Wed, 8am-4.15pm Tue & Thu, 8am-4pm Fri, 8-11am Sat Oct-Apr)

Museum of the Ghetto (Muzeum ghetta; ☎ 416 782 576; www.pamatnik-terezin.cz; Komenského, Terezín; adult/child 160/130Kč; ☼ 9am-6pm Apr-Oct, to 5.30pm Nov-Mar) Combined ticket for Muzeum Ghetta and Malá pevnost is 180/140Kč. The museum has good multilingual self-guide pamphlets, a large selection of books for sale, and guides (some of them ghetto survivors).

North Bohemia Fine Arts Gallery (Severo česká galerie výtvarného umění; ☎ 416 732 382; Michalská 7, Litoměřice; adult/concession 32/16Kč; ☼ 9am-noon & 1-6pm Tue-Sun Apr-Sep, to 5pm Oct-Mar)

Eating

Music Café Viva (☎ 608 437 783; Mezibraní 5, Litoměřice; mains 80-200Kč; ☼ 11am-midnight) Housed in a former bastion in the old city walls opposite the train station, this music-oriented eatery has a cocktail bar below, a restaurant above and creaking wooden beams galore.

Restaurace Atypik (☎ 416 782 780; Máchova 91, Terezín; mains 60-100Kč; ☼ 11am-10pm) Atypik by name, but rather typical by nature, this bustling place offers all the predictable local favourites, with an emphasis on stodge and unapologetic meatiness.

Sleeping

Hotel Salva Guarda (☎ 416 732 506; www.salva-guarda .cz; Mírové náměstí 12, Litoměřice; s/d 920/1450Kč; P) Litoměřice's top hotel is set in the lovely Renaissance House at the Black Eagle. It also has the best restaurant on the square.

Pension Prislin (☎ 416 735 833; www.prislin.cz; Na Kocandě 12, Litoměřice; s/d 700/1200Kč; P) A view across the river and breakfast in the garden are good reasons for choosing the family-friendly Prislin. It's five minutes' walk east of the town square, along the main road.

U Svatého Václava (☎ 416 737 500;
usvatehovaclava@seznam.cz; Svatováclavská 12,
Litoměřice; s/d 600/1000Kč) Tucked away in the shadow of St Wenceslas Church, this pretty villa houses a tip-top pension with sauna, well-equipped rooms and a homely apron-toting owner who whips up a fine breakfast.

KUTNÁ HORA

Now dwarfed by 21st-century Prague, Kutná Hora once marched in step with the capital and, with a little help from fate, might even have stolen its crown as the heart and soul of Bohemia. Enriched by the silver ore that ran in veins through the surrounding hills, the medieval city once enjoyed explosive growth, becoming the seat of Wenceslas II's royal mint in 1308 and the residence of Wenceslas IV just under 100 years later. The silver *groschen* that were minted here at that time represented the

www.lonelyplanet.com

TRANSPORT

Distance from Prague 65km
Direction East
Travel time 1½ hours
Train There are direct trains from Prague's main train station to Kutná Hora Hlavní Nádraží (98 Kč, 55 minutes, seven daily).
Bus There are about six direct buses a day, on weekdays only, from stop No 2 at Prague's Florenc bus station to Kutná Hora (58Kc, 1¼ hours).

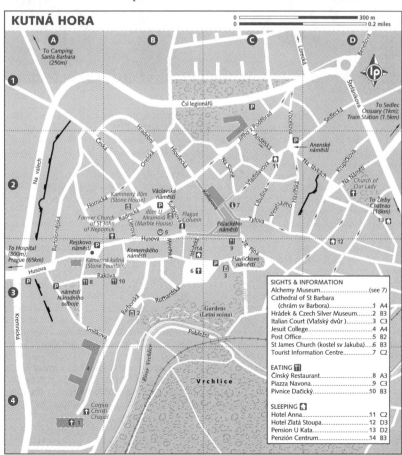

KUTNÁ HORA

0 — 300 m
0 — 0.2 miles

SIGHTS & INFORMATION	
Alchemy Museum..........................(see 7)	
Cathedral of St Barbara	
(chrám sv Barbora)........................1	A4
Hrádek & Czech Silver Museum........2	B3
Italian Court (Vlašský dvůr)............3	C3
Jesuit College..................................4	A4
Post Office.....................................5	B2
St James Church (kostel sv Jakuba)...6	B3
Tourist Information Centre...............7	C2

EATING	
Čínský Restaurant...........................8	A3
Piazza Navona.................................9	C3
Pivnice Dačický..............................10	B3

SLEEPING	
Hotel Anna....................................11	C2
Hotel Zlatá Stoupa........................12	D3
Pension U Kata..............................13	D2
Penzión Centrum...........................14	B3

Sedlec Ossuary (below)

hard currency of Central Europe. But while boom-time Kutná Hora was Prague's undisputed understudy, the town tripped out of history when the silver mines began to splutter and run dry in the 16th century; a demise hastened by the Thirty Years' War and finally certified by a devastating fire in 1770. While the capital continued to expand, its sister city largely vanished from sight.

Which is not to say everyone has forgotten about it. Kutná Hora today is an A-list tourist attraction – it was added to Unesco's World Heritage List in 1996 – luring visitors with a smorgasbord of historic sights and more than a touch of nostalgic whimsy. Standing on the ramparts surrounding the mighty Cathedral of St Barbara, looking out across rooftops eerily reminiscent of Prague's Malá Strana, it's all too easy to indulge in spot of melancholic what-might-have-been.

If you arrive by train, a natural first stop is the remarkable **Sedlec Ossuary** (Kostnice), just a 10-minute walk south from Kutná Hora train station. When the Schwarzenberg family purchased Sedlec monastery in 1870 they allowed a local woodcarver to get creative with the bones that had been piled in the crypt for centuries. But this was no piddling little heap of bones; it was the remains of no fewer than 40,000 people. The result was spectacular: garlands of skulls and femurs are strung from the vaulted ceiling like Addams Family Christmas decorations, while in the centre dangles a vast chandelier containing at least one of each bone in the human body. Four giant pyramids of stacked bones squat in each of the corner chapels, and crosses, chalices and monstrances of bone adorn the altar. There's even a Schwarzenberg coat-of-arms made from bones.

From Sedlec it's another 20-minute walk (or five-minute bus ride) into central Kutná Hora. Palackého náměstí, the main square, is unremarkable; the most interesting part of the old town lies to its south. But first, take a look at the **Alchemy Museum**, in the same building as the information centre, complete with basement laboratory, Gothic chapel and mad-scientist curator.

From the upper end of the square a narrow lane called Jakubská leads directly to the huge **St James Church** (kostel sv Jakuba; 1330). Just east of the church lies the **Italian Court** (Vlašský dvůr), the former Royal Mint – it got its name from the master craftsmen from Florence brought in by Wenceslas II to kick-start the business, and who began stamping silver coins here in 1300. The oldest remaining part, the (now bricked-up) niches in the courtyard, were minters' workshops. The original treasury rooms now hold an exhibit on coins and minting. The guided tour (with English text) is worth taking for a look at the few historical rooms open to the public, notably a 15th-century **Audience Hall** with two impressive 19th-century murals depicting the election of Vladislav Jagiello as king of Bohemia in 1471 (the angry man in white is Matthias Corvinus, the loser), and the Decree of Kutná Hora being proclaimed by Wenceslas IV and Jan Hus in 1409.

From the southern side of St James Church, a narrow cobbled lane (Ruthardská) leads down and then up to the **Hrádek** (Little Castle). Originally part of the town's fortifications, it was rebuilt in the 15th century as the residence of Jan Smíšek, administrator of the royal mines, who grew rich from silver he illegally mined right under the building. It now houses the **Czech Silver Museum** (České Muzeum Stříbra). The exhibits celebrate the mines that made Kutná Hora wealthy, including a huge wooden device once used to lift loads weighing as much as 1000kg from the 200m-deep shafts. You can even don a miner's helmet and lamp and join a 45-minute guided tour (adult/child 110/70Kč) through 500m of **medieval mine shafts** beneath the town.

Just beyond the Hrádek is the 17th-century former **Jesuit college**, fronted by a terrace with a row of 13 baroque statues of saints, an arrangement inspired by the statues on Prague's Charles Bridge. All are related to the Jesuits and/or the town; check out the second one – the woman holding a chalice, with a stone tower at her side, is St Barbara, the patron saint of miners and therefore of Kutná Hora.

At the far end of the terrace is Kutná Hora's greatest monument, the Gothic **Cathedral of St Barbara** (chrám sv Barbora). Rivalling Prague's St Vitus in size and magnificence, its soaring nave culminates in elegant, six-petalled ribbed vaulting. Work was started in 1380, interrupted during the Hussite Wars and abandoned in 1558 when the silver began to run out. It was finally completed in neogothic style at the end of the 19th century. The **ambulatory chapels** preserve some original 15th-century frescoes, some of them showing miners at work. Take a walk around the outside of the church, too; the terrace at the east end enjoys the finest view in town.

Sights & Information

Alchemy Museum (☎ 327 511 259; Palackého náměstí 377; adult/concession 40/25Kč; ☷ 10am-5pm Apr-Oct, to 4pm Nov-Mar)

Cathedral of St Barbara (chrám sv Barbora; ☎ 776 393 938; adult/concession 30/15Kč; ☷ 9am-5.30pm Tue-Sun May-Sep, 10-11.30am & 1-4pm Apr & Oct, 10-11.30am & 2-3.30pm Nov-Mar)

Czech Silver Museum (České Muzeum Stříbra; ☎ 327 512 159; adult/concession 60/30Kč; ☷ 10am-6pm Jul & Aug; 9am-6pm May, Jun & Sep; 9am-5pm Apr & Oct; closed Mon year-round)

Italian Court (Vlašský dvůr; ☎ 327 512 873; Havlíčkovo náměstí 552; adult/concession 80/50Kč; ☷ 9am-6pm Apr-Sep, 10am-5pm Mar & Oct, 10am-4pm Nov-Feb)

Sedlec Ossuary (Kostnice; ☎ 327 561 143; Zámecká 127; adult/concession 45/30Kč; ☷ 8am-6pm Apr-Sep, 9am-noon & 1-5pm Oct, to 4pm Nov-Mar)

Tourist Information Centre (☎ 327 512 378; www.kh.cz; Palackého náměstí 377; ☷ 9am-6pm Apr-Oct; 9am-5pm Mon-Fri, 10am-4pm Sat & Sun Nov-Mar) Books accommodation, rents bicycles and offers internet access (1Kč per minute, 15Kč minimum).

Eating

Čínský Restaurant (☎ 327 514 151; náměstí Národního odboje 48; mains 90-200Kč; ☷ 11am-10pm Tue-Sat, to 2.30pm Sun) Set in a plush old house with a garden out back, the imaginatively named 'Chinese' is a little heavy on the MSG but still manages a tasty chicken kung-po.

Piazza Navona (☎ 327 512 588; Palackého náměstí 90; mains 100-130Kč; ☷ 9am-midnight May-Sep, to 8pm Oct-Apr) Feed up on pizza at this homely Italian café-bar, plastered with Ferrari flags and Inter Milan pennants; tables spill onto the main square in summer.

Pivnice Dačický (☎ 327 512 248; Rakova 8; mains 60-100Kč; ☷ 11am-midnight) Get some froth on your moustache at this old-fashioned, wood-panelled Bohemian beer hall, where you can dine on dumplings and choose from five different draught beers, including Hoegaarden.

Sleeping

Hotel Anna (☎ 327 516 315; hotel.anna@seznam.cz; Vladislavova 372; s/d 730/1150Kč; ℗) Offers comfortable, modern rooms with shower, TV and breakfast in a lovely old building with an atmospheric stone-vaulted cellar restaurant.

Hotel Zlatá Stoupa (☎ 327 511 540; zlatastoupa@iol.cz; Tylova 426; s/d from 1220/1980Kč; **P**) If you feel like spoiling yourself, the most luxurious place in town is the elegantly furnished 'Golden Mount'. We like a hotel room where the minibar contains full-size bottles of wine.

Penzión Centrum (☎ 327 514 218; www.centrum .penzion.cz; Jakubská 57; d/tr 1000/1400Kč; **P**) Tucked away in a quiet, flower-bedecked courtyard off Kutná Hora's main drag, this place offers snug rooms and a sunny garden.

Penzión U Kata (☎ 327 515 096; www.ukata.cz; Uhelná 596; s/d from 450/600Kč; **P**) This quiet, backstreet pension has basic but comfortable rooms, all with private shower and WC.

Directory

Directory

The practical information in this chapter is divided into two parts, Transport and Practicalities. Within each section, information is presented in strictly alphabetical order.

TRANSPORT

AIR

The national carrier, **Czech Airlines** (ČSA; Map pp268–9; ☎ 239 007 007; www.csa.cz; V celnici 5, Nové Město), has direct flights to Prague from many European cities, including London, Edinburgh, Paris and Frankfurt, and from New York and Toronto.

Airlines

Main international airlines serving Prague:

Aer Lingus (EI; ☎ 224 815 373; www.aerlingus.ie)

Aeroflot (SU; ☎ 227 020 020; www.aeroflot.ru)

Air France (AF; ☎ 221 662 662; www.airfrance.com/cz)

Alitalia (AZ; ☎ 224 194 150; www.alitalia.com)

Austrian Airlines (OS; ☎ 227 231 231; www.aua.com)

British Airways (BA; ☎ 239 000 299; www.britishairways.com)

Croatia Airlines (OU; ☎ 222 222 235; www.croatiaairlines.hr)

Czech Airlines (OK; ☎ 239 007 007; www.csa.cz)

EasyJet (EZY; www.easyjet.com)

El Al (LY; ☎ 224 226 624; www.elal.co.il)

FlyGlobespan (B4; ☎ 220 113 171; www.flyglobespan.com)

GermanWings (4U www.germanwings.com)

JAT Airways (JU; ☎ 224 942 654; www.jat.com)

KLM (KL; ☎ 233 090 933; www.klm.com)

LOT (LO; ☎ 222 317 524; www.lot.com)

Lufthansa (LH; ☎ 224 422 911; www.lufthansa.com)

Malev (MA; ☎ 220 113 090; www.malev.com)

SAS (SK; ☎ 220 116 031; www.scandinavian.net)

SkyEurope (NE; ☎ 900 14 15 16; www.skyeurope.com)

SN Brussels Airlines (SN; ☎ 220 116 352; www.flysn.com)

Turkish Airlines (TK; ☎ 234 708 708; www.turkishairlines.com)

Airport

Prague-Ruzyně Airport (☎ 220 113 314; www.csl.cz; bus 100, 119, 179) is 17km west of the city centre. There are two international terminals – Terminal North 2 is for flights to/from Schengen Agreement countries (most EU nations, plus Switzerland, Iceland and Norway), and Terminal North 1 is for flights to/from non-Schengen countries (including the UK, Ireland and non-European destinations).

In both terminals the arrival hall and departure hall are next to each other, on the same level. The arrival halls have exchange counters, ATMs, accommodation and car-hire agencies, public-transport information desks, taxi services and 24-hour left-luggage counters. The departure halls have restaurants and bars, information offices, airline offices, an exchange counter and travel agencies. Once you're through security, there are shops, restaurants, bars and internet access (including wi-fi).

There's a **post office** (☼ 8am-6pm Mon-Fri, to 1pm Sat) in the administrative centre across the car park from the arrival hall of Terminal North 1.

GETTING INTO TOWN

To get into town, buy a ticket from the public transport (Dopravní podnik; DPP) desk in arrivals and take bus No 119 (20Kč, 20 minutes, every 15 minutes) to the end of the line (Dejvická), then continue by metro into the city centre (another 10 minutes; no new ticket needed). Note that you'll also need a half-fare (10Kč) ticket for your backpack or suitcase if it's larger than 25cm x 45cm x 70cm.

Alternatively, take a **Cedaz minibus** (☎ 220 114 296; www.cedaz.cz) from outside arrivals; buy a ticket from the driver (90Kč, 20 minutes, every 30 minutes 5.30am to 9.30pm). There are city stops near metro Dejvická and at the **Czech Airlines office** (Map pp268–9), near náměstí Republiky. You can also get a Cedaz minibus to your hotel or any other address (480Kč for one to four people, 960Kč for five to eight) – book and pay at the Cedaz desk in the arrivals hall.

Airport Cars (☎ 220 113 892) taxi service, with prices regulated by the airport administration, charges 650Kč (20% discount for the return trip) into the centre of Prague (a regular taxi fare *from* central Prague should be about 450Kč). Drivers usually speak some English and accept Visa credit cards.

Websites

As well as airline websites, there are a number of efficient online resources for buying good-value flight tickets. A couple of the best include:

Cheap Flights (www.cheapflights.co.uk) Lists discount flights to Prague from the UK and Ireland.

Opodo (www.opodo.co.uk) Site owned by consortium of European airlines; often cheaper than no-frills airlines for short-notice flights.

BICYCLE

Prague is not the best city for getting around by bike. Traffic is heavy, exhaust fumes can be choking, tram tracks can be dangerous and there are few dedicated bicycle lanes. That said, the city now has about 180km of signposted cycle routes, about 60km of which are traffic-free (see http://wgp.praha-mesto.cz for an interactive map, in Czech only), and the popularity of cycling is steadily increasing.

Bikes must be equipped with a bell, mudguards, a white reflector and white light up front, a red reflector and flashing red light at the rear, and reflectors on pedals – if not, you can be fined up to 1000Kč. Cyclists up to the age of 15 must wear helmets.

If you're aged at least 12 you can take your bicycle on the metro, but you must place it near the last door of the rear carriage, and only two bikes are allowed. Bikes are not permitted if the carriage is full, or if there's already a pram in the carriage.

Bicycle Hire

City Bike (Map pp268–9; ☎ 776 180 284; www.citybike-prague.com; Králodvorská 5, Staré Město; ⏰ 9am-7pm Apr-Oct; metro Náměstí Republiky) Rental includes helmet, padlock and map; two hours costs 280/340Kč for a cruiser/mountain bike.

Praha Bike (Map pp268–9; ☎ 732 388 880; www.praha bike.cz; Dlouhá 24, Staré Město; 4/8hr 360/500Kč; ⏰ 9am-7pm 15 Mar-15 Nov; tram 5, 8, 14) Good, new bikes with lock, helmet and map, plus free luggage stor-

age. Also offers student discounts and group bike tours (also see p57).

BUS

All international and long-distance domestic buses (and many regional services) use **Florenc bus station** (Map pp278–9; ☎ 12 999; www.jizdnirady.cz; Křižíkova 4, Karlín). Bus companies include the following:

Capital Express (Map pp276–7; ☎ 220 870 368; www.capitalexpress.cz; U výstaviště 3, Holešovice; ⏰ 8am-6pm Mon-Thu, to 5pm Fri) Daily bus service between London and Prague via Plzeň.

Eurolines (Map pp268–9; ☎ 224 239 318; www.eurolines.cz, in Czech; Senovážné náměstí 6, Nové Město 6, Nové Město; ⏰ 8am-6pm Mon-Fri) Links Prague with cities all over Western and Central Europe; there's another Eurolines ticket office in Florenc bus station.

CAR & MOTORCYCLE

Driving in Prague is no fun, especially in the narrow, winding streets of the city centre. Trying to find your way around – or to park legally – while coping with trams, buses, other drivers, cyclists and pedestrians can make you wish you'd left the car at home.

Prague Information Service (Pražská informační služba or PIS; see p238) publishes a *Transport Guide* with many useful tips for drivers, including emergency breakdown services, where to find car-repair shops (by make) and all-important parking tips.

Car Hire

The main international car-hire chains all have airport pick-up points as well as offices in the city centre. Rates begin at around 1900/10,700Kč per day/week for a Škoda Fabia, including unlimited mileage, collision-damage waiver and value-added tax (VAT; or DPH in Czech). There's a 400Kč surcharge to pick up your vehicle from the airport, but delivery to hotels in central Prague is free.

Small local companies such as Secco, Vecar and West Car Praha offer much better rates, but are less likely to have fluent English-speaking staff – it's often easier to book by email than by phone. Typical rates for a Škoda Fabia are around 800Kč a day, including unlimited mileage, collision-damage waiver and VAT.

Directory

TRANSPORT

A-Rent Car/Thrifty (Map pp272–3; ☎ 224 233 265; www.arentcar.cz; Washingtonova 9, Nové Město; metro Muzeum)

Avis (Map pp268–9; ☎ 221 851 225; www.avis.com; Klimentská 46, Nové Město; tram 5, 8, 14)

CS-Czechocar (Map pp280–1; ☎ 261 222 079; www .czechocar.cz; Congress Centre, 5.května 65, Vyšehrad; metro Vyšehrad)

Europcar (Map pp268–9; ☎ 224 810 515; www.europcar .cz; Pařížská 28, Staré Město; tram 17)

Hertz (Map pp272–3; ☎ 225 345 000; www.hertz.cz; Karlovo Náměstí 15, Nové Město; metro Karlovo náměstí)

Secco Car (Map pp262–3; ☎ 220 802 361; www.seccocar .cz; Přístavní 39, Holešovice; tram 1, 3, 12, 15, 25)

Vecar (Map p275; ☎ 224 314 361; www.vecar.cz; Svatovítská 7, Dejvice; metro Dejvická)

West Car Praha (Map pp262–3; ☎ 235 365 307; www .westcarpraha.cz, in Czech; Veleslavínská 17, Veleslavín; tram 20, 26)

Emergencies

In case of an accident the police should be contacted immediately if repairs are likely to cost over 20,000Kč or if there is an injury. Even if damage is slight, if you're driving your own car it's a good idea to report the accident, as the police will issue an insurance report that will help avoid problems when you take the car out of the country.

For emergency breakdowns, the **ÚAMK** (Central Automobile & Motorcycle Club; Map pp262–3; ☎ 1230 for breakdowns, 261 104 33 for info; www.uamk.cz; Na strži 9, Nusle) provides nationwide assistance 24 hours a day.

ÚAMK has agreements with numerous national motoring organisations across the world through its affiliation to the Alliance Internationale de Tourisme and the Fédération Internationale de l'Automobile. If you are a member of any of these, ÚAMK will help you on roughly the same terms as your own organisation would. If not, you must pay for all services.

Parking & Regulations

Parking in most of central Prague is regulated with permit-only and parking-meter zones. Meter fees are 30Kč or 40Kč per hour (effective 8am to 6pm), with time limits from two to six hours. Traffic inspectors are always keen to hand out fines, clamp wheels or tow away vehicles. Parking in

one-way streets is normally allowed only on the right-hand side.

There are several car parks at the edges of Staré Město, and Park-and-Ride car parks around the outer city (most are marked on city maps), close to metro stations.

In Prague you may overtake a tram only on the right, and only if it's in motion. You must stop behind any tram taking on or letting off passengers where there's no passenger island. A tram has the right of way when making any signalled turn across your path.

PUBLIC TRANSPORT

Prague has an excellent integrated public transport system that combines metro, tram and bus. It's operated by **Dopravní podnik hlavního město Prahy** (DPP; ☎ 296 191 817; www.dpp.cz), which has information desks at Ruzyně airport (7am to 10pm) and in four metro stations – Muzeum (7am to 9pm), Můstek, Anděl and Nádraží Holešovice (all 7am to 6pm) – where you can get tickets, directions, a multilingual transport-system map, a map of night services (*noční provoz*) and a detailed English-language guide to the whole system.

On metro trains and newer trams and buses, an electronic display shows the route number and the name of the next stop, and a recorded voice announces each station or stop. As the train, tram or bus pulls away, the announcer says '*Příští stanice…*' (The next station is…) or '*Příští zastávka…*' (The next stop is…), perhaps noting that it's a *přestupní stanice* (transfer station). At metro stations, signs point you towards the *výstup* (exit) or to a *přestup* (transfer to another line).

The metro operates from 5am to midnight. There are three lines: Line A runs from the northwestern side of the city at Dejvická to the east at Skalka; line B runs from the southwest at Zličín to the northeast at Černý Most; and line C runs from the north at Ladví to the southeast at Háje. Line A intersects line C at Muzeum, line B intersects line C at Florenc and line A intersects line B at Můstek.

After the metro closes, night trams (Nos 51 to 58) and buses (Nos 501 to 512) still rumble across the city about every 40 minutes through the night. If you're planning a late evening, find out if one of these services passes near where you're staying.

Tickets

You need to buy a ticket before you board a bus, tram or metro. Tickets are sold from machines at metro stations and major tram stops, at newsstands, Trafiky snack shops, PNS newspaper kiosks, hotels, PIS tourist information offices (see p238), all metro station ticket offices and DPP information offices.

A transfer ticket (*jízdenka*) valid on tram, metro, bus and the Petřín funicular costs 20/10Kč per adult/child aged six to 15 years; kids under six ride free. You'll also need a 10Kč ticket for each large suitcase or backpack if it's larger than 25cm x 45cm x 70cm. Validate (punch) your ticket by sticking it in the little yellow machine in the metro station lobby or on the bus or tram the first time you board; this stamps the time and date on it. Once validated, transfer tickets remain valid for 75 minutes if stamped between 5am and 8pm on weekdays, and for 90 minutes at all other times. Within this time period you can make unlimited transfers between all types of public transport (you don't need to punch the ticket again).

There's also a short-hop 14/7Kč ticket, valid for 20 minutes on buses and trams, or for up to five metro stations. No transfers are allowed with these (except between metro lines), and they're not valid on the Petřín funicular or on night trams (Nos 51 to 58) or buses (Nos 501 to 512). Being caught without a valid ticket entails a 400Kč on-the-spot fine (50Kč for not having a luggage ticket). The plain-clothes inspectors travel incognito, but will show a red-and-gold metal badge when they ask for your ticket. A few may demand a higher fine from foreigners and pocket the difference, so insist on a receipt (*doklad*) before paying.

You can also buy tickets valid for 24 hours (80Kč) and three/seven/15 days (220/280/320Kč). Again, these must be validated on first use only; if a ticket is stamped twice, it becomes invalid. With these tickets, you don't need to pay an extra fare for your luggage.

TAXI

Prague City Council has finally cracked down on the city's notoriously dishonest taxi drivers by raising the maximum fine for overcharging to one million Kč and providing a website detailing legitimate fares (http://panda.hyperlink.cz/taxitext/etaxi web.htm). However, hailing a taxi on the street – at least in a tourist zone – still holds the risk of an inflated fare. The taxi stands around Wenceslas Square, Národní třída, Na příkopě, Praha hlavní nádraží, Old Town Square and Malostranské náměstí are the most notorious rip-off spots; even the locals are not safe.

You're much better off calling a radio-taxi than flagging one down, as they're better regulated and more responsible. From our experience the following companies have honest drivers (some of whom speak a little English) and offer 24-hour services.

AAA Radio Taxi (☎ 14 014)

Airport Cars (☎ 220 113 892)

Halo Taxi (☎ 244 114 411)

ProfiTaxi (☎ 844 700 800)

If you hail a taxi in the street, ask the approximate fare in advance and ask the driver to use the meter (*zapněte taximetr, prosím*). If it's 'broken', find someone else or establish a price before setting off. If you get the rare driver who willingly turns on the meter, they deserve a tip just for that (Czechs usually leave the change).

The official maximum rate for licensed cabs is 34Kč minimum plus 25Kč per kilometre, and 5Kč per minute while waiting. On this basis, any trip within the city centre – say, from Wenceslas Square to Malá Strana – should cost around 110Kč to 170Kč. A trip to the suburbs should not exceed 300Kč, and to the airport 450Kč. Journeys outside Prague are not regulated.

Regulations state that official taxis must have a yellow roof light, the business name and taxi ID number on both front doors, and a list of fares inside. The meter must be at zero when you get in, and at the end of the journey the driver must give you a meter-printed receipt showing company name, taxi ID number, date and times of the journey, end points, rates, the total, the driver's name and their signature. Get one before you pay, and make sure it has all these things in case you want to make a claim. Complaints about overcharging should be directed to **City Hall** (Pražské radnice; Map pp268–9; ☎ 236 002 269; www.prague-city.cz; Office 405, 4th fl, Platnéřská 19, Staré Město; ☉ noon-5pm Mon, 8am-6pm Wed).

TRAIN

The railway system is operated by České dráhy (ČD; Czech Railways; www.cd.cz). Most international trains arrive at Prague's main station, Praha hlavní nádraží (Map pp272–3). A few go to Praha-Holešovice (Map pp276–7) or Praha-Smíchov (Map pp262–3); all three stations have their own metro stops. Masarykovo nádraží (Map pp268–9), two blocks north of the main train station, is the main domestic station.

Note – Praha hlavní nádraží is set to undergo a major redevelopment between 2006 and 2009; during this period the layout of the station may be changed.

Arriving in Prague by Train

On arriving at Praha hlavní nádraží, the underpass from the platforms leads you to level 3 of the four-level station complex; turn left here to find the AVE accommodation agency (opposite). Continue down a short flight of stairs to level 2, the main concourse, where you'll find the helpful PIS Tourist Information Booth (9am-7pm Mon-Fri, to 5pm Sat & Sun) beside the metro entrance at the southern (left) end.

Ramps to each side of the ticket counters in the main concourse lead down to level 1, with a 24-hour left-luggage office (úschovna; 15 or 30Kč per bag per day) and luggage lockers (60Kč; accepts 5, 10 and 20Kč coins).

There are four metro station entrances in the concourse – the two nearer the stairs from level 3 lead to the northbound platform (direction Ladví), the two nearer the exits are southbound (direction Haje). Public transport tickets and information are available at the DPP booths beside the southbound metro entrances. There are taxi ranks at either end of the concourse. To find the nearest tram stop (tram Nos 5, 9 and 26) exit the main concourse and turn right; the stop is at the far end of the park.

Try not to arrive in the middle of the night – the station closes from 12.40am to 3.40am, and the surrounding area is a magnet for pickpockets and drunks.

Leaving Prague by Train

You can buy international train tickets in advance from train stations, ČD Travel (Map pp268–9; 972 233 930; V Celnici 6, Nové Město) and Čedok travel agencies.

At Prague's main train station, you can get information on international train services at the ČD info centre at the south end of the main concourse, and from ticket windows Nos 2 to 8 (usually only one of these windows – look for a sign advertising information in English). Full printed timetables are displayed on level 3; timetable information is also available online at www.idos.cz.

YOU'RE GOING WHERE?

Although most staff at the international ticket counters in Prague's main train station speak at least some English, those selling domestic tickets rarely do. In order to speed up the process of buying a ticket, and to avoid misunderstandings, it's often easier to write down what you want on a piece of paper and hand it to the clerk (this works for bus tickets, too).

Write it down like this:

- od: departure station, eg PRAHA
- do: destination station
- čas: departure time using 24-hour clock
- datum: date, eg for 2.30pm on 20 May, write '14.30h. 20/05'. Or just dnes (today)
- osoby: number of passengers
- jednosměrný (one way) or zpáteční (return)

If you're making a reservation on an EC or IC train, you may also want to specify 1. třída or 2. třída (1st or 2nd class), and whether you want a okno (window) or chodba (aisle) seat.

One-way domestic train tickets for distances of more than 50km are valid for 24 hours from time of purchase, but for distances under 50km only until 6am the next day. Note that domestic return tickets (about 10% more expensive than singles) are only valid for 48 hours from time of purchase – if you plan to be away for more than two days, buy two singles.

The big display board on the main concourse lists departures with columns marked *druh vlaku* (type of train – EC, IC etc), *číslo vlaku* (train number), *cílová stanice* (final destination), *směr* (via), *odjezd* (departure time) and *nášt.* (platform number). To make sure you're on the correct train, makes sure its number (displayed on a panel on the side of the coach) matches the train number of the service you want.

You can buy domestic tickets *(vnitrostátní jízdenky)* at the odd-numbered ticket windows (marked with an A) to the left of the departures board on the main concourse; for international advance reservations *(mezínárodní rezervace)* go to windows 2 to 8 (marked B), and for international tickets *(mezínárodní jízdenky)* go to windows 12 to 24 (marked C) to the right.

PRACTICALITIES

ACCOMMODATION
Accommodation listings in this book (see p194) are broken down first by neighbourhood, then alphabetically within each neighbourhood heading. Check out p194 for details of accommodation styles, price ranges and longer-term rentals.

Accommodation Agencies
Recommended agencies with English-speaking staff:

Alfa Tourist Service (Map pp268–9; ☎ 224 230 037; www.alfatourist.cz; Opletalova 38, Nové Město; ☷ 9am-5pm Mon-Fri) Can provide accommodation in student hostels, pensions, hotels and private rooms.

Apartments.cz (Map pp272–3; ☎ 224 990 900; www.apartments.cz; Ostrovní 7, Nové Město; ☷ 9am-5pm Mon-Fri) Long-established specialist in holiday apartments near the city centre.

AVE (Map pp272–3; ☎ 251 551 011; www.avetravel.cz; Praha-hlavní nádraží, Nové Město; ☷ 6am-11pm) Convenient offices at the airport, main train station and Praha-Holešovice train station. The branch at the main train station specialises in finding last-minute accommodation.

Happy House Rentals (Map pp272–3; ☎ 224 946 890; www.happyhouserentals.com; Jungmannova 30, Nové Město; ☷ 9am-5pm Mon-Fri) Specialises in rental apartments, both short-term and long-term.

Hostel.cz (☎ 415 658 580; www.hostel.cz) Website database of around 60 hostels, with a secure online booking system.

Mary's Travel & Tourist Service (Map pp278–9; ☎ 222 253 510; www.marys.cz; Italská 31, Vinohrady; ☷ 9am-9pm) Friendly and efficient agency offering private rooms, hostels, pensions, apartments and hotels in all price ranges in Prague and surrounding areas.

Prague Apartments (☎ 323 641 476; www.prague-apartment.com) Web-based service with range of comfortable, IKEA-furnished flats. Availability of apartments displayed online.

Stop City (Map pp272–3; ☎ 222 521 233; www.stopcity.com; Vinohradská 24, Vinohrady; ☷ 10am-9pm Apr-Oct, to 8pm Mon-Sat Nov-Mar) Specialises in apartments, private rooms and pensions in the city centre, Vinohrady and Žižkov areas.

BUSINESS HOURS
Shops tend to open from 8.30am to 5pm or 6pm Monday to Friday, and 8.30am till noon or 1pm on Saturday. Department stores close at 8pm Monday to Friday, at 6pm on Saturday and Sunday. Touristy shops in central Prague are open later at night and all day Saturday and Sunday.

Banks generally open 8am to 4.30pm Monday to Friday. The city's main post office opens 7am to 8pm every day, while other post offices open 8am to 6pm or 7pm Monday to Friday and until noon on Saturday. Restaurants tend to open between 10am and 11pm (cafés generally open around 8am), while bars usually open 11am till midnight (though some in the city centre stay open till 3am or 4am).

Most museums and galleries open from 9am or 10am to 5pm or 6pm year-round. Many are closed on Monday, and on the first working day after a holiday. Some of Prague's bigger churches are open similar hours.

Castles, chateaux and other historical monuments outside the city are open May to September, from 8am or 9am to 5pm or 6pm, except for a lunch break, daily except Monday and the first working day after a holiday. Most shut down from November to March, with some limited to weekends in October and April. If you plan to take a guided tour, remember that ticket offices close an hour or so before the official closing time, depending on the length of the tour.

CHILDREN
Czechs are very family oriented and there are plenty of activities for children around

the city. Although few Prague restaurants cater specifically for children, with play areas and so on, many offer a children's menu *(dětský jídelníček)*; even if they don't, they can usually provide smaller portions for a lower price.

Museums of possible interest to children include the Toy Museum (p74), though, frustratingly, its many displays are hands off; the Public Transport Museum (p115), where kids will love climbing on the vintage trams and buses; and the Aircraft Museum (p114), which offers the chance to see Russian MiG fighter planes up close.

For outdoor activities try the Prague Zoo (p113) or Petřín (p83), a large park on a hill where parents and kids alike can take a break from sightseeing. In the park itself you can climb up the Petřín Lookout Tower for terrific views over Prague. For the best views of all, go to the TV Tower (p111) in Žižkov.

In summer there are rowing and paddle boats for hire along the Vltava river as well as river cruises and boat tours (p58), and there are safe, fenced playgrounds by the entrance to Petřín park on náměstí Kinských (Map pp270–1); at the northern end of Kampa island (Map pp264–5); on Children's Island (p82); and on Vlašská, just west of the German embassy (Map pp264–5).

March is the time of the St Matthew Fair (p9), when the exhibition grounds in Holešovice are full of fairground rides, shooting galleries and candy floss. If there's a circus in town it will most likely be in Letná Park, opposite the AC Sparta Praha Stadium (Toyota Arena; Map pp276–7).

At weekends and on holidays between April and mid-November, vintage tram cars trundle along a special sightseeing route, No 91, around the city centre (see p58 for more information). And don't miss the changing of the guard at Prague Castle (see p70 for details) – but get in position before the crowds do, or the kids won't see a thing.

See also the boxed text on p115.

Babysitting

PIS (p238) usually has a list of babysitting *(hlídání dětí)* agencies, and most top-end hotels provide a babysitting service; rates are generally around 120Kč per hour. **Prague Family** (☎ 224 224 044; www.praguefamily .cz) is an agency that can provide English-speaking baby-sitters.

CLIMATE

Prague has warm, occasionally showery summers and cold, often snowy winters with generally changeable conditions. A typical day in Prague from June to August sees the mercury range from about 12° to 22°C. Temperatures from December to February push below freezing. Wide variations are common, sometimes surpassing 35°C in summer and -20°C in winter. The summer's long, sunny, hot spells tend to be broken by sudden, heavy thunderstorms. In general, May and September enjoy the most pleasant weather.

See p9 for advice on the best time to visit.

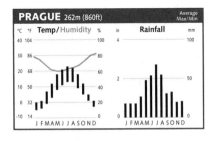

COURSES

The **Information-Advisory Centre of Charles University** (Informačmě-poradenské centrum, IPC; Map pp272–3; ☎ 222 232 452; ipc@ruk .cuni.cz; Školská 13a, Nové Město; ❂ 9am-6pm Mon-Fri) is the place to go for general information on university courses.

Places that offer courses to English-speaking visitors:

Institute for Language & Preparatory Studies (Ústav jazykové a odborné přípravý; Map pp280–1; ☎ 224 990 411; www.ujop.cuni.cz; Vratislavova 10, Vyšehrad; metro Vyšehrad) ÚJOP runs six-week Czech language courses for foreigners. No prior knowledge of the Czech language is required. The course fee is €585, not including accommodation. You can also opt for individual lessons (45 minutes) at €20 each. Further details and an application form are available on the website.

London School of Modern Languages (Map pp280–1; ☎ 222 515 018; www.londonschool.cz; Budečká 6, Vinohrady; tram 4, 22, 23) Czech courses for both individuals and companies, including specialised Czech language courses for business, law or IT. Individual tuition costs 610Kč an hour.

PCFE Film School (Map pp272–3; ☎ 257 534 013; www .prague-center.cz; Pstrossova 19, Nové Město; tram 17, 21)

Offers four-week intensive film-making workshops in summer, covering screenwriting, directing, cinematography, editing and sound design.

CUSTOMS

Travelling between the Czech Republic and other EU countries you can import/export 800 cigarettes, 400 cigarillos, 200 cigars, 1kg of smoking tobacco, 10L of spirits, 20L of fortified wine (eg port or sherry), 90L of wine and 110L of beer, provided the goods are for personal use only (each country sets its own guide levels; these figures are minimums). Note – until the end of 2007 you can export only 200 cigarettes from the Czech Republic to Austria, Belgium, Germany, the UK, Denmark, Sweden, Finland, France and Ireland; from 2008 on, the figure will be 800.

Travellers from outside the EU can import/export, duty-free, a maximum of 200 cigarettes *or* 100 cigarillos *or* 50 cigars *or* 250g of tobacco; 2L of still table wine; 1L of spirits *or* 2L of fortified wine, sparkling wine or liqueurs; 60mL of perfume; 250mL of eau de toilette; and €175 worth of all other goods (including gifts and souvenirs). Anything over this limit must be declared to customs officers. People under 17 do not get the alcohol and tobacco allowances.

Any goods you buy in the Czech Republic can be taken to any other EU country without paying additional VAT. If you are resident outside the EU, you may be able to reclaim VAT on your purchases (see p183). You're not permitted to export genuine antiques.

There is no limit to the amount of Czech or foreign currency that can be taken in or out of the country, but amounts exceeding 500,000Kč must be declared.

DISABLED TRAVELLERS

Increasing, but still limited, attention is being paid to facilities for people with disabilities in Prague. Wheelchair ramps are becoming more common, especially at major street intersections, in newer shopping malls and in top-end hotels (in the Sleeping chapter we identify hotels with facilities for wheelchair users). For people who are blind or vision-impaired, most pedestrian crossings in central Prague have a sound signal to indicate when it's safe to cross. McDonald's and KFC entrances and toilets are wheelchair-friendly.

Much of Prague Castle is wheelchair-accessible, but the cobbled streets, narrow pavements and steep hills of the surrounding Hradčany and Malá Strana districts are not. The Estates Theatre (p161) is equipped for the hearing-impaired, while the Convent of St Agnes (p89) has a ground-floor presentation of medieval sculptures with explanatory text in Braille; these venues and several other theatres are wheelchair-accessible. (The monthly what's-on booklet *Přehled* – which is published by PIS in Czech only – indicates venues with wheelchair access.)

Few buses and no trams have wheelchair access; special wheelchair-accessible buses operate Monday to Friday on bus line Nos 1 and 3, including between Florenc bus station and náměstí Republiky, and between Holešovice train station and náměstí Republiky (visit the website at www.dpp.cz for more information).

Prague's main train station (Praha hlavní nádraží), Praha-Holešovice train station and a handful of metro stations (Hlavní Nádraží, Hůrka, Luka, Lužiny, Nádraží Holešovice, Stodůlky and Zličín) have self-operating lifts. Other metro stations (Chodov, Dejvická, Florenc C line, Háje, IP Pavlova, Opatov, Pankrác, Roztyly and Skalka) have modified lifts that can be used with the help of station staff. Czech Railways (ČD) claims that every large station in the country has wheelchair ramps and lifts, but in fact the service is poor.

When flying, travellers with special needs should inform the airline of their requirements when booking, and again when reconfirming, and again when checking in. Most international airports (including Prague's) have ramps, lifts and wheelchair-accessible toilets and telephones. Aircraft toilets, on the other hand, present problems for wheelchair users, who should discuss this early on with the airline and/or their doctor.

Some useful organizations include the following:

Czech Blind United (Sjednocená organizace nevidomých a slabozrakých v ČR; Map pp272–3; ☎ 221 462 146; www.braillnet.cz; Krakovská 21, Nové Město) Represents the vision-impaired; provides information but no services.

Prague Wheelchair Users Organisation (Pražská organizace vozíčkářů; Map pp268–9; ☎ 224 827 210; www.pov.cz in Czech; Benediktská 6, Staré Město) Can organise a guide and transportation at about half the cost of a taxi, and has a CD-ROM guide to barrier-free Prague in Czech, English and German.

DISCOUNT CARDS

The Prague Card is a combined public-transport pass and admission card that is valid for one year (the transport ticket is valid only for three consecutive days, allowing you unlimited travel on metro, trams and buses). It provides the holder with free entry to more than a dozen city sights, including the Army Museum and the Vyšehrad Casemates, as well as discounted fees (from 10% to 50%) at a couple of dozen more, including Troja Chateau, the TV Tower and a range of guided walks. However, it does not include major attractions such as Prague Castle, the Church of St Nicholas in Malá Strana and the Prague Jewish Museum.

The pass costs 860Kč (or €30 if bought via the internet), and can be purchased from the EuroAgentur desk at Prague Airport, the **Prague Card Change Office** (Map pp272–3; Vodičkova 34, Nové Město) and online at www.praguecard.info.

ELECTRICITY

Electricity in Prague is 230V, 50Hz AC. Outlets have the standard European socket with two small round holes and a protruding earth (ground) pin. If you have a different plug, bring an adaptor (see www.kropla.com for info). North American 110V appliances will also need a transformer if they don't have built-in voltage adjustment.

EMBASSIES & CONSULATES

Australia (Map pp268–9; ☎ 296 578 350; www.embassy .gov.au/cz.html; 6th floor, Klimentská 10, Nové Město) Honorary consulate for emergency assistance only (eg a stolen passport); nearest Australian embassy is in Vienna.

Austria (Map pp270–1; ☎ 257 090 511; www.austria.cz in German and Czech; Viktora Huga 10, Smíchov)

Canada (Map p275; ☎ 272 101 800; www.canada.cz; Muchova 6, Bubeneč)

France (Map pp264–5; ☎ 251 171 711; www.france.cz, in French and Czech; Velkopřerovské náměstí 2, Malá Strana)

Germany (Map pp264–5; ☎ 257 113 111; www.deutsch land.cz, in German and Czech; Vlašská 19, Malá Strana)

Ireland (Map pp264–5; ☎ 257 530 061; prague embassy@dfa.ie; Tržiště 13, Malá Strana)

Israel (Map p275; ☎ 233 097 500; info@prague.mfa .gov.il; Badeniho 2, Bubeneč)

Netherlands (Map p275; ☎ 233 015 200; www .netherlandsembassy.cz; Gotthardská 6/27, Bubeneč)

New Zealand (Map pp262–3; ☎ 222 514 672; egermayer@nzconsul.cz; Dykova 19, Vinohrady) Honorary consulate providing emergency assistance only (eg stolen passport); the nearest NZ embassy is in Berlin.

Poland (Map pp264–5; ☎ 257 099 500; www.prague .polemb.net; Valdštejnská 8, Malá Strana) This is the embassy; go to the consular department for visas.

Poland (Map pp262–3; ☎ 224 228 722; konspol@mbox .vol.cz; V úžlabině 14, Strašnice) This is the consular department; come here for visas.

Russia (Map pp276–7; ☎ 233 374 100; embrus@tiscali .cz; Pod Kaštany 1, Bubeneč)

Slovakia (Map pp264–5; ☎ 233 113 051; www.slovak emb.cz, in Slovak; Pod Hradbami 1, Dejvice)

South Africa (Map pp262–3; ☎ 267 311 114; saprague@ terminal.cz; Ruská 65, Vršovice)

UK (Map pp264–5; ☎ 257 402 111; www.britain.cz; Thunovská 14, Malá Strana)

USA (Map pp264–5; ☎ 257 022 000; www.usembassy.cz; Tržiště 15, Malá Strana)

EMERGENCY

Ambulance (☎ 155)

Breakdown Assistance for Motorists (ÚAMK; ☎ 1230)

EU-wide emergency hotline (☎ 112)

Fire (☎ 150)

Municipal Police (☎ 156)

State Police (☎ 158)

GAY & LESBIAN TRAVELLERS

Homosexuality is legal in the Czech Republic (the age of consent is 15), but Czechs are not accustomed to seeing same-sex couples showing affection to each other in public; it's best to be discreet. The city's gay bars and clubs are concentrated in the city centre, and in the districts of Vinohrady and Žižkov.

The bimonthly gay guide and contact magazine *Amigo* has a few pages in English, and a useful English website (www.amigo .cz/en). The Gay Guide Prague (www.gay guide.net/europe/czech/prague) is another useful source of information. See also the boxed text on p176 for gay-friendly venues and accommodation options.

Gay Iniciativa (Gay Initiative; Map pp268–9; ☎ 224 223 811; www.gay.iniciativa.cz, in Czech; Senovážné náměstí 2; tram 3, 9, 14, 24) is a gay and lesbian organisation that campaigns for legal rights and registered partnerships, offers help and support, and provides info on events and resources.

HOLIDAYS

Banks, offices, department stores and some shops will be closed on public holidays. Restaurants, museums and tourist attractions tend to stay open. See also p9.

New Year's Day 1 January

Easter Monday March/April

Labour Day 1 May

Liberation Day 8 May

SS Cyril & Methodius Day 5 July

Jan Hus Day 6 July

Czech Statehood Day 28 September

Republic Day 28 October

Struggle for Freedom & Democracy Day 17 November

Christmas Eve (Generous Day) 24 December

Christmas Day 25 December

St Stephen's Day 26 December

INTERNET ACCESS

Prague has dozens of internet cafés. Conveniently located ones:

Bohemia Bagel (Map pp270–1; ☎ 257 310 694; www.bohemiabagel.cz; Újezd 16, Malá Strana; per min 1.50Kč; 7am-midnight; tram 6, 9, 12, 20, 22, 23) Also provides low-cost international phone calls.

Bohemia Bagel (Map pp268–9; ☎ 224 812 560; www.bohemiabagel.cz; Masná 2, Staré Město; per min 1.50Kč; 7am-midnight; metro Náměstí Republiky) This café is also a popular eatery; see p138 for details.

Globe Bookshop & Café (Map pp272–3; ☎ 224 934 203; www.globebookstore.cz; Pštrossova 6, Nové Město; per min 1.50Kč; 10am-midnight; metro Karlovo Náměstí) No minimum. Also has ethernet sockets where you can connect your own laptop (same price; cables provided, 50Kč deposit).

Internet (Map pp268–9; Rytířská 18, Staré Město; per min 1.60Kč; 9am-11pm Mon-Fri, 10am-9pm Sat, 11am-9pm Sun; metro Můstek) 25Kč minimum; low-cost international phone calls.

net k@fe (Map pp268–9; Na poříčí 8; Nové Město; per min 1Kč; 9am-11pm; metro Náměstí Republiky) Cheapest in the city centre.

Pl@neta (Map pp278–9; ☎ 267 311 182; Vinohradská 102, Vinohrady; per min 0.40-0.80Kč; 8am-11pm; metro Jiřího z Poděbrad) Cheapest rates before 10am and after 8pm Monday to Friday, all day Saturday and Sunday; 5Kč minimum.

Spika (Map pp268–9; ☎ 224 211 521; http://netcafé.spika.cz; Dlážděná 4, Nové Město; per min 20Kč; 8am-midnight; metro Náměstí Republiky)

V Síti (Map pp280–1; ☎ 222 524 071; Jana Masaryka 46, Vinohrady; per min 1Kč; 10am-10pm Mon-Fri, 2-10pm Sat & Sun; tram 4, 22, 23) An internet teahouse, with 53 varieties of tea as well as internet access on PCs ands iMacs.

You should be able to log on from your hotel room for the cost of a local call by registering with an internet roaming service such as **MaGlobe** (www.maglobe.com), which has access numbers for Prague. Most midrange and top-end hotels have telephone jacks, usually US standard (RJ-11), which you can plug your modem cable into, or ethernet sockets for sharing the hotel's broadband connection. Buy a line tester – a gadget that goes between your computer and the phone jack – so that you don't inadvertently fry your modem. Get on and off quickly; calls from hotels are expensive. For more information on travelling with a laptop check out www.kropla.com.

Increasing numbers of hotels, bars, fast-food restaurants and internet cafés offer wi-fi hotspots where you can access the internet with your own wi-fi-enabled laptop. You can find an international directory of wi-fi hotspots on www.jiwire.com; see also the 'Computers, Cameras, Phones' branch on the Thorn Tree at www.lonelyplanet.com.

If you access your account at home through a smaller ISP or your office or school network, your best option is to open a webmail account, such as Yahoo or Hotmail, before you leave, and either give your new webmail address to your friends and family, or use the account's 'Check Other Mail' option to download mail from your home account (this may not work for work-based accounts).

LEGAL MATTERS

If you find yourself under arrest for any reason whatsoever, you are entitled to call your embassy (see opposite for listings). Note that it is technically illegal not to carry some form of identification (normally your passport). If you can't prove your identity, police have the right to detain you for up to 48 hours. Some older police officers retain a communist-era mistrust of foreigners; younger officers are easier to deal with, but almost none speak fluent English.

Penalties for possession of drugs are harsh and it's unlikely that your embassy can do much to help if you are caught. In the Czech Republic it is illegal to possess 'more than a small amount' of drugs. Unfortunately the law does not define 'a small amount' or specify which drugs, giving the police a free hand to nick anyone in possession of any amount of any drug. This will change in 2007 when a new law is introduced.

Drink-driving is strictly illegal; there is a zero blood-alcohol limit for drivers. Traffic fines are generally paid on the spot (ask for a receipt). A smoking ban levies a 1000Kč on-the-spot fine for smoking at bus and tram stops, even though they are in the open air.

WHEN YOU'RE LEGAL

The following minimum legal ages apply in the Czech Republic:

- Drinking alcohol – 18
- Driving – 18
- Heterosexual/homosexual sex – 15
- Smoking – 16
- Marriage – 18
- Voting – 18

MAPS

City maps are available at newsagents, bookshops and travel agencies. A detailed plan of the city centre and inner suburbs is Kartografie Praha's *Praha – plán města* (1:10,000). It includes public transport and parking information, an index, a metro map, plans of the castle and Charles Bridge, and a brief description of the major historical sites.

Lonely Planet's plastic-coated *Prague* city map is handy and hard-wearing, and has sections covering central Prague, Prague Castle, greater Prague, the Prague metro and the region around Prague, and an index of streets and sights.

PIS (p238) stocks a free English-language pamphlet called *Welcome to the Czech Republic,* which is produced by the Ministry of Interior. It features a map of the historical centre, transport routes in the centre, and information such as emergency phone numbers and embassy addresses.

If you are staying in Prague for a significant amount of time, Kartografie Praha's pocket atlas *Praha – plán města – standard* (1:20,000), covering all of Prague, is invaluable.

A public-transport map showing all day and night services (metro, tram and bus) is available from any of the public information offices of Dopravní podnik Praha (DPP; see p226), the city transport department.

MEDICAL SERVICES

Emergency treatment and nonhospital first aid are free for all visitors to the Czech Republic; in a serious medical emergency (eg suspected heart attack), call ☎ 112 (English- and German-speaking operators available).

Citizens of EU countries can obtain a European Health Insurance Card (EHIC), which replaces the old E111 form in the UK; this entitles you to free state-provided medical treatment in the Czech Republic. Non-EU citizens must pay for treatment, and at least some of the fee must be paid upfront. Everyone has to pay for prescribed medications.

There are plenty of pharmacies *(lékárna)* in Prague, and most city districts have one that stays open 24 hours. In Nové Město you'll find it at the **district clinic** (Map pp272–3; ☎ 224 946 982; Palackého 5, Nové Město; ⏰ 7am-7pm Mon-Fri, 8am-noon Sat; metro Národní třída). In Vinohrady go to **Lékárna U sv Ludmily** (Map pp272–3; ☎ 222 513 396; Belgická 37, Vinohrady; ⏰ 7am-7pm Mon-Fri, 8am-noon Sat; metro Náměstí Míru).

For emergency service after hours, ring the bell – you'll see a red button with a sign *zvonek lékárna* (pharmacy bell) and/or *první pomoc* (first aid). Some prescription medicines may not be available, so it's wise to bring enough for your trip.

Clinics

American Dental Associates (Map pp268–9; ☎ 221 181 121; www.americandental.cz; 2nd floor Atrium, Stará

Celnice Bldg, V celnici 4; Nové Město; metro Náměstí Republiky) Entirely English-speaking.

Canadian Medical Care (Map pp262–3; ☎ 235 360 133, after hrs ☎ 724 300 301; www.cmc.praha.cz; Veleslavínská 1, Veleslavín; 🕑 8am-6pm Mon-Fri; tram 20 or 26 from metro Dejvická) A pricey but professional private clinic with English-speaking doctors; an initial consultation will cost from US$50 to US$200.

Na Homolce Hospital (Map pp262–3; ☎ 257 271 111; www.homolka.cz; 5th fl, Foreign Pavilion, Roentgenova 2, Motol; bus 167 from metro Anděl) The best hospital in Prague, equipped and staffed to Western standards, with staff who speak English, French, German and Spanish.

Polyclinic at Národní (Poliklinika na Národní; Map pp272–3; ☎ 222 075 120, 24hr emergencies ☎ 720 427 634; www.poliklinika.narodni.cz; Národní 9, Nové Město; 🕑 8.30am-5pm Mon-Fri; metro Národní třída) A central clinic with staff who speak English, German, French and Russian. Expect to pay around 800Kč to 1200Kč for an initial consultation.

METRIC SYSTEM

Czechs use the metric system. A comma is used instead of a decimal point, and full stops are used to indicate thousands, millions etc. A dash is used after prices rounded to the nearest koruna. For example, thirty thousand koruna would be written 30.000,- rather than 30,000.00. See the inside front cover of this guidebook for a conversion table.

MONEY

The Czech crown (Koruna česká, or Kč) is divided into 100 hellers or haléřů (h). Banknotes come in denominations of 20, 50, 100, 200, 500, 1000, 2000 and 5000Kč; coins are of 50h and one, two, five, 10, 20 and 50Kč.

Keep small change handy for use in public toilets and tram-ticket machines, and try to keep some small-denomination notes for shops, cafés and bars – getting change for the 2000Kč notes that ATMs often spit out can be a problem.

See the inside front cover of this guidebook for the exchange-rates table.

ATMs

There is a good network of ATMs, or *bankomaty,* throughout the city. Most accept Visa, MasterCard, Cirrus and Maestro cards.

Changing Money

The easiest, cheapest way to carry money is in the form of a debit card from your bank, which you can use to withdraw cash either from an ATM or over the counter in a bank. Using an ATM will result in your home bank charging a fee (usually 1.5% to 2.5%), but you'll get a good exchange rate and provided you make withdrawals of at least a couple of thousand koruna at a time, you'll pay less than the assorted commissions on travellers cheques. Check with your bank about transaction fees and withdrawal limits.

The main Czech banks – Komerční banka, Česká spořitelna, Československá obchodní banka (ČSOB) and Živnostenská banka – are the best places to change cash. They charge 2% commission with a 50Kč minimum (but always check, as commissions can vary from branch to branch). They will also provide a cash advance on Visa or MasterCard without commission.

Hotels charge about 5% to 8% commission, while Čedok travel agencies and post offices charge 2% – similar rates to the banks.

Try to avoid the many private exchange booths *(směnárna)* in central Prague – they lure tourists in with attractive-looking exchange rates that turn out to be 'sell' rates (if you want to change foreign currency into Czech crowns, the 'buy' rate applies). There may also be an even worse rate for transactions under a certain amount, typically around €500. Check the small print carefully, and ask exactly how much you will get before parting with any money.

Credit Cards

Many midrange and top-end hotels and restaurants accept credit cards. You can use a card to get a cash advance in a bank or to withdraw money from ATMs, but charges will be higher than with a debit card.

You can report lost credit cards (or travellers cheques) to the following:

Amex (☎ 222 800 222)

Diners Club (☎ 267 197 450)

MasterCard/Eurocard & Visa (☎ 272 771 111)

Travellers Cheques

Banks charge 2% with a 50Kč minimum for changing travellers cheques. Amex and

Travelex offices change their own-brand cheques without commission, but charge 2% or 3% for other brands, 3% or 4% for credit-card cash advances, and 5% for changing cash.

Lost travellers cheques can also be reported to the same telephone numbers listed for lost credit cards (see above).

American Express (Map pp272–3; ☎ 234 711 711; Václavské náměstí 56, Nové Město; ☺ 8am-10pm; metro Muzeum)

Travelex (Map pp272–3; ☎ 224 946 066; Národní třída 28, Nové Město; ☺ 9am-1.30pm & 2-6.30pm; metro Národní třída)

NEWSPAPERS & MAGAZINES

The kiosks on Wenceslas Square, Na příkopě and náměstí Republiky sell a wide range of international newspapers and magazines, including British papers such as the *Times*, *Independent* and *Guardian* (international edition), which are available on the day of publication.

See p13 for information about local newspapers.

POST

The **main post office** (Map pp272–3; ☎ 221 131 111; www.cpost.cz; Jindřišská 14, Nové Město; ☺ 2am-midnight; metro Můstek) is just off Wenceslas Square. There's an information desk just inside the main hall to the left.

The main post office uses an automatic queuing system. Take a ticket from one of the machines in the entrance corridors – press button No 1 for stamps, letters and parcels, or No 4 for Express Mail Service (EMS), and take a ticket. Then watch the display boards in the main hall – when your ticket number appears (flashing), go to the desk number shown.

Most of the city's other post offices open from 8am to 6pm or 7pm Monday to Friday, and until noon Saturday.

Postal Rates

The Czech postal service (Česká Pošta) is fairly efficient. Anything you can't afford to lose, however, should go by registered mail (*doporučený dopis*) or by EMS.

A postcard or letter up to 20g costs 9Kč to other European countries; for destina-

tions outside Europe, a postcard/letter costs 12/14Kč. A 2kg parcel by EMS costs 900Kč to Europe, 1200Kč to North America and 1600Kč to Australia. You can send parcels of books (or printed matter such as magazines, newspapers etc) up to 30kg at lower rates.

Receiving Mail

You can pick up poste-restante mail (*výdej listovních zásilek*) at desk Nos 1 and 2 (at the far left) in the main post office from 7am to 8pm Monday to Friday and until noon Saturday. Mail should be addressed to Poste Restante, Hlavní pošta, Jindřišská 14, 110 00 Praha 1, Czech Republic. You must present your passport to claim mail (check under your first name, too). Mail is held for one month.

Holders of Amex cards or travellers cheques can have letters and faxes held for up to one month at the American Express office on Wenceslas Square (see p235).

Sending Mail

You can buy stamps from street vendors and newspaper kiosks as well as from post offices. Letters go in the orange boxes found outside post offices and around the city.

Small-packet services and EMS close at noon on Saturday, and are closed Sunday. Always get a receipt (*potvrzení*) when sending anything larger than a letter by airmail, or when using a more expensive service, to ensure it goes by the service you have paid for.

If you need a professional courier service, **DHL** (Map pp272–3; ☎ 800 103 000; www.dhl.cz; Václavské náměstí 47, Nové Město; ☺ 8am-6.30pm Mon-Fri, 9am-3pm Sat) has a convenient office just off Wenceslas Square, with English-speaking staff.

RADIO

Radio Prague (www.radio.cz; 92.6MHz FM) broadcasts 15-minute-long programmes in English covering Czech news, culture and current affairs at 7.07pm Monday to Thursday. The city's best alternative music station is **Radio 1** (91.9MHz FM), though good things are also being said about the newest kid on the block, commercial-free **Radio Wave** (100.7MHz FM).

The **BBC World Service** (www.bbc.co.uk /worldservice) broadcasts both English-language and Czech news and cultural programmes locally on 101.1MHz FM, 24 hours a day.

SAFETY

Although Prague is as safe as any European capital, the huge influx of money to the city has spawned an epidemic of petty crime. Where tourists are concerned, this mainly means pickpockets. The prime trouble spots are Prague Castle (especially at the changing of the guard), Charles Bridge, Old Town Square (in the crowd watching the Astronomical Clock), the entrance to the Old Jewish Cemetery, Wenceslas Square, the main train station, in the metro (watch your backpack on escalators) and on trams (notably on the crowded Nos 9, 22 and 23).

There's no need to be paranoid, but keep valuables well out of reach, and be alert in crowds and on public transport. A classic ruse involves someone asking directions and thrusting a map under your nose, or a woman with a baby hassling you for money – anything to distract your attention – while accomplices delve into your bags and pockets. If anything like this happens, immediately check your bags and look around you.

Lost or Stolen Belongings

If you have lost your passport, wallet, or other valuables, report the loss to the **Foreigners Police Station** (Map pp262–3; Sdružení 1, Pankrac; 🕑 7.30-11.30am & 12.15-3pm Mon, Tue & Thu, 8am-12.15pm & 1-5pm Wed; metro Pankrac).

If your passport, wallet or other valuables have been stolen, obtain a police report and crime number from the **State Police Station** (Map pp264–5; Vlašská 3, Malá Strana; 🕑 24hr; tram 12, 20, 22, 23); you will need this to make an insurance claim. Unless you speak Czech, forget about telephoning the police, as you will rarely get through to an English speaker. You can apply to your embassy for a replacement passport.

For anything except travel documents, you might get lucky at the city's **lost & found office** (ztráty a nálezy; Map pp272–3; ☎ 224 235 085; Karoliny Světlé 5; 🕑 8am-noon & 12.30-5.30pm Mon & Wed, to 4pm Tue & Thu, to 2pm Fri; tram 6, 9, 18, 22, 23), east of the National Theatre (Národní divadlo).

There's another **lost & found office** (☎ 220 114 283; 🕑 24hr) at the airport.

Racism

You may be surprised at the level of casual prejudice directed against the Roma, whom people are quick to blame for the city's problems. Overt hostility towards visitors is rare, though there have been some assaults by skinheads on dark-skinned people.

Scams

Beware of men who claim to be plain-clothes police officers investigating counterfeiting or illegal moneychanging. They approach tourists and ask to see their money, which is returned after being examined. When you check your wallet you'll find that a substantial amount of money has been taken. No genuine police officer has the right to inspect your money.

Another ploy involves a 'lost tourist' asking for directions (usually in halting English). Once you have been in conversation for a few minutes, two of the tourist's 'friends' interrupt, claiming to be plain-clothes policemen and accusing you of changing money illegally. They will demand to see your wallet and passport, but if you hand them over they are likely to run off with them.

TELEPHONE

All Czech phone numbers have nine digits – you have to dial all nine for any call, local or long distance (ie there is no separate area code). All land-line numbers in Prague begin with a 2; mobile numbers begin with a 6 or 7.

There are payphones all over the place which can be used to make local, long-distance and international calls. Blue coin-phones accept only 2Kč, 5Kč, 10Kč and 20Kč coins; a more common and convenient alternative is a prepaid calling card, which allows you to make domestic and international calls from any phone or payphone in the Czech Republic.

Local prepaid cards include Smartcall (www.smartcall.cz) and TeleCard (www.telecard.cz) – you can buy them from hotels, newspaper kiosks and tourist information offices for 150Kč to 1000Kč. To use one, folllow the instructions on the card –

dial the access number, then the PIN code beneath the scratch-away panel, then the number you want to call (including any international code). Rates from Prague to the UK, USA and Australia with Smartcall can be as low as 2.6Kč a minute; the more expensive the card, the better the rate.

You can also make international calls from the telephone bureau at the main post office (to the left inside the right-hand entrance) – pay a deposit and make your call in a soundproof booth, where a little meter ticks off the rate.

The telephone bureau has directories for Prague and other major cities. You can also look up business phone numbers online at www.zlatestranky.cz. See also this book's inside front cover for useful phone numbers and codes.

Mobile Phones

The Czech Republic uses GSM 900, which is compatible with the rest of Europe, Australia and New Zealand but not with the North American GSM 1900 or the totally different system in Japan. Some North Americans, however, have dual-band GSM 1900/900 phones that do work here; check with your service provider about using your mobile abroad, and beware of calls being routed internationally (which is very expensive for a 'local' call). The main mobile networks in Prague are Eurotel, T-Mobile and Vodafone.

If your mobile phone is unlocked, you can buy a Czech SIM card from any mobile phone shop for around 450Kč (including 300Kč of calling credit) and make local calls at local rates. In this case, of course, you can't use your existing mobile number.

TELEVISION

The only regular English-language programming on the two state-run TV channels is the 45-minute 'Euronews' bulletin on ČT 2, which is broadcast at noon Monday to Thursday and 7.15pm Friday to Sunday. There are two independent commercial channels: TV Nova and Prima TV, which shows a lot of dubbed American and European movies, drama series and sitcoms. Anyone with a satellite dish can choose from an extensive menu of European stations.

TIME

The Czech Republic is on Central European Time, ie GMT/UTC plus one hour. Clocks are set to daylight-saving time in summer, that is, forward one hour on the last weekend in March and back one hour on the last weekend in October. Czechs use the 24-hour clock.

TIPPING

It's normal practice in pubs, cafés and mid-range restaurants to add 10% if service has been good (or to round up the bill to the next 10Kč if it's under about 150Kč); for more information on tipping in restaurants see p132. The same applies to tipping taxi drivers. If your driver is honest and turns on the meter then you should round up the fare at the end of your journey.

TOILETS

Public toilets are free in state-run museums, galleries and concert halls. Elsewhere, such as in train, bus and metro stations, public toilets are staffed by attendants who charge 5Kč to 10Kč for admission. Most places are clean and well kept. Men's are marked *muži* or *páni*, and women's *ženy* or *dámy*.

In the main tourist areas, there are public toilets in Prague Castle; opposite the tram stop on Malostranské náměstí; next to the Kinsky Palace on Old Town Square; on Templova, just off Celetná close to the Powder Gate; on Uhelný trh in the Old Town; and next to the Laterna Magika on Národní třída.

TOURIST INFORMATION

The **Prague Information Service** (Pražská informační služba, PIS; ☎ 12 444 or ☎ 221 714 444 in English & German; www.prague -info.cz) is the main provider of tourist information: it has good maps and detailed brochures (including accommodation options and historical monuments), all free. PIS also publishes the detailed what's-on guide *Přehled* (in Czech only) and other general material.

There are three PIS offices:

Main train station (Praha hlavní nádraží; Map pp272–3; Wilsonova 2, Nové Město; ☾ 9am-7pm Mon-Fri, to 6pm Sat & Sun Apr-Oct; to 6pm Mon-Fri, to 5pm Sat & Sun Nov-Mar)

Malá Strana Bridge Tower (Map pp264–5; Charles Bridge; ☽ 10am-6pm Apr-Oct)

Old Town Hall (Map pp268–9; Staroměstské náměstí 5, Staré Město; ☽ 9am-7pm Mon-Fri, to 6pm Sat & Sun Apr-Oct; to 6pm Mon-Fri, to 5pm Sat & Sun Nov-Mar)

Overseas Offices

Czech Tourism (www.czechtourism.com) offices around the world provide information about tourism, culture and business in the Czech Republic.

Austria (☎ 01-535 2360; Herrengasse 17, 1010 Vienna)

France (☎ 01 53 73 00 22; rue Bonaparte 18, 75006 Paris)

Germany (☎ 030-208 2592; Friedrichstrasse 206, 10969 Berlin-Kreuzberg)

Netherlands (☎ 070-356 1477; Paleistraat 4, 2514 JA Den Haag)

Poland (☎ 022-629 7271; Al. Róż 16, 00-556 Warsaw)

UK (☎ 020-7631 0427, brochure requests ☎ 09063-640641; 13 Harley St, London W1G 9QG)

USA (☎ 212-288 0830; 1109 Madison Ave, New York, NY 10028)

VISAS

Everyone is required to have a valid passport (or ID card for EU citizens) to enter the Czech Republic. Citizens of EU and EEA (Europe Economic Area) countries do not need a visa for any type of visit. Citizens of Australia, Canada, Israel, Japan, New Zealand and the USA can stay for up to 90 days without a visa; other nationalities can check their visa requirements on www.czech.cz. Visas are not available at border crossings or at Prague's Ruzyně airport; you'll be refused entry if you need one and arrive without one.

Non-EU citizens who want to stay in the Czech Republic for more than 90 days must apply for a long-term visa, employment visa or residency permit; get details from your nearest Czech embassy, and apply at least four months in advance.

Visa regulations change from time to time, so check www.czech.cz.

Extensions

Non-EU citizens can apply for a visa extension or residency permit at entrance B of the drab **Foreigners' Police & Passport Office**

www.lonelyplanet.com

(Úřadovna cizinecké policie a pasové služby; Map pp278–9; Olšanská 2, Žižkov; ☽ 7.30-11.30am, noon-4.30pm & 5-7pm Mon-Thu). Take tram No 9 or 26 to the Olšanská stop (opposite the bright-yellow Telepoint sign). An extension costs 1000Kč, and is payable with special stamps *(kolky)* sold at the passport office or at any post office. The fact that visas and residency permits are still handled by the police is a hangover from the communist era – be prepared for long queues, grumpy staff and no English speakers.

WOMEN TRAVELLERS

Walking alone on the street is as safe – or as dangerous – as in most large European cities. Avoid the park in front of Prague's main train station after dark, and be aware that the area around the intersection of Wenceslas Square and Na příkopě is effectively a red-light district at night. The city has developed a burgeoning sex industry, with strip clubs, lap-dancing clubs, brothels and street workers all in evidence. Women (especially solo travellers) may find the atmosphere in some traditional Czech pubs a bit raw, as they tend to be exclusively male territory.

There are few services for women such as helplines and refuge or rape crisis centres. The main organisation in Prague is the **White Circle of Safety** (Map pp262–3; Bílý kruh bezpečí; ☎ 257 317 110; www.bkb.cz; Duškova 20, Smíchov), which provides help and counselling to victims of crime and violence.

WORK

Unemployment in Prague is low – around 2.5% – and although there are job opportunities for foreigners in English teaching, IT, finance, real estate and management firms, competition for jobs is fierce and finding one is increasingly difficult.

EU citizens do not need a work permit to work in the Czech Republic; non-EU citizens do. You can find short- or long-term employment teaching English (or other languages) at the numerous language schools in Prague – language teachers were in great demand in 2006. Alternatively, you might find employment in the city's many expat-run restaurants, hostels and bars. Possibilities also exist in foreign-owned businesses. Investment banking, real estate, IT and

Directory

PRACTICALITIES

management firms need experienced staff and often employ non-Czech speakers, but the odds of getting such a job are better if you apply from home rather than waiting until you are in Prague.

You can research the employment market on websites such as www.jobs.cz, www.expats.cz and www.prague.tv, and look for jobs in the classified-ad section of the *Prague Post* (www.praguepost.cz).

Language

Language

It's true – anyone can speak another language. Don't worry if you haven't studied languages before or that you studied a language at school for years and can't remember any of it. It doesn't even matter if you failed English grammar. After all, that's never affected your ability to speak English! And this is the key to picking up a language in another country. You just need to start speaking.

Learn a few key phrases before you go. Write them on pieces of paper and stick them on the fridge, by the bed or even on the computer – anywhere that you'll see them often.

You'll find that locals appreciate travellers trying their language, no matter how muddled you may think you sound. So don't just stand there, say something! If you want to learn more Czech than we've included here, pick up a copy of Lonely Planet's comprehensive but user-friendly *Czech Phrasebook*.

PRONUNCIATION
It's not easy to learn Czech pronunciation, and you may have to learn a few new linguistic tricks to do so. It is, however, spelt the way it's spoken, and once you become familiar with the sounds, it's easy to read. Stress is usually on the first syllable.

Vowels
Vowels have long and short variants; they have the same pronunciation, but the long vowels are simply held for longer. The long vowels are indicated by an acute accent. The following approximations reflect British pronunciation:

a	as the 'u' in 'cut'
á	as the 'a' in 'father'
e	as in 'bet'
é	as the word 'air'
ě	as the 'ye' in 'yet'
i/y	as the 'i' in 'bit'
í/ý	as the 'i' in 'marine'
o	as in 'pot'
ó	as the 'aw' in 'saw'
u	as in 'pull'
ú/ů	as the 'oo' in 'zoo'

Diphthongs

aj	as the 'i' in 'ice'
áj	as the word 'eye'
au	as the 'ow' in 'how'
ej	as the 'ay' in 'day'
ij/yj	short; as 'iy'
ij/ýj	longer version of ij/yj
oj	as the 'oi' in 'void'
ou	as the 'o' in 'note', though each vowel is more strongly pronounced than in English
uj	as the 'u' in 'pull', followed by the 'y' in 'year'
ůj	longer version of uj

Consonants

c	as the 'ts' in 'lets'
č	as the 'ch' in 'chew'
ch	like 'ch' in Scottish *loch*
f	as in 'fever', never as in 'of'
g	as in 'get', never as in 'age'
h	as in 'hand'
j	as the 'y' in 'year'
r	a rolled 'r' (at the tip of the tongue)
ř	no English equivalent; a rolled 'rzh' sound, as in the composer, Dvořák
s	as in 'sit', never as in 'rose'
š	as the 'sh' in 'ship'
ž	a 'zh' sound, as the 's' in 'treasure'
ď, ľ, ť	very soft palatal sounds, ie consonants followed by a momentary contact between the tongue and the hard palate, as if followed by 'y' (like the 'ny' in canyon). The same applies to d, n and t when followed by i, í or ě.

All other consonants are similar to their English counterparts, although the letters k, p and t are unaspirated, meaning they are pronounced with no audible puff of breath after them.

SOCIAL
Greetings & Civilities

Hello/Good day.
Dobrý den.
Ahoj. (informal)
Goodbye.
Na shledanou.
Ahoj/Čau. (informal)
Yes.
Ano/Jo. (polite/informal)
No.
Ne.
May I? (asking permission)
Dovolte mi?
Sorry/Excuse me. (apologising or seeking assistance)
Promiľte.
Could you help me, please?
Prosím, můžete mi pomoci?
Please.
Prosím.
Thank you (very much).
(Mockrát) děkuji.
You're welcome.
Není zač.
Good morning.
Dobré jitro/ráno.
Good afternoon.
Dobré odpoledne.
Good evening.
Dobrý večer.
How are you?
Jak se máte?
Well, thanks.
Děkuji, dobře.

Going Out

What's there to do in the evenings?
Kam se tady dá večer jít?
What's on tonight?
Co je dnes večer na programu?
In the entertainment guide.
V kulturním programu.

I feel like going to a/an/the ...
Mám chuť jít ...

bar	do baru
café	do kavárny
cinema	do kina
disco	na diskotéku
opera	na operu
restaurant	do restaurace
theatre	do divadla

Do you know a good restaurant?
Znáš nejakou dobrou restauraci?

Are there any good nightclubs?
Jsou tady nějaké dobré noční podniky?

Language Difficulties

Do you speak English?
Mluvíte anglicky?
I understand.
Rozumím.
I don't understand.
Nerozumím.
Could you write it down, please?
Můžete mi to napsat, prosím?

PRACTICAL
Directions

Do you have a local map?	Máte mapu okolí?
Where is ...?	Kde je ...?
Go straight ahead.	Jděte přímo.
Turn left.	Zatočte vlevo.
Turn right.	Zatočte vpravo.
behind	za
in front of	před
far	daleko
near	blízko
opposite	naproti

Numbers

It's quite common for Czechs to say the numbers 21 to 99 in reverse; for example, *dvacet jedna* (21) becomes *jedna dvacet*.

0	nula
1	jedna
2	dva
3	tři
4	čtyři
5	pět
6	šest
7	sedm
8	osm
9	devět
10	deset
11	jedenáct
12	dvanáct
13	třináct
14	čtrnáct
15	patnáct
16	šestnáct
17	sedmnáct
18	osmnáct
19	devatenáct
20	dvacet
21	dvacet jedna

22	dvacet dva
23	dvacet tři
30	třicet
40	čtyřicet
50	padesát
60	šedesát
70	sedmdesát
80	osmdesát
90	devadesát
100	sto
1000	tisíc

Banking

Where's a/the ...?
Kde je ...?

ATM	bankomat
bank	banka
exchange office	směnárna

I want to change (a) ...
Chtěl/a bych vyměnit ... (m/f)

| cash/money | peníze |
| (travellers) cheque | (cestovní) šek |

What time does the bank open?
V kolik hodin otevírá banka?

Post Office

Where's a/the post office?
Kde je pošta?

I want to buy ...
Rád/a bych koupil/a ... (m/f)

| postcards | pohlednice |
| stamps | známky |

I want to send a ...
Chtěl/a bych poslat ... (m/f)

fax	fax
letter	dopis
parcel	balík
postcard	pohled

Phones & Mobiles

Where's the nearest public phone?
Kde je nejbližší veřejný telefon?
Could I please use the telephone?
Mohu si zatelefonovat?
I want to call ...
Chci zavolat ...
I want to make a long-distance call to ...
Chtěl/a bych volat do ... (m/f)
I want to make a reverse-charge/collect call.
Chtěl/a bych zavolat na účet volaného. (m/f)
I want to buy a phonecard.
Chtěl/a bych koupit telefonní karta. (m/f)

Internet

Is there a local internet café?
Je tady internet kavárna? (m/f)
I'd like to get internet access.
Chtěl/a bych se připojit na internet. (m/f)
I'd like to check my email.
Chtěl/a bych si skontrolovat můj email. (m/f)

Paperwork

name	jméno
address	adresa
date of birth	datum narození
place of birth	místo narození
age	věk
sex	pohlaví
nationality	národnost
passport number	číslo pasu
visa	vizum
driving licence	řidičský průkaz

Question Words

Who?	Kdo?
What?	Co?
When?	Kdy?
Where?	Kde?
How?	Jak?

Shopping & Services

Where's (a/the) ...?
Kde je ...?
I'm looking for (a/the) ...
Hledám ...

art gallery	uměleckou galérii
city centre	centrum
embassy	velvyslanectví
main square	hlavní náměstí
market	tržiště
museum	muzeum
public toilet	veřejné záchody
tourist office	turistická informační kancelář

What time does it open/close?
V kolik hodin otevírají/zavírají?

Signs

Kouření Zakázáno	No Smoking
Otevřeno	Open
Umývárny/Toalety	Toilets
Páni/Muži	Men
Dámy/Ženy	Women
Vchod	Entrance
Vstup Zakázán	No Entry

Východ	Exit
Zákaz	Prohibited
Zavřeno	Closed

Time & Dates

What time is it?	Kolik je hodin?
in the morning	ráno
in the afternoon	odpoledne
in the evening	večer
today	dnes
now	teď
yesterday	včera
tomorrow	zítra
next week	příští týden

Monday	pondělí
Tuesday	úterý
Wednesday	steda
Thursday	čtvrtek
Friday	pátek
Saturday	sobota
Sunday	neděle

January	leden
February	únor
March	březen
April	duben
May	květen
June	červen
July	červenec
August	srpen
September	září
October	říjen
November	listopad
December	prosinec

Dates in Museums

year	rok
century	století
millennia	milénium/tisíciletí
beginning of ...	začátek ...
first half of ...	první polovina ...
middle of ...	polovina ...
second half of ...	druhá polovina ...
end of ...	konec ...

Transport

What time does the train/bus leave?
V kolik hodin odjíždí vlak/autobus?
What time does the train/bus arrive?
V kolik hodin přijíždí vlak/autobus?
Excuse me, where is the ticket office?
Prosím, kde je pokladna?
I want to go to ...
Chci jet do ...

I'd like ...
Rád/a bych ... (m/f)

a one-way ticket	jednosměrnou jízdenku
a return ticket	zpáteční jízdenku
two tickets	dvě jízdenky

FOOD

breakfast	snídaně
lunch	oběd
dinner	večeře

Is service included in the bill?
Je to včetně obsluhy?

For more detailed information on food and dining out, see p47-54.

EMERGENCIES

Help!
Pomoc!
It's an emergency!
To je naléhavý případ!
Could you please help me?
Prosím, můžete mi pomoci?
Call an ambulance/a doctor/the police!
Zavolejte sanitku/doktora/policii!
Where's the police station?
Kde je policejní stanice?

HEALTH

Where's the ...?
Kde je ...?

chemist/pharmacy	lékárna
dentist	zubař
doctor	doktor
hospital	nemocnice

I need a doctor who speaks English.
Potřebuji lékaře, který mluví anglicky.
I'm sick.
Jsem nemocný/nemocná. (m/f)

Symptoms

I have (a) ...
Mám ...

diarrhoea	průjem
fever	horečku

I have a headache.
Bolí mě hlava.
It hurts here.
Bolí mě zde.

Glossary

You may encounter these terms and abbreviations while in Prague. For more on food terms see pages 48 to 54.

bankomat(y) – ATM(s)

čajovná – teahouse
ČD – Czech Railways, the state railway company
Čedok – the former state tour operator and travel agency, now privatised
chrám – cathedral
ČSA – Czech Airlines, the national carrier
ČSAD – Czech Automobile Transport, the state bus company
ČSSD – Social Democratic Party
cukrárna – cake shop

divadlo – theatre
doklad – receipt or document; see also *potvrzení*
dům – house or building

galérie – gallery, arcade

hlavní nádraží (hl nád) – main train station
hora – hill, mountain
hospoda – pub
hostinec – pub
hrad – castle
hřbitov – cemetery

jízdenka – ticket

kaple – chapel
kavárna – café or coffee shop
Kč (Koruna česká) – Czech crown
kino – cinema
knihkupectví – bookshop
kolky – duty stamps, for payment at certain government offices, such as for a visa extension; sold at post offices and elsewhere
kostel – church
kreditní karta – credit card

lékárna – pharmacy

město – town
most – bridge

nábřeží (nábř) – embankment
nádraží – station
náměstí (nám) – square

ODS – Civic Democratic Party
ostrov – island

palác – palace
pekárna – bakery
penzión – pension
pěší zóna – pedestrian zone
pivnice – small beer hall
pivo – beer
pivovar – brewery
potraviny – grocery or food shop
potvrzení – receipt or confirmation; see also *doklad*
Praha – Prague
provozní doba – business hours, opening times
přestup – transfer or connection

restaurace – restaurant

sad(y) – garden(s), park(s), orchard(s)
samoobsluha – self-service, minimarket
stanice – train stop or station
sv (svatý) – Saint

třída (tř) – avenue

ulice (ul) – street

Velvet Divorce – separation of Czechoslovakia into fully independent Czech and Slovak republics in 1993
Velvet Revolution (Sametová revoluce) – bloodless overthrow of Czechoslovakia's communist regime in 1989
věž – tower
vinárna – wine bar
vlak – train
výdej listovních zásilek – poste restante mail

zahrada – gardens, park
zámek – chateau
zastávka – bus, tram or train stop

Behind the Scenes

THE LONELY PLANET STORY

The story begins with a classic travel adventure: Tony and Maureen Wheeler's 1972 journey across Europe and Asia to Australia. There was no useful information about the overland trail then, so Tony and Maureen published the first Lonely Planet guidebook to meet a growing need.

From a kitchen table, Lonely Planet has grown to become the largest independent travel publisher in the world, with offices in Melbourne (Australia), Oakland (USA) and London (UK). Today Lonely Planet guidebooks cover the globe. There is an ever-growing list of books and information in a variety of media. Some things haven't changed. The main aim is still to make it possible for adventurous travellers to get out there – to explore and better understand the world.

At Lonely Planet we believe travellers can make a positive contribution to the countries they visit – if they respect their host communities and spend their money wisely. Every year 5% of company profit is donated to charities around the world.

THIS BOOK

This guidebook was commissioned in Lonely Planet's London office, and produced by the following:

Commissioning Editor Janine Eberle

Coordinating Editor Kate James

Coordinating Cartographers Natasha Velleley, Bonnie Wintle

Coordinating Layout Designer Jim Hsu

Managing Cartographer Shahara Ahmed

Assisting Editor Jackey Coyle

Cover Designer Marika Kozak

Project Manager Sarah Sloane

Language Content Coordinator Quentin Frayne

Thanks to Trent Paton, Jennifer Garrett, Helen Christinis, Celia Wood, Sally Darmody

Cover photographs 'Nationale Nederlanden' Architect: Frank O Gehry, Damian Heinisch/Bilderberg (top); A woman reading in a metro station, Mark Thomas/Alamy (bottom); Couple on bench on Vlatva River, Izzet Keribar/Lonely Planet Images (back).

Internal photographs p66 (#4) Cheryl Forbes/Lonely Planet Images; p2 (#5) Geopix/Alamy; p64 (#4) Oldrich Karasek/Alamy; p64 (#1) Izzet Keribar/Lonely Planet Images; p64 (#3) Paul Lindsay/Alamy; p220 Martin Moos/Lonely Planet Images; p2 (#1), p8, p12, p19, p21, p23, p25, p28, p30, p33, p32, p35, p34, p39, p49, p52, p58, p59, p60 (#1, #2,#4), p61 (#1, #3, #4), p62 (#1), p63 (#2, #3), p65 (#1, #2, #3, #4), p66 (#1, #2, #3), p72, p76, p80, p83, p87, p90, p95, p98, p102, p109, p111, p114, p119, p121, p125, p127, p135, p139, p143, p146, p149, p154, p157, p162, p163, p164 (#1, #2, #3), p165 (#1, #2, #3), p166 (#1, #2, #3), p167 (#1, #2, #3), p168, p169 (#2, #3, #4), p170 (#1, #2, #3, #4), p173, p176, p178, p182, p187, p190, p195, p198, p202, p206, p213, p212, p214, p217 Richard Nebesky/Lonely Planet Images; p60 (#3), p62 (#3), p164 (#4) Jonathan Smith/Lonely Planet Images; p2 (#3, #4) Jan Stromme/Lonely Planet Images; p61 (#2) Oliver Strewe/Lonely Planet Images; p2 (#2) Phil Robinson/Alamy; p64 (#2) roughguidespictures.com/Alamy; p63 (#1, #4) Neil Wilson/Lonely Planet Images; p62 (#2) Brent Winebrenner/Lonely Planet Images.

OUR READERS

Many thanks to the travellers who used the last edition and wrote to us with helpful hints, useful advice and interesting anecdotes:

A Sanne Aabjerg Kristiansen, Sally Amis, Diane Armson **B** Dennis Baca, Andrea Barbati, Kathryn Barrett, Hanna Benseman, Richard Bingham, Sylvia Brewer **C** Eimear Carvill, John Chapman, L Clark, Nicolas Contat, Ron Corral, Robert Coup, Columba Cryan **D** Maggie Dalton **E** AJ Edwards, Matthew Emery, Sven Eriksson **F** Rob Fairy, Theo Fikke, Roger Forder **G** Jesús García, Richard Goldstein **H** Timo Hartikainen, Derek & Judy Henchliffe, Will Henderson, Gerald Hermüller, Nina Hill, Kate Hunter, Martin Husbands **I** Ina Inglingstad, Rebecca Isles **J** Alex Johnstone, Eddie Joseph **K** Martina Kamenikova, Farah Karim, Brian Kelly, Dewey Kiley, Austin Kinsella, Andre Kirchberger, James Kirkin **L** Lucie Lafontaine, Vanessa Lal, Jamie Leigh, Frantisek Lengal, Vincent Lock, Martin Machovec, Michelle McAvoy, Ross McGibbon, Cari Merkley, Sandra Modry, Susanna Morgan **N** Carolyn Normanton **P** Ken Parkes, David Patel, Fred Pattison, Mike Payne, Gordon Pinder, Karen Playfair, Kerstin Plichta **R** Colm Rafferty, Gavin Riggs, Andy Roberts, Pesach Rogoway, Jim Roland, Paul Rosenberg, Armin Rosencranz, Julia Rout **S** Susana Santos, Valerie Schnee, Susan Smith, Rachel Smylie, Tom & Anne Marie Snabl, Peter Snoeckx, Roger van de Sompel, Christian Strauf, John Streets **T** Nicole Taylor, Gianluca Tempesti, Mario Toups, Gillian Twigg **W** Frank & Sally Wallbridge, Yvonne Warners, Eddi Warres, Liz Wheeler, Sherryl Woodhams **Z** Sarah Zarrow

ACKNOWLEDGMENTS

Prague Transit Map © DP Praha, akciová společnost

Notes

Notes

Index

See also separate indexes for Eating (p258), Drinking (p258), Shopping (p258) and Sleeping (p259).

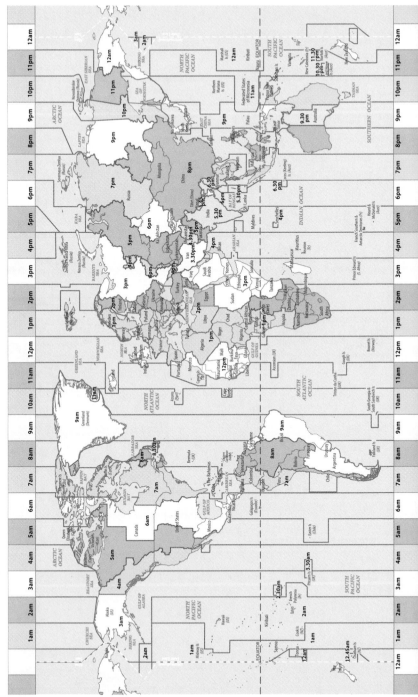

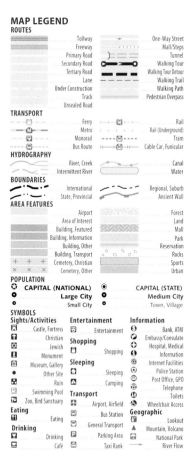

MAP LEGEND
ROUTES

Tollway
Freeway
Primary Road
Secondary Road
Tertiary Road
Lane
Under Construction
Track
Unsealed Road

One-Way Street
Mall/Steps
Tunnel
Walking Tour
Walking Tour Detour
Walking Trail
Walking Path
Pedestrian Overpass

TRANSPORT

Ferry
Metro
Monorail
Bus Route

Rail
Rail (Underground)
Tram
Cable Car, Funicular

HYDROGRAPHY

River, Creek
Intermittent River

Canal
Water

BOUNDARIES

International
State, Provincial

Regional, Suburb
Ancient Wall

AREA FEATURES

Airport
Area of Interest
Building, Featured
Building, Information
Building, Other
Building, Transport
Cemetery, Christian
Cemetery, Other

Forest
Land
Mall
Park
Reservation
Rocks
Sports
Urban

POPULATION

CAPITAL (NATIONAL)
Large City
Small City

CAPITAL (STATE)
Medium City
Town, Village

SYMBOLS

Sights/Activities
Castle, Fortress
Christian
Jewish
Monument
Museum, Gallery
Other Site
Ruin
Swimming Pool
Zoo, Bird Sanctuary

Eating
Eating

Drinking
Drinking
Café

Entertainment
Entertainment

Shopping
Shopping

Sleeping
Sleeping
Camping

Transport
Airport, Airfield
Bus Station
General Transport
Parking Area
Taxi Rank

Information
Bank, ATM
Embassy/Consulate
Hospital, Medical
Information
Internet Facilities
Police Station
Post Office, GPO
Telephone
Toilets
Wheelchair Access

Geographic
Lookout
Mountain, Volcano
National Park
River Flow

Maps

GREATER PRAGUE

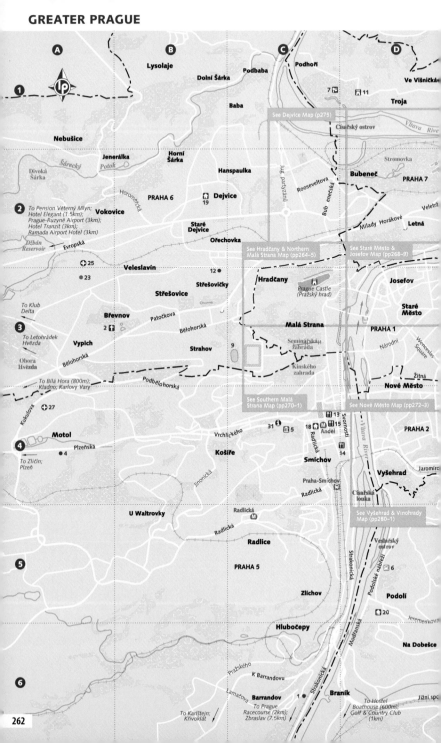

A **B** **C** **D**

1

Lysolaje

Dolní Šárka

Podbaba

Podhoří

Ve Višničce

7

11

Troja

Baba

See Dejvice Map (p275)

Císařský ostrov

Vltava River

Nebušice

Šárecký Potok

Jenerálka

Horní Šárka

Hanspaulka

Stromovka

Divoká Šárka

Bubeneč

PRAHA 7

2

To Pension Větrný Mlýn;
Hotel Elegant (1.5km);
Prague-Ruzyně Airport (3km);
Hotel Tranzit (3km);
Ramada Airport Hotel (3km)

Horoměřická

PRAHA 6

Dejvice

19

Rooseveltova

Bub eneckú

Jug. partyzánů

Milady Horákové

Veletrž

Letná

Vokovice

Staré
Dejvice

Džbán
Reservoir

Evropská

Ořechovka

25

See Hradčany & Northern
Malá Strana Map (pp264–5)

See Staré Město &
Josefov Map (pp268–9)

23

Veleslavín

12

Hradčany

Josefov

Střešovičky

Prague Castle
(Pražský hrad)

Staré
Město

Střešovice

To Klub
Delta

Břevnov

Patočkova

Bělohorská

Malá Strana

PRAHA 1

3

To Letohrádek
Hvězda

2

Vypich

Seminářská
zahrada

Národní

Wenceslas
Square

Strahov

9

Obora
Hvězda

Bělohorská

Kinského
zahrada

Žitná

To Bílá Hora (800m);
Kladno; Karlovy Vary

Podbělohorská

Nové Město

Kukulova

27

See Southern Malá
Strana Map (pp270–1)

See Nové Město Map (pp272–3)

13

Svornosti

Vltava River

PRAHA 2

4

Vrchlického

31

5

18

15

Anděl

Radlická

Motol

Plzeňská

4

Košíře

14

To Zličín;
Plzeň

Jinonická

Smíchov

Vyšehrad

Jaromiro

Praha-Smíchov

Radlická

Císařská
louka

U Waltrovky

Radlická

Radlická

M

See Vyšehrad & Vinohrady
Map (pp280–1)

5

Radlice

Veslařský
ostrov

PRAHA 5

Strakonická

6

Zlíchov

Podolské nábřeží

Podolí

20

Jeremenkov

6

Hlubočepy

Na Dobešce

Modřanská

Pražského

K Barrandovu

Strakonická

Braník

Lamačova

Barradov

1

To Prague
Racecourse (2km);
Zbraslav (7.5km)

To Hostel
Boathouse (600m);
Golf & Country Club
(1km)

Jižní spo

To Karlštejn;
Křivoklát

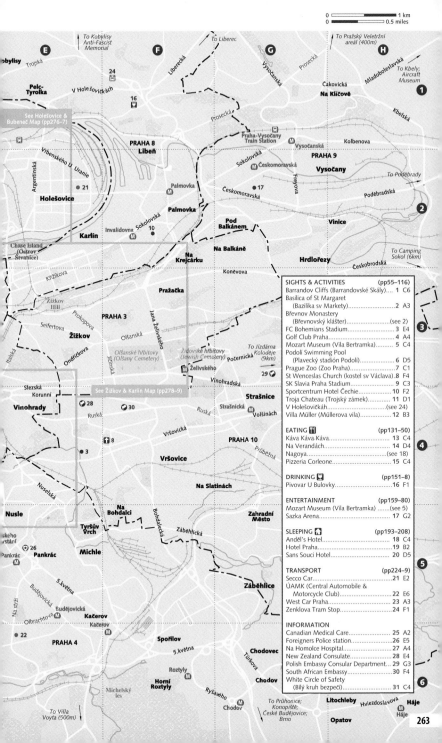

SIGHTS & ACTIVITIES (pp55–116)
Barrandov Cliffs (Barrandovské Skály).... 1 C6
Basilica of St Margaret
(Bazilika sv Markety)........................ 2 A3
Břevnov Monastery
(Břevnovský klášter)......................(see 2)
FC Bohemians Stadium.......................... 3 E4
Golf Club Praha.................................... 4 A4
Mozart Museum (Vila Bertramka)........... 5 C4
Podolí Swimming Pool
(Plavecký stadión Podolí)................... 6 D5
Prague Zoo (Zoo Praha)........................ 7 C1
St Wenceslas Church (kostel sv Václava).8 F4
SK Slavia Praha Stadium........................ 9 C3
Sportcentrum Hotel Čechie.................. 10 F2
Troja Chateau (Trojský zámek)............ 11 D1
V Holešovičkách................................(see 24)
Villa Müller (Müllerova vila)................. 12 B3

EATING (pp131–50)
Káva Káva Káva.................................. 13 C4
Na Verandách.................................... 14 D4
Nagoya..(see 18)
Pizzeria Corleone............................... 15 C4

DRINKING (pp151–8)
Pivovar U Bulovky.............................. 16 F1

ENTERTAINMENT (pp159–80)
Mozart Museum (Vila Bertramka) ......(see 5)
Sazka Arena...................................... 17 G2

SLEEPING (pp193–208)
Anděl's Hotel.................................... 18 C4
Hotel Praha...................................... 19 B2
Sans Souci Hotel................................ 20 D5

TRANSPORT (pp224–9)
Secco Car... 21 E2
ÚAMK (Central Automobile &
Motorcycle Club)............................ 22 E6
West Car Praha.................................. 23 A3
Zenklova Tram Stop............................ 24 F1

INFORMATION
Canadian Medical Care........................ 25 A2
Foreigners Police station..................... 26 E5
Na Homolce Hospital.......................... 27 A4
New Zealand Consulate....................... 28 E4
Polish Embassy Consular Department.... 29 G3
South African Embassy........................ 30 F4
White Circle of Safety
(Bílý kruh bezpečí)........................... 31 C4

See pp270-1

See p275

Na valech

Na bašté sv. Jiří

Mickie wiczova

Badeniho

Tram 18; 57;

Písek Gate

🏛 3

🏛 13

Tychonova

Chotkovy sady

Tram 22; 23

Mariánské hradby

🏛 33

Královská zahrada

Chotkova

Pod Bruskou

Tram 18; 22; 23; 57

Tram 12

nábřeží

• 2

Stag Moat (Jelení příkop)

Brusnice

Castle Steps (Zámecké schody)

Palace Gardens Beneath Prague Castle (Palácové zahrady pod Pražským bradem)

Malostranská Ⓜ

Prague Castle (Pražský hrad)

84 🅟

39

🅟 73

🏛 46 22 •

Valdštejnská

Klárov

Gardens on the Ramparts (Zahrada Na Valech)

Wallenstein Square (Valdštejnské náměstí)

Wallenstein Garden (Valdštejnská zahrada)

Mánes Bridge (Mánesův most)

Tram 18

78 🏠 4

🅟 80

14

🏛 38

See pp258-9

Sněmovní

Tomášská

Thunovská

Tram 12; 20; 22; 23; 57

Letenská

Vojanovy sady

seminaře

Klárov

29 🏛

18 • 56 🅿

🏛 32

Little Quarter Square (Malostranské náměstí)

Malá Strana

Cihelná

Nerudova

52 🏠

61 🅟

🅟

🏠 30

🅿 62

Josefská

🅿 85

Dražického náměstí

U lužického

26 • 🏛 15

🏛 43

49

55 🅿

57

25 🅿

🏠 59

Mostecká

23 • 🏠 72

Mišeňská

65

44 🏛

37 🏠

88 🅿 83

54 🏛

40 •

8 •

5

Tržiště

🏠 67

63 🅿

Prokopská

Saská

77 🅿

Charles Bridge (Karlův most)

🏛 51

42

Lázeňská

9

Vrtbov Garden (Vrtbovská zahrada)

50

20 •

Na Kampě

76 •

Karmelitská

Maltese Square (Maltézské náměstí)

Velkopřevorské náměstí

🅿 81

Čertovka

Hroznová

Vltava River

🏠 11

Harantová

Nebovidská

Seminářská zahrada

Kampa

0 — 500 m
0 — 0.3 miles

HRADČANY & NORTHERN MALÁ STRANA

STARÉ MĚSTO & JOSEFOV

A　**B**　**C**　**D**

1

2

3

4

5

6

PRAHA 7

Letná Gardens
(Letenské sady)

🏛 Metronome

Letná terása

nábřeží Edvarda Beneše

Tram 12, 17, 51, 54

🏛 81

Tram 12

Dvořákovo nábřeží

Čechův most

Tram 17, 53

23

54

Josefov

U milosrdných

Kozí

U obecního dvora

🏛 104

Bílkova

2

Dušní

76

Elišky Krásnohorské

20

87

177

96

Vězeňská

90

56

98

91

U starého hřbitova

45

Červená

83

153

102

22

36

Maiselova

26

33

143

68

V kolkovně

Dlouhá

53

17. listopadu

42

Old Jewish Cemetery
(Starý židovský hřbitov)

Široká

132

128

Masná

70

48

Široká

16

142

67

159

Pařížská tř.

Vltava River

Dvořákovo nábřeží

Tram 17, 53

Jan Palach
Square
(náměstí
Jana Palacha)

173

Máneův most

Tram 18

38

Salvátorská

88

Jáchymova

97

130

140

Týnská ul.

Tynsk

Kaprova

126

69

Staroměstská Ⓜ

151

191

61

15

112

46

136

25

163

27

80

Štup

Dlouhá

Tynská

116

Žatecká

Valentinská

U radnice

182

32

Old Town
Square
(Staroměstské
náměstí)

29

9

59

4

64

Alšovo nábřeží

Veleslavínova

Křižovnická

Tram 17, 18, 53

51

152

Platnéřská

Mariánské
náměstí

44

28

Little Square
(Malé náměstí)

Linhartská

Husova

Železná

60

3

Staré Mě

106

8

Křižovnické
náměstí

11

City Library
(Městská
knihovna)

37

7

62

157

Kamzíková

Charles Bridge
(Karlův most)

172　43

169

17

1

10

Karlova

93

107

144

Melantrichova

Michalská

121

186 @

Open-Air
Market

125

12

154

95

131

Smetanovo nábřeží

39

170

Liliová

21

105

119

124

148

145

73

113

55

Novotného
lávka

Anenská

Anenské
náměstí

120

Řetězová

79

Rétězová

158

Zlatá

13

168

Pikli

Havelská

V kolích

Provar

164

Karolíny
Světlé

268

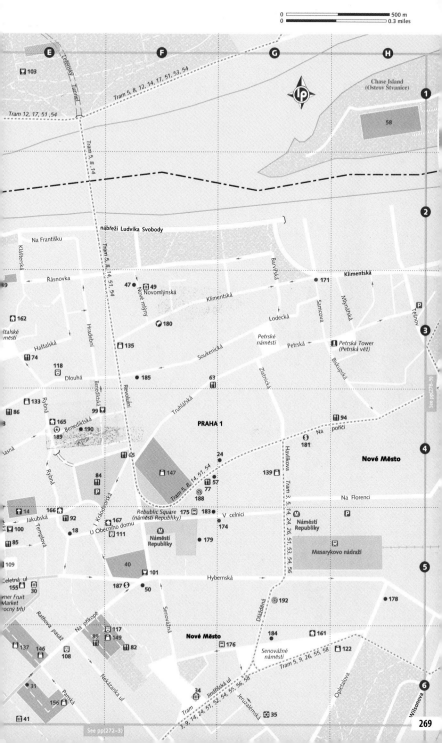

A   B   C   See pp264-5   D

See pp264-5

1

The Hunger Wall (Hladová zeď)

Petřín Hill

10   8

3

2

Olympijská

Růžový
sad

5 ●

11

17

Strahov
Stadium

Vaníčkova

27

Chaloupeckého

3

Strahov

Jezdecká

Šermířská

Kinský Garden
(Kinského
zahrada)

Atletická

4

9

SIGHTS & ACTIVITIES (pp55–116)
Children's Playground.................... 1 F3
Church of St John at the Laundry
  (kostel sv Jana Na prádle)........ 2 G2
Church of St Lawrence
  (kostel sv Vavřince)................. 3 C1
Church of St Michael
  (kostel sv Michala)................. 4 D4
Esquo Squashcentrum................ 5 A2
Futura Gallery............................ 6 C6
Kampa Museum (Muzeum Kampa).7 G1
Mirror Maze (Bludiště)............... 8 C1
Musaion.................................... 9 D4
Petřín Lookout Tower
  (Petřínská rozhledna).............. 10 C1
Štefánik Observatory
  (Štefánikova hvězdárna).......... 11 D2

EATING (pp131–50)
Bar Bar..................................... 12 F2
Bohemia Bagel.......................... 13 F2
Cantina.................................... 14 F2
La Bastille................................ 15 F2
Meduzzy................................... 16 F3
Restaurant Nebozízek................ 17 D2
Rybářský klub........................... 18 G2
Sushi Bar.................................. 19 G2

U modré kachničky..................... 20 F1
Wigwam.................................... 21 G3

DRINKING (pp151–8)
Café Savoy................................ 22 G2
Futurum.................................... 23 G6
Klub Újezd................................ 24 F2
Letní bar................................... 25 H2

ENTERTAINMENT (pp159–80)
Angel Club................................ 26 C6
Klub 007 Strahov...................... 27 B2
Palace Cinema Multiplex..........(see 30)

SHOPPING (pp181–92)
Capriccio.................................. 28 F3
Mapis....................................... 29 F4
Nový Smíchov........................... 30 F6
Vetešnictví............................... 31 F2

SLEEPING (pp193–208)
Hotel Julian.............................. 32 F4
Hotel William............................ 33 F1
Travellers' Hostel Island............ 34 H3

INFORMATION
Austrian Embassy...................... 35 E5

5

Holečkova

6   6

26

Kmochova

Grafická

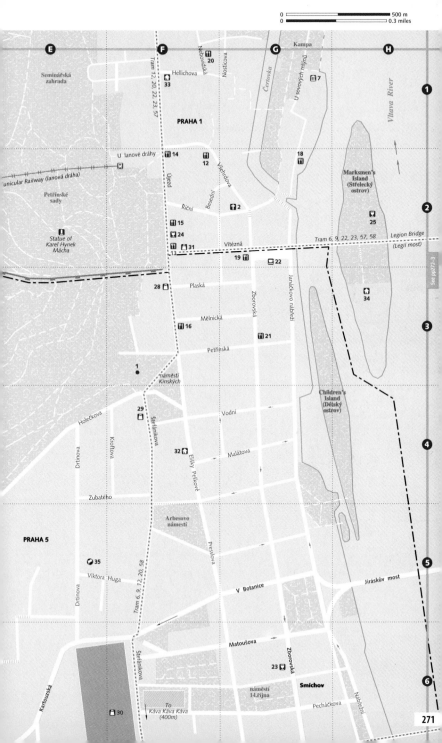

A B C D

1

Náprstkova   60   3   52   40   Na můstku   Můstek

42   Karoliny Světlé   25   Bethlehem Square (Betlémské náměstí)   Husova   V kotcích   104   Rytířská   28 října   132   20

Betlémská   Skořepka   Uhelný trh   73   Jungmannovo náměstí   4

Konviktská   68   89   75   Martinská   51   1   120

100   5   Na perštýně   7   125   Františkán. zahrada

34   63   109   108   96   134   Národní Třída

Smetanovo nábřeží Tram 17, 18, 53   Divadelní   Bartolomějská   128   133   39   Národní třída   Tram 6, 9, 18, 21, 22, 23, 51, 54, 57   37   83   61   85   Mikulandská   Purkyňova   92   124   Palackého

67   29   Voršilská   11   Ostrovní   Spálená   Vladislavova   Jungmannova   78

80   119   V jirchářích   57   72   M.Rettigové   47   44   Vodičkova   69   Školská

112   113   114   Na struze   16   Opatovická   Lazarská   Tram 3, 9, 14, 24, 51, 52, 54, 55, 56, 58

Slav Island (Slovanský ostrov)   Masarykovo nábřeží   Šítkova   58   71   Klementská   Černá   Ostní   79   Navrátilova   53

See pp270-1   Vojtěšská   130   Pštrossova   87   dinářů   28   Řeznická

17   Myslíkova   Odborů   74   Na zbořenci   Příčná   95

21   35   Charles Square (Karlovo náměstí)   116   Malá   Štěpánská

Záhořanského   Karlovo Náměstí   M

Jiráskův most   Jirásek Square (Jiráskův náměstí)   26   10   Tram 4, 6, 10, 22, 23   Ječná   6   70

Resslova   9   Nové Město   Charles Square (Karlovo náměstí)

12   55   Václavská   Salmovská

32   Dittrichova   Trojanova   Lípová

31   Rašínovo nábřeží   Vltava River   Tram 17, 21   Tram 3, 4, 10, 14, 16, 18, 24   Cogazova   Vyšehradská   PRAHA 2

Na Moráni   Tram 3, 4, 10, 14, 16   U nemocnice

Palackého most   Palackého náměstí   15   Karlovo Náměstí   M   14   98

272   Tram 4, 7, 10, 14

0 ⊨══════════ 500 m
0 ⊨══════════ 0.3 miles

E **F** **G** **H**

Panská 24

Růžová

Uljíčovny

Opletalova

Wilsonova

1

V cípu

Hlavní
Nádraží
131
121

Praha hlavní nádraží
(Main Train Station)

48
135

49

56

Jindřišská

129

Politických vězňů

Vrchlického
sady

Wenceslas Square

Můstek
2

M

99
94 102

97

PRAHA 1

105

101

Washingtonova

2

76

41

86

88 22
19
117 77 45

93

30

Lucerne Palace
(palác Lucerna)

50

123

U divadla

81

Španělská

Novák Arcade
(pasáž U Nováků)

111

V jámě 66

110

118
65 23
Muzeum

Mánesova
136

54

3

36
M

27

122

Metránská

Vinohradská

Tram 11

Italská

64

Legerova
59

Štěrková

Řimská

Balbínova

4

Žitná

Anglická

Tram 11

5

8
33

Na Rybníčku II

Na Rybníčku

82

náměstí
Míru

Tram 4, 6, 10, 16, 22, 23, 51, 56, 57

106

IP Pavlova
M M
91 Lublaňská

Rumunská
46

103

107 Legerova

Belehradská

127

Belgická

115

6

Kateřinská

Ke Karlovu

13

Na bojišti

38

Sokolská

Rumunská

Lublaňská

Tram 6, 11

Londýnská

Uruguayská

273

Tyršova

NOVÉ MĚSTO

DEJVICE

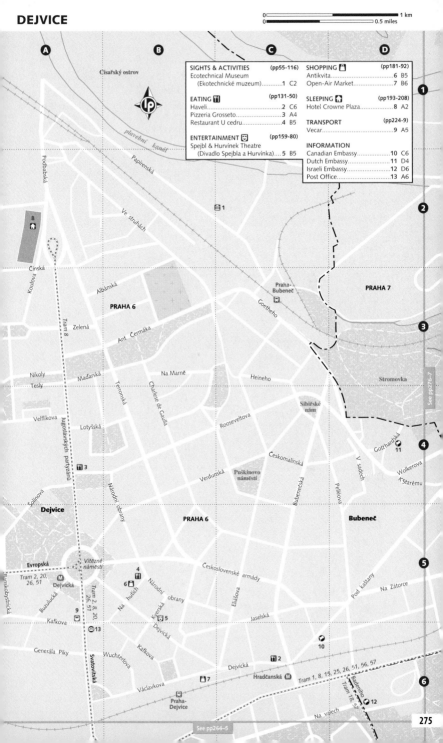

0 ——————— 1 km
0 ——————— 0.5 miles

SIGHTS & ACTIVITIES	(pp55-116)
Ecotechnical Museum	
(Ekotechnické muzeum)............1	C2

EATING	(pp131-50)
Haveli....................................2	C6
Pizzeria Grosseto.....................3	A4
Restaurant U cedru..................4	B5

ENTERTAINMENT	(pp159-80)
Spejbl & Hurvínek Theatre	
(Divadlo Spejbla a Hurvínka)....5	B5

SHOPPING	(pp181-92)
Antikvita................................6	B5
Open-Air Market......................7	B6

SLEEPING	(pp193-208)
Hotel Crowne Plaza..................8	A2

TRANSPORT	(pp224-9)
Vecar....................................9	A5

INFORMATION	
Canadian Embassy...................10	C6
Dutch Embassy.......................11	D4
Israeli Embassy......................12	D6
Post Office............................13	A6

Císařský ostrov

plavební kanál

Papírenská

Ve struhách

PRAHA 7

Praha-
Bubeneč

Goetheho

Podbabská

Čínská

Koulova

Albánská

PRAHA 6

Zelená

Ant. Čermáka

Na Marně

Stromovka

Heineho

See pp276-7

Nikoly
Tesly

Maďarská

Terronská

Charlese de Gaulla

Roosveltova

Sibiřské
nám.

Velflíkova

Lotyšská

Tram 8

Jugoslávských partyzánů

Gotthardská

Wolkerova

K Starému

Šolínova

Národní obrany

Verdunská

Puškínovo
náměstí

Bubenečská

Pelléova

V sadech

Českomalínská

Dejvice

PRAHA 6

Bubeneč

Evropská

Vítězné
náměstí

Československé armády

Pod kaštany

Na Zátorce

Hanšpaulská

Tram 2, 20,
26, 51

Dejvická

Tram 2, 8, 20,
26, 51

Buzulucká

Na hutích

Národní
obrany

Eliášova

Jaselská

Kafkova

Generála Píky

Wuchterlova

Dejvická

Václavkova

Dejvická

Hradčanská

Tram 1, 8, 15, 25, 26, 51, 56, 57

Na valech

Svatovítská

Praha-
Dejvice

Tram 18, 57

Badeniho

See pp264-5

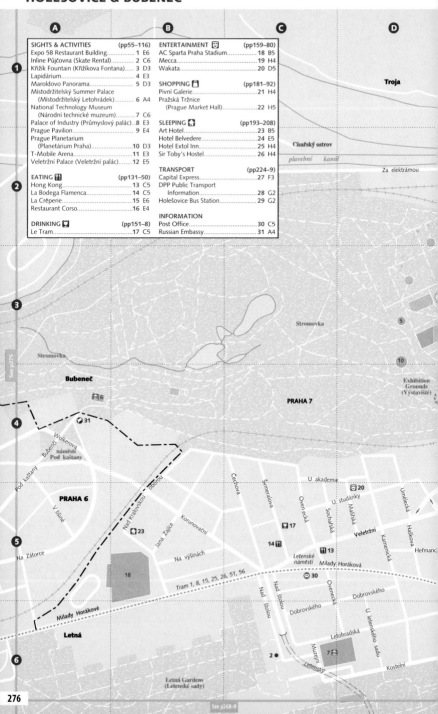

SIGHTS & ACTIVITIES	(pp55–116)
Expo 58 Restaurant Building	1 E6
Inline Půjčovna (Skate Rental)	2 C6
Křížík Fountain (Křižíkova Fontana)	3 D3
Lapidárium	4 E3
Maroldovo Panorama	5 D3
Místodržitelský Summer Palace (Místodržitelský Letrhrádek)	6 A4
National Technology Museum (Národní technické muzeum)	7 C6
Palace of Industry (Průmyslový palác)	8 E3
Prague Pavilion	9 E4
Prague Planetarium (Planetárium Praha)	10 D3
T-Mobile Arena	11 E3
Veletržní Palace (Veletržní palác)	12 E5

EATING	(pp131–50)
Hong Kong	13 C5
La Bodega Flamenca	14 C5
La Crêperie	15 E6
Restaurant Corso	16 E4

DRINKING	(pp151–8)
Le Tram	17 C5

ENTERTAINMENT	(pp159–80)
AC Sparta Praha Stadium	18 B5
Mecca	19 H4
Wakata	20 D5

SHOPPING	(pp181–92)
Pivní Galerie	21 H4
Pražská Tržnice (Prague Market Hall)	22 H5

SLEEPING	(pp193–208)
Art Hotel	23 B5
Hotel Belvedere	24 E5
Hotel Extol Inn	25 H4
Sir Toby's Hostel	26 H4

TRANSPORT	(pp224–9)
Capital Express	27 F3
DPP Public Transport Information	28 G2
Holešovice Bus Station	29 G2

INFORMATION	
Post Office	30 C5
Russian Embassy	31 A4

Troja

Císařský ostrov

plavební kanál

Za elektrámou

Stromovka

Stromovka

Bubeneč

PRAHA 7

Exhibition Grounds (Výstaviště)

Wolkerova náměstí
Pod kaštany

Pod kaštany

PRAHA 6

V tišině

Na Zátorce

Nad Královskou oborou

Jana Zajíce

Korunovační

Na výšinách

Čechova

Šmeralova

Over ecká

U akademie

U studánky

Sochárská

Mališská

Veletržní

Kamenická

Umělecká

Haškova

Hefmanc

Letenské náměstí

Milady Horáková

Tram 1, 8, 15, 25, 26, 51, 56

Nad štolou

Nad štolou

Over ecká

Dobrovského

Dobrovského

U letenského sadu

Milady Horákové

Letná

Letohradská

Muzejní

Letenský

Kostelní

Letná Gardens (Letenské sady)

See p275

See p268–9

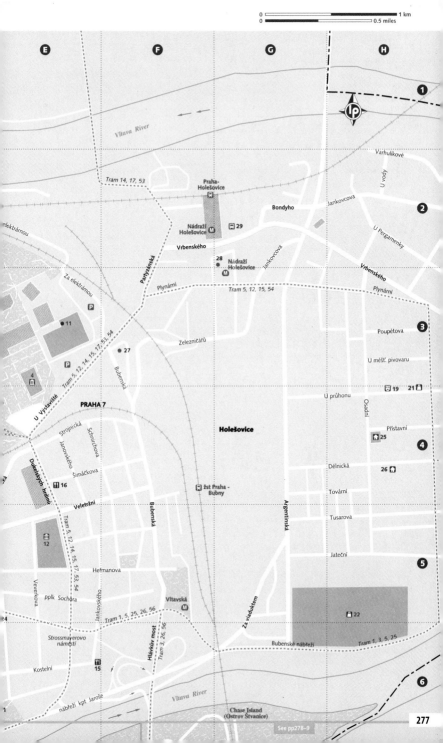

0 _____ 1 km
0 _____ 0.5 miles

E   **F**   **G**   **H**

1

Vltava River

Varhulíkové

Tram 14, 17, 53

Praha-
Holešovice

U vody

Bondyho

Jankovcova

2

U Pergamenky

Nádraží
Holešovice Ⓜ   🚋 29

Vrbenského

28   Nádraží
     Holešovice Ⓜ

Jankovcova

Vrbenského

elektrárnou

Plynární

Za elektrárnou

Partyzánská

Plynární

Tram 5, 12, 15, 54

3

Poupětova

● 11

Železničářů

U měšť. pivovaru

● 27

Tram 5, 12, 14, 15, 17, 53, 54

Bubenská

🚋 19   21 🏛

U průhonu

Osadní

U Vystaviště

PRAHA 7

Holešovice

Přístavní

🏠 25

4

Strojnická

Šmichrova

Délnická

26 🏛

Janovského

Šimáčkova

Tovární

🍴 16

Veletržní

Bubenská

Tusarová

🏛 12

Argentinská

Za viaduktem

Jatečni

5

Heřmanova

🚋 22

Veverkova

pplk Sochora

Vltavská Ⓜ

Jankovského

Tram 1, 5, 25, 26, 56

🖼 žst Praha -
Bubny

6

Hlávkův most

Tram 3, 26, 56

Bubenské nábřeží

Tram 1, 3, 5, 25

Strossmayerovo
náměstí

Kostelní

🏛 15

Vltava River

nábřeží kpt Jaroše

Chase Island
(Ostrov Štvanice)

See pp278–9

277

ŽIŽKOV & KARLÍN

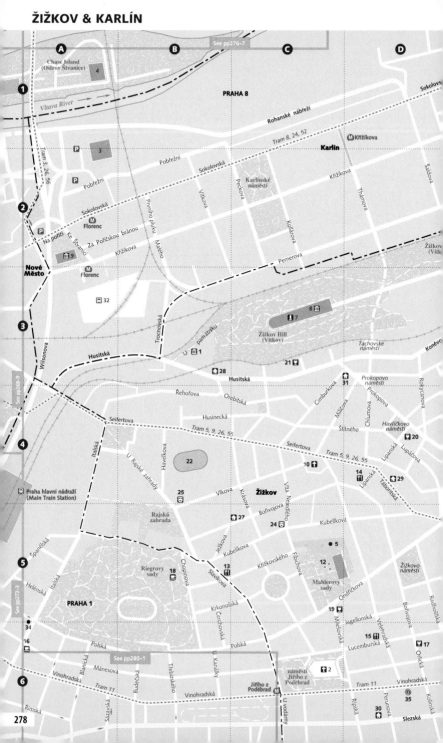

Chase Island
(Ostrov Štvanice)

Vltava River

PRAHA 8

Rohanské nábřeží

Sokolovs

Tram 8, 24, 52

Karlín

Křižíkova

Pobřežní

Sokolovská

Peckova

Křižíkova

Karlínské
náměstí

Thámova

Šaldov

Sokolovská

Prvního pluku

Vítkova

Kollárova

Žižkov
(Vítk

Na poříčí

Ke Štvanici

Za Poříčskou bránou

Maltho

Pernerova

Florenc

Křižíkova

9

**Nové
Město**

Florenc

32

Trocnovská

U památníku

1

7

8

Žižkov Hill
(Vítkov)

Tachovské
náměstí

Konevo

Husitská

Wilsonova

21

28

31

Prokopovo
náměstí

Husitská

Cimburkova

Milíčova

Prokopova

Rokycanova

Řehořova

Orebitská

Husinecká

Štítného

Havlíčkovo
náměstí

Seifertova

Tram 5, 9, 26, 55

Lipanská

Lupáčova

20

Italská

U Rajské zahrady

Havlíčkova

22

Seifertova

Tram 5, 9, 26, 55

Víta Nejedlého

10

14

29

Lipanská

Táboritská

Žižkov

Praha hlavní nádraží
(Main Train Station)

25

Vlková

Krásova

Bořivojova

Kubelíkova

27

24

Žižkovo
náměstí

Jeseniova

Kubelíkova

Křížkovského

Fibichova

5

12

Španělská

Italská

Rajská
zahrada

Riegrovy
sady

18

13

Slavíkova

Mahlerovy
sady

Ondříčkova

Borivojova

Radhošťská

PRAHA 1

Helénská

19

Milešovská

Jagellonská

Velehradská

15

17

34

Chopinova

Krkonošská

Čerchovská

Polská

U Kanálky

Lucemburská

Kolínská

16

Polská

Blanická

Mánesova

Třebízského

Budečská

Sázavská

Vinohradská

Tram 11

**náměstí
Jiřího z
Poděbrad**

2

Tram 11

Vinohradská

Rímská

**Jiřího z
Poděbrad**

U vodárny

Vinohradská

Rípská

30

Perunova

35

Kolínská

Slezská

See pp272–3

See pp280–1

See pp268–9

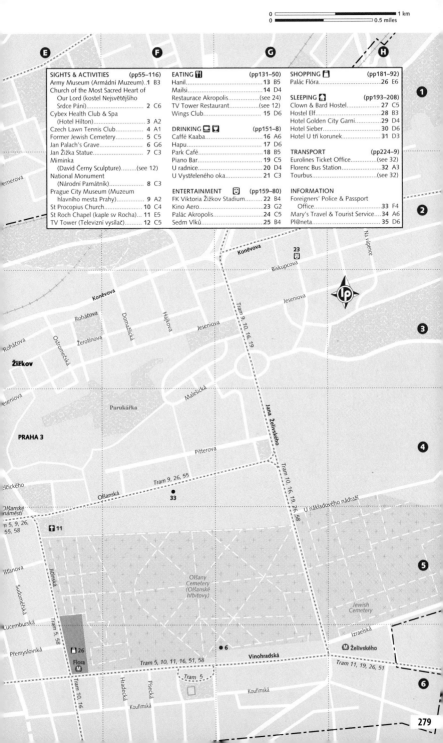

SIGHTS & ACTIVITIES	(pp55–116)
Army Museum (Armádní Muzeum)..1	B3
Church of the Most Sacred Heart of	
Our Lord (kostel Nejsvětějšího	
Srdce Páni).................................. 2	C6
Cybex Health Club & Spa	
(Hotel Hilton)............................. 3	A2
Czech Lawn Tennis Club.................. 4	A1
Former Jewish Cemetery.................. 5	C5
Jan Palach's Grave.......................... 6	G6
Jan Žižka Statue............................. 7	C3
Miminka	
(David Černy Sculpture)........(see 12)	
National Monument	
(Národní Památník).......................... 8	A2
Prague City Museum (Muzeum	
hlavního mesta Prahy)................ 9	A2
St Procopius Church...................... 10	C4
St Roch Chapel (kaple sv Rocha)... 11	E5
TV Tower (Televizní vysílač)........ 12	C5

EATING 🍴	(pp131–50)
Hanil.. 13	B5
Mailsi... 14	D4
Restaurace Akropolis..................(see 24)	
TV Tower Restaurant..................(see 12)	
Wings Club..................................... 15	D6

DRINKING 🖵 🖵	(pp151–8)
Caffé Kaaba.................................... 16	A6
Hapu... 17	D6
Park Café....................................... 18	B5
Piano Bar.. 19	C5
U radnice.. 20	D4
U Vystřeleného oka........................ 21	C3

ENTERTAINMENT 🎭	(pp159–80)
FK Viktoria Žižkov Stadium............ 22	B4
Kino Aero....................................... 23	G2
Palác Akropolis.............................. 24	C5
Sedm Vlků..................................... 25	B4

SHOPPING 🛍	(pp181–92)
Palác Flóra..................................... 26	E6

SLEEPING 🛏	(pp193–208)
Clown & Bard Hostel...................... 27	C5
Hostel Elf....................................... 28	B3
Hotel Golden City Garni.................. 29	D4
Hotel Sieber................................... 30	D6
Hotel U tří korunek........................ 31	D3

TRANSPORT	(pp224–9)
Eurolines Ticket Office................(see 32)	
Florenc Bus Station........................ 32	A3
Tourbus.....................................(see 32)	

INFORMATION	
Foreigners' Police & Passport	
Office.. 33	F4
Mary's Travel & Tourist Service.... 34	A6
Pl@neta.. 35	D6

VYŠEHRAD & VINOHRADY

Slav Island
(Slovanský
ostrov)

A **B** **C** **D**

Navrátilova

Řeznická

Vojtěšská

Petrossova

Myslíkova

Křemencová

Černá

Na zbořenci

Odborů

PříčnÁ

Kraľovská

Žitná

Záhořan-
ského

Charles Square
(Karlovo náměstí)

Malá

Štěpánská

Na Rybníčku II

Štěpánská

Karlovo
Náměstí

M

Ječná

Tram 4, 6, 10, 16, 22, 23, 51, 56, 57

Resslova

**Nové
Město**

Václavská

Vyšehradská

Charles
Square
(Karlovo
náměstí)

Salmovská

Lipová

Kateřinská

Na bojiš

Jiráskův most

Gorazdova

Dittrichova

Trojanova

Na Moráni

Karlovo
Náměstí

Palackého
náměstí

M

Rašínovo nábřeží

U nemocnice

See pp272–3

Vinčná

Palackého most

Vltava River

Pod Slovany

Na Slovanech

Vyšehradská

Benátská

PRAHA 2

Ke Karlovu

10

3

Charles University
Botanical Garden
(Botanická zahrada
Univerzity Karlovy)

Apolinářská

37

3

Trojická

Podskalská

Charles University
Botanical Garden

38

Hořejší nábřeží

Plavecká

Vyšehradská

Na slupi

Albertov

Studničková

Horská

6

Rašínovo nábřeží

Svobodova

Tram 7

Tram 3, 7, 16, 17, 21, 54

Horská

Na slupi

Sekanin

Vnislavova

Tram 18, 24, 53, 55

22

Libušina

Vratislavova

Hostivítova

Neklanova

Vnislavova

Ostrčilovo
náměstí

27

Oldřichova

46

8

42

Tram 7, 18, 24, 53

Štulcovy
sady

16

2

Jaromírova

Vyšehrad

Vyšehrad
Cemetery

20

V pevnosti

Karlachovy
sady

19

Ševcova

39

Čiklova

Štulcova

28

5

9

K rotundě

18

Lumírova

24

Vyšehrad Gardens
(Vyšehradské
sady)

11

14

1

Strakonická

13

12

51

Na Bučance

Vyšehrad Rock
(Vyšehradské
skála)

17

Krokova

Imperial
Meadow
(Císařská
louka)

Podolské nábřeží

21

PRAHA 4

Na Pankráci

Pank
nám

0 — 500 m
0 — 0.3 miles

SIGHTS & ACTIVITIES (pp55–116)
Basilica of St Lawrence
 (Bazilika sv Vavřince)..................1 B5
Brick Gate (Cihelná brána)............2 B5
Casemates (Kasematy)..............(see 2)
Church of St John of Nepomuk on
 the Rock (kostel sv Jana
 Nepomuckého na Skalce)...........3 B3
Church of St Ludmilla
 (kostel sv Ludmily)....................4 F2
Church of SS Peter & Paul
 (kostel sv Petra a Pavla)............5 B5
Church of the Assumption of the
 Virgin Mary & Charlemagne
 (kostel nanebevzetí Panny
 Marie a Karla Velikého).............6 D4
Church of the Beheading of John
 the Baptist (Kostelík Stětí sv
 Jana Křtitele)........................(see 19)
Congress Centre
 (Kongresové centrum)...............7 D6
Cubist Apartment Block................8 C4
Cubist Houses..............................9 B5
Emmaus Monastery
 (klášter Emauzy).....................10 B3
Gothic Cellar (Gotický sklep).......11 B5
Leopold Gate (Leopoldova brána)..12 C5
Libuše's Bath.............................13 B5
Myslbek Statues.........................14 B5

National House (Národní dům).....15 F2
New Provost's House
 (Nové proboštství)...................16 B5
Peak Gate (Špička brána)............17 C6
Rotunda of St Martin
 (Rotunda sv Martina)...............18 C5
Royal Palace..........................(see 24)
St Mary Chapel in the Ramparts (kaple
 Panny Marie v hradbách)..........19 C5
Slavín......................................20 B5
Tábor Gate (Táborská brána)......21 C6
Villa Libušina (Cubist House).......22 B4
Vinohrady Theatre
 (Divadlo Na Vinohradech).........23 F1
Vyšehrad Gallery
 (Galerie Vyšehrad)..................24 B5

EATING (pp131–50)
Ambiente...................................25 G1
Aromi.......................................26 H1
James Cook...............................27 D5
Rio's Vyšehrad...........................28 B5
Tiger Tiger................................29 F1
U Neklana..............................(see 8)

DRINKING (pp151–8)
Club Stella.................................30 G2
Kavárna Medúza.........................31 F3
Zvonařka..................................32 F3

ENTERTAINMENT (pp159–80)
Termix......................................33 G1

SHOPPING (pp181–92)
Orientální Koberce Palácka...........34 G1
Shakespeare & Sons....................35 H3
Vinohradský Pavilón....................36 G1

SLEEPING (pp193–208)
Admirál Botel.............................37 A3
Hostel U Melounu.......................38 D3
Hotel Amadeus...........................39 D5
Hotel Anna................................40 G2
Hotel Green Garden.....................41 E3
Hotel Union...............................42 D5
Le Palais Hotel...........................43 F3
Pension Arco..............................44 H3
Pension Beetle...........................45 G3

TRANSPORT (pp224–9)
CS-Czechocar..........................(see 7)

INFORMATION
Institute for Language & Preparatory
 Studies (Ústav jazykové a odborné
 připravý)................................46 B4
London School of Modern
 Languages...............................47 G2
Police Station.............................48 F3
Stop City Accommodation.............49 F1
V Síti.......................................50 G2
Vyšehrad Information Office..........51 C6

Nusle

281

METRO & TRAM MAP

Orientační plán · **Metro**

Dopravní podnik hl. m. Prahy,
akciová společnost

STANICE METRA
METRO STATION

STANICE PŘESTUPNÍ
POINT OF CHANGE

TRATĚ METRA
METRO ROUTES

BEZBARIÉROVÝ PŘÍSTUP
BARRIERLESS ACCESS

ZÁCHYTNÁ PARKOVIŠTĚ
PARKING FACILITIES